INSIDES AND OUTSIDES

Interdisciplinary Perspectives on Animate Nature

Maxine Sheets-Johnstone

D1739163

imprint-academic.com

Published in the UK by
Imprint Academic, PO Box 200, Exeter EX5 5YX, UK

Distributed in the USA by
Ingram Book Company,
One Ingram Blvd., La Vergne, TN 37086, USA

ISBN 9781845409043

A CIP catalogue record for this book is available from the
British Library and US Library of Congress

Contents

Prologue

[T]here belongs within my psychic being the whole constitution of the world existing for me and... the differentiation of that constitution into the systems that constitute what is included in my peculiar ownness and the systems that constitute what is other... If perchance it could be shown that everything constituted as part of my peculiar ownness... belonged to the concrete essence of the constituting subject as an inseparable internal determination, then, in the Ego's self-explication, his peculiarly own world would be found as "inside" and, on the other hand, when running through that world straightforwardly, the Ego would find himself as a member among its "externalities" and would distinguish between himself and "the external world."

—Husserl (1973, pp. 98–9)

How might ideas, processes, and things that seem entirely different and separate actually be reconciled as inextricable complementary aspects of complementary pairs... To see how, first appreciate that very little in life, even at the most elementary molecular level, happens unless two or more individual things come together... But things don't just come together, do they? They must also be able to move apart again. This is the complementary nature at perhaps its most basic.

—Kelso and Engstrøm (2006, p. 85)

This Prologue sets the stage for the chapters that follow. It situates the chapters in the most basic aspects of insides and outsides, aspects having to do with both our subject–world relationship and our personal relationship with others as those relationships are present from the beginning. It identifies these most basic aspects of inside and outside in terms of Husserl's phenomenology of the "Ego," the "I" who is the subject of any and all subject–world relationships, including relationships with other animate beings, and of Kelso and Engstrøm's complementarity thesis that shows how, rather than being polar opposites, inside and outside are complementary. The chapters that follow are from this perspective widely varying and highly detailed interdisciplinary elaborations of the real-life, real-time aspects of inside and outside set forth in the Prologue.

I: Husserl's Abstractive Epoché and Kelso and Engstrøm's "Complementary Nature"

In the first epigraph above, Husserl is describing what is present in the "abstractive epoché" by which he distinguishes what is "I" from "Other." This distinguished "I" is not a matter of "I 'alone' remain" (Husserl 1973, p. 93), but a matter of "I" *in relation to all that is alien*. What Husserl finds in this methodologically abstracted "I" is an "animate organism" that is "*uniquely* singled out," that "is not just a body but precisely an animate organism: the sole Object... to which, in accordance with experience, I ascribe *fields of sensation...* the only Object 'in' which I *'rule and govern' immediately*" (ibid., p. 97). Husserl goes on to specify three further dimensions of this "sole Object" that is an animate organism, namely, doings and "I cans" and thus the ability, by way of "the *kinesthesias*," to "'*act*' somatically"; a reflexive relationship between organs of sense and objects of sense, as in one hand touching the other; and "*psycho-physical unity*" (ibid.). In his further methodological abstraction, Husserl proceeds to a descriptive analysis of "externalities," of what is in fact alien and hence Other. In this analysis there is recognition of both subject–world relationships and corporeal–intercorporeal relationships. In effect, Husserl is essentially distinguishing between insides and outsides.

It is important to realize that though Husserl specifies the realm of the abstractive epoché as "the sphere of ownness," and speaks over and over of "ownness," of "my" and "mine" (ibid., pp. 92 ff.), he is not claiming *owner- ship* of "my animate organism" as a possession. He is delineating basic I/Other ontological distinctions, elucidating to begin with essential features of the "I," and on that basis and in turn, concerning himself with how that "I" "*wholly transcends his own being*" (ibid., p. 105) in the consti- tution of the world. "Ownness" is thus indeed not a matter of possession; it is a matter of ontology, what one might designate a *primordial* ontology (see ibid., pp. 103–06), and of an epistemology on the basis of that ontology. In light of this terminological-semantic clarification, the following comparison can in fact be made.

Just as Husserl describes the Body as the "*zero point*" of orientation with respect to all appearances in the world (1989, p. 166)—to the nearness or farness of things, to their being above or below, to the right or left, and so on—and thus describes subject–world relationships, so the "sphere of ownness"—fields of sensation, "I govern," "I can," and so on—describes *the zero point of the subject tout court*, the zero point of purely "*personal*" happenings, abilities, and relationships (Husserl 1973, p. 97). The zero point of the subject *tout court* is indeed the "*uniquely* singled out" animate organism within the abstractive epoché, the Body that, as Husserl states with respect to the zero point of orientation, is "always here" (Husserl 1989, p. 166). Thus, precisely as with the zero point of orientation, what is specified in the zero point of the subject *tout court* is a hereness, an "ultimate central here" of the subject in relation to any "there," a hereness that is "not just a body but precisely an animate organism: the sole Object within my abstract world-stratum to which, in accordance with experience, I ascribe *fields of sensation...*" (ibid.). In short, whatever the happenings, abilities, and relationships, they are ontological dimensions of the "*uniquely singled out*" animate organism that constitute the experiential ground on which the Objective world is constituted and thus the ground of a veridical epistemology. Hence clearly, Husserl's use of the term "ownership," "my," and "mine" is properly understood not in the vernacular or colloquial sense of *possession*, but in the sense of the subject *tout court*, the subject divorced as it were from the world, from all that is alien. Being a question of the subject *tout court*, and in turn, of the subject in relation to the world, it is a question of how, as animate organisms, we are individually gifted with sense modalities and capacities, and how on the basis of these modalities and capacities we progressively make sense of "externalities": the Objective world, both the world of things and the world of other animate beings.

In *The Complementary Nature*, Kelso and Engstrøm cite researchers from many different fields of study, all of whom in one way and another view their own research and findings as encompassing complementarities rather than contraries—"both/and" rather than "either/or." Kelso and Engstrøm quote William James, for example, who describes the stream of consciousness in terms of a bird's "perchings and flight" (Kelso and Engstrøm 2006, pp. 175–6). They quote Isaac Newton's description of nature as "generating fluids out of solids, and solids out of fluids, fixed things out of volatile and volatile out of fixed, subtle out of gross and gross out of subtle, some things to ascend and make terrestrial juices, Rivers and Atmosphere; and consequence others to descend. ..." (ibid., p. 72). They quote Niels Bohr whose coat of arms reads "Contraries are complementary" and who wrote with respect to the dual wave and particle nature of light, "The quantum postulate forces us to adopt a new mode of description designated as complementary" (ibid., p. 62). Kelso and Engstrøm point out that "In the last few hundred years ... the complementary nature has become increasingly important to human beings, as they have developed more and more sophisticated methods to study and manipulate nature in order to understand it" (ibid., p. 252). They give as examples James Maxwell's discovery of the "inextricable complementarity" of electricity and magnetism in the phenomenon of electromagnetism and Einstein's astrophysical discoveries showing that time and space are "inextricably connected as complementary aspects" (ibid.).

Kelso and Engstrøm introduce a semantically rich diacritical mark to designate this inextricable complementarity. They term this mark "~" a "squiggle" or tilde (ibid., p. xiv), a mark placed between two words and indicating a "complementary pair" (ibid., p. 7). The mark will be used at times in the Prologue text that follows. Kelso and Engstrøm give as an example "body" and "mind," which are "complementary aspects of the complementary pair "body~mind." They pointedly explain, "We use the tilde ~ not to concatenate words or as an iconic bridge between polarized aspects, but to signify that we are discussing complementary pairs. Equally if not more important, the tilde symbolizes the *dynamic nature* of complementary pairs" (ibid.). As they later state, "complementary pairs *move*" (ibid., p. 8), and as they later quote Sheets-Johnstone, "In coordination dynamics, the real-life coordination of neurons in the brain and the real-life coordinated actions of animals are cut, fundamentally, from the same dynamic cloth. Integrity is in turn preserved because it is never threatened. Psychophysical unity is undergirded at all levels by coordination dynamics" (ibid., p. 9).

What Kelso and Engstrøm are at pains to describe in their classic study and reformulation of classic polarizations is precisely how "[p]olarized aspects of a complementary pair appear as modes of a dynamical system that is capable of moving between boundaries even as it includes them" (ibid.). They later specify examples of how coordination dynamics informs complementary pairs. One of these examples concerns "togetherness~ apartness": "Tendencies for togetherness coexist with tendencies of apartness. This is likely an inherent property of all complex organizations. For example, successful groups are loosely bound both by a commitment to a common goal and by the diverse needs and capabilities of their members. This is the essence of metastable coordination dynamics" (ibid., p. 225). One could easily extend the metastable dynamics of togetherness~ apartness to science~philosophy, for example, to familiarity~strangeness, emotion~reason, abnormal~normal, nature~culture, enemy~friend, part~ whole, as well, of course, to subject~world, self~other—and to insides~ outsides.

II: Insides and Outsides from the Beginning

Objective determinations define space as three-dimensional: up/down, right/left, front/back—all obviously complementary pairs warranting a tilde rather than a slash. The three pairs are further described in terms of planes: frontal, sagittal, and transverse. While there is much received wisdom in these determinations, they overlook a fundamental spatial reality of animate nature, namely, insides and outsides. All animate forms of life are in fact identified and identifiable in terms of their insides and outsides, their inner morphological structures and organs and their outer morphological structures and organs that together make them the animate forms they are. Their morphologies are not simply assemblages of parts. They define the whole as a living organism, an organism that moves, that is motivated by its senses, instincts, and affects to respond to its surrounding world and to those animate creatures within it. Morphology and responsivity go hand in hand. Humans do not bark and dogs do not crow. Indeed, responsivity is a differential as well as distinctive biological marker of life: it is a marker not just in the overall sense of advantageous, life-enhancing movement, but in the particular sense of the capacity to be moved to move in the first place, and, with respect to many forms of animate life such as prey and predator species, to think in movement (on the latter topic, see Sheets-Johnstone 1981, exp. version of same in Sheets-Johnstone 1999a/2011, 2009). Precisely in this sense insides are not oppositional but complementary to outsides and outsides are not oppositional but complementary to insides: where there is a world, there is a subject and where there is a subject, there is a world; where there is intercorporeal life, there is corporeal life, and where there is corporeal life, there is intercorporeal life, and this from the beginning in forms of animation inside and out.

An infant puts its thumb in its mouth. It sucks on breast and bottle nipples. It swallows what it sucks in. It gurgles. It cries. It kicks. It waves its arms. It is alive to its bodily insides. It is alive to their kinesthetically and tactilely felt dynamics. It is alive furthermore to its viscerally felt churnings, cramps, and tensions. It feels, for example, what infant psychiatrist and clinical psychologist Daniel Stern describes as a "hunger storm" (Stern 1990, pp. 31–5, 36–43). In turn, it is alive to the hands that pick it up, to the arms that cradle it, to the smells that now envelop it, to the voice that whispers and hums. Further still, when it closes its eyes, it shuts out a visually enlivened world. It encloses itself in an inside-felt darkness. A prime sense of distance, of near-ness and far-ness, is muted. It now senses whatever is immediately and directly outside by touch, sound, and smell. With eyes closed, the surrounding world indeed closes inward. It no longer reverberates in the fullness of visually perceived outsides. It is closed in on its insides, whether enlivened by feelings, images, or thoughts.

Insides and outsides are of singular moment in infancy, which perhaps explains why toilet training can be upsetting, curious, or a challenge for an infant and young child. What is inside is in a sense treasured: it is part of oneself. There is thus a felt difference between defecating and urinating into what is tactilely felt close-up, a contiguous part of oneself, and defecating and urinating into a wholly foreign object. Putting one's tactilely and kinetically felt outward-moving insides into a thoroughly foreign object and flushing them away can be an affectively dramatic, alarming, and even puzzling event. Moreover given that we initially explore objects by putting them in our mouths, not just the affective significance, but the cognitive significance of insides and of our tactile-kinesthetic bodies can hardly be denied. That cognitive significance is apparent in the fact that *in, inside, and being inside* are singularly prominent in myriad ways in infant experience: taking a nipple into its mouth, closing an object inside its hand, being put in a crib, putting its arm in a sleeve—all attest to the tactile-kinesthetic foundations of the prominence of insides. It is thus hardly surprising that the word *in* is the first preposition an infant understands, both as locative state and locative act (Clark 1979, 1973; Cook 1978; Grieve, Hoogenraad and Murray 1977; see also Bower 1974; Piaget and Inhelder 1967; Piaget 1967, 1968. For a discussion of same, see Sheets-Johnstone 1990, pp. 236–43).

Fundamental human concepts, *nonlinguistic corporeal concepts*, derive from tactile-kinesthetic and kinetic experiences (Sheets-Johnstone 1990). Archetypal corporeal-kinetic forms and relations, precisely as in putting an arm in a sleeve or closing an object in one's hand, are conceptual by their very nature (Sheets-Johnstone 1999b, pp. 149–54/2009, pp. 219–23). They *embody* concepts in the proper sense of that word, a sense in which we say that someone is the *embodiment* of courage, or that someone *embodies* qualities we value. Elemental spatial concepts such as inside~outside, open~close, and up~down, elemental temporal concepts such as sudden~attenuated, elemental force concepts such as weak~strong, and elemental spatio-temporal concepts such as approaching~receding are concepts contingent on tactile-kinesthetic and kinetic experience. In the beginning, we explore the world and come to know it in and through movement and touch. In the beginning we share a world with others and come to know that world of others in and through movement and touch.

As indicated above, insides resonate affectively from the beginning. Contentment, apprehension, curiosity, fear, excitement—all such feelings reverberate in distinctively felt qualitative ways, which is to say that what-ever the affect, its corporeal-kinetic dynamics are palpably felt. A dynamic congruency indeed exists between emotions and movement (Sheets-Johnstone 1999a/2011, pp. 454–7; 2009, Chapter 8; 2008, pp. 461–3). Their congruency is *felt*; it is lived through from beginning to end. Elemental qualitative concepts such as intense, soft, smooth, quick, gentle, sharp, and sluggish are dynamically embodied in affective experience and are grounded in the affective/tactile-kinesthetic body. An intense fear, for example, is felt throughout the body; it moves through us and moves us to move, whether to flee or to freeze on the spot. A hesitancy to disturb is similarly felt throughout the body; it too moves through us and moves us to move, in soft footsteps perhaps or to close the door. We could hardly feign or restrain an emotion were there not a natural dynamic congruency.

As neonates, our lives were strongly focused on insides, not as opposed to outsides, but as the felt center of learning one's body and learning to move oneself, of dramas such as "hunger storms" and toilet training, of contentment in being softly cradled, and so on. As we grow and mature, insides recede in prominence. We become habituated to feeding ourselves, i.e. to putting food on utensils and then into our mouths and to chewing and swallowing, just as we become habituated to the darkness on closing our eyes and to putting one thing inside another as milk in a glass and a key in a lock. What is inside can also, however, be publically embarrassing. As we grow and mature, limitations are put on insides: sneezing, coughing, hiccuping are on the safe side, so to speak; flatulence and burping are commonly not. Safe-side bodily happenings do not divulge secrets about digestive or eliminative processes. While eating and drinking are fully sanctioned public acts, what they lead to are aspects of bodily insides to be kept under cover, not to be made public except in textbooks, medical schools, closed-door medical offices, or operating rooms.

Yet insides have a decidedly public forum, adult as well as infant, when it comes to pain or discomfort from earaches, stomachaches, toothaches, headaches, muscle cramps, bee stings, or itchings from insect bites, for example. From infancy onward, indeed throughout our life, we are incontestably subject to "the slings and arrows that flesh is heir to." It is thus not surprising that outward expressions of pain are publicly sanctioned. In a sense, it could not be otherwise since the expressions are not just spontaneous but difficult to suppress, whether the pain is a throbbing pain, a stabbing pain, a dull pain, or whatever. Depending upon the severity of the pain, however, its expression can at least in some instances be restrained and in fact is restrained when it is a question of showing fortitude, stoicism, or manliness. Moreover pain can be mimed as well: one can pretend to be hurting just as one can pretend not to be hurting and duly convince others in the process. An overlooked fact of such pretense, however, is its dependence on kinesthesia. The fact that one can go through the motions of pain testifies to the seminal significance of the realities of a particular sense modality, namely, the sense modality that is kinesthesia, the sense through which one experiences the spatio-temporal-force dynamics of one's movement and thus the various spatio-temporal-energic dynamics that constitute feelings of pain, and thus, too, the sense that grounds one's concomitant visual experience of the kinetic dynamics of pain in others. One knows through kinesthetic experience the linear contortions, for example, the twists and turns, the rhythmic writhings, the tensional modulations, the temporal spurts and shadings, the outstretched reachings, and so on, that constitute differential expressions of pain. One is, in short, already primed in the bodily kinetic dynamics of pain on the basis of one's own kinesthetically lived-through experiences of pain. In effect, one knows pain *not only from the inside but implicitly on that basis from the outside.*

III: Further Delineations of Inside and Outside

An exceptional omission is apparent in the above beginning under-standings of the foundational dynamic significance of corporeal insides and outsides. Swallowing, closing one's eyes, urinating, defecating, sneezing, coughing, flatulence, and so on are all staples of life from the beginning. Pains—earaches, stomachaches, toothaches, muscular spasms and tensions, and the like—are similarly staples in the sense that they are fundamental bodily phenomena, felt inside in distinctive qualitatively inflected ways and visually apparent outside in distinctive qualitatively inflected ways. They are, in short, part and parcel of *the experienced corporeal and intercorporeal dynamics of human life.* But an even more fundamental bodily phenomenon is there from beginning to end. This fundamental bodily phenomenon that is involuntary yet substantively essential to life dynamically embodies the foundational animate complementarity of inside and outside—*embodies* again in the genuinely linguistically and con-ceptually proper sense of the word.

Breathing itself is not embodied. It is itself already a living corporeal reality that needs to be neither provided with nor incorporated in a body in order to be properly recognized and properly understood. It is a corporeal reality at the core of animate life, an existential reality that constitutes *the* foundational complementarity of insides and outsides, *the* foundational complementarity in both a temporal and existential sense, temporal in terms of its own dynamics, existential in terms of an individual's life span. Moreover it is a corporeal reality whose dynamics can be, and at times are, directly and immediately experienced not only in spontaneous yawnings, sneezes, and laughter, but in stretching on getting out of bed, in panting after a race or an intense run, and so on. The current freely-applied lexical band-aid of embodiment can indeed find no home here, for what is already a living corporeal reality, a dynamically vibrant one, is in no need of a perfunctory or automatic business-like packaging that makes otherwise immaterial or seemingly free-floating phenomena—e.g. self, mind, sub-jectivity, or even experience—ready for check-out into the real world.[1]

---

1   An embodied courier has in fact no place within a genuinely real and true epistemology and metaphysics of animate life; such a courier is *hors du phénomène propre*, the latter being the foundational dynamic realities of life itself, dynamic realities such as the in and out of breath. Present-day discourse does indeed seem at times to suggest that we need to be

Breathing is a felt flowing in and flowing out. Coincident with this felt flow in and out is a felt opening and closing of a passageway and an expansion outward or upward and a recession inward or downward. In a literally extended sense, a breath inward brings in what is communal and outer-worldly; a breath outward releases what is individual and inner-worldly. Breath might thus be thought a paradigm of conjunction and separation, a complementarity of subject and world and of self and Other. In other words, as well as being in and of themselves complementary, flowing in and flowing out, opening and closing, rising and falling are in distinctively corresponding ways complementary to a subject–world relationship in terms of inhaling and exhaling; in terms of a passageway that opens and lets in, then lets out and closes; and in terms of a directionally expanding volume, then a directionally receding volume. Breath is at the same time complementary to self and Other in the sheer communality of air, air that one shares with Others in breathing in and breathing out. In short, breathing is a kinetic phenomenon that connects us in multiple ways to a complementarity of insides and outsides. In doing so, it describes what Husserl might include as a further "double reality" of animate nature (see Husserl 1989, pp. 297-8), a further "intertwining" or further example of "double–sided unities" (ibid., p. 352; see also Husserl 1977, pp. 151-3), all of which are aptly described both epistemologically and ontologically as a complementarity. The double reality of breath is indeed not an either/or but a both~and (Kelso and Engstrøm 2006; see also Sheets-Johnstone 2004 on conceptual complementarities), an in and out at the core of animate life.

The dynamics of breath are intimately connected with what we are doing, hence with movement, whether we are sleeping, dreaming, sitting placidly in an armchair, racing to a finish line, feeling angry, waiting anxiously for news, grieving, watching a film, or whatever. Whatever our doing or circumstance, our breath is ever-accommodating, timing its in and out dynamics automatically to the dynamics of our lives. It is indeed connected with our animation, with movement, both its own in and out kinetic dynamics that can be kinesthetically and tactilely felt and the kinesthetic and kinetic dynamics that engage us in our daily lives. These kinesthetic and kinetic dynamics are normally in sync with one another in terms of effort and release. For example, when we stretch our arms over-head, our breath automatically complies: it flows inward. When we release

---

"embedded" in the world, that our doings and movement in and through the world need to be "enacted," and that our mental processes need to be located environmentally in an "extended mind." If one were to generalize, one would say that it is as if *everything* about us that is inside needs to be housed outside, in a larger container of some kind.

our upward reach and our arms proceed downward, our breath flows outward. If we try to stretch overhead and exhale, and release our arms downward and inhale, we find our stretch awkwardly impeded and in fact impossible to achieve. The coordination of the kinesthetic-kinetic dynamics of breath and everyday movement is not something we orchestrate, though we certainly can take a deep breath, then plunge into whatever the daunting task at hand, for example, and on completing the task, exhale in great relief and with pleasurable forcefulness. Here too, when we do inhale and exhale voluntarily, we are involved in a whole-body way with movement, from top to bottom and from the neurological to the experiential—and, we might add, at times with the quintessential dynamic congruency of emotions and movement as well, precisely as when we feign or restrain a smile, for example, or the outward expression of laughter. The natural coordination of all aspects of our lives as animate forms testifies to the foundational significance of the inside~outside nature of breath and of animate movement.

IV: Inside and Outside Sense Modalities

Movement is not only like breath in being foundational to our being but is coincident with breath in the ongoing in-and-out streamings of breath. This existential truth may well have inspired Greek writers who extolled *pneuma*, precisely as William James recalls in his reference to what was "ever the original of 'spirit', breath moving outwards, between the glottis and the nostrils" (James 1987, pp. 1157–8). Moreover movement is in and of itself foundational to an assessment of whether a person or creature is living or dead. Its essential centrality was dramatically evident in the medical aftermath of a gunman's shooting of US House of Representative Gabrielle Giffords. In the immediate aftermath, *responsivity* was the critical center of attention. At the time of the shooting, Gifford's husband Mark Kelly "was encouraged by her responsiveness, which included the ability to signal with her hand and move both arms," and this in spite of his realization that there was a "rough road ahead" in terms of recovery ("Gabrielle Giffords," *Wikipedia*). Since Giffords was on a ventilator for several days before her neurosurgeon determined that she could breathe on her own, the clear determinant of whether she was alive and remained alive was responsivity. This fact is not surprising given that responsivity is a biologically recognized "sign of life" (Curtis, 1975, pp. 27–8). In biological terms, it specifies the capacity to "*respond to stimuli*" (ibid., p. 28; italics in original), a capacity that is "a fundamental and almost universal characteristic of life" (ibid.). Examples of that capacity abound: "Plant seedlings bend toward light; meal-worms congregate in dampness; cats pounce on small moving objects; even certain bacteria move toward or away from particular chemicals" (ibid.). Though movement is not specifically mentioned, it is implicit in responsivity, namely, 1) in the ability to move, 2) in the distinction of what is animate from what is inanimate, 3) in the distinction of what is living from what is dead.

As the example of Giffords's responsivity shows, our immediate and direct experience of inside and outside is not limited to breath. We experience that further inside~outside relationship, that "being-in-the-world," from the beginning. Essential aspects of that foundational relationship can nonetheless go largely unrecognized or insufficiently elaborated to the point of remaining basically unacknowledged or unelucidated. For example, Husserl's pointed insight into the dynamic nature of consciousness—"consciousness of the world… is in constant motion" (Husserl 1970, p. 109)—goes unrecognized in static or "state" notions of consciousness, as, for instance, those anchored in the excitation of singular neurons such as "mirror neurons."[2] Similarly, a quintessential sensory dimension of intercorporeal life remains unelucidated, its attempted naming by various researchers—e.g. interkinesthesia (Behnke 2008), enkinesthesia (Stuart 2012), "kinesthetic exchanges" (Rothfield 2005)—being a wayward sensory elaboration. In both instances, not only what Husserl terms the "two-sided" relationship between the internal and external goes unrecognized (Husserl 1977, e.g. pp. 100, 101, 150–3), but the inherently dynamic nature of the relationship goes unrecognized. What is thus essential is an attentive focus on movement itself, beginning with movement that we experience in terms of our own moving bodies and the distinctively different ways in which that experience may unfold in terms of inside and outside.

Though ignored in typical specifications of "the five senses," we are clearly indebted to a sixth sense, the sense modality of kinesthesia, and through that sense modality to an awareness of our own movement. We spontaneously experience directly its distinctive qualitative dynamics: we feel those dynamics from the moment we awake and move ourselves. They flow forth in familiar ways as we get out of bed and stand up, whether rushing because we are late or whether lazily stretching this way and that because it is a holiday. That they commonly flow forth in familiar ways is testimony to the fact that they exist along a gradient of awareness running

---

2   As Kelso remarks, "Even when we know what single neurons do (and keep in mind the neuron itself is a complex system), we still have to understand how they work together to support behavioral function" (Kelso 1995, p. 228). He later states, "the linkage between coherent events at different scales of observation from the cell membrane to the cerebral cortex is *by virtue of shared dynamics*, not because any single level is more or less fundamental than any other" (ibid., p. 229). Moreover as Kelso and Engstrøm point out, "multiple oscillations from widely distributed brain regions are coupled or 'bound' together into a coherent network when people attend to a stimulus, perceive, think, remember, and act" (Kelso and Engstrøm 2006, p. 145).

from background to foreground, thus anywhere from a recessive awareness to a focal awareness. This gradient of awareness is a *felt* kinesthetic
awareness that may indeed be in the background rather than the foreground as we wash the dishes, for example, or climb the stairs. Our dish-
washing and climbing are dynamic patterns that were once learned and are
now ingrained in kinesthetic memory on the basis of their familiarity. They
run off, as it were, by themselves. Yet any time we care to attend focally to
the ongoing kinesthetic experience of washing or climbing, there it is: a
particular qualitative dynamic. We feel a certain rhythm that is punctuated
by certain pauses and accelerations, for example, and certain kinetically
generated spatial contours as well. We furthermore have the possibility at
any time of turning attention away from a particular felt qualitative
dynamics, whether foregrounded or backgrounded, to aspects of those
dynamics as they play out in the world. In such instances we attend to our
movement from an observer point of view. We might, for example, pay
attention to changing bodily contours and linear relationships as we move
from a horizontal position to a vertical position in getting out of bed and
standing up, and to the temporal and energy aspects of those movements,
whether they are tense and speeded up or whether they are lax and
languid. When we do so, we are no longer *feeling* those dynamics as they
spontaneously flow forth; we are *perceiving* those dynamics, attending to
them objectively. We are in effect parsing them, as it were, from the outside. In either instance, the inherently dynamic structure of movement
obtains as does the sensory modality of kinesthesia, which is to say that
whatever our movement, it is inherently both an inside and an outside
phenomenon, and in whichever mode we experience that phenomenon
and wherever our experience along a gradient of awareness, the experience
cannot be suppressed short of pathology. Indeed, as well-known neuro-
physiologist Marc Jeannerod concluded from his own research studies and
the studies of others, "There are no reliable methods for suppressing
kinesthetic information arising during the execution of a movement"
(Jeannerod 2006, p. 56; see also Sheets-Johnstone 1999a/2011, p. 520; 2014,
pp. 249–50/this volume, Chapter II).[3]

A further aspect of the inside and outside of movement has to do with
the fact that any and all movement creates its own distinctive space, time,
and force, its own distinctive qualitative dynamic. That it does so is the
basis of habits, that is, of our ability to form everyday sequences of

---

[3]   "Information" terminology aside, Jeannerod's declarative finding speaks
      reams about the foundational ongoing reality and significance of
      kinesthesia, reams that should certainly lead scientists, phenomenologists,
      and philosophers generally to take kinesthesia seriously and the challenge
      of elucidating its *insuppressible living dynamics* of signal importance.

movement such as brushing teeth and pouring milk into a glass as well as our ability to master complex skills such as pitching a ball in baseball and making a surgical incision, and, moreover, of our ability to feel the familiarity of the dynamics of such habits and skills to the degree that, changes in circumstance notwithstanding, the particular qualitative dynamic that constitutes the habit or skill runs off by itself. In virtue of its particular qualitative dynamics, the habit or skill is, in neuropsychologist Aleksandr Luria's words, a "kinesthetic melody" (Luria 1966, 1973). The fact that any and all movement creates its own space, time, and force, its own distinctive qualitative dynamic, is in fact straightforwardly evident in our recognizing someone by the way he or she walks, by the way he or she laughs, by the way he or she expresses doubt, surprise, cheerfulness, dejection, and so on. That any and all movement creates its own space, time, and force, and that these integral aspects of movement coalesce in forming distinctive qualitative dynamics is of course straightforwardly evident as well in species across the Kingdom Animalia and in natural world phenomena: in the undulating way in which a worm rounds and elongates its body and in doing so crawls along the earth; in the charging swiftness and directional determination with which lionesses pursue a prey animal; in the cresting, peaking, and suspension of a wave before it plunges into the ocean.

When we turn attention from familiarly felt or perceived qualitative dynamics of movement to movement as a purely objective happening, we experience movement as a force *in space* and *in time*. In other words, and as indicated above, we perceive movement as a happening "out there," a distinctive world phenomenon. We experience movement in just this way when we turn attention to where or how we ourselves are moving or where or how an object other than ourselves is moving. In such instances, we perceive movement as a kinetic happening in *a three-dimensional, time-clocked* world. But furthermore, and most commonly, we perceive movement not as a sheer dynamic but as *an object in motion*, precisely as in perceiving not only the spatial, temporal, and force aspects of our moving body in getting out of bed and standing up, but the spatial, temporal, and force aspects of the plane on which we have just traveled in its approach to a gate in the terminal—in which direction the gate lies with respect to our plane, for example, and how slowly or quickly our plane is closing the distance to the gate. As noted above, movement remains a dynamic phenomenon, but a dynamic phenomenon that in one way and another is being analytically perceived, monitored, and judged as an object in motion. Perhaps the most typical intercorporeal experiences of objects in motion are in walking down a crowded street, entering a crowded elevator, or walking down a narrow corridor. We not only commonly adjust our straight line forward movement, but may adjust as well the line of our body, tilting right or left, for example, or drawing an arm inward so that we do not bump into others. We commonly expect others to do the same. In effect, we coordinate movement in such ways that, as objects in motion, we move in harmony with one another. We move in harmony too when we help some-one with an injured arm, for example, or assist a toddler in crossing the street. Combining kinesthetic with kinetic-visual and/or kinetic-tactile awarenesses, we move in sensitively attuned ways with others.

That all animate movement has both an inside and an outside explains why movement is at the heart of both subject~world relationships and corporeal~intercorporeal relationships. Whether reaching for a cup or a salt shaker, or kicking a ball in a way that manoeuvers it toward a goal, we 'subjects' have a sequential dynamic relationship with an object in the world, a relationship that is both a kinesthetic and kinetic-visual/kinetic-tactile relationship: we are moving with respect to a seen object in the world, then moving hand to grasp the object or foot to strike the object. With respect to corporeal~intercorporeal relationships, we may be shaking hands with a friend or riding a horse over obstacles. Again, in such experiences, we have a sequential dynamic relationship that is both a kinesthetic and kinetic-visual/kinetic-tactile relationship. Clearly, the sense modality of kinesthesia and the complex sense modalities of the kinetic-visual and kinetic-tactile are basic to both subject~world and corporeal~intercorporeal relationships. Moreover a double reality obtains in each instance in terms of the inside~outside complementarity of the kinesthetic and the kinetic-visual and/or kinetic-tactile themselves. Perhaps because kinesthesia and the combined sense modalities are such a staple, such a built-in of every-day life, they are taken for granted—that is, unless or until through accident, ageing, or illness, or through misjudgement, interruption, or inattentiveness, they become the center of attention. With respect to the above examples, our hand may knock over the salt shaker; the kicked ball may go astray; our handshake may be aborted because of a sneeze; we may be jostled because the horse stumbles. What customarily and even normally flows forth in a smooth and unimpeded dynamic is suddenly disrupted, and the expected confluence of kinesthetic and kinetic-visual/kinetic-tactile dynamics is cut short. The coordination dynamics that normally obtain between the kinesthetic and kinetic, *between inside and outside*, are indeed thwarted. We are no longer moving in harmony, whether in relation to something in the world or in relation to others.

The inside of movement grounds everyday thinkings and doings as well, thinkings in terms of trains of thought and ultimate decisions to do such and such—for example, the decision to leave at such and such a time and to take this route rather than that—and most notably, the ability to think in movement itself, as in lifting a leg just the right height over a log as one moves continuously along in a walk through the woods. The inside of movement thus grounds both consequent doings in light of thinkings and immediate doings in light of thinking in movement itself. In this context, one might furthermore consider the myriad instinctive, reactive, or reasoned actions individuals take in relation to others and to the surrounding world and parse those actions in terms of movement inside and outside, such as one's instinctive withdrawal of one's hand from a hot stove, one's reactive response to the smile or insult of another, or one's reasoned participation in a protest march. Clearly, the relationship between the inside and outside of movement has significance all the way from having learned our bodies and learned to move ourselves, and thereby move in the ways we now do in the first place, to movements having social and ecological significance. Moreover and as indicated earlier, the inside~ outside relationship of movement has emotional significance: feelings move through us and move us to move in the world in distinctive ways. Fear, for example, may move a person to move in the proverbial modes of "freeze or flight," though fear may also take an individual pathologically away from the everyday world. Yet as each breath shows, pathology notwithstanding, the everyday world remains "the *life-world* for us all" (Husserl 1973, p. 136). The communal and the individual are indeed inextricably linked, and linked furthermore in "a *common time-form*" (ibid., p. 128). A common lifeworld and a common time form, in fact ground our capacity to move in concert with others and to harm others as well. In virtue of being the bodies we are, and in virtue of experiencing immediately and directly the bodies we are, *and at will from both inside and outside*, we know the powers and vulnerabilities of being the bodies we are, and thus not only *that* we can move in harmony or disharmony with others, but *how* we can move in harmony or disharmony with others.

The inside~outside complexity of movement is mirrored in many ways by the inside~outside complexity of tactility. Tactility is immediately and directly experienced in both the felt in-and-out flow of breath and the felt opening and closing of a passageway. It is, of course, immediately and directly experienced in all corporeal~intercorporeal and subject~world relationships in which we touch and are touched by others and by things in our surrounding world. In fact and in truth, we are always in touch with something (Sheets-Johnstone 1990, 1999a/2011). Indeed, as Aristotle astutely observed, "Without touch, an animal cannot be" (Aristotle 435b16-17): "the loss of this one sense alone must bring about the death of an animal… it is indispensably necessary to what is an animal" (Aristotle 435b4–9). Husserl specifies these existential insights in exacting terms when he states, "By means of the sense of touch, I am always in the world perceptually" (Husserl 1989, p. 74). He later describes the double reality of touching and touched, affirming specifically in focusing on the experience of one hand touching the other, that each part of the body involved "is then precisely for the other an external thing that is touching and acting upon it, and each is at the same time Body" (ibid., pp. 152–3).

Husserl's elucidation of the double reality of tactility, its double-sided unity or intertwining, was transformed by Merleau-Ponty into a "chiasm" and "reversibility" that focus not just on the fact that the right hand that touches the left can become the hand that is touched by the left, but extends that reversibility to seer and seen: the look, Merleau-Ponty states, "palpates" things (Merleau-Ponty 1968, p. 133). That it does so, he declares, is simply "a remarkable variant" of "tactile palpation" (ibid.). What is experientially crossed and reversible in tactility is thus, according to Merleau-Ponty, experientially crossed and reversible in vision. While it might appear that Merleau-Ponty is extending what Husserl describes as the self-reflexivity of an animate organism, that is, the reflexive relationship of an animate organism to itself, a relationship in which a "functioning organ" of the organism "*become[s] an Object and the Object a functioning organ*" (Husserl 1973, p. 97), that extension on behalf of a visual subject–world reflexivity is beyond credibility. In fact, Husserl's observations a good number of years earlier contest such an extension. While Husserl points out, "To be sure, sometimes it is said that the eye is, as it were, in touch with the Object by casting its glance over it," he immediately proceeds to note, "But we immediately sense the difference. An eye does not appear to one's own vision, and it is not the case that the colors which would appear visually on the eye as localized sensations... would be the same as those attributed to the object in the apprehension of the seen external thing and Objectified in it as features." He furthermore rather jovially points out, "And similarly, we do not have a kind of extended occularity such that, by moving, one eye could rub past the other and produce the phenomenon of double sensation" (Husserl 1989, p. 155). He concludes, "I do not see myself, my Body, the way I touch myself. What I call the seen Body is not something seeing which is seen, the way my Body as touched Body is something touching which is touched" (ibid.). In effect, Merleau-Ponty's extension of palpation to vision—"We must habituate ourselves to think that every visible is cut out in the tangible" (Merleau-Ponty 1968, p. 134)—is what might be termed an excess existential exuberance over the double reality of tactility. Moreover his claim of a "pre-established harmony" of "[t]he look" with "visible things" in the world "as though [the look] knew them before knowing them" (ibid., p. 133), is oddly adultist, especially in light of his three-year lectureship on child psychology at the Sorbonne and his writings on infants in which he states, "In the beginning of the child's life, external perception is impossible for very simple reasons: visual accommodation and muscular control of the eyes are insufficient. As has been often said, the body is at first 'buccal' in nature" (Merleau-Ponty 1964, p. 122).

Turning a blind eye to the essential developmental role of tactility and its relationship to visual discernment and acuity is indeed a surprising neglect, for while as adults we commonly categorize tactile experience in the simple terms of either/or possibilities, those possibilities exist along a gamut of possibilities that run along a gradient: from blunt to sharp, smooth to jagged, wet to dry, warm to cold, loose to tight, soft to hard, heavy to light, and round to straight, for example—all of them being differentially apparent tactile qualities, some being experienced by an infant in inspecting a fork, a spoon, a cup, or a plate, and in picking up and moving any of these items about to begin with, or in lifting a toy from the pillow and in lifting itself up by the bars of its crib. They are furthermore differentially apparent in a felt three-dimensional sense in the handling of all kinds of objects, from round to rectangular, for example, and are thus apparent in the felt difference between a ball and a block. They are differentially apparent too in being dressed for bed and being dressed in a coat, in being given a bath and being dried afterward, in being picked up in rigid, tightly closed arms and in relaxed, soft arms. Given the gamut of tactile experiences from birth onward, it is hardly surprising that what is distinguished in the close-up tactile terms of texture, weight, temperature, shape, and so on, comes to inform vision of our surrounding world, both our developing subject~world relationships and corporeal~intercorporeal relationships. In sum, an avowed 'non-analogical' but 'literal' extension of "palpation" to vision (Merleau-Ponty1968, p. 133) overrides the essential tactile ways in which we come to know the world and build our knowledge of it. If indeed, "We must habituate ourselves to think that every visible is cut out in the tangible," then that foundational tactile ground requires meticulous elucidation as do the myriad ways in which it comes to inform vision.

Our immediate and direct experience of inside and outside is clearly not limited to breath or to movement but includes our tactile "being-in-the-world," an inside~outside relationship from the beginning that is substantively tethered to corporeal~intercorporeal experience: in nursing, in being fed, in being put inside a crib, in being diapered and clothed, and so on. However rudimentary in the beginning, our awareness of inside and outside is palpable, *literally* palpable. We do indeed touch and are touched by others and by things outside us. We furthermore touch and are touched by our own bodily parts when we flex an elbow or a knee and bring forearm and upper arm together or the backsides of our calf and thigh together, or when we bring our leg upward toward our torso, or when we make a fist or clap our hands, or when bring our lips together and sound the consonant "m." We should note too that to distinguish between touching and touched in these instances is oftentimes a matter of the felt pressure of one part on another and that hands joined as in prayer are virtually indistinguishable in terms of touching and touched except by the application of pressure. Hands commonly exert pressure simply by their weight on another bodily part, as a hand resting on a thigh, for example, but they can also readily exert additional pressure by pressing on that bodily part. One's hand can thus be readily recognized as that which is touching and one's thigh as being touched. One's thigh, in contrast, can exert pressure on one's hand only by pressing, i.e. by one's moving one's thigh upward to exert pressure on one's hand. It cannot otherwise be recognized as touching rather than touched. Movement in fact allows one to distinguish that which is touching from that which is touched as when one's hand rests on one's chest, for example, and, simply in virtue of breath, one feels the rising or expansion of the chest as a pressure against one's hand. In a way akin to the indistinguishability of touching and touched in hands joined in prayer, a static pressure may in fact be inchoate with respect to distinguishing between touching and touched, which may explain why there is need for an applied pressure by way of movement to make the distinction. These facts may themselves explain why philosopher Marjorie Greene, a long-time and well-known aficionado of Merleau-Ponty, remarked, "As with no other thinker, I say, yes, so it is—but what about that hand trick? Alas, I cannot make it work" (Greene 1976, p. 619).

In everyday life, touching is not usually a static phenomenon, not even in sitting or in a hand resting upon a leg. Touching is commonly a dynamic phenomenon, a matter not only of one's running one's hand along a surface or picking up a book, for example, but of small yet remarkable movements and shifts in position in sitting or standing. Like fingers pressing on keys or scratching a head, everyday touchings are commonly a kinesthetic as well as tactile experience. In effect, the relationship inherent in the double reality of touching and touched is complex, far more complex than an easy and straightforward reversibility. Husserl's descriptive references to intertwining, to double-sided unities, to intentional unities, and the like, incline one toward that complexity by specifying both/and relationships, relationships that implicitly recognize a relational together-ness and apartness. They thereby enlarge our understandings of insides and outsides beyond a singular and simple reversibility. What nevertheless remains striking in Merleau-Ponty's as well as Husserl's analyses of the sensory modality of touch is a concern with a double reality, an inside and an outside, and in particular, a quest to elucidate the essential character of that double reality, on the one hand by way of an "existential analysis" (Merleau-Ponty 1962, p. 136), on the other by way of the rigors of a phenomenological methodology.

It is of course of the very nature not just of movement and tactility but of all sensory modalities to conjoin insides and outsides, thus to conjoin subject and world, and corporeal and intercorporeal life. The conjunction can be complex as with kinetic-visual and kinetic-tactile modalities. In fact, movement and tactility enter into smell and taste, making them a kinetic-tactile-olfactory and a kinetic-tactile-gustatory modality respectively, thus anchoring them too in the tactile-kinesthetic body. We could hardly smell smoke or taste peanuts were we tactilely and kinesthetically deficient. The modality of hearing, specifically with respect to our making sounds, similarly conjoins insides and outsides. Hearing oneself speak, cry, shout, or laugh is exemplary of the self-reflexive relationship of an animate organism to itself, a double reality akin to the "self-reflexivity" that Husserl describes (Husserl 1973, p. 97). While Husserl astutely observes, "I do not see myself, my Body, the way I touch myself," I do hear myself, my Body, in a way analogous to the way I touch myself. An awareness of oneself as a sound-maker is in fact and to begin with not only essential to the realization of self-reflexivity, but is the ground floor of the origin of language (Sheets-Johnstone 1990). The modality of hearing, specifically with respect to oneself as sound-maker, incorporates both the articulation of sound and the airborne sound itself and is thus a tactile-kinesthetic-aural modality. There is obviously no such self-reflexivity in the hearing of sounds in the world, but there is nevertheless an inside and outside not only in terms of meaning, but in terms of dynamics. We may be startled when we hear the close rolling sound of thunder, for example, or we may be puzzled by sounds that we do not recognize as familiar in any way, or we may be entranced by the sheer dynamics of a Bach cantata, or we may be excited by the news someone is relating to us. Whether the sounds of other individuals, the sounds of nature, the sounds of music, or whatever, we experience a double reality. In short, hearing is in all instances an inside~outside phenomenon.

However cold the air taken in, it is all warm and toasty when it flows out. Inside~outside complementarities are foundational to life, even a paradigm of life and living beings. The double reality not only anchors the animate nature of life but avoids terms such as "embodiment," "embedded," "enaction," "extended," and so on, all of which package, locate, or attempt to animate what are already formal aspects of life as well as the animate form of life that is the subject of discussion and that exists among other animate forms of life in the world. We come into the world moving, breathing, and tactilely alive; we are precisely not stillborn. Moreover though we have no memory of the phenomenon personally, we come out of the womb in birth and into the world. We indeed travel in the very beginning from inside to outside. In doing so, we begin life-long subject~world relationships and life-long corporeal~intercorporeal relationships. May the chapters that follow elucidate basic dimensions of these developing relationships and inspire others to further investigations of insides and outsides.

References

Aristotle (1984) *De Anima*, in Barnes, J. (ed.) *The Complete Works of Aristotle*, vol. I, Smith, J.A. (trans.), Princeton, NJ: Princeton University Press.

Behnke, E.A. (2008) Interkinaesthetic affectivity: A phenomenological approach, *Continental Philosophy Review*, 41, pp. 143–161.

Bower, T.G.R. (1974) *Development in Infancy*, San Francisco, CA: W.H. Freeman.

Clark, E.V. (1979) Building a vocabulary: Words for objects, actions and relations, in Fletcher, P. & Garman, M. (eds.) *Language Acquisition*, pp. 149–160, Cambridge: Cambridge University Press.

Cook, N. (1978) In, on and under revisited again, *Papers and Reports on Child Language Development 15*, pp. 38–45, Stanford, CA: Stanford University Press.

Curtis, H. (1975) *Biology*, 2nd ed., New York: Worth Publishers.

Grene, M. (1976) Merleau-Ponty and the renewal of ontology, *The Review of Metaphysics*, 29 (4), pp. 605–625.

Grieve, R., Hoogenraad, R. & Murray, D. (1977) On the young child's use of lexis and syntax in understanding locative instructions, *Cognition*, 5, pp. 235–250.

Husserl, E. (1970) *The Crisis of European Sciences and Transcendental Phenomenology*, Carr, D. (trans.), Evanston, IL: Northwestern University Press.

Husserl, E. (1973) *Cartesian Meditations*, Cairns, D. (trans.), The Hague: Martinus Nijhoff.

Husserl, E. (1977) *Phenomenological Psychology*, Scanlon, J. (trans.), The Hague: Martinus Nijhoff.

Husserl, E. (1989) *Ideas Pertaining to a Pure Phenomenology and to a Phenomenological Philosophy: Studies in the Phenomenology of Constitution, Book II*, Rojcewicz, R. & Schuwer, A. (trans.), Dordrecht: Kluwer Academic Publishers.

James, W. (1987) *William James: Writings 1902–1910*, New York: Library of America.

Kelso, J.A.S. (1995) *Dynamic Patterns: The Self-Organization of Brain and Behavior*, Cambridge, MA: Bradford Book/MIT Press.

Kelso, J.A.S. & Engstrøm, D.A. (2006) *The Complementary Nature*, Cambridge, MA: Bradford Book/MIT Press.

Luria, A.R. (1966) *Human Brain and Psychological Processes*, Haigh, B. (trans.), New York: Harper & Row.

Luria, A.R. (1973) *The Working Brain: An Introduction to Neuropsychology*, Haigh, B. (trans.), Harmondsworth: Penguin Books.

Merleau-Ponty, M. (1962) *Phenomenology of Perception*, Smith, C. (trans.), New York: Routledge & Kegan Paul.

Merleau-Ponty, M. (1964) The child's relation with others, Cobb, W. (trans.), in Edie, J.M. (ed.) *The Primacy of Perception*, pp. 96–155, Evanston, IL: Northwestern University Press.

Merleau-Ponty, M. (1968) *The Visible and the Invisible*, Lefort, C. (ed.), Lingis, A. (trans.), Evanston, IL: Northwestern University Press.

Piaget, J. (1967) *La construction du réel chez l'enfant*, Neuchatel: Delachaux et Niestlé.

Piaget, J. (1968) *La naissance de l'intelligence chez l'enfant*, 6th ed., Neuchatel: Delachaux et Niestlé.

Piaget, J. & Inhelder, B. (1967) *The Child's Conception of Space*, Langdon, F.J. & Lunzer, J.L. (trans.), New York: W.W. Norton.

Rothfield, P. (2005) Differentiating phenomenology and dance, *Topoi*, 24, pp. 43–53.

Sheets-Johnstone, M. (1981) Thinking in movement, *Journal of Aesthetics and Art Criticism*, 39 (4), pp. 399–407. Expanded version in Sheets-Johnstone, M. (1999a/exp. 2nd ed. 2011) Chapter 12, and Sheets-Johnstone, M. (2009) Chapter II.

Sheets-Johnstone, M. (1990) *The Roots of Thinking*, Philadelphia, PA: Temple University Press.

Sheets-Johnstone, M. (1999a/exp. 2nd ed. 2011) *The Primacy of Movement*, Amsterdam/Philadelphia, PA: John Benjamins Publishing.

Sheets-Johnstone, M. (1999b) Sensory-kinetic understandings of language: An inquiry into origins, *Evolution of Communication*, 3 (2), pp. 149–183.

Sheets-Johnstone, M. (2004) Preserving integrity against colonization, *Phenomenology and the Cognitive Sciences*, 3, pp. 249–261.

Sheets-Johnstone, M. (2009) *The Corporeal Turn: An Interdisciplinary Reader*, Exeter: Imprint Academic.

Sheets-Johnstone, M. (2014/this volume, Chapter II) Animation: Analyses, elaborations, and implications, *Husserl Studies*, 30 (3), pp. 247–268.

Stern, D.N. (1990) *Diary of a Baby*, New York: Basic Books.

Stuart, S.A.J. (2012) Enkinaesthesia: The essential sensuous background for co-agency, in Radman, Z. (ed.) *Knowing without Thinking: Mind, Action, Cognition, and the Phenomenon of the Background*, pp. 167–186, New York: Palgrave Macmillan.

Chapter Abstracts and Acknowledgments of Original Publication

CHAPTER I: KINESTHETIC EXPERIENCE:
UNDERSTANDING MOVEMENT INSIDE AND OUT

Body, Movement and Dance in Psychotherapy (2010), Vol. 5, No. 2: 111–127.

This chapter focuses phenomenological and empirical attention on kinesthetic experience. In doing so, it illuminates key experienced aspects of movement: its felt spatial dynamics on the one hand and its perceived three-dimensional form on the other. On this basis, the chapter proceeds to consider in turn: (1) the ontogenetic and phylogenetic significance of animate movement and its kinesthetic underpinnings; (2) the fundamental import of recognizing animation as the starting point for studies of animate life; and (3) the need to recognize common misconceptions of movement that distract us from the dynamic realities of movement itself. The clinical relevance of the analysis and the concepts it engenders are set forth in the conclusion.

CHAPTER II: ANIMATION: ANALYSES,
ELABORATIONS, AND IMPLICATIONS

Husserl Studies (2014), Vol. 30: 247–268.

This chapter highlights a neglected if not wholly overlooked topic in phenomenology, a topic central to Husserl's writings on animate organism, namely, animation. Though Husserl did not explore animation to the fullest in his descriptions of animate organism, his texts are integral to the task of fathoming animation. The chapter's introduction focuses on seminal aspects of animate organisms found within several such texts and elaborates their significance for phenomenological understandings of animation. The chapter furthermore highlights Husserl's pointed recognition of "the

problem of movement," movement being an essential dimension of animation if not definitive of animation itself. Succeeding sections of the chapter
testify to "the problem of movement" and the need to address it. They do
so by answering the following basic questions: What is livingly present in
the experience of movement, whether our own movement and the movement of other animate beings, or the movement of leaves, clouds, and so
on? What distinguishes kinesthetic from kinetic experiences of movement?
How are movement and time related? Just what is the problem of movement and how in fact do we address it? In what way is movement pertinent to the phenomenological concept of receptivity and the biological
concept of responsivity? Throughout these sections the chapter sets forth
phenomenological analyses, elaborations, and implications of animation.

CHAPTER III: ON THE ORIGIN, NATURE, AND GENESIS OF HABIT

Phenomenology and Mind (2014), Vol. 6: 76–89.

Brushing one's teeth, tying a shoelace or a knot, hammering a nail and not
one's thumb, writing one's name, walking down stairs—each is a
distinctive qualitative dynamic, a sequence of movements that has a
distinctive beginning, a distinctive contour with distinctive intensity
changes, for example, and a distinctive end. Each is a dynamic pattern of
movement. We are born with none of these dynamic patterns, which is to
say that they are not ready-made or innate in any sense. Each is learned.
The lesson to be learned from this existential truth concerns the origin of
habits: whatever habits we develop in what we do and the way we do
things, they exist because we learn the dynamics that constitute them,
whether by trial and error, by assiduous practice, by resting and taking up
the challenge again at a later time, or whatever. The mode of one's learning
may vary, but the formation of a habit in each instance is basically an
enlargement of one's kinetic repertoire. When we begin not with an
adultist perspective and speculative entities to explain various phenomena,
but with a veritable reconstructive or constructive phenomenology that
allows one to "get back" to those nonlinguistic days in which we learned
our bodies and learned to move ourselves and in the process formed nonlinguistic corporeal concepts in concert with developing synergies of
meaningful movement, we approach veritable understandings of mind. We
find that those synergies of meaningful movement are orchestrated not by
an embodied mind but by a mindful body alive to and cognizant of its
surrounding world, a mindful body developing fundamental abilities to
move effectively and efficiently within that world from infancy and in fact
from *in utero* onward.

CHAPTER IV: GETTING TO THE HEART OF
EMOTIONS AND CONSCIOUSNESS

In *Handbook of Cognitive Science*, ed. Paco Calvo and Antoni Gomila (2008), Amsterdam: Elsevier: 453–465.

The realities of life itself are of fundamental significance. Because they are, they warrant serious investigation and study from the beginning, the beginning in precisely a phylogenetic, ontogenetic, and phenomenological sense. A substantive sense of these realities is implicit throughout the writings of Charles Darwin. From the beginning of his studies as a biologist on The Beagle to his last studies of earthworms, Darwin's morphological concerns were consistently tied to animation, that is, to how animate forms make a living given the animate forms they are. Animation indeed tells us why distinguishing between behavior and movement is of vital significance; it tells us why concepts emanating from movement are of vital significance to animate life; it tells us how emotions are descriptively declinable in terms of force, space, and time, how they are manifestations of dynamic bodily feelings, and thus how they animate animate forms of life, moving animate forms of life to move; and finally, it tells us why emotions and movement are dynamically congruent. Animation is thus the "stable foundation" that Darwin sought for understanding the relationship of mind and body, and by extension, for understanding emotions and consciousness in their multiple and varied forms.

CHAPTER V: SCHIZOPHRENIA AND "THE COMET'S TAIL
OF NATURE": A CASE STUDY IN PHENOMENOLOGY
AND HUMAN PSYCHOPATHOLOGY

Philoctetes (journal co-sponsored by NY Psychoanalytic Institute), (2007), Vol. 1, No. 2: 5–45 (target article with commentaries and response).

In the context of fleshing out his concept of primal sensibility, Husserl turns attention to the development of the ego, specifically its actions and affections, stating that "the Ego always lives in the medium of its 'history'." His ensuing descriptive account of primal sensibility, summed in his notion of the comet's tail of Nature, is doubly significant: it provides a broad and direct phenomenological base from which to present a new and veritably rich historical perspective on schizophrenia and at the same time opens phenomenology itself to the task of setting forth a bona fide phenomenology of nature. The new perspective set forth in this chapter is not meant as an ultimate key to schizophrenia but as a penetrating new vista from which to view the pathology. The new vista grounds abnormalities of the psyche in foundational understandings of nature, understandings that complement in exacting ways the notable expositions and analyses of schizophrenia set forth by Louis Sass, specifically in the continuities Sass describes between the normal and abnormal by way of modern artists and schizophrenics; by Luc Ciompi, specifically in his integration of affect and cognition, and in the specific kind of atmosphere Ciompi cultivates at his Soteria treatment center; by Natalie Depraz, specifically in her attempt to elucidate affect in light of the unexpected; by Josef Parnas, specifically in his delineation of the immobilizing perplexity and incertitude typical of pre-psychotic individuals and their feelings of anxiety and "imminent disaster"; and by Shaun Gallagher, specifically in his sustained emphasis on the "disruption of protention" in the temporal flow of experience in schizophrenia. The new vista furthermore offers substantive empirical grounds for bridging a fundamental dichotomy in present-day neuroscientific research, notably, the chasm between experience and *the brain*. Indeed, phylogenetic and ontogenetic facts of life provide neuroscientific researchers with what dynamic systems theorists term "real-time" phenomena and thus with bona fide empirical bases on which to ground otherwise speculative forays into neurological patternings in the brain. These same phylogenetic and ontogenetic facts of life are seminal to classical psychoanalysis, i.e. to Freud's deep belief in the biological foundations of the psyche—e.g. "in the psychical field the biological factor is really the rock-bottom"—and in this biological sense to his disowned *Project* that attempted a neurological grounding of psychic functioning.

CHAPTER VI: *THE DESCENT OF MAN,* HUMAN NATURE, AND THE NATURE/CULTURE DIVIDE

Anthropological Theory (2010), Vol. 10, No. 4: 343–360.

How does human nature, especially as typically construed within a nature/culture divide, fit into Darwin's keen and detailed descriptions of animate life? This chapter points out omissions on each side of the nature/culture divide, a divide academically evident in the division between "the humanities" on the one side and "the sciences" on the other. On this basis, the chapter proceeds to concentrate attention pre-eminently on an inexplicable lacuna in today's scientific research, and in research generally over the 138 years since *The Descent of Man and Selection in Relation to Sex* was published, namely, on the lack of recognition of, and in turn the lack of penetrating and self-enlightening research on, "the law of battle" as a real human phenomenon. As described by Darwin, "the law of battle" is a biological matrix, natural to humans as to other animals, though tempered in humans by human "civilization." As the chapter shows, variously aided and abetted, the matrix has not only been reduced to a cellular phenomenon, i.e. sperm competition, but has been culturally elaborated—culturally "exapted," to borrow Gould and Vrba's term—to subserve strictly cultural ends, ends that reach far beyond the original ends and that have to do with the pursuit of various forms of "cultural fitness," and this from the beginnings of recorded human history.

CHAPTER VII: ON THE HAZARDS OF BEING A STRANGER TO ONESELF

Psychotherapy and Politics International (2008), Vol. 6, No. 1: 17–29.

This chapter traces out the socio-political consequences of self-ignorance and self-deception. These consequences were clearly recognized more than 2,000 years ago by early Greek philosophers, in part along the lines of "a conceit of wisdom." The consequences were more recently spelled out in striking ways by Carl Jung in his psychoanalytic analyses of "mass-minded man" who, through self-ignorance and self-deception, wreaks havoc and cruelty on others. The chapter furthermore points up both the challenge of attaining self-knowledge and possible paths to its attainment that bolster or augment classic psychotherapeutic approaches.

CHAPTER VIII: ON THE ELUSIVE NATURE OF THE HUMAN SELF: DIVINING THE ONTOLOGICAL DYNAMICS OF ANIMATE BEING

In *Interdisciplinary Perspectives on Personhood*, ed. Wentzel van Huyssteen and Erik P. Wiebe (2011), Grand Rapids, MI: William B. Eerdmans Publishing: 198–219.

Notable methodological and experiential similarities exist between Husserl's phenomenology and Vipassana (Buddhist) meditation that have sizeable import in themselves and sizeable import for divining the nature of the self, divining not in the sense of prophesizing or conjecturing—or of endowing with a divine spirit—but in the sense of experiencing outside the natural attitude, hence in the methodologically nuanced sense of following along lines of the "supernatural." Divining rods are thus in this instance empirically-proven rods, i.e. bona fide methodologies. Methodological and experiential similarities between a Western philosophy and an Eastern practice provide mutually validating evidence of a consciousness beyond the natural attitude—a "supernatural" consciousness. The mutually validating evidence might well intensify present-day interests of scientists in phenomenology and correlatively motivate them to study meditational practices to the point they approach the study of these areas of experience with the same vigor and zeal they study deficits such as blindsight, for example, and conditioned "motor" responses such as eye-blinking. The mutually validating evidence would in fact ordinarily count as experimental replication, cross-cultural replication at that, of a methodologically

arrived at ontological truth about humans, a fact testifying to the importance of understanding consciousness or mind from what we might call the
cultivated end of the cognitional spectrum. Such understanding ultimately
involves not merely an acknowledgement but an illumination of "the
subjective." With that illumination comes the possibility of insight into the
nature of "the self." The self is not equated to consciousness but is understood in the context of the lived and living temporal dynamics of
consciousness.

CHAPTER IX: THE BODY AS CULTURAL OBJECT/ THE BODY AS PAN-CULTURAL UNIVERSAL

In *Phenomenology of the Cultural Disciplines*, ed. Lester Embree and Mano
Daniel (1994), Boston, MA: Kluwer Academic Publishers: 85–114.

In addition to implicitly carrying forward a Cartesian-inspired depreciative
assessment of the body, many cultural disciplines (including philosophy)
have been heavily influenced by postmodern dogma, which basically
regards the body as little more than a cultural artifact. Received wisdom
and dogma together preclude an appreciation of the body as pan-cultural
universal. A consideration of early stone tools in the light of phenomenological corporeal matters of fact shows how the body is the source of
fundamental meanings, a semantic template. The analogy between the two
major hominid tooth forms—molars and incisors—and the major early
stone tools—core tools and flake tools—is in fact obvious once animate
form and the tactile-kinesthetic body—the sensorial felt body—is
recognized. A consideration of the experience of eyes as windows on two
worlds exemplifies a further dimension of the body as pan-cultural universal. The experience of eyes as centers of light and dark is tied to an
intercorporeal semantics that is rooted in morphological/visual relationships and attested to by biologist Adolf Portmann's notion of inwardness.
The experience is furthermore shown to be the basis of cultural practices
and beliefs related to the creation of circular forms such as the mandala.
Phenomenological attention to corporeal matters of fact as exemplified by
paleoanthropological artifacts, by the experience of inwardness, and by
cultural drawings of circular forms underscores the desirability of a
corporeal turn, an acknowledgement of animate form and of tactile-
kinesthetic experiences that consistently undergird hominid life.

CHAPTER X: DESCRIPTIVE FOUNDATIONS

Interdisciplinary Studies in Literature and Environment (2002), Vol. 9, No. 1:
165–179.

Darwin's descriptive accounts of the natural living world reveal not just facts but truths about the living world, including both the lives of others and our own lives. These descriptive foundations are laid by direct experience. Descriptive foundations are similarly at the core of phenomenological analyses. These analyses too reveal not just facts but truths about the living world as it is experienced. The grounding import of descriptive foundations to studies in evolutionary biology and phenomenology readily leads to an appreciation of the challenge of languaging experience, that is, the challenge of quintessentially capturing the dynamics of life in words. Only if and where an otherwise purely objective veridicality passes over into a resonating experiential veridicality does language have the possibility of becoming descriptive of life as it is lived from the inside out. Ecocritical writings, literary writings on the natural environment, answer to the challenge of languaging experience in just this way. They too are rooted in descriptive foundations. They neither represent nature nor take language for granted as a ready-made, but resonate veridically with experience of the world and animate nature. In doing so, they authenticate both a world of living subjects and the dynamic livingness of nature.

CHAPTER XI: THE ENEMY:
A TWENTY-FIRST CENTURY ARCHETYPAL STUDY

Psychotherapy and Politics International (2010), Vol. 8, No. 2: 146–161.

This chapter delineates the biologically based archetype of the enemy, showing how it derives ideationally and affectively from the archetype of the stranger, the latter an evolutionary given in the lives of animate creatures. In doing so, it extends Jung's classic exposition of archetypes and sustains the relationship of archetypes to instincts. It shows how globalization magnifies the archetype of the enemy; how, in a living sense, stranger and enemy archetype are taxonomically distinct; and how, just as the enemy is the cultural elaboration of the biologically based archetype of the stranger, so war is the cultural elaboration of male–male competition. In elucidating these aspects of the enemy, it makes explicit reference to Darwin's lengthy descriptive writings about male–male competition across invertebrate and vertebrate species. Key implications and ramifications are discussed on the basis of both Jung's and Darwin's insights into what is commonly known as "the mind/body problem."

CHAPTER XII: STRANGERS, TRUST, AND RELIGION:
ON THE VULNERABILITY OF BEING ALIVE

Human Studies (2015), Vol. 38, No. 3: doi 10.1007/s10746-015-9367-z.

Strangers, trust, and religion are critical dimensions within the sphere of human vulnerability. How are they experientially related? This chapter articulates commonly unexplored lines that connect commonly recognized dots. It begins with an epistemological account of the stranger as an Other in the Sartrean sense of otherness: someone who is the embodiment of possible harm, a threat to both our existence and the very meanings and values our life embodies, hence an existential source of fear. The chapter then sets forth an account of trust as a palliative to fear, trust being a socio-affective "compensation" for all its risks. On the basis of observations by both Thomas Merton and Huston Smith concerning the stranger, the paper in turn investigates the relationship of strangers, trust, and religion in the terms of life and death. In doing so, it draws on and extends citations from the writings of Michel Foucault and Elaine Scarry who, in different ways, highlight provocative conceptions of the Other. The chapter ends with reflections upon what Rudolph Otto termed the "mysterium tremendum" —the experienced mystery of life itself—upon the fact that we are vulnerable in the mere fact of being alive, and upon the fact that we have ways of transcending our vulnerability through a recognition and even celebration of our common humanity.

CHAPTER XIII: MOVEMENT:
OUR COMMON HERITAGE AND MOTHER TONGUE

In *Dance Knowledge*, ed. Anne Margrete Fisvik and Egil Bakka (2002), (Proceedings of the 5th NOFOD Conference, Trondheim, Norway, 10–13 January 2002): 37–50.

The world of dance is testimonial to the kinetic possibilities of human bodies. The possibilities are not merely anatomical ones. Their significance is in fact inadquately understood when specified simply in terms of a facilitating anatomy. Their fundamental significance lies in having a foundation in human ontogeny, namely, in the spontaneous disposition to learn one's body and to move oneself, and in the correlatively spontaneous disposition to think in movement. These native dispositions of infancy are ontogenetically pan-cultural and as such are basic to dance in any culture. Because they are human universals that define foundational aspects of our humanness, they warrant study in themselves. Such study can pinpoint ways in which standard conceptions of infancy are wayward. The characterization of infants as pre-linguistic is a prime example. When we examine closely the corporeal facts of the matter, or more specifically, the corporeal-*kinetic* facts of the matter, we find that, rather than infants being pre-linguistic, *language is post-kinetic*. An inquiry into the basis of our kinetic possibilities brings to light just such corporeal-kinetic matters of fact, not only correcting our illusions concerning infancy, but pointing us in the direciton of basic truths about ourselves. It does so by elucidating both the essentially kinetic way in which humans—like all other animate forms—come to make sense of themselves and the world, and the kinetic structures at the foundation of dance across cultures. The major focus of the chapter is on the former, that is, on the conceptual import of our common kinetic ontogeny and its cultural aspects and implications.

CHAPTER XIV: GLOBABLIZATION AND THE OTHER: LIFEWORLD(S) ON THE BRINK

Psychotherapy and Politics International (2012), Vol. 10, No. 3: 246–260.

This chapter specifies how globalization is not only an economic reality, but a socio-political–psychological-ecological reality. It demonstrates how globalization as an institution created by humans not only fosters fear and greed among humans, but also decimates non-human animal lifeworlds, and further, how in doing so, it threatens planet Earth itself. The chapter explores the relationship of globalization to Otherness in the form of the "enemy," whether religious, national, ethnic, political, or ecological, the latter specifically with respect to coral reefs. The exploration highlights the fact that if there are endangered species, it is because a dangerous species exists, namely, humans. Globalization foments an "us against them" mentality; heightens human competition between groups; and, not surprisingly, draws on what Darwin described as "the law of battle," namely, male–male competition. What in a phylogenetic sense originated in the service of mating now functions in the service of power and war. Recognition of this socio-political–psychological-ecological reality leads to an inquiry into the enemy that is not only outside but also within. Notable descriptions of the "Other within" are found in Socrates' and Plato's commentaries on the nature of humans, in Jung's concept of the Shadow, and, strikingly, in the observations of David Shulman and Mahmoud Darwish on the Israeli–Palestinian conflict and impasse. This investigation of the relationship between globalization and the Other leads ultimately to the realization that, if socio-political–psychological-ecological ills are to be treated and cured, then humans are obliged to an examination of the Other within.

Chapter I

Kinesthetic Experience
Understanding Movement Inside and Out[1]

Abstract: This chapter focuses phenomenological and empirical attention on kinesthetic experience, describing key experienced aspects of movement: its felt spatial dynamics on the one hand and its perceived three-dimensional form on the other. It proceeds on this basis to consider: (1) the ontogenetic and phylogenetic significance of animate movement and its kinesthetic underpinnings; (2) the fundamental import of recognizing animation as the starting point for studies of animate life; and (3) the need to recognize common misconceptions of movement that distract us from the dynamic realities of movement itself. The clinical relevance of the analysis and the concepts it engenders are set forth in the conclusion.

Introduction

What I would like to do in this chapter is: (1) set forth and clarify fundamental aspects of kinesthetic experience; (2) point out common misconceptions of movement that occlude its dynamic realities; and (3) underscore the necessity of being conceptually and linguistically true to the truths of experience. In doing so, I want to highlight three topics or areas of concern: methodology, dynamics, and meaning. Let me specify in a beginning way why I want to highlight each of these topics.

First, present-day usage of the term 'embodiment' and its derivatives is grounded in the assumption that there are methods that, by their very nature, inherently take the body into account, and that, by appeal to these methods, we can illuminate the bodily nature of cognition, mind, knowing, self-awareness, and so on. In this respect, *phenomenology* is of foundational import; it cannot be ignored. Why is this? Because its fundamental concern is with experience and with giving veridical descriptive accounts of

---

[1] First published in *Body, Movement and Dance in Psychotherapy* (2010), Vol. 5, No. 2: 111–127.

experience. If we leave experience behind, we leave life (real life) behind, with all its lived through meanings, motivations, feelings, thoughts, and so on. Second, we are not simply bodies, morphological forms having such and such parts, but dynamically moving and dynamically attentive creatures. As Darwin consistently recognized, animal morphologies are in the service of movement. Hence, like all animate forms in the animal kingdom, we humans are basically and essentially not simply a taxonomically recognizable morphology but taxonomically recognizable *morphologies-in-motion* that are dynamically motivated and attentive to their surrounding world. Third, in the course of their everyday activities, animals (humans included) are typically engaged in the world in ways that promote their well-being. They move in ways that sustain or enhance their survival, which is to say that they create *synergies of meaningful movement*. These three topics (methodology, specifically phenomenology; dynamics, specifically morphologies-in-motion; and meaning, specifically synergies of meaningful movement) will thread their way throughout this chapter. As will be evident, they are all realities of the fundamental phenomenon of *animation* and are declinable in terms of that fundamental phenomenon.

I. Phenomenology

As an introduction to understanding movement from the inside out, I begin with insights of the phenomenological philosopher Edmund Husserl regarding the nature of movement as both an internal and external phenomenon. Husserl's insights occur in the context of his investigations of empathy in his Fifth Cartesian Meditation. He does not offer an extended descriptive analysis of the experience of empathy in that meditation, an analysis of what we might describe in simple terms as our pairing with others, but leaves three clues that might lead to such an analysis, and these clues bear directly on understandings of movement and kinesthesia. In particular, certain unspecified aspects of empathy appear in his reduction of the sense of self to what he terms a "sphere of ownness" (Husserl 1973, pp. 92-9). The first clue turns on the fact that the five characteristics he cites as belonging to the sphere of ownness (fields of sensations, I govern, I cans, self-reflexivity, and psychophysical unity) are all rooted in experiences of our kinetic/tactile-kinesthetic bodies.[2] For example, with reference to "I cans", not only can I play the piano and walk to the store, but I can speak, perform calculations involving long division, make surgical incisions, and so on. In short, I have kinetic/tactile-kinesthetic faculties emanating from

---

[2]   Husserl's omission of feeling from his account of the "sphere of ownness" and his specification of "fields of sensation" within that sphere, blind us to the *dynamics* of self-movement and to the foundationally kinetic nature of empathy.

capacities accrued in the course of my developmental and educational history. The second clue has to do with similarity. Husserl speaks of similarity as undergirding my pairing of myself with others, ostensibly tying similarity simply to formal appearance, but intimating a similarity in kinetic dynamics by references to a person's style and conduct. Such references indicate that a similarity in movement as well as form binds me to others in a common humanity. This is because others present themselves as *animate* and, in their animation, move in ways dynamically similar to the ways in which I move. Again, we are pointed in the direction of kinetic/tactile-kinesthetic bodies, in particular species-specific kinetic/tactile-kinesthetic bodies. The third clue has to do with harmoniousness. Husserl speaks of "harmonious behavior," "harmonious systems," and "harmonious verification"; all in the context of explaining pairing or the analogical in analogical apperception. He gives no extended example of harmoniousness, though he remarks, for example, that "the outward conduct of someone who is angry or cheerful... I easily understand from my own conduct under similar circumstances" (Husserl 1973, p. 120). If we take harmoniousness as a clue, however, we are readily led to a kinetic dynamics. In other words, at the most basic level of analysis, harmoniousness points us not toward behaviors but toward movement; it refers to a "qualitative kinetic concordance," not to behavioral categories. In effect, we are led once again to kinetic/tactile-kinesthetic bodies.

On the basis of his readings of Husserl's archival texts on empathy and intersubjectivity, Danish philosopher Søren Overgaard shows how Husserl homes in on and prominences movement in attempting to elucidate the nature of pairing. Overgaard's exegetical aim is not to explicate intersubjectivity, but to answer to the question of how pairing is possible to begin with. His amplifications of Husserl's texts are of considerable import because they show, not explicitly but in a readily discernible manner, that Husserl approaches the problem of pairing from a direction essentially different from that in his Cartesian Meditations. Rather than the problem of pairing being a problem of "the other body," it is a problem of "my body." In other words, what Husserl attempts to pinpoint is not how the other body is a lived body, a feeling, thinking being, but how my body is "a physical, spatial body," that is, an object in the world. As Overgaard states, "Husserl... reaches the insight that kinesthetic "subjective' movement must at the same time be 'objective' (physical, spatial) movement," that "the 'internal' and the 'external' of my movement are inseparably realised (*verwirklicht*) as one." Overgaard tells us that Husserl "sometimes underscores [this conclusion] by saying that 'the kinesthetic movement brings with it *its* external side, and that the kinesthesis itself is the spatial movement'" (Overgaard 2003, p. 63).

Overgaard's illumination of how pairing could even get started, in essence answering to the question of what motivates it, vindicates Husserl's notion of pairing at the same time that it deepens our understanding of it by focusing attention on self-movement and what it reveals. Phenomenological understandings of self-movement nonetheless remain incomplete. They remain incomplete because the phenomenon of self-movement is under-examined, specifically in terms of what Husserl and Overgaard term "kinesthetic movement." From a phenomenological perspective, "kinesthetic movement" can only mean the actual experience of one's own movement, an experience, we might note, that is readily accessible to any human even if readily passed over by many. An examination of the experience reveals not only the fact that any movement creates its own qualitative dynamics, including specifically *spatial* dynamics, i.e. directional and areal qualities,[3] but that the mover has the possibility of experiencing space in an objective sense in any act of moving merely by paying attention to the three-dimensionality of his or her movement, hence its direction and amplitude. There is thus no reason for "musts," as in Husserl's and Overgaard's statement, "'subjective' movement must at the same time be 'objective' (physical, spatial) movement"; or in the statement, "there is a way in which my movement can and indeed must have the status of an external movement for me" (Overgaard 2003, p. 64). "Musts" are properly replaced by descriptive accounts of kinesthetic/kinetic experience, i.e. by a bona fide phenomenology of self-movement. A phenomenological examination of kinesthetic/kinetic experience readily shows that spatial qualities, both direc tional and areal, are fundamental to the three-dimensionality experientially manifest in self-movement. In effect, any movement I make creates a certain spatial dynamic in virtue of its spatial qualities and is at the same time a three-dimensional happening: it is both kinesthetic and kinetic. In Husserl's terms, it is both an internal and external happening.

Perceiving my movement as a three-dimensional happening is not contingent on vision. The "inner" and "outer" of my movement are directly experienced (or experience-able) in my movement itself. Indeed, movement is inherently spatial in the double sense of my *kinesthetically feeling* a certain qualitative spatial dynamics (curved, jagged, twisted, straight, constricted, confined, expansive, open, and so on) and of my *kinesthetically perceiving* the three-dimensional reality of my movement. I might note in passing phenomenologists' dedicated attention to the double sense of touch, "the touching and the touched," and their remarkably blindered and

---

[3]   Of course, any movement I make creates not just a spatial dynamic but a spatio-temporal-energic dynamic. Because space and physicality are of specific moment here, I omit the fuller descriptive term.

consequentially far-reaching neglect of the double sense of movement. When I hammer a nail, for example, I can experience space objectively in the three-dimensional expanse in and through which my downward-arcing arm moves, or I can turn my attention to the qualitative feel of my movement and experience a downward accelerating qualitative spatio-temporal-energic dynamic; when I scratch my head, I can experience space objectively in the three-dimensionality of the movement of my arm as it travels upward toward my head and of the back and forth movement of my fingers across a surface, or I can turn my attention to the qualitative dynamics of the upward lift and scratching movement. Correlative spatial experiences, in reality, spatio-temporal-energic experiences, obtain with any other so-called "kinesthetic movement." There would in fact be no space, no objective "out there," short of movement; there would be no concept of space or of being "in space" to begin with. The concept of space derives from movement. It is anchored in kinesthetic/kinetic experience, specifically in the dual experience of a qualitative spatial dynamics and the three-dimensionality of movement.

The problem of trying to get my movement "in space" out there in a world of others is thus a pseudo-problem when the experience of self-movement is phenomenologically examined and understood. We are alerted to this understanding even by neurophysiologists. In a textbook on the scientific bases of movement, Gowitzke and Milner state, "The voluntary contribution to movement is almost entirely limited to initiation, regulation of speed, force, range, and direction, and termination of the movement" (Gowitzke & Milner 1988, p. 193). Though their way of putting the matter is negative because of their central focus on what is neurophysiologically transpiring in self-movement, i.e. on what is involuntary rather than voluntary, their straightforward acknowledgement of range and direction (among other facets of movement) leaves no doubt but that movement is inherently spatial and, being voluntary, is open to experiential investigation. In the present instance, the challenge is to flesh out the nature of that spatiality and, as a spin-off, to shed initial light on the constitution of pairing or intersubjectivity; in particular, it is to show precisely through a phenomenological analysis of movement how it is that "the kinesthesis itself *is* the spatial movement." Further clarifications (or perhaps better, admonishments) warrant mention in the context of this challenge.

Overgaard remarks that "Some of [Husserl's] most fascinating reflections center on the... notion of something appearing 'there', in near- and far-perspectives," and that "There would be no space, and nothing at all would appear 'out there', according to Husserl, if I myself—with my kinesthetic movements—did not move *in* space" (Overgaard 2003, p. 62). Ironically, the concern with "here" and "there," and with "near" and "far," leads one to conceive of pairing in static rather than dynamic spatial terms. In fact, the common understanding of empathy in terms of "here" and "there," i.e. my imagining myself there where the other is, is grounded in static images. Movement is implied but precisely not prominenced in the foundationally dynamic way it should be prominenced, "should" not out of theoretical or explanatory necessity, but in recognition of the fact that movement is in fact central, quintessentially so. The same is true of "near" and "far": space is implied by way of movement, and movement is itself merely implied. Moreover, the very words "here," "there," "near," and "far" take for granted the very space they want to instantiate and docu- ment by way of experience. This may well be because space itself is already construed as a static container, a holder of things that are "here" or "there," "near" or "far." Husserl's conclusion, that "the kinesthesis itself *is* the spatial movement," is from this perspective less a point of arrival than a point of departure for a phenomenological analysis of self-movement that would do justice to the qualitative dynamics of movement that not only ground pairing and in turn ground the dynamic underpinnings of inter- subjectivity and empathy, but that, to begin with, are not simply spatial in character, but encompass temporal and energic dimensions and thereby constitute the conceptual spatio-temporal-energic backbone of our lives as animate beings. Near and far, sudden and prolonged, straight and curved, intense and weak: all such concepts are basically nonlinguistic concepts deriving from our experiences of movement. They are the bedrock of our foundational capacity to think in movement, a thinking that is grounded in nonlinguistic corporeal concepts.

Furthermore, in following through on a phenomenological analysis of self-movement, the sphere of ownness that Husserl describes would be properly augmented to include feelings. Feelings are a vital dimension of the sphere of ownness. As Freud rightly observed, we have both sensations and feelings "from within" (Freud 1923/1955, p. 19). But it is important that we distinguish between the two. In particular, we do not have "sensations" of movement, as we have sensations of touch or smell, or as we might say we have sensations of light and of sound; as indicated above, we have *feelings* of movement, just as we have kinetic motivational feelings, bodily felt urges and impulsions, and affective feelings of joy, disgust, fear, and so on. The assumption that we have sensations of movement distorts the dynamic reality of self-movement. The terminological problem is complex. The distinction between sensation and perception commonly if implicitly rests on a distinction between inner and outer: whatever the modality of objects sensed "out there" in the world, we have "perceptions" of them; whatever the modality of objects sensed in our bodies, we have "sensations" of them. The sensation/perception distinction, however, does not hold when it comes to self-movement. Self-movement is not sensational like pains, itches, a scratchy throat, and so on. Sensations are not dynamic events but punctual ones having no inherent connection or flow. Movement is in contrast an unfolding dynamic event and, as such, demands close analysis and elucidation in its own right. We indeed have "perceptions" of movement as well as "feelings" of movement as noted above, precisely in terms of our double spatial sense of movement: we "perceive" our movement as a three-dimensional happening; we "feel" the qualitative dynamics of our movement.

It is notable in this respect that in his Fifth Cartesian Meditation, Husserl remarks that empathy is through and through "indicated somatically," even to "the *higher psychic sphere*" (Husserl 1973, p. 120). As shown earlier by way of the clues I mentioned at the beginning, he could equally say that everything is indicated somatically in the sphere of ownness. In both instances, however, it is not merely a question of a body, but of a body-in-movement. Husserl's further statement indirectly underscores this very point: "Higher psychic occurrences," he observes, "diverse as they are and familiar as they have become, have furthermore their style… and take their course in forms of their own, which I can understand associatively on the basis of my empirical familiarity with the style of my own life" (Husserl 1973). Clearly, the core phenomenon is not simply a body but a *moving* body, a familiar moving body having a certain style of moving about in the world. Accordingly, we should be considering not *embodiment* and intersubjectivity, the former a thoroughly static concept like sensations, but *animation* and intersubjectivity, a dynamic concept proper to the phenomenon being investigated and described. Husserl himself intimates as much when he speaks consistently throughout his writings of "animate organism" and of "the animate bodily organism of the other Ego" (Husserl 1973, p. 122).

II. Fundamental Ontogenetic and Phylogenetic Realities of Animate Life

Infant psychiatrist Daniel Stern's descriptions of affect attunement are strikingly relevant in this context. They implicitly demonstrate the import of understanding movement inside and out, for they show: (1) that the dynamics of movement are indeed both kinesthetically and kinetically apparent, that is, that they are simultaneously experienced individually and socially; (2) that the experienced movement dynamics are congruent with an affective dynamics; and (3) that the qualitative character of the movement dynamics is cognized, hence that the spatio-temporal-energic qualities inherent in movement are recognizable and duly recognized. Let me give two examples from Stern (1985, p. 140):

A nine-month-old boy bangs his hand on a soft toy, at first in some anger but gradually with pleasure, exuberance, and humor. He sets up a steady rhythm. Mother falls into his rhythm and says, "kaaaaa-*bam*, kaaaaa-*bam*", the "*bam*" falling on the stroke and the "kaaaaa" riding with the preparatory upswing and the suspenseful holding of his arm aloft before it falls.

A nine-month-old girl becomes very excited about a toy and reaches for it. As she grabs it, she lets out an exuberant "aaah!" and looks at her mother. Her mother looks back, scrunches up her shoulders, and performs a terrific shimmy with her upper body, like a go-go dancer. The shimmy lasts only about as long as her daughter's "aaaah!" but is equally excited, joyful, and intense.

Stern analyses such instances of affect attunement in terms of "intensity," "timing," and "shape." He breaks these dimensions down in greater detail, describing how a mother matches the "absolute intensity," "intensity contour," "temporal beat," "rhythm," "duration," and "shape" of her infant's dynamics (Stern 1985, pp. 146–9). The immediate point of note here is that whatever the mode of attunement, whether aural, oral, or kinetic, it is not a question of imitation but of dynamics; dynamics created by infant and mother together through some mode of bodily movement. In each instance, the kinetic dynamics resound meaningfully for infant and mother alike. Infant and mother are thus cognitively as well as affectively and kinetically attuned. Together, through their common recognition of the dynamics, they create *synergies of meaningful movement*.

Such ontogenetical realities of life itself are of fundamental significance. When theories or linguistic fads overtake real-life observations, or when ready- made categories of behavior (eating, mating, fighting, playing, and so on) triumph over finely-detailed descriptive accounts of the actual movement dynamics of animate beings (whether beavers building dams, birds building nests, humans building houses, businesses, hopes, philosophies, or a complementary dynamics) the basic realities of life itself are elided. These realities are implicit in the original descriptive foundations set forth by Darwin. Indeed, the center pin of Darwin's extensive as well as lifelong studies of animals was precisely living forms that move themselves. From his beginning studies as a biologist on *The Beagle* (Darwin 1958) to his last studies of earthworms (Darwin 1881/1976), his morphological concerns were consistently tied to animation; that is, how, given the particular animate forms they are, diverse species of animals make a living. His emphasis was thus not on static morphologies, but on *morphologies-in-motion*. Morphologies-in-motion (animation) are first and foremost subject–world relationships. Perception, emotion, cognition, and imagination all derive from the basic fact that, whatever the animate form, it lives not in a vacuum or in ambiguity but in a world particularized for it by its being the animate form it is. Precisely because it does not live in a vacuum or in ambiguity, it is unnecessary to "embed" it (its perceptions, cognitions, and affective experiences) in a world, just as it is unnecessary to "embody" its actions, cognitions, experiences, emotions, and so on. Its interest, curiosity, hesitation, fright, and so on, its turning toward or turning away, and its approach or avoidance, are emblematic of its affective motivations to move in distinctive ways with respect to the particular world in which it lives, including the particular social world in which it lives and which it cognizes. Indeed, those animate forms that survive and reproduce (those morphologies-in-motion that successfully bear young) have developed synergies of meaningful movement. Accordingly, instead of trying to correct originally misconceived human joints through linguistic therapies of one kind and another, that is, instead of trying to remedy both centuries-old and recent carvings that separate mind and body, subject and world, emotion and cognition, and so on, carvings made in error to begin with, we should begin at the beginning, with life itself.

As Socrates admonished, to achieve a clear description of things, we adhere to their "natural formation," which means "dividing where the joint is, not breaking any part as a bad carver might" (*Phaedrus*, p. 265). Moreover, as he later admonished, "we certainly should divide everything into as few parts as possible" (*Statesman*, p. 287). In finer terms, then, instead of taking up a pre-eminently "cognitive" science, for example, and trying to reshape it to match the realities of life itself through linguistic implants on the order of embodied action (Varela, Thompson & Rosch 1991, pp. 172–80), embodied language (Gibbs, 2006), embodied cognition (Varela et al. 1991, pp. 147–84), embodied subjectivity (Zahavi 2005, pp. 156–63), embodied self-awareness (Zahavi 2002), embodied simulation (Gallese 2007), embodied self-experience (Zahavi 2005, pp. 197–206), embodied mind (Thompson 2007), and even embodied movement (Gibbs 2006, pp. 127, 130, 134), or through linguistic transplants that conceptually disfigure the truths of experience by encasing them in a motorology, as in talk of sensorimotor subjectivity (Hanna & Thompson 2003; Thompson 2007; Zahavi 2005), sensorimotor profiles (Noë 2004), motor intentionality, motor control (Merleau-Ponty 1962), and the like, we should begin with the fundamental fact of animation that integrally and explicitly informs the evolution of animate forms of life and that indeed constitutes the basic evolutionary fact of animate life.

III. Animation

As noted earlier, that we are first and foremost "animate" organisms is a truth Husserl consistently recognized. The truth merits highlighting if not accentuating. In his lifelong studies of sense-making (of constitution, meaning, sedimentations, horizons, protentions, retentions, and more), Husserl wrote not about "active" or "enactive" organisms; he wrote not about "embodied" organisms; he wrote not about "embedded" organisms; he wrote throughout about *animate organisms* (Husserl 1970, 1973, 1980, 1989). Though Darwin did not write about animate organisms as such, he certainly wrote similarly of human and nonhuman animals, their mental powers and their emotions (Darwin 1871/1981, 1872/1965), giving attention throughout to evolutionary continuities. Animation is the ground floor of our being alive in all its affective, perceptual, cognitional, and imaginative guises and stages, and in a surrounding world to begin with. In other words, animation grounds the full range of those intricate and varying dynamics that constitute and span the multiple dimensions of our livingness. Moreover, it bears emphasizing that animate organisms are by nature subjects of a world. Indeed, animate organisms, being subjects, are never without a surrounding world. Husserl actually makes this point sharply and in an extended descriptive manner in the context of contrasting the natural and human sciences. In the human sciences, he writes, scientists are oriented

> toward men and animals not as bodies to be investigated in the attitude oriented toward nature ["nature" as in physics, for example, or chemistry] but as men (or animals) who have their bodies as living bodies, who have their personal surrounding world, oriented around their living bodies as the near-far world and, at the same time, in the manners of appearing of right-left, up-down—all these manners of appearing standing in a successive relation of dependence to subjective manners of "I move my living body" in a system of kinesthesis... (Husserl 1970, pp. 331–2)

In short, Husserl is at pains to underscore the fact that living bodies (animate organisms) are not entities in a vacuum but are experientially anchored and engaged in dynamically meaningful ways in a surrounding world.

Animation (by animation, I mean precisely the fundamental kinetic realities that inherently conjoin cognition and affectivity and make synergies of meaningful movement possible) is theoretically of a piece with the biological concept of "responsivity."[4] As a biology textbook notes, "Plant seedlings bend toward light; meal-worms congregate in dampness; cats pounce on small moving objects; even certain bacteria move toward or

---

[4] I would like to thank the first reviewer of this article for her/his insightful suggestion of referring to philosophers Emmanuel Levinas and Bernhard Waldenfels in conjunction with "responsivity." A delineation of the complementarity between their understandings and expositions of responsivity and the biological notion set forth here would be intriguing and highly profitable, and would thereby warrant, at least to my mind, a separate article.

away from certain chemicals… [T]he capacity to respond is a fundamental and almost universal characteristic of life" (Curtis 1975, p. 28). It is notable that we find just such observations throughout Darwin's writings with respect to emotions: they implicitly limn life along the lines of responsivity, that is, animation. For example, Darwin observes, "Terror acts in the same manner on them [the lower animals] as on us, causing the muscles to tremble, the heart to palpitate, the sphincters to be relaxed, and the hair to stand on end" (Darwin 1871/1981, p. 39). He goes on to write of courage and timidity being "variable qualities in… individuals of the same species," of suspicion in "most wild animals," of some animals of a species being good-tempered and others ill-tempered, and of maternal affection in nonhuman animal life (Darwin 1871/1981, pp. 39–40). In short, and even before he examines emotions at length in his well-known book *The Expression of the Emotions in Man and Animals*, Darwin dwells at length on the responsivity of living creatures: on the primordial "animation" that is at the heart of life across virtually the whole of the animal kingdom.

Precisely in this context, it is of moment to note Darwin's estimation of the philosophically, psychologically, and neuroscientifically vexed relationship of mind and body, of the challenge it presents, and of the proper mode of conceiving and approaching the challenge of understanding that relationship. He writes, "Experience shows the problem of the mind cannot be solved by attacking the citadel itself—the mind is function of body—we must bring some *stable* foundation to argue from." While further comment will be made presently on this insightful observation, the point of moment here is that "animation" is indeed the "stable" foundation from which to argue, for animation is inclusive of the whole of life, and is thus integral to all-inclusive and penetrating understandings of cognition, emotion, consciousness, and more. In particular, animation tells us why concepts emanating from movement are of vital significance to animate life; it tells us why emotions are dynamic and dynamically-felt bodily feelings that, like movement, are descriptively declinable in terms of force, space, and time; it tells us why emotions and movement are dynamically congruent.

IV. Kinesthesia and Primary
Misconceptions about Movement

Aristotle regarded movement a *sensu communis*; a common sense or sense common to all other senses. He specified only five senses: vision, hearing, touch, smell, and taste. He described touch as a primary sense, a sense without which we could not live. Indeed, taking up Aristotle's observation, I pointed out in *The Roots of Thinking* that we are always in touch with something: walking, sitting, standing, lying, eating, pulling, pushing, hugging, kissing, scratching, rubbing. By the same token, we are always alive kinesthetically not only to felt postural attitudes and bodily tensions, but to our everyday kinetic dynamics that unfold with a familiarity that commonly goes unnoticed precisely because, as adults, the dynamics are familiar to us. A prime example I give to illustrate this fact is the everyday practice of brushing your teeth. Were someone else to brush your teeth, you would immediately recognize the fact that you yourself were not brushing your teeth, not simply because you saw someone standing before you holding your toothbrush and moving it about, but because *you would definitively feel a foreign dynamics inside your mouth.* Tactility and kinesthesia are indeed commonly intertwined: our tactile-kinesthetic bodies are the bedrock of the dynamic invariants that shape our everyday lives. In essence, J.J. Gibson takes up Aristotle's notion of movement as a *sensu communis* but in doing so diminishes its own fundamental import, prominencing "information pick-up" and vision, and overlooking precisely the foundational reality of our tactile-kinesthetic bodies and the synergies of meaningful movement that develop in the course of learning our bodies and learning to move ourselves (see Sheets-Johnstone 1999a, chapter 5). In short, Gibson's variation on and elaboration of what is basically Aristotle's notion of movement as a *sensu communis* distracts us from the dynamic realities of movement itself and from penetrating understandings of those dynamics; understandings that illuminate the qualitative structures inherent in the kinesthetic dynamics that inform our lives conceptually as well as kinetically, and the corresponding ways in which those dynamics are congruent to the affective dynamics that similarly inform our lives. To arrive at bona fide understandings of these dynamic relationships, we need to alert ourselves to the ways in which received ignorance masquerades as received wisdom about movement and thereby distracts us precisely from an awareness and recognition of the dynamics inherent in our being the animate forms we are. Received ignorance is evident in three primary domains.

To begin with, however much dictionaries tell us that movement is a change of position, movement is not a change of position, for movement has no position. Only objects have positions and, when they move, *they* change position.[5] Movement is the change itself, the dynamic happening, and needs to be phenomenologically analyzed and properly understood as such.

Second, movement does not simply occur *in* space and *in* time; movement *creates* its own space, time, and force, and it is precisely the creation of its own space-time-force that gives any movement its distinctive qualitative

---

5   Not only are airplanes experienced as objects in motion, but people may be
     similarly experienced: Mary's standing up and sitting down may be experi-
     enced as taking place in space and in time just as John's getting into his car
     may be.

character: its waxings and wanings, its hesitancies and surges, its amplitudes and constrictions, its linear contours, its intensities, and so on, what I
have described phenomenologically as its tensional, linear, areal, and projectional qualities (Sheets-Johnstone 1966/1979/1980, 1999a). In short, any
movement creates its own distinctive spatio-temporal-energic dynamics;
dynamics that are occluded in conceptions of movement as a phenomenon
simply taking place *in* time and *in* space.

It is relevant to point out that the common notion of movement as a
change of position is of a conceptual piece with the notion that movement
takes place in time and in space. In both instances, the dynamics of movement itself go unnoticed. Moreover as is evident, there is commonly the
same conflation of movement and objects in motion (see Sheets-Johnstone
1979). Positional displacements of objects occur precisely *in* time and *in*
space. Given the overlap in misconceptions, it is not surprising that the in
space and in time misconception of movement similarly nullifies an
appreciation of the qualitative kinesthetic dynamics that are definitive of
movement; definitive because they specify the basic experiential character
of movement.

The third misconception has to do with language. The challenge of
being conceptually and linguistically true to the truths of animate experience means taking up the challenge of understanding movement inside
and out, and describing it accordingly, in the manner of famed neuropsychologist Aleksandr Romanovich Luria, who recognized kinetic/
kinaesthetic melodies. Received ignorance disregards Luria's insights,
turning instead to what I specified earlier as linguistic implants and transplants, apparently operating under the illusion that linguistic implants and
transplants suffice to remedy what are basically manmade carvings at
unnatural joints. When we duly heed Socrates's admonishment to heed the
"natural formation" of things, we straightaway recognize both the need to
be true to the truths of experience and the challenge of languaging experience according to those truths. I might add that an epiphenomenal perk of
the actual practice of phenomenology puts one directly in touch with that
double recognition. One faces directly the challenge of languaging experience, languaging what is actually there, sensuously present in experience,
and languaging the ways in which one goes and has gone beyond what is
actually there sensuously present toward a constellation of meanings and
values that accrue in the present and that have accrued over the course of
one's life.

In sum, what the phenomenological procedure of bracketing allows is
precisely a suspension of encumbered and encumbering misconceptions of
movement. One finds indeed that cognition is not embodied; experience is
not embodied; self-awareness is not embodied; agents are not embodied;
and movement is certainly not embodied. One finds the term "embodi-

ment" in all its forms to be, on the one hand, a lexical band-aid that covers over a 250 year-old suppurating wound and, on the other hand, a linguistic implant that plumps up facets of humanness by giving them a body. It removes all thought of animation from the scene of discussion, and passes over recognition of animation as foundational to the discussion itself. It thus passes over kinesthesia and proprioception. Proprioception is indeed not a faculty up for human grabs as it were, "a matter of debate among philosophers", as Evan Thompson views it (Thompson 2007, p. 464, note 3). Proprioception, like kinesthesia, is through and through an evolutionary phenomenon and warrants recognition and study as such. Moreover, subjectivity is not only not embodied, but it is not a sensorimotor phenomenon any more than intentionality is a motor phenomenon. Motorology talk deflects us from the realities of kinesthesia and proprioception no less than embodiment talk; that is, it too deflects us from the dynamics of movement itself and of the cognitional and affective dynamics that constitute the synergies of meaningful movement that informs the lives of animate beings. Motors, after all, do not have feeling; they are incapable of affectivity. By the same token, they lack agency. Motors do not go forth in the world in search of a lost companion any more than they go forth in search of food; they have neither friends nor hunger. Motorologists, like embodiers, need to wean themselves away from embodiment and sensory-*motor* talk and work toward languaging the realities of sensory-*kinetic/ kinesthetic* experience. Kinesthesia and proprioception are foundational aspects of animation and as such require straightforward analysis and study in their own right.[6] Through such study, the synergies of meaningful movement that inform all facets of creaturely life can come to be properly and finely described in the fullness of their dynamic experiential realities and, concomitantly, animate forms can come to be seen finally in the context of their phylogenetic and ontogenetic heritages as morphologies-in-motion.

---

[6] Other forms of movement analysis exist in addition to a phenomenological analysis, the most prominent one being Labananalysis. I have been told by practitioners of Labananalysis that it is closely related to the phenomenological analysis of movement.

V. Clinical Implications[7]

The clinical relevance of the above analysis together with the concepts it engenders can be set forth in relation to three basic dimensions of human experience: agency, modalities of kinesthetic awareness, and dynamic congruency of emotions and movement. Each of these dimensions is central to therapeutic work and will be elucidated briefly to mark out paths that therapists themselves may hone and develop.

(a) Agency

Individuals who feel helpless or incapable, who lack self-confidence and the like, can be led, through movement, to appreciate the authority that they can enjoy with respect to their own movement. In such experiences, they can discover that they are basically free to move as they wish to move. Moreover, they can discover that they can stop a movement in which they are engaged at any time that they wish. Most importantly, they can discover that they can change the qualitative dynamics of their movement. In making such discoveries, they become aware of the ways in which and the circumstances in which their movement dynamics have been and remain habitual. They thus come to realize, in the same way that they readily recognize the movement style of others in the course of their every-day lives, that they have their own style of moving, a style that they are now aware of, that they can now assess and evaluate, and that they can now change or modify if they so desire. In short, their sense of agency comes to the fore and can be appreciated and enhanced through attention to their own experiences of movement. On this basis, and in phenomeno-logical terms, they develop a living sense of their "I cans." Their sense of their bodies can shift accordingly. They are not just these arms, these legs, this torso, this head, for example. They are all-of-a-piece autonomous individuals who have the capacity to move as they choose and whose bodies are expressive of who they are. Through attention to their own self-movement, their sense of agency has the possibility of taking root and flowering. In *The Primacy of Movement* (Sheets-Johnstone 1999a), I discussed the sense of agency in multiple contexts; particularly in a chapter titled 'On Learning to Move Oneself' with reference to infant psychiatrist Daniel Stern's concept of the "core self" (Stern 1985, pp. 45–6) and psychologist

---

[7] Although I am not a therapist, I have led movement workshops for, or involving, psychologists and psychiatrists (Psychiatric Institute, University of Heidelberg; Department of Social Science, University of Cardiff; Philoctetes Center, New York), have done a considerable amount of research and writing in psychology and psychiatry (e.g. Sheets-Johnstone 2007, 2008a, 2008b, 2010), and have recently been interviewed for an online publication by a clinical psychologist (see reference section for details).

Jerome Bruner's concept of "agentivity" (Bruner 1990, pp. 77–8), a concept originating in conjunction with his studies of infants and young children in which he noted their consummate attention to "agent and action" in the beginning stages of speech.

(b) Modalities of Kinesthetic Awareness

An enhanced sense of agency is obviously related to enhanced kinesthetic awarenesses. Such awarenesses can also lead to fine-grained under-standings of the social synergies of meaningful movement that abound in everyday life. Modalities of kinesthetic awareness are thus of considerable moment. Experiencing movement as having an "inside" and an "outside" opens possibilities of awareness of how one's own movement resounds semantically not only in one's own kinesthetic experience but in the visually-attuned kinetic experience of others. The two experiences are sensorily different, but they are both anchored in the semantic congruency that obtains between movement and meaning. In other words, whatever the synergy of meaningful movement, it is on the one hand meaningfully motivated and articulated; on the other hand it, it resonates with meaning for those in one's immediate surrounding world. It does so in virtue of its dynamics. For example, two friends greeting each other or two individuals shaking hands on meeting for the first time are engaging in a comple-mentary qualitative dynamic in which there is a kinetic-semantic con-gruency. Social synergies of meaningful movement are not of course by any means all sweetness and light. In a heated argument, for example, synergies of meaningful movement are obviously antagonistic. The out-pouring of words in the unfolding verbal interchange is not simply a buccal or oral synergy of meaningful movement but a whole-body synergy that feeds into and indeed can readily escalate the kinetic-semantic dynamic resonating for both individuals. Attendance to kinesthetic modalities of awareness can enhance social awareness in just this sense, for whatever the kinesthetically-felt, semantically-resonant dynamics of one's own movement, those dynamics resonate in the kinetically-sensitive eyes of others. They resonate in kinetically-sensitive eyes because we are all of us, from the beginning, self-schooled in movement and in the integral relationship of movement and meaning, and further, because we are all of us, from the beginning, attracted to movement. As psychoanalyst René Spitz observed, movement in infancy is the attractor *par excellence* (Spitz 1983, p. 149). Dance/movement therapists can lead people to appreciate how it remains the attractor and how modalities of kinesthetic awareness ground our social interactions.

(c) Dynamic Congruency of Emotions and Movement

Understanding the natural dynamic congruency of emotions and movement is of prime clinical significance. Emotions are not "states" of being but dynamic phenomena that are experienced in the flesh. Though sizeably under-researched and seemingly unrecognized, their dynamic congruency to movement is clinically significant precisely in terms of this fact. Individuals could hardly feign an emotion or restrain an emotion if a natural congruency between affect and movement did not already exist; that is, there would be no basis for feigning or restraining if one were not already experientially aware of "what comes naturally." Moreover, that emotions can be and are reworked culturally and familially attests to their foundation in Nature; that is, cultures, and families, can and do suppress, exaggerate, distort, or elaborate what is evolutionarily given (for examples of such reworkings with respect to power, see Sheets-Johnstone 1994). Dynamics are the key to understanding the natural relationship of affect and movement. In an article and chapter titled 'Emotion and Movement: A Beginning Empirical-Phenomenological Analysis of Their Relationship' (Sheets-Johnstone 1999b, 2009, Chapter VIII), I exemplified the dynamic congruency of emotions and movement in phenomenological, biological, and literary terms, drawing in the latter two instances on the writings of ethologist Konrad Lorenz and novelist William Faulkner. As the exemplifications demonstrate, feelings (both affective *feelings* and kinesthetic) have a particular unfolding spatio-temporal-energic form. To become aware of the subtle and complex dynamic dimensions of fear or reticence or delight or anger or any emotion as it is lived through and to become aware of *how it moves us to move* (Sheets-Johnstone 2006) is to become aware not only of motivations but of the way in which we kinetically take up its dynamic, commonly in habitual ways; which habitualities readily lead us back to a consideration of the import of "agency" and the importance of recognizing "modalities of kinesthetic awareness." As Jung notes, "as long as [a person] is unable to control his moods and emotions, or to be conscious of the myriad secret ways in which unconscious factors insinuate themselves into his arrangements and decisions, he is certainly not his own master" (Jung 1968, p. 72).

In sum, the dimensions of human experience set forth above are open to further explorations and refinements. They are basic avenues of research that are of substantive clinical relevance and, as such, call out to dance/movement therapists to forge ahead, to reflect, and to develop them in the light of their own clinical experience.

Acknowledgements

The original version of this chapter was presented as a Keynote Address at a conference titled 'Kinesthsia and Motion', at the University of Tampere, Finland, in October 2008. A second version of the chapter was presented as a guest lecture at the Institute for Advanced Study at the University of Minnesota in March 2009.

References

Bruner, J. (1990) *Acts of Meaning*, Cambridge, MA: Harvard University Press.

Curtis, H. (1975) *Biology*, 2nd ed., New York: Worth Publishers.

Darwin, C. (1958) *The Voyage of the Beagle*, New York: Bantam Books.

Darwin, C. (1965) *The Expression of the Emotions in Man and Animals*, Chicago, IL: University of Chicago Press. (Original work published 1872.)

Darwin, C. (1976) *Darwin on Earthworms: The Formation of Vegetable Mould through the Action of Worms with Observations on their Habits*, Ontario: Bookworm. (Original work published 1881.)

Darwin, C. (1981) *The Descent of Man, and Selection in Relation to Sex: Vol. 1*, Princeton, NJ: Princeton University Press. (Original work published 1871.)

Freud, S. (1955) The ego and the id, in Strachey, J. (ed.) *The Standard Edition of the Complete Psychological Works of Sigmund Freud*, vol. 19, pp. 19–27, London: Hogarth Press. (Original work published 1923.)

Gallese, V. (2007) Intentional attunement. The mirror neuron system and its role in interpersonal relations, *Interdisciplines*, [Online], http://www. Interdisciplines.org/mirror/papers/1 [1 june 2010].

Gibbs, R. (2006) *Embodiment and Cognitive Science*, New York: Cambridge University Press.

Gowitzke, B.A. & Milner, M. (1988) *Scientific Bases of Human Movement*, 3rd ed., Baltimore, MD: Williams and Wilkins.

Hanna, R. & Thompson, E. (2003) Neurophenomenology and the spontaneity of consciousness, in Thompson, E. (ed.) *The Problem of Consciousness: New Essays in the Phenomenological Philosophy of Mind*, pp. 133–161, Calgary: University of Calgary Press.

Husserl, E. (1970) *The Crisis of European Sciences and Transcendental Phenomenology*, Carr, D. (trans.), Evanston, IL: Northwestern University Press.

Husserl, E. (1973) *Cartesian Meditations*, Cairns, D. (trans.), The Hague: Martinus Nijhoff.

Husserl, E. (1980) *Ideas Pertaining to a Pure Phenomenology and to a Phenomenological Philosophy: Book 3 (Ideas III)*, Klein, T.E. & Pohl, W.E. (trans.), The Hague: Martinus Nijhoff.

Husserl, E. (1989) *Ideas Pertaining to a Pure Phenomenology and to a Phenomenological Philosophy: Book 2 (Ideas II)*, Rojcewicz, R. & Schuwer, A. (trans.), Boston, MA: Kluwer Academic Publishers.

Jung, C.G. (1968) *Man and His Symbols*, New York: Dell Publishing.

Merleau-Ponty, M. (1962) *Phenomenology of Perception*, Smith, C. (trans.), New York: Routledge and Kegan Paul.

Noë, A. (2004) *Action in Perception*, Cambridge, MA: MIT Press.

Overgaard, S. (2003) The importance of bodily movement to Husserl's theory of Fremderfarung, *Recherches Husserliennes*, 19, pp. 55–65.

Phaedrus, in *Dialogues of Plato: Vol. 1*, Jowett, B. (trans.), pp. 233–284, New York: Random House.

Sheets-Johnstone, M. (1966; 2nd eds. 1979/1980; 50th anniversary ed. 2015) *The Phenomenology of Dance*, Madison, WI: University of Wisconsin Press; Exeter: Dance Books Ltd; New York: Arno Press; Philadelphia, PA: Temple University Press.

Sheets-Johnstone, M. (1979) On movement and objects in motion, *The Journal of Aesthetic Education*, 13 (2), pp. 33–46.

Sheets-Johnstone, M. (1994) *The Roots of Power: Animate Form and Gendered Bodies*, Chicago, IL: Open Court Publishing.

Sheets-Johnstone, M. (1999a/expanded 2nd ed. 2011) *The Primacy of Movement*, Amsterdam/Philadelphia, PA: John Benjamins Publishing.

Sheets-Johnstone, M. (1999b) Emotion and movement: A beginning empirical-phenomenological analysis of their relationship, *Journal of Consciousness Studies*, 6 (11–12), pp. 259–277.

Sheets-Johnstone, M. (2006) Sur la nature de la confiance, in Ogien, A. & Quéré, L. (eds.) *Les moments de la confiance*, pp. 23–41, Paris: Economica.

Sheets-Johnstone, M. (2007/this volume, Chapter V) Schizophrenia and the 'comet's tail of nature': A case study in phenomenology and human psycho-pathology (target article with commentaries by Jaak Panksepp, Luc Ciompi, and Louis Sass, and response), *Philoctetes*, 1 (2), pp. 5–45.

Sheets-Johnstone, M. (2008a/this volume, Chapter VII) On the hazards of being a stranger to oneself, *Psychotherapy and Politics International*, 6 (1), pp. 17–29.

Sheets-Johnstone, M. (2008b) *The Roots of Morality*, College Park, PA: Pennsylvania State University Press.

Sheets-Johnstone, M. (2009) *The Corporeal Turn: An Interdisciplinary Reader*, Exeter: Imprint Academic.

Sheets-Johnstone, M. (2010/this volume, Chapter XI) The enemy: A 21st century archetypal study, *Psychotherapy and Politics International*, 8.

Sheets-Johnstone, M. (2016) The psychopathology of disembodiment and reconnection through enactment: A conversation with Maxine Sheets-Johnstone by Nancy Eichhorn, *Somatic Psychotherapy Today*, 6 (1) Winter 2016.

Spitz, R.A. (1983) Dialogues from infancy, in Emde, R.N. (ed.) *Dialogues from Infancy; Selected Papers*, New York: International Universities Press.

Statesman, in *Dialogues of Plato: Vol. II*, Jowett, B. (trans.), pp. 293–340, New York: Random House.

Stern, D.N. (1985) *The Interpersonal World of the Infant: A View from Psycho-analysis and Developmental Psychology*, New York: Basic Books.

Thompson, E. (2007) *Mind in Life: Biology, Phenomenology, and the Sciences of Mind*, Cambridge, MA: Harvard University Press.

Varela, F., Thompson, E. & Rosch, E. (1991) *The Embodied Mind: Cognitive Science and Human Experience*, Cambridge, MA: MIT Press.

Zahavi, D. (2002) First-person thoughts and embodied self-awareness: Some reflections on the relation between recent analytical philosophy and phenomenology, *Phenomenology and the Cognitive Sciences*, 1, pp. 7–26.

Zahavi, D. (2005) *Subjectivity and Selfhood*, Cambridge, MA: Bradford Books/ MIT Press.

Chapter II

Animation

Analyses, Elaborations,
and Implications[1]

Abstract: This chapter highlights a neglected, if not wholly overlooked, topic in phenomenology, a topic central to Husserl's writings on animate organism, namely, animation. Though Husserl did not explore animation to the fullest in his descriptions of animate organism, his texts are integral to the task of fathoming animation. The chapter's introduction focuses on seminal aspects of animate organisms found within several such texts and elaborates their significance for a phenomenological understanding of animation. The chapter furthermore highlights Husserl's pointed recognition of "the problem of movement," movement being an essential dimension of animation if not definitive of animation itself. Succeeding sections testify to "the problem of movement" and the need to address it. They do so by answering the following basic questions: What indeed is livingly present in the experience of movement, whether our own movement and the movement of other animate beings, or the movement of leaves, clouds, and so on? What distinguishes kinesthetic from kinetic experiences of movement? How are movement and time related? Just what is the problem of movement and how do we address it? In what way is movement pertinent to receptivity and responsivity? Throughout these sections the chapter encompasses phenomenological analyses, elaborations, and implications of animation.[2]

I. Animate Organism: An Introduction

To be animate is to have the capacity to move oneself and to experience the spatio-temporal-energic dynamics of one's movement. An animate organism is thus not just a living organism but a moving organism, an organism

---

[1]   First published in *Husserl Studies* (2014), Vol. 30: 247–268.
[2]   This chapter is a sizeably expanded version of the paper given at the inaugural Satellite Session of the Society for Phenomenology of the Body taking place at the 2013 conference of the Society for Phenomenology and Existential Philosophy, Eugene, Oregon. The session was dedicated to "Husserl's Concept of Animate Organism."

that feels the dynamic flow of its movement: its direction and amplitude, its intensity, its duration and speed. Moreover it feels an affective impulsion to move in the first place, and that affective character informs the flow of its movement throughout—every step, turn, or pause along the way. Animate organisms are moved to move and kinesthetically experience in felt bodily ways the particular qualitative dynamics of their movement: a slow, hobbling walk; a striding, forceful rush forward; a dawdling, circular strolling about; and so on. In short, what is experienced is a tactile-kinesthetic body-in-motion, tactile in Aristotle's sense, a sense born out in phenomenological investigations of experience, namely, that animate forms of life are never out of touch with something, both in simply being alive and in making their way in the world (Aristotle, *De Anima* 435a14; 435b4–5; 435b6–7; Sheets- Johnstone 2011a, Chap. 2, Part II).

In *Ideas II*, Husserl states that "primal sensibility, sensation, etc. *does not arise out of immanent grounds*, out of psychic tendencies; it is simply there, it emerges" (Hua IV, pp. 335/346). He ties this "sphere of passivity" to receptivity, "[t]he lowest Ego-spontaneity or Ego-activity" (Hua IV, pp. 336/347), which he characterizes as "a *primal sphere of intentionality*," albeit "*an unauthentic one*, since there can be no question here of a genuine 'intention toward', for which the Ego is required" (Hua IV, pp. 335–336/ 346–347). Thus, and above all in the form of "sensations," Husserl tends clearly to tether primal sensibility to a passive subject/world relationship.

Primal sensibility, however, is first and foremost not a primal sensibility of the world; it is a primal sensibility of one's living body, which is to say one's *animate* organism. In effect, primal sensibility rests on the ground of *primal animation*, the foundational reality of being a moving being, and a moving being from fetal development onward, including being an affectively moving being (Johnstone 2012). If being animate were just a matter of being alive and being alive were just a matter of primal sensibility, we would be static, posturally-defined creatures whose world would come forth involuntarily. We would be the equivalent of Condillac's statues. Primal sensibility is indeed properly and even necessarily described as a fundamental dimension of primal animation and this because sensibility to one's own movement "is simply there." We are kinesthetically attuned to our own movement, to its inherent qualitative dynamics, which is to say that we are alive, in a felt bodily sense, to the temporal, spatial, and energic qualities that give our movement its overall defining character—its vigorous explosiveness as in kicking, its sustained expansiveness as in stretching, and so on. In short, and to use Husserl's descriptive term, primal animation is "the root soil" (Hua IV, pp. 279/292). Animate organisms are thus at bottom gifted not simply with primal sensibility but with primal animation, which is "simply there," and there from the beginnings of life in utero. One might even say that animate organisms are developmentally and ever after made of movement and endowed with movement, inside and out.

It is of moment to note in this context that while the question "why is there something rather than nothing?" can be asked in relation to any physical body in the world—a mountain, a skeleton, a stone, and even a flower or tree or an animate organism—the question "why is there movement rather than stillness?" can be asked only in relation to an animate body—an ocean, a raindrop, the wind, an ant, a frog, a lion, a human.[3] What is animate is not basically something rather than nothing. It is indeed not basically a thing to begin with: it is not a static spatial entity but a spatio-temporal-energic phenomenon. An animate body is indeed movement through and through, movement that with respect to some animate organisms is on behalf of learning their body and learning to move themselves to begin with. Such learning is foundational to their exploring the world and coming to know it, to satisfying hunger, to escaping a predator, to procreation, and so on. When we ask why there is movement rather than stillness, we come face to face with the question of life, the nature of life, the nature of animate forms of life, and, we could add— especially given Husserl's consistent recognition of nonhuman animate life (e.g. Hua IV, pp. 175–176/185; Hua III, pp. 130–132/124–127; Hua IX, pp. 130–133/99–101)—even the nature of their evolutionary relationships and provenience.

In this context too, we can point out that, however neglected, there is no doubt but that Husserl explicitly recognized the foundational significance of movement in his combined epistemological-ontological insight that "I move" precedes "I do" and "I can" (Hua IV, pp. 261/273; see also Hua IV, pp. 259/271). Landgrebe appears to be the single phenomenologist who has taken this insight seriously or at least realized its fundamental, indeed essential significance (Landgrebe 1977, pp. 107–108; 1981, Chaps. 1 and 2). In the context of describing the significance of "I move," i.e. this "pre-linguistic acquaintance with oneself as the center of a spontaneous ability to move," Landgrebe writes, "kinaesthetic motions, without which there can be no constitution of time, are the most fundamental dimension of transcendental subjectivity, the genuinely original sphere, so that even the body (Leib), as functioning body, is not just something constituted *but is itself constituting as the transcendental condition of the possibility of each higher level of consciousness and of its reflexive character*" (Landgrebe 1977, p. 108; italics added). As indicated above, movement is the ground floor of learning our bodies and learning to move ourselves effectively and efficiently in the world, in effect of achieving a repertoire of "I cans" in the

---

3   Flora such as a rose and a linden, for example, are of course animate in the sense of being living and even moving in terms of growth and change. See also Pollan (2013) for burgeoning new understandings of flora.

first place (Sheets-Johnstone 2011a, Chap. 5). It should in fact be noted that any kind of "action" or "activity" involves movement: by its very nature, any so-termed "action" or "activity" — be it kicking a ball, shopping for bread, reading a book, or writing a letter — is not only by nature *constituted* in and through movement but could not be conceived as a packaged unit of some kind short of movement. Moreover we might point out in this context that kinesthesia, the sense modality that gives us an immediate and direct experience of our own movement, is insuppressible. In the context of examining "conscious knowledge about one's actions" and experimental research that might address the question of such knowledge, including experimental research dealing with pathologically afflicted individuals, psychologist Marc Jeannerod affirms, "There are no reliable methods for suppressing kinesthetic information arising during the execution of a movement" (Jeannerod 2006, p. 56). "Information" terminology aside, especially in the context not of position or posture but of movement, Jeannerod's declarative finding speaks reams about the foundational ongoing reality and significance of kinesthesia, reams that should certainly lead phenomenologists to take kinesthesia seriously and the challenge of elucidating its *insuppressible living dynamics* of signal importance.[4]

---

4   Clearly — and particularly in light of the insuppressibility of kinesthesia — we do not have to wait until something untoward occurs that awakens us into awareness and deters us from continuing on our way. On the contrary, precisely because movement is a dynamic happening and because the dynamics of our everyday movement have become habitual and are within our repertoire of what Husserl terms our "I cans," we can consult them at any time. In short, and as I have elsewhere shown (Sheets-Johnstone 2011a), any time we care to pay attention to our own movement, there it is. Further-more, we all learned our bodies and learned to move ourselves as infants and young children (ibid.). From this pan-human ontological perspective, the idea of starting with "action" is actually adultist; movement obviously comes first. There would indeed be no *action* if movement were not present from the first day and before, present and there to be honed and perfected. In learning our bodies and learning to move ourselves by attending to our own movement, we forged an untold number of dynamic patterns that became habitual. Familiar dynamics — tying a knot, brushing one's teeth, buttering one's toast, writing one's name, pulling weeds, sweeping, typing, playing a Bach prelude, and so on — are woven into our bodies and played out along the lines of our bodies. They are kinesthetic/kinetic melodies in both a neurological and experiential sense (Luria 1966, 1973). When we turn attention to these familiar dynamics, to our own *coordination dynamics* (Kelso 1995; Kelso and Engstrøm 2006), we recognize kinesthetic melodies; they bear the stamp of our own qualitatively felt movement patterns, our own familiar synergies of meaningful movement (Sheets-Johnstone 2009a,b).

In short, if we ask where the "skilled-ego," the "practical subject," and our "I cans" come from, there can be no doubt but that they come from primal animation and its spontaneous experienced existential reality: "I move." Indeed, "movement forms the I that moves before the I that moves forms movement" (Sheets-Johnstone 2011a, p. 119). Given this spontaneously emergent and experienced kinetic existential reality, a genetic phenomenology is essential. We cannot "get back," we cannot re-experience our infancy and early childhood development, but we can "reconstruct" as Husserl recognized (Hua VI, Beilage III/Appendix VI); we can carry out a "constructive phenomenology" as Fink recognized (Fink 1995, p. 63; see also Sheets-Johnstone 2011a, Chap. 5); and we can most definitely initiate a sorely lacking domain within phenomenology: *the phenomenology of learning*. We otherwise hazard being adultist in our phenomenological quests, forgetting that we all came into the world moving; we were precisely not stillborn.

Moreover in this context we can focus attention specifically on the general neglect of movement together with the specific neglect of the static phenomenology that elucidates its inherent qualitative spatio-temporal-energic structure (see Section III below and Sheets-Johnstone 1966/2nd ed., 1979/1980). Addressing this dual neglect is all the more urgent in light of Husserl's interest in and support of Heidegger's concern with "the *enigma of motion*" (Heidegger 1962, p. 444). Heidegger's concern with the enigma of motion is a matter of historicality; Husserl's concern with "the problem of movement" resides in the fundamental nature of animate organisms. Husserl's concern is evident not only in his marginal notes to *Sein und Zeit* (to be discussed below in Section IV), but in his own affirmation of "the problem of movement" in *Analyses Concerning Passive and Active Synthesis*. He writes, "one's own lived-body [...] is constituted phenomenologically in a fundamentally different way than [sic] other things. The question in all of this is how 'it gets on as it does'. Many new problems radiate out from here: like the problems of change and above all the problem of movement whose possibility belongs to the fundamental nature of a bodily thing" (Hua XXXI, pp. 299/585). We might parenthetically note that Husserl's specification of "the problems of change" along with "above all the problem of movement" recalls Aristotle's clear-sighted realization: "Nature is a principle of motion and change. [...] We must therefore see that we understand what motion is; for if it were unknown, nature too would be unknown" (Aristotle, *Physics* 200b:12–14). In brief, the problem of movement "above all" warrants our attention.

Of further significance is the fact that primal animation and its spontaneously emergent and experienced existential reality, "I move," are not lacking in cognitional awarenesses, however inchoate or burgeoning these awarenesses might be, as of the in-and-out flow of one's breath, or the rising and falling of one's chest, or the blinking or fluttering of one's eyelids. Neither are they lacking in inchoate or burgeoning concepts. On the contrary, they are informed or in the process of being informed by nonlinguistic corporeal concepts from fetal development onward. When lips open and close at eleven weeks, a fetus can feel their movement and hence begin to distinguish open and closed. Such experiences of the felt tactile-kinesthetic body are the bedrock of corporeal concepts and undergird later linguistic formulations. Moreover, post-natally an infant determines how tightly it must clasp a particular block or glass so that it does not drop, and hence develops a concept of weight—the heaviness or lightness of things—and a correlated concept of effort, how it must modulate the tensional quality of its movement to accommodate a particular weight. Furthermore, in nursing or being bottle-fed, an infant feels the softness and pliability of a nipple, and by its tongue movements, feels the hardness of its gums, the moistness of its lips, and so on. At a later age, it discovers the kinesthetically felt temporal and energic difference between pushing a toy away and flinging it or knocking it away, as well as the kinesthetically felt tensional difference between holding a doll and letting it drop and the kinesthetically felt spatial difference between reaching for a toy that is close and one that is further away. Just such discriminating experiences are the generative source of corporeal concepts, concepts that themselves are the foundation of concepts later formulated in language (Sheets-Johnstone 1990). Further still, in such experiences as these, infants and young children not only learn their bodies and learn to move themselves; they discover in exacting ways their capacity *to make things happen*. Such kinesthetic/kinetic discoveries are the cornerstone of their sense of agency.[5]

In sum, our first relation to a surrounding world is in and through movement. "I govern" (Hua I, pp. 128/97) is a *learned* ability, capacity, or accomplishment. I cannot and do not govern what I do not know and I do not come into the world *knowing*. I come into the world *moving* and with a capacity to learn, and my first learning consists in learning my body and learning to move myself, learning in ways that promote moving effectively and efficiently in my surrounding world. What undergirds our

---

5   "Agency" is actually an adultist term that fails to take Husserl's insight into the origin of "I cans" into account, namely, that "I move" precedes "I do," and "I can." Agency as a repertoire of I cans (and an ever-expanding or possibly expanding repertoire of I cans) is basically a matter of "making things happen": I can pull that toy toward me; I can close my mouth, turn my head, and refuse the spoon filled with food that someone is trying to put in my mouth. Moreover from infancy onward, we experience spontaneous dispositions to move: when something is put into one's mouth, or when one puts something oneself into one's mouth, one does not just let it sit there.

foundational learning is indeed primal animation, what dynamic systems theorists—specifically, coordination dynamics researchers—term an *intrinsic dynamics* (Kelso 1995), the intrinsic dynamics of *animate organisms*. Just as such animation or dynamics undergird our learning our bodies and learning to move ourselves, so they undergird our correlative build-up of kinesthetic learnings into "I cans" with respect to our surrounding world, a world that includes other animate beings and objects, thus in general terms, *both other entities that move and entities that are still*, entities that, like tables, chairs, towels, and soap, are still unless I or other animate beings move them. In sum, my first relation to the world is kinesthetic/kinetic: I move toward, I turn away, I suck, I kick, I make inchoate reaching movements, and so on. Moreover I babble and cry and discover myself as a sound-maker. Indeed, though etymology decrees otherwise, *infants are not pre-linguistic; language is post-kinetic* (Sheets-Johnstone 2010a, 2011a,b).

I turn now to four clarifying perspectives on animation that are in essence elaborations of Husserl's concept of animate organism. Though the first two are more detailed, the second two are no less essential. The perspectives culminate in concluding remarks about the concept of animate organism and its implications.

II. The Living Present, Movement, and Self-Movement

The living present is a matter of movement, and self-movement is a matter not of sensations but of dynamics. Sensations are temporally punctual and spatially pointillist: a push, a shove, an itch, a stabbing pain, a piercing sound, a flash of light, and so on. Sensations do not and cannot give you *flow*.[6] Everyday human movement is replete with flow, flowing habitualities—stepping off a curb and crossing the street; picking up a fork laden with food and bringing it to your opening mouth. Habitualities are *synergies of meaningful movement* that precisely flow forth without our having to monitor them in a focused way (Sheets-Johnstone 2009a, 2010b, 2011a,b, 2012a,b). We kinesthetically *feel* familiar dynamics running off as we focus attention on the keys we have dropped, for example, and

---

6   Sensations, specifically *kinesthetic sensations*, can, however, give one a static overall sense of one's body, as when one is gripped with pain or startled rigid in fear. Even so, it is notable that sensations commonly and simply "happen to you." They are commonly the result of something, precisely as with a flash of light or an itch. Dynamics, in contrast, are something "you make happen." You create them when you kick a ball, dry yourself after a shower, and so on. All such patterns of movement constitute a particular dynamic flow of energy that has equally particular spatial and temporal contours. For a further elaboration and discussion of sensations as spatially pointillist and temporally punctual phenomena in contrast to kinesthetically felt qualitative dynamics, see Sheets-Johnstone (2006).

spontaneously stoop to pick them up. Indeed, we feel familiar dynamics running off in stooping to pick up the keys. Were it not for our experiencing these familiar dynamics, experiencing them *in a felt kinesthetic sense*, we would never know what we were doing, i.e. that we had dropped the keys and were doing something to correct the situation. In short, we would never know that as so-called "received wisdom" puts it, "something is wrong," a "breakdown" has occurred (Searle 1992, p. 184). As noted elsewhere (Sheets-Johnstone 2011a, p. 215), "the belief that we know of the Background only when something goes wrong is an interesting but biased way of appreciating the Background." Husserl's fuller observation on "the background" is revealing:

> [C]oncerning the constitution in consciousness of the object prior to the turning of the attention and the taking of a specific position regarding it, we are referred back to the constitution in consciousness of previous objects, to previous acts of attention [...] Ultimately we arrive at the "obscure", [the] "hidden" [... where] [i]nsofar as attention plays a role, [...] we have there implicitly an Ego that is accomplishing some kind of comportment. The ultimate, however, is a *background that is prior to all comportment* and is instead presupposed by all comportment. [...] In a certain sense there is, in the obscure depths, a root soil. (Hua IV, pp. 279/291–292; italics in original)

The background or root soil is clearly animation, a kinesthetically-felt body whose familiar movement dynamics are felt as they run off in all comportments, felt not commonly in focal ways but along a conscious gradient of awareness in everyday life. The familiar felt awareness of our movement as we reach for a glass, jog down a path, sit down, or jump up from a chair, is similarly a dynamic kinesthetically felt experience through and through. In each instance, it is indeed a matter not of localized "kinesthetic sensations" but of a familiar whole body kinesthetically experienced *dynamic*. Accordingly, our vast repertoire of I cans—dynamic patterns of movement or coordination dynamics that we have learned—is not an amalgam of localized movement sensations, even "so-called 'movement sensations'" (Hua XXXI, pp. 13/50), but a repertoire of *familiar kinesthetic flows* that constitute a particular qualitative spatio-temporal-energic dynamic that we feel as such, a particular qualitative spatio-temporal-energic dynamic that is itself precisely a qualitative variation on a particular theme—reaching, stooping, sitting, and so on—depending on the particular situation or circumstance in which we find ourselves.

The very fact of this repertoire shows that, with respect to *flow* and its inherent temporal dynamics, movement is of a piece with the nature of life itself. Why else would Husserl write of "this elusively flowing life" (Hua VI, pp. 181/178), and go on to describe that elusive flowing in terms that accord precisely with Heraclitus's observation that one never crosses the same river twice (Heraclitus Fr. 91, 12 in Wilbur and Allen 1979, p. 67)? Why else would Husserl be led to declare that "We, as living in wakeful world-consciousness, are constantly active on the basis of our passive having of the world; it is from there, by objects pregiven in consciousness, that we are affected; it is to this or that object that we pay attention, according to our interests; with them we deal actively in different ways; through our acts they are 'thematic' objects" (Hua VI, pp. 110/108)? Further still, why else would Husserl be led to observe that "consciousness of the world […] is in constant motion" (Hua VI, pp. 111/109), and that "[a]ll past and future, even [the temporal givenness] of memorial objects is oriented to this flowing Now" (Hua XXXI, pp. 297/584)? Indeed, like movement itself, life flows; it is not a state of being but the animated dynamic of animate organisms.

It is hardly surprising, then, that what Husserl writes of inner time consciousness in terms of flow and streaming present is equally descriptive of movement. The "source point" — the beginning of any temporal Object or "now" — he declares, is "in a continuous line of advance," an advance that is the "running off" of a "continuity" (Husserl 1966, pp. 48–50). Whether a question of a falling leaf, of tying a shoelace, or of sweeping the floor, the same description holds: in each instance, there is a source point and a "continuous line of advance," the "running off" of a "continuity." Aristotle's keen observations on the integral relation of time and movement are of moment in this respect. Aristotle points out to begin with that "[T]ime is neither movement nor independent of movement. We must take this as our starting-point and try to discover — since we wish to know what time is — what exactly it has to do with movement" (*Physics* 219a1–3). He begins by observing that "we perceive movement and time together" (*Physics*, 219a4), that we apprehend time "only when we have marked motion, marking it by before and after" and that "only when we have perceived before and after in motion that we say that time has elapsed" (*Physics*, 219a23–25). He thus goes on to observe that "[h]ence time is not movement, but only movement insofar as it admits of enumeration" (*Physics*, 219b3–4), and later concludes that "Time is a measure of motion and of being moved" (*Physics*, 220b35). In short, Aristotle consistently ties time and movement together. Without movement, there would be no befores and afters, or in terms of internal time consciousness, no pro-tentions and retentions. Without movement, the world and all in it would be stilled. Indeed, the end of time and spatial stillness are of a piece.

Aristotle's observations are similar to those of Husserl, not specifically in terms of internal time consciousness, of course, but simply in terms of the inherent motion of time, of what Husserl describes as a "running off," a "continuity," a "continuous alteration," or in other words, as a continual conjoining of a "now" with "before" and "after." Husserl's observations in

fact hold for both time and motion: "now is constantly changed into something that has been"; an ever fresh now "passes over into modification,
peels off"; "a stable continuum" exists in which the present flows unbroken
into the past, the source point into retention, and into a "series of
retentions" from source point onward (Husserl 1966, pp. 50-1). In short,
movement is integral to time and time is integral to movement. Husserl in fact
writes at one point explicitly of the inherent temporality of movement in
relation to retentions using the image of a comet's tail to describe that
inherent temporality. He states, "During the perception of motion, there
takes place, moment by moment, a 'comprehension-as-now'; constituted
therein is the now actual phase of the motion itself. But this now-
apprehension is, as it were, the nucleus of a comet's tail of retentions
referring to the earlier now-points of the motion" (1966, p. 52).[7] The image
of a comet's tail, it should be noted, is perhaps more essential to the linkage
of time and motion than Husserl realizes insofar as "motion," like the
comet's tail, has no "nows" except insofar as it changes direction, for
example, or speed, or intensity, and so on. In short, any particular movement—a ripple in the water, the breaking of a wave, a turning of one's
head, the raising of one's arm—has no "nows" but only a certain qualitatively inflected temporal flow: it is quick or slow, sustained or abrupt.
Indeed, the comet's tail, like Zeno's arrow, strikingly captures the
"elusively flowing" character of movement.

   Time and movement are clearly inherently related, even structurally of
a piece, but unlike the qualitative dynamics of our own movement, we do
not *feel* time.[8] We feel only movement, our own animation, or we *perceive*
the animation, the qualitative kinetic dynamics, of other bodies. Nonetheless, what Husserl writes of inner time consciousness in terms of flow and
streaming present is equally descriptive of movement, whether our own or
that of others in the world about us. In particular, the primal impression of
movement generated by the "source point" of a falling leaf, for example, or

---

7   The comet's tail makes an appearance in relation to life as well when
    Husserl writes that "The Ego always lives in the medium of its 'history'"
    (Hua IV, pp. 339/350). Heidegger's historical *"enigma of motion"* is close to
    the surface in such observations.
8   Heidegger's meticulously resonant descriptive analysis of boredom
    (Heidegger 1995) might seem to come close to being a refutation of the
    claim, as might the simple expression that "time flies," i.e. one feels that
    time is flying by. In no instance, however, does one feel time directly, and
    this because time is a concept, a fundamental human concept. The concept
    is definitively tied to movement, but while movement is experienced or
    experientially possible, time is not. Words definitive of movement are
    commonly ascribed to time, as in time flying, dragging, creeping along, and
    so on, just as words describing feelings such as boredom or enduring are
    commonly ascribed to underlying indirect feelings of time.

of tying one's shoelace, is the beginning of a "continuous alteration." The actual movement, like consciousness of the actual movement "is constantly changed into something that has been; constantly, [… it] passes over into modification, peels off" (Husserl 1966, p. 50). Similarly, when Husserl writes of a "continuum" in which the present flows unbroken into past, the source point into retention, and into a series of retentions from source point onward (ibid., pp. 50–1), he could well be describing the very nature of movement. We might ask, then, why what Husserl describes as the flow and streaming present of inner time-consciousness is not recognized as fundamentally descriptive of movement and in fact of the nature of *animate life* — the very nature of *animate organisms*. The question is pointedly and critically entailed in taking seriously the fact that "consciousness of the world […] is in constant motion" and that "we are constantly active on the basis of our passive having of the world." Moreover the moment we delve into just what constitutes "active," or "action" — that is, the moment we begin to question just what these common terms mean and ask ourselves precisely in what they consist — we come face to face with *movement*, thus inevitably with our understanding of movement or lack thereof, and thus face to face with the "problem of movement," "*the enigma of motion.*"

It is of critical import in this context to single out and to elucidate more closely the temporal and its relationship to movement. Conceiving — and perceiving — "the body" as simply a spatial entity has its liabilities. Our bodies are temporal through and through and this not only because they change over time — growing, ageing, contracting an illness, and so on — but because, *being animate, they move; they are animated bodies*. Indeed, *lived* bodies are *animated* bodies. As pointed out earlier, animate organisms are not simply *alive*; animate organisms *move*. We in fact affirm that someone or something is alive because it moves; we see it capable of self-generated movement. Accordingly, the temporal nature of animate organisms can be ignored only at the cost of compromising veridical understandings of animate organisms. Perceived and conceived as simply a spatial object, an animate organism tends to be a posturally-defined and essentially visual entity, and one that is furthermore primarily visually oriented (Gallagher and Zahavi 2012, pp. 162, 237; Gallagher 2005, p. 43; Zahavi 1999, p. 97; Hua IV, pp. 159/166–7; Hua XXXI, pp. 297–300/584–7).[9] It does not suffice

---

9 Specification of the body as the "zero-point of orientation", as the "here" of every "there," and so on, reinforces a purely spatial concept of "the body." This sense and concept of "the body" reflects a purely spatial under-standing of the world that is in large measure due to a concern with cog-nition, particularly cognition of objects in a surrounding world. The spatial perspective ties in with sensations rather than dynamics, and in terms not just of "the body" but of the surrounding world itself. In reality, that world is never the same from one moment to the next, in large part because of my

to bring in tactility in an effort to *animate* or *enliven* this spatial object. Moreover it is not simply insufficient to describe an animate organism—a lived body, a *Leib*—in terms of "action" or "behavior" (much less "embodiment") as is presently the common practice; *it is not phenomenological to describe it in such terms.* Neither behavior nor action is conceptually or analytically adequate with respect to understanding animate movement, and this because "behavior" and "action" wrap the body in a closed

---

very movement in it, but in large part too because the sky darkens, the air outside is now cold, the breeze from the north has picked up, the clouds are changing patterns, a cluster of leaves are swirling, and so on.

A further point may be added with respect to a postural notion of the body and a lack of recognition of kinesthesia in preference to talk of proprioception. With respect to the latter, Zahavi, for example, writes that "Not only can I be, live, feel, and move my body, I can also know and describe it theoretically as a complex of physiological organs" (Zahavi 1999, p. 109). What is lacking are precisely phenomenological analyses of *living, feeling, and moving my body,* but these can be accomplished only through a recognition of *kinesthesia* in the first place, and a recognition of the fact that we do not come into the world ready-made with all our habits in place and all of the familiar dynamics that go with those habits. Telling too is the fact that if one avers that in the course of everyday life "I do not have observational access to my body in action" but only "non-observational proprioceptive and kinaesthetic awareness of my body in action" (Gallagher and Zahavi 2012, p. 162), there can hardly be reason for saying "I live, feel, and move my body."

As to proprioception, it is vital to distinguish postural from kinetic experiences, particularly when one writes, for example, that with respect to what Husserl describes as the co-articulation of perception and "the kinestheses" (Hua IV, pp. 58/63) "the kinaesthetic experiencing [manifests] positions in a system of possible movements" (Zahavi 1999, p. 97). Distinguishing between proprioception and kinesthesia is as phenomenologically essential as distinguishing between sensations and dynamics. In short, to say that "I have a proprioceptive sense of whether I am sitting or standing, stretching or contracting my muscles" and to claim that "these postural and positional senses of where and how the body is [...] are what phenomenologists call a 'pre-reflective sense of myself as embodied'" (Gallagher and Zahavi 2012, p. 155) are a phenomenological overreach in each instance. While we may certainly "sense ourselves" stretching, for example, and contracting, we do not have a "sense of ourselves" stretching or contracting *muscles,* at least not in the everyday sense Gallagher and Zahavi describe. We have direct and immediate experiences not of *muscles* but of *movement,* and in particular, of distinctively different *kinesthetically-felt* spatial dynamics in stretching and contracting. In fact, we have distinctively different overall dynamics in stretching and contracting that include temporal and intensity differences as well, precisely as Luria's description of movement and "complex sequential activity" as *kinesthetic melodies* so perfectly captures (Luria 1966, 1973).

unilluminated "doing" of some kind, a packaged physical happening. Neither comes close to an elucidation of dynamics, the inherent qualitative dynamics of movement, much less the inherent living significance of movement and its sensory modality of kinesthesia. In effect, it is hardly surprising that action and behavior miss any awareness of the integral relationship of time and movement.

Husserl himself misses an awareness of this relationship because he falls short of a full understanding of kinesthesia[10] and thus a full understanding of animate organisms. These lapses occur, however, because his essential concern is with worldly cognitions, with perceiving objects in the world and with the constitution of meaning in relation to these perceived objects. Understandably, then, he overlooks the dynamic realities of kinesthesia and the import of animation.[11] In doing so, he also overlooks the fact that self-movement is both originarily, and with respect to all later habitualities, a qualitative dynamic that is *felt*, a qualitative dynamic that not only inherently encompasses a temporal dimension but a temporal dimension that is *cardinal* rather than *ordinal* (see Sheets-Johnstone 2011a, Chap. 3). In particular, the inherent and originary temporality of movement and its developmental habitualities are not a series of "befores" and "afters" in relation to a "now," but precisely and invariantly a "streaming present," a "flow," as in reaching for and picking up a toy or glass, throwing or kicking a ball, walking down the street or down the stairs, sawing a piece of wood, and so on. The tripartite *ordinal* ordering of time is a sophisticated reflective attainment that, in terms of the inherent and originary qualitative temporal structure of movement, imposes divisions where none exist, divisions that if present would in fact disrupt what is experienced as a global and globally-felt qualitative dynamic.

---

[10] In truth, Husserl unwittingly deflects attention from the *kinesthetic dynamics* of animate life by consistently writing of *"kinesthetic sensations."* See Sheets-Johnstone (2006) for further elucidation of *the felt dynamics of life*.

[11] It is in these dynamic kinesthetic realities and animation, for example, that an awareness of the three-dimensionality of space originates, i.e. it originates in the context of perceiving one's own movement as having a three-dimensional character. When an infant stretches its arms overhead, reaches for a toy, kicks its legs, or runs its hands over a ball, it forms or begins to form a conception—specifically, a nonlinguistic corporeal conception—of the three-dimensionality of space. This objectifying perceptual dimension of self-movement is secondary to the original felt kinesthetic dynamics of self-movement. It might be noted that when spatial subjectivity is "enclosed in the body," i.e. "embodied," the temporal is not surprisingly put "all in the head" via internal time-consciousness. But in fact, it is only when the foundational reality of constitution passes over the foundational reality of animation that temporality is "all in the head."

Moreover in originary self-movement and later habitualities, what is constituted and has been constituted is not an object, nor does it have profiles. *What is being created and what is constituted are one and the same*: the dynamic pattern or coordination dynamics that I am now in a literal sense bringing to life are of a piece with the dynamics being constituted. Thus, something quite different is going on in the *felt* experience and constitution of self-movement than in the *perceptual* experience and constitution of an object in the world. In self-movement, a particular unfolding dynamic is *kinesthetically present* that cannot be otherwise *kinesthetically present* except by our moving differently and thereby creating and constituting a different qualitative dynamic. Temporal aspects of movement are indeed malleable: we can, temporally speaking, soften or accentuate the flow of our move-ment, its ebbings, surges, punctuations, explosions, attenuations, accelera-tions, brakings, and so forth. In effect, we can qualitatively vary temporal aspects of our movement because all such aspects are *qualitative* to begin with and are experienced as such. We see thus that movement creates its own time. By the same token, it creates its own space and force. In effect, movement does not simply take place *in* space and *in* time; it creates a certain temporality, spatiality, and force in the very way it flows forth, in the way it "runs off."

It is worth noting that Husserl comes close to recognizing the import of a global qualitative dynamic when he writes of "style" (Hua IV, pp. 270–1/283), and particularly when he writes of "qualitative change" and the "style of change" (Husserl 1981, pp. 239–40). In such instances what is commonly conceived as ordinal in nature—a quantitative or additive con-ception of time that essentially measures off moments of time in befores and afters—comes close to the realization of cardinal temporality. The latter is not a numerical experience of self-movement but a physiognomic experience of self-movement, precisely a *qualitative dynamic*. In short, when we listen to our *"internal movement consciousness"*, we find a distinctively felt temporal flow or streaming present that is constituted in the very process of its being created. We might ask, then, whether what Husserl writes of internal time consciousness in terms of *flow* and *streaming present* is not equally descriptive of everyday self-movement, and indeed whether Husserl's critical questions with respect to Brentano's account of "the origin of time" and his own question of "how time-consciousness is possible" (Husserl 1966, p. 40) cannot find substantive phenomenological clues in the experience of self-movement that lead to substantive answers. Such clues might show, for example, that an originary and even proper elucidation of how time-consciousness is possible lies not in the examina-tion of something external to us, like a melody, but in the very nature of our being the animate organisms we are, that is, in the very nature of self-movement.[12]

III. Distinguishing Between Kinesthetic and Kinetic Experiences of Movement

The distinction between kinesthetic and kinetic experiences is absolutely essential both to understandings of the individual nature of kinesthetic experience, and within that individual experience the difference between a *felt* qualitative dynamic and a *perceived* quasi-objectified dynamic, and to understandings of the difference between those kinesthetic experiences and kinetic experiences of the movement of others, whether those others are objects such as an airplane or a leaf, or whether they are other individuals, that is, living beings, forms of animate life, *animate organisms*.

To begin with, what I kinesthetically experience in a *felt* bodily sense is a first-hand—or first-body—*felt qualitative dynamic experience of movement itself*. I feel the dynamics of my movement, "my" *not in the sense of owner-ship* (cf. Gallagher 2005; Gallagher and Zahavi 2012), but in the sense of "I move," without the "I" being in any way substantively part of the immediate and direct experience, let alone reflectively constructed or inserted into that experience. One could from a Buddhist as well as phenomenological perspective specify simply "moving, moving," the inherently qualitative dynamics of "moving, moving" being what is experientially present and all that is experientially present (Kornfield and Goldstein 1987, pp. 22, 144). In fact, the moment I put an "I" or an "ownership" into the experience, I am perceiving the movement, not feeling its dynamics pure and simple. I am answering to a question perhaps—"Are you really doing this?"—or perhaps thinking to myself—"I am finally on my way!"; "I have almost completed this project"; "I have in fact succeeded in calculating the sum"; and so on. As discussed in the previous section, the pure and simple dynamics that run off in kinesthetic experience are commonly familiar dynamics. They undergird our "elusively flowing life" in a way akin to a sub-melodic presence.[13] They are indeed most commonly

---

12 We might in this context recall Husserl's words: "consciousness of the world is [...] in constant motion" (Hua VI, pp. 111/109). That observation implicitly validates the inherent animation of animate organisms. Harking back to the question of why there is movement rather than stillness, we might in fact posit in answer that movement is the temporal measure of all things.

13 It is of interest to point out the similarity between Husserl's phrase, "elusively flowing life"—"Not even the single philosopher by himself, within the epoche, can hold fast to anything in this elusively flowing life"— and Kornfield and Goldstein's phrase, "this process of flowing change"— "The truth of our being is simply this process of flowing change" (Kornfield

synergies of meaningful movement, synergies so familiar they run off without direct attention. Yet any time we care to pay attention to them, there they are, which is to say we pre-reflectively feel their unfolding dynamics (Sheets-Johnstone 2011a, 2012c).

What I kinesthetically experience in a *perceived* bodily sense are not uncommonly the spatio-temporal-energic realities of self-movement in terms of their *"out-thereness,"* realities *in space* and *in time,* such as the precise arc through which I am now moving my arm in perfecting my tennis serve and the exact timing of my throwing the ball in the air in relation to that arc, and energetic realities such as the degree of force I am now exerting in executing the serving movement and in throwing the ball in the air. As might be apparent, perceiving one's movement kinesthetically is common when one is learning a new skill or perfecting its execution. Perceptual awarenesses of one's movement, however, are evident too in those instances when one decides to change the manner in which one is moving, as, for example, when one decides to slow down or to move more energetically. Perceptual awarenesses are furthermore evident in those situations in which one feigns an emotion, that is, when one purposefully goes through the motions of smiling, for example, and of greeting someone joyously when no such feelings are felt. In all such instances, one's movement is quasi-objectified, "quasi" because one can never be a full-fledged object to oneself. As Sartre astutely noted, it is impossible to take a point of view on one's body in the sense of accessing different profiles of it (Sartre 1956, pp. 329–30). All the same, one can certainly perceive one's body going through the motions of a tennis serve or of smiling. Perceiving oneself going through the motions is in fact as much of an outside, i.e. objective, view as is possible. That perceptual experience is clearly different from feeling the kinesthetic flow of a qualitative dynamics. In the latter instance, *I am not moving through a form; the form is moving through me.*

Perceptual awarenesses of movement exist not only in various circumstances pertaining to one's own movement alone but in the broader context of oneself among others, i.e. oneself in a social and objective surrounding world. These perceptual awarenesses are commonly if not regularly geared toward tempering one's movement to accord (as Husserl might well say) *"harmoniously"* with the "thereness" of objects and persons in that world, whether those persons and objects are moving or still. One might tip-toe

---

and Goldstein 1987, p. 56). A further similarity is of moment with respect to an awareness of the dynamic nature of consciousness or mind, namely, in Husserl's affirmation that "consciousness of the world [...] is in constant motion" and Kornfield and Goldstein's affirmation that in meditating, "We can begin to study the whole process of the movement of mind" (ibid., p. 55).

into a room, for example, perceptually monitoring one's movement in order not to disturb someone who is working or sleeping, just as one might carefully monitor the angle and speed through which one goes through a newly painted doorway. In all such instances, the out-thereness of one's movement and the thereness of other persons and objects are *perceptual* data that are attended to spatially, temporally, and energically so that anything from modest consideration to outright deference is given to their presence. What may indeed be properly described as *moving in concert with others* in an everyday sense—and in an aesthetic sense as well, as in performing in an orchestral concert, an opera, a dance concert, or a theater play—rests on our pre-reflective awareness of *the foundational qualitative dynamics of movement and their variational possibilities*, in more precise terms, on the inherent tensional, linear, areal, and projectional qualities of movement, any movement, our own or that of others (see Sheets-Johnstone 1966/1979, 1980, 1999/2011). Attention to these foundational dynamics and in particular a brief specification of their qualitative nature are requisite prior to exemplifying the phenomenon of moving in concert with others.

As pointed out in the previous section, any particular movement—a ripple in the water, the breaking of a wave, a turning of one's head, the raising of one's arm—has no "nows" but only a certain qualitatively inflected temporal flow: it is quick or slow, sustained or abrupt. More than this, any particular movement has a certain spatial and energic quality as well, thus a certain overall kinetic dynamic that can be analyzed phenomenologically in terms of its intensity, directional thrust, amplitude, and the manner in which it unfolds. In other words, any movement can be analyzed in detail in terms of its tensional, linear, areal, and projectional qualities. When we see people raising their arm and waving it to hail a taxi, for example, or pushing a grocery cart, or stumbling on an unseen obstacle on their path, or when we see the breaking of a wave or the falling of a leaf, we see a certain unfolding kinetic dynamic. If we take pushing a grocery cart as an example of any unfolding kinetic dynamic, we can give a brief itemization of the specific qualitative possibilities within any dynamic: the *intensity* of one's movement may change from strong to light when one gradually slackens the pressure of the push as one passes an interesting assortment of goods on a shelf; the *direction* of one's movement obviously shifts when one rounds the corner from one aisle to another or when one looks here and there in the store for a particular item; the *range* of one's movement within the store may be limited or extensive depending on the extent of one's grocery list and the time one has to shop; the *manner in which one moves* may be sustained or abrupt, for example, depending upon whether one is leisurely strolling down an aisle or whether one unexpectedly meets another cart coming toward one from the opposite direction.

In addition to the dynamics created by the tensional quality of any movement (its intensity), the linear quality (its direction), the areal quality (its range), and its projectional quality (the manner in which it unfolds), two further spatial qualities are part of any kinetic dynamic. They derive from a body-in-movement as distinct from movement itself. In particular, linear and areal qualities — in vernacular terms, direction and range — are pertinent to moving bodies as well as to movement itself, thus to the linear and areal designs of moving bodies as well as to the linear and areal patterns of movement itself. The linear design of a body-in-movement may be vertical, for example, or twisted, bent over, tilted diagonally forward, and so on. A body's linear design naturally changes in the course of any synergy of meaningful movement, precisely as in the simple movement of extending one's arm and reaching for a glass, of sitting down or of rising from sitting to standing, and in getting into or out of bed. Its linear design is indeed a combination of lines, not only as in sitting down, but as in twisting one's head and upper torso in the process of walking down the street to see something behind one. The areal design of a body-in-movement has a certain qualitative character in terms of its expansiveness or contractiveness that is apparent not only when we crouch in order to hide, for example, but when we crouch in fear. Indeed, our expansiveness or contractiveness is particularly evident in our affective dynamics: we indeed crouch in fear just as we open our arms in delight, increase the length of our stride, and even run outstretched toward a friend whom we see approaching ahead of us.

While kinesthetically experienced qualitative dynamics are felt, precisely as in familiar synergies of meaningful movement, kinesthetically felt qualitative dynamics readily give way to kinesthetically perceived quantitative dynamics in the process of learning or perfecting new skills. As the earlier tennis serve example suggests, a determination of how far we must reach, or how fast we must proceed, or how strongly we must push forward or pull back, and so on, are integral to our learning and perfecting. Accordingly, it is not surprising that in such situations our perceptual attention is dominated by an attention to objective aspects of our movement, not to its felt quality. Yet its felt quality is commonly precisely what is aimed for, for it is when that felt quality is achieved that the movement is learned or perfected: it runs off smoothly, effectively, efficiently. In short, when we pass from monitoring dynamics to feeling dynamics, we are no longer moving through a form: the form is moving through us. Indeed, as renowned choreographer and dancer Merce Cunningham metaphorically put it in the context of explaining how he learned a complex set of separate movements for arms, legs, head, and torso: "The separate movements were arranged in continuity by random means, allowing for the superimposition (addition) of one or more, each having its own rhythm and time-length. But each succeeded in becoming continuous if I could wear it long enough, like a suit of clothes" (Cunningham 1968, unpaginated).

Felt and perceptual awarenesses that eventuate in "becoming continuous" are apparent in our everyday lives beyond their interweaving and integral necessity in learning a new sequence of movements or perfecting a skill. Interweaving awarenesses can enter our everyday lives at work and at play, as when we are sweeping the floor, for example, or making a surgical incision, or playing ping pong, or backing the car to park it alongside the curb. We may be focusing attention on the force of our movement, for example, or its direction or speed. Interweaving awarenesses are nearly certain to be involved in navigating a crowded sidewalk or a tight and narrow path where quantitatively as well as qualitatively inflected spatio-temporal-energic dynamics enter into movements such as swerving, tilting, slowing down, quickening, twisting, stepping aside, dashing forward, and so on. It is precisely in such social contexts that our *natural kinetic awareness of other persons* is central to our experience. While that kinetically-anchored experience is necessarily perceptual rather than felt, it is nonetheless basically an experience of a qualitative dynamics, the foundational qualitative dynamics of movement. While we may possibly note the degree to which a person moves to the side of a tight and narrow path as we near each other, for example, we are not so much gauging the person's movement quantitatively as we are engaged in the dynamic flow of his or her movement, its qualitative dispositions, propensities, inclinations, and transitions that move him or her toward the side. This qualitative form of engagement is present in our interpersonal relations with infants and young children, relations that are fundamentally not just animated but dynamically interanimate in qualitatively-inflected ways. In his descriptions of affect attunement, infant psychiatrist and clinical psychologist Daniel N. Stern has written meticulously of these interanimate dynamics (Stern 1985). His descriptions unequivocally if implicitly validate the fact that movement is our mother tongue, a tongue that allows us from the very beginning to *communicate nonlinguistically* by way of the qualitative dynamics of movement. We might further note that a qualitative engagement is clearly dominant in personal aesthetic performances in music, dance, and theater where, as mentioned earlier, one is attentive both to the perceived qualitative kinetic dynamics of the music, the dance, or the movement of other actors and to one's own kinesthetically felt qualitative dynamics.

When we focus attention directly on our natural kinetic awareness of movement in our surrounding world—whoever or whatever the moving others in that world—we necessarily experience a dynamic world in which the foundational qualitative dynamics of movement are of singular moment. Their fundamental spatio-temporal-energic nature is indeed at the heart of our experience, both kinesthetically and kinetically. It is because we are gifted with this dual awareness of movement that we are able to move in harmony with others. We have a common language that we commonly speak quite fluently. In effect, because we perceive the kinetic qualitative dynamics of other persons and kinesthetically feel the qualitative dynamics of our own movement, we are able to move in concert with others.

Yet our perceptual awareness of a kinetic qualitative dynamics is complex. It perforce involves sensory modalities beyond kinesthesia. Indeed, moving in concert draws precisely on a recognition of Aristotle's description of movement as a *sensu communis*.

The integral relationship of movement to audition and tactility is readily evident, evident over and beyond moving one's lips, tongue, and glottis separately or conjointly in speaking or in making any sounds, and over and beyond moving one's hand across a surface to feel its texture or one's fingers along an edge to determine its sharpness or bluntness. With respect to making music together, for example, moving in concert requires not only attending to the qualitative dynamics of the sounds one is making or wants to bring forth, but attending to the qualitatively unfolding dynamics of the communally made audible music itself, its kinetic rises and falls, accelerations and decelerations, its changing intensities, and so on. Movement is similarly integral to tactility whenever or wherever it is a question of moving in concert, thus not only in lifts in the context of a dance, for example, but in love-making and in riding a horse. In all such tactile instances of moving in concert, one's own movement and the movement of another being unfold in dynamic harmony with one another, and this because both oneself and the other are mutually attuned to the tactile-kinesthetic and tactile-kinetic dynamics of movement. In brief, the *sensu communis* nature of movement allows us to move in concert with others, to listen, as it were, to a kinetic dynamics outside ourselves, as in the qualitative flow of a piece of music as it unfolds and the qualitative dynamics of other animate beings. What basically conjoins us in concert is the integral conjunction of a felt and perceived qualitative dynamics, the qualitative dynamics that are definitive of movement.

The import of recognizing the foundational qualitative dynamics of movement, whatever the movement might be and whoever the moving individuals might be, of recognizing the fundamental difference between kinesthetic and kinetic experiences of those dynamics, and of recognizing the *sensu communis* nature of movement with respect to moving in concert —all are of particular note with respect to terms such as "interkinesthesia" (Behnke 2008), "enkinesthesia" (Stuart 2012), and "kinesthetic exchanges" (Rothfield 2005). Phenomenologically and empirically there are no such phenomena; the terms are misguided neologisms or labels. Although kinesthesia is a pan-human sensory modality and one that in fact cannot be suppressed (Jeannerod 2006), kinesthesia is a wholly individual experiential modality. The necessity of inquiring into, and phenomenologically analyzing the nature of, kinesthetic experience and thus of ascertaining the structural dimensions of its qualitative dynamics cannot be overemphasized. There can indeed be no shared kinesthesia any more than there can be such phenomena as "intervision" or "intervisuality," "envision" or "envisuality," or for that matter, "interolfaction," "entactility," "gustatory exchanges," and so on. On the other hand, we should note that phenomena such as *joint attention* indirectly attest to the reality of movement as a *sensu communis* and to the possibility of moving in concert. Joint attention is in fact a common animate phenomenon, one that has been empirically studied over a period of many years and is commonly regarded a staple in developmental infant studies (e.g. Scaife and Bruner 1975; Collis and Schaffer 1975; Stern 1985; Carpendale and Lewis 2012). We should note too the fact that although people cannot have kinesthetic exchanges, they may certainly exchange glances.

The basis of these shared experiences warrants specification, which is to say that what makes movement a *sensu communis* warrants fine-grained phenomenological examination. Such examination shows that *moving in concert* is not just a natural interpersonal movement phenomenon, but one in which the *visually perceived movement of another conjoins with one's kinesthetically felt movement*. In short, the foundational qualitative dynamics of movement remain the foundational qualitative dynamics of movement whether the movement is visually perceived and is thus experienced kinetically or whether it is kinesthetically experienced, i.e. felt rather than perceived as an ongoing dynamic. Where a fluid moving in concert does not spontaneously obtain, as in people failing to get out of each other's way on a crowded sidewalk, one's otherwise unbroken kinesthetically felt movement may be perceptually interrupted and monitored. In other words, habitual and accommodating ways of movement that simply "run off" may be interspersed with perceptions of movement. In such situations, the dynamics of one's movement are both perceptual and felt. Moving in concert with others is thus clearly a phenomenon that is both kinetic and kinesthetic and in which what is kinesthetic may be perceived as well as felt. What obtains in either instance, however, and as noted above, are *the inherent and abiding qualitative dynamics of movement*. Accordingly, what warrants phenomenological attention and indeed phenomenological elucidation is precisely the way in which a conjoined visual-kinetic awareness of an individual in one's surrounding world resonates dynamically with the kinesthetic dynamics of one's own movement, and beyond this, the way in which conjoined auditory-kinetic awarenesses, and conjoined tactile-kinetic awarenesses of an individual in one's surrounding world do the same. In sum, both the kinesthetic and kinetic dynamic realities and possibilities of movement are integral to moving in concert with other beings. One might almost be tempted to say that the harmony of the world hangs in the balance.[14]

IV. The Essential Coupling of Body and World, the Foundational Phenomenological Trinity, and the "Enigma" or "Problem" of Movement

The world one puts together is in conjunction with the body one is — the body one has learned and learned to move. The two go together. In effect, that "I govern" at all is only because I have learned my body and learned to move myself in effective and efficient ways. The ground floor of I govern thus lies in the foundational phenomenological trinity: "I move," "I do," "I can do," or "I can". To forget or to pass over the originary "I move" is indeed to forget or to pass over the ground floor of the trinity. More than this, it is actually a breach of phenomenological methodology to take movement for granted. Of considerable interest in this context are Husserl's marginal notes in *Being and Time*[15] where Heidegger writes of "the *enigma of motion*" (Husserl 1997, p. 414; Heidegger 1962, p. 444), and earlier indicates that "being-in-movement" (*Bewegtheit*) "cannot be understood in terms of motion as change of place" (Husserl 1997, p. 413; see alternate translation in Heidegger 1962, p. 441).[16] In both places, Husserl

---

14 It might be noted that appeals to tactility in particular on behalf of grounding intersubjectivity in the exteriority of one's own body overlook completely the phenomenological realities of movement (e.g. Zahavi 1999, p. 169). Kinesthetic perceptions are notably three-dimensional, not only as when one is learning to walk and to throw efficiently but as when one is learning to make surgical incisions and to drive. Kinesthetic perception is equally integral to understanding foundational forms of "bodily awareness" that ground "our ability to encounter an Other with an internal manifestation of alterity" (ibid.). It is indeed unnecessary to opine that "When my left hand touches my right, I am experiencing myself in a manner that anticipates both the way in which an Other would experience me and the way in which I would experience an Other" (ibid.). In short, when movement is consistently passed over by tactility and examples of touching (e.g. ibid., p. 105), a kind of functionalism obtains, a functionalism that in the end instrumentalizes the body and conceals its kinesthetic melodies (Luria 1966, 1973), obliterating the qualitative dynamics that undergird, structure, and sustain its movement.

15 All references that follow adhere to Thomas Sheehan's translated textual quotations from *Sein und Zeit* in Husserl (1997).

16 It is important to emphasize that Heidegger's concern is not with the phenomenon of movement itself — which, being ignored or passed over, itself constitutes a veritable phenomenological gaping hole as well as an "enigma" — but with the *historicality of Being*.

writes in the margin "enigma of motion" (Husserl 1997, pp. 413, 414). Moreover, alongside Heidegger's first mention of "being-in-movement," Husserl writes in the margin "being-in- movement" (1997, p. 413). Perhaps most striking too is the fact that, as noted earlier, Husserl himself writes of "the problem of movement" (Hua XXXI, pp. 299/585).

Clearly, the problem or enigma of movement can be resolved only by taking seriously the challenge of probing in depth the phenomenon "being-in-movement." Being-in-movement is indeed more than a historically formulated fact of life; it is an apt description of animate life itself. As noted earlier, we come into the world moving; we are precisely not stillborn. Apart from being asleep and apart from being rapt in wonder or in an aesthetic experience of some kind, being-in-movement describes our every-day lives as infants, growing children, and adults. Moreover even in sleeping and being caught up in wonder or in an aesthetic experience, we are far from breathless. Our breath moves us ceaselessly throughout our lives. Being-in-movement is existentially descriptive of our lives as animate organisms; it is indeed descriptive of the lives of all animate organisms. Precisely how it anchors I do and I can—that is, how "I move" ultimately grounds "I govern"—is a vexing question that warrants dedicated phenomenological examination. The question is not and cannot be answered by ready-made appeals to or writings about agency, even "pre-reflective" experiences of agency (e.g. Gallagher 2005, 2012; Gallagher and Zahavi 2012).

V. Receptivity and Responsivity

Husserl wrote pointedly and assiduously of receptivity (Husserl 1973; Hua XXXI). But receptivity is one half of a dyad. The other half is responsivity, precisely as in interest and turning toward. Again, as with the phenomenology of learning and the phenomenological trinity, this animate aspect requires phenomenological attention, not only attention to movement, but attention to affect and the qualitative dynamics of movement that are dynamically congruent with affect (Sheets-Johnstone 1999, included in 2009b, Chap. VIII). In this attention lies the possibility of expanding understandings of receptivity, which, after all, may be negative rather than positive and thus result in disinterest rather than interest and in a turning away or against rather than a turning toward.

The receptive and responsive realities of animate life extend across a broad and complex range. We may feel attracted to, repulsed by, confronted by, and so on. Surely given the foundational reality of receptivity and responsivity in animate life—and in fact the way in which that reality plays out in *style*—phenomenologists would do well to consider how "Every man [...] has his style of life in affection and action" and how it is that "one can to a certain extent expect how a man will behave in a given case if one has correctly apperceived him in his person, in his style" (Hua IV, pp. 270-1/282-3). The moment we replace the easy labels "action" and "behavior" (or "embodied") with *movement*, "the thing itself"—the real stuff—comes into view in the full measure of its qualitative dynamics. In turn, we begin to realize the possibility of elucidating a broad and complex range of possibilities within receptivity and responsivity.

VI. Concluding Remarks

Were it not for our being *animate organisms*, for *being* bodies (not merely *having* bodies), we would obviously be inanimate if not stillborn. Bodies are not just little go-carts for minds any more than brains are ready-made oracles at Delphi (the place to go for solutions to any puzzle about humans). All the original putting together from egg and sperm onward eventuates in mindful bodies capable of creating synergies of meaningful movement on their own behalf and on behalf of their progeny. The qualitative dynamics of movement are the basis of their forming *synergies of meaningful movement*. In the everyday world, these synergies commonly run off without focused attention, but only because they are inscribed in kinesthetic memory and run off on the basis of that memory (Sheets-Johnstone 2003, 2009b, Chap. X, 2012d). In contrast, we are aware when a synergy of meaningful movement "goes wrong" because we have a pre-reflective awareness of its familiar dynamics, familiar dynamics that we once learned and that are no longer present. What these experiential realities show is that consciousness is not a one-dimensional faculty but runs along a gradient of awarenesses. Habitualities that run off with pre-reflective attention were originally *learned* patterns of movement—patterns such as tying a shoelace, buttoning a shirt, and so on—and moreover not simply learned patterns of movement in relation to objects in the world, but learned patterns of movement *tout court*, such as turning over in one's crib, reaching and grasping, walking, running, skipping, throwing, and even speaking. Consciousness is indeed "in constant motion" as a whole-body, tactile-kinesthetically-grounded phenomenon linked foundationally and essentially to our "being-in-movement," which is to say to our being animate organisms.

References

Aristotle (1984) *De Anima*, in Barnes, J. (ed.) *The Complete Works of Aristotle*, Smith, J.A. (trans.), pp. 641-692, Bollingen Series LXXI.2, Princeton, NJ: Princeton University Press.

Aristotle (1984) *Physics*, in Barnes, J. (ed.) *The Complete Works of Aristotle*, Hardie, R.P. & Gaye, R.K. (trans.), pp. 315-446, Bollingen Series LXXI.2, Princeton, NJ: Princeton University Press.

Behnke, E. (2008) Interkinaesthetic affectivity: A phenomenological approach, *Continental Philosophy Review*, 41, pp. 143–161.

Carpendale, J.I.M. & Lewis, C. (2012) Reaching, requesting and reflecting: From interpersonal engagement to thinking, in Foolen, A., Lüdtke, U.M., Racine, T.P. & Zlatev, J. (eds.) *Moving Ourselves, Moving Others*, pp. 243–259, Amsterdam/Philadelphia, PA: John Benjamins Publishing.

Collis, G.M. & Schaffer, H.R. (1975) Synchronization of visual attention in mother-infant pairs, *Journal of Child Psychiatry*, 16, pp. 315–320.

Cunningham, M. (1968) *Changes: Notes on Choreography*, Starr, F. (ed.), New York: Something Else Press.

Fink, E. (1995) *Sixth Cartesian Meditation*, Bruzina, R. (trans.), Bloomington, IN: Indiana University Press.

Gallagher, S. (2005) *How the Body Shapes the Mind*, Oxford: Clarendon Press/Oxford University Press.

Gallagher, S. (2012) *Phenomenology*, Basingstoke: Palgrave Macmillan.

Gallagher, S. & Zahavi, D. (2012) *The Phenomenological Mind*, 2nd ed., London: Routledge.

Heidegger, M. (1962) *Being and Time*, Macquarrie, J. & Robinson, E. (trans.), New York: Harper & Row.

Heidegger, M. (1995) *The Fundamental Concepts of Metaphysics: World, Finitude, Solitude*, McNeill, W. & Walker, N. (trans.), Bloomington, IN: Indiana University Press.

Hua III. Husserl, E. (1950) *Ideen zu einer reinen Phänomenologie und phänomenologische Philosophie, Erstes Buch*, Biemel, W. (ed.), Den Haag: Martinus Nijhoff; *Ideas Pertaining to a Pure Phenomenology and to a Phenomenological Philosophy, First Book*, Kersten, F. (trans.), The Hague: Martinus Nijhoff, 1983.

Hua IV. Husserl, E. (1962) *Ideen zu einer reinen Phänomenologie und phänomenologische Philosophie, Zweites Buch*, Biemel, M. (ed.), Den Haag: Martinus Nijhoff; *Ideas Pertaining to a Pure Phenomenology and to a Phenomenological Philosophy, Second Book*, Rojcewicz, R. & Schuwer, A. (trans.), Dordrecht: Kluwer Academic Publishers, 1989.

Hua VI. Husserl, E. (1954a) *Die Krisis der europäischen Wissenschaften und die transcendentale Phänomenologie*, Biemel, W. (ed.), Den Haag: Martinus Nijhoff; *The Crisis of European Sciences and Transcendental Phenomenology*, Carr, D. (trans.), Evanston, IL: Northwestern University Press, 1970.

Hua VI. Husserl, E. (1954b) Der Ursprung der Geometrie als intentional-historisches Problem, in *Die Krisis der europäischen Wissenschaften und die transcendentale Phänomenologie*, Biemel, W. (ed.), Beilage III, pp. 365–386, Den Haag: Martinus Nijhoff; The origin of geometry, in *The Crisis of European Sciences and Transcendental Phenomenology*, Carr, D. (trans.), pp. 353–378, Evanston, IL: Northwestern University Press, 1970.

Hua XXXI. Husserl, E. (2000) *Aktive Synthesen: Aus der Vorlesung 'Transzendentale Logik' 1920/21. Ergänzungsband zu den 'Analysen zur passiven Synthesis'*, Breeur, R. (ed.), Den Haag: Kluwer Academic Publishers; *Analyses Concerning Passive and Active Synthesis: Lectures on Transcendental Logic*, Steinbock, A. (trans.), Dordrecht: Kluwer Academic Publishers, 2001.

Husserl, E. (1966) *The Phenomenology of Internal Time-Consciousness*, Heidegger, M. (ed.), Churchill, J.S. (trans.), Bloomington, IN: Indiana University Press.

Husserl, E. (1973) *Experience and Judgment*, Landgrebe, L. (ed.), Churchill, J.S. & Ameriks, K. (trans.), Evanston, IL: Northwestern University Press.

Husserl, E. (1981) The world of the living present and the constitution of the surrounding world external to the organism, Elliston, F.A. & Langsdorf, L. (trans.), in *Husserl: Shorter Works*, McCormick, P. & Elliston, F.A. (eds.), pp. 238–250, Notre Dame, IN: Notre Dame Press.

Husserl, E. (1997) *Psychological and Transcendental Phenomenology and the Confrontation with Heidegger (1927–1931)*, Sheehan, T. & Palmer, R.E. (eds. & trans.), Dordrecht: Kluwer Academic Publishers.

Jeannerod, M. (2006) *Motor Cognition: What Actions Tell the Self*, Oxford: Oxford University Press.

Johnstone, A.A. (2012) The deep bodily roots of emotion, *Husserl Studies*, 28 (3), pp. 179–200.

Kelso, J.A.S. (1995) *Dynamic Patterns*, Cambridge, MA: MIT Press/Bradford Books.

Kornfield, J. & Goldstein, J. (1987) *Seeking the Heart of Wisdom*, Boston, MA: Shambhala.

Landgrebe, L. (1977) Phenomenology as transcendental theory of history, Huertas-Jourda, J. & Feige, R. (trans.), in *Husserl: Expositions and Appraisals*, McCormick, P. & Elliston, F.A. (eds.), pp. 101–113, Notre Dame, IN: Notre Dame Press.

Landgrebe, L. (1981) *The Phenomenology of Edmund Husserl: Six Essays*, Welton, D. (ed.), Ithaca, NY: Cornell University Press.

Luria, A.R. (1966) *Human Brain and Psychological Processes*, Haigh, B. (trans.), New York: Harper & Row.

Luria, A.R. (1973) *The Working Brain: An Introduction to Neuropsychology*, Haigh, B. (trans.), Harmondsworth: Penguin Books.

Pollan, M. (2013) A radical new way of understanding flora, *The New Yorker*, December 23 and 30, pp. 92–105.

Rothfield, P. (2005) Differentiating phenomenology and dance, *Topoi*, 24, pp. 43–53.

Sartre, J.-P. (1956) *Being and Nothingness*, Barnes, H.E. (trans.), New York: Philosophical Library.

Scaife, M. & Bruner, J.S. (1975) The capacity for joint visual attention in the infant, *Nature*, 253, pp. 265–266.

Searle, J. (1992) *The Rediscovery of Mind*, Cambridge, MA: Bradford Books/MIT Press.

Sheets-Johnstone, M. (1966; 2nd eds. 1979/1980; 50th anniversary ed. 2015) *The Phenomenology of Dance*, Madison, WI: University of Wisconsin Press; Exeter: Dance Books Ltd.; New York: Arno Press; Philadelphia, PA: Temple University Press.

Sheets-Johnstone, M. (1990) *The Roots of Thinking*, Philadelphia, PA: Temple University Press.

Sheets-Johnstone, M. (1999) Emotions and movement: A beginning empirical-phenomenological analysis of their relationship, *Journal of Consciousness Studies*, 6 (11–12), pp. 259–277. Also in Sheets- Johnstone (2009b, Chap. VIII).

Sheets-Johnstone, M. (2003) Kinesthetic memory, *Theoria et Historia Scientiarum: An International Journal for Interdisciplinary Studies*, VII (1), pp. 69–92. (Special issue on "Embodiment and Awareness", Gallagher, S. & Depraz, N. [eds.]). Also in Sheets-Johnstone (2009b, Chap. X.)

Sheets-Johnstone, M. (2006) Essential clarifications of "self-affection" and Husserl's sphere of ownness: First steps toward a pure phenomenology of (human) nature, *Continental Philosophy Review*, 39, pp. 361–391.

Sheets-Johnstone, M. (2009a) Animation: The fundamental, essential, and properly descriptive concept, *Continental Philosophy Review*, 42, pp. 375–400.

Sheets-Johnstone, M. (2009b) *The Corporeal Turn: An Interdisciplinary Reader*, Exeter: Imprint Academic.

Sheets-Johnstone, M. (2010a) Why is movement therapeutic?, *American Journal of Dance Therapy*, 32, pp. 2–15.

Sheets-Johnstone, M. (2010b) Kinesthetic experience: Understanding movement inside and out, *Body, Movement and Dance in Psychotherapy*, 5 (2), pp. 111–127.

Sheets-Johnstone, M. (2011a) *The Primacy of Movement*, expanded 2nd ed., Amsterdam/Philadelphia, PA: John Benjamins Publishing.

Sheets-Johnstone, M. (2011b) Embodied minds or mindful bodies? A question of fundamental, inherently inter-related aspects of animation, *Subjectivity*, 4, pp. 451–466.

Sheets-Johnstone, M. (2012a) On movement and mirror neurons: A challenging and choice conversation, *Phenomenology and the Cognitive Sciences*, 11, pp. 385–401.

Sheets-Johnstone, M. (2012b) From movement to dance, *Phenomenology and the Cognitive Sciences*, 11, pp. 39–57.

Sheets-Johnstone, M. (2012c) Steps entailed in foregrounding the background: Taking the challenge of languaging experience seriously, in Radman, Z. (ed.) *Knowing without Thinking: Mind, Action, Cognition, and the Phenomenon of the Background*, pp. 187–205, New York: Palgrave Macmillan.

Sheets-Johnstone, M. (2012d) Kinesthetic memory: Further critical reflections and constructive analyses, in Koch, S.C., Fuchs, T., Summa, M. & Müller, C.

(eds.) *Body Memory, Metaphor and Movement*, pp. 43–72, Amsterdam/ Philadelphia, PA: John Benjamins Publishing.

Stern, D.N. (1985) *The Interpersonal World of the Infant: A View from Psycho- analysis and Developmental Psychology*, New York: Basic Books.

Stuart, S.A.J. (2012) Enkinaesthesia: The essential sensuous background for co- agency, in Radman, Z. (ed.) *Knowing without Thinking: Mind, Action, Cognition and the Phenomenon of the Background*, pp. 167–186, New York: Palgrave Macmillan.

Wilbur, J.B. & Allen, H.J. (1979) *The Worlds of the Early Greek Philosophers*, Buffalo, NY: Prometheus Books.

Zahavi, D. (1999) *Self-awareness and Alterity: A Phenomenological Investigation*, Evanston, IL: Northwestern University Press.

Chapter III

On the Origin, Nature, and Genesis of Habit[1]

Abstract: *This chapter details fundamental aspects of habits, beginning with the fact that habits are dynamic patterns that are learned, and that, in coincidence with this learning, habits of mind are formed, as in the formation of expectations, thus of certain if/then relationships. It points out that, in quite the opposite manner of the practice of phenomenology, the strange is made familiar in the formation of habits. It shows how clear-sighted recognition of the seminal significance of movement and phenomenologically-grounded understandings of movement are essential to understandings of habits and the habits of mind that go with them. The article differentiates non-developmentally achieved habits from developmentally achieved habits, but elucidates too the relationship between instincts and habits. It elucidates the relationship in part by showing how, contra Merleau-Ponty, "in man" there is a "natural sign" – or rather, natural signs. By relinquishing an adultist stance and delving into our common infancy and early childhood, we recognize the need for what Husserl terms a "regressive inquiry" and thereby recover 'natural signs' such as smiling, laughing, and crying. At the same time, we honor Husserl's insight that "habit and free motivation intertwine." As the chapter shows, resolution of the relationship between habit and free motivation requires recognition of nonlinguistic corporeal concepts that develop in concert with synergies of meaningful movement, concepts and synergies achieved not by embodied minds but mindful bodies.*

Brushing one's teeth, tying a shoelace or knot, hammering a nail and not one's thumb, writing one's name, walking down stairs—each is a distinctive qualitative dynamic, a sequence of movements that has a distinctive beginning, a distinctive contour with distinctive intensity changes, for example, and a distinctive end. Each is a dynamic pattern of movement. We are born with none of these dynamic patterns, which is to say that they are not ready-made or innate in any sense. Each is learned.

---

[1]   First published in *Phenomenology and Mind* (2014), Vol. 6: 76–89.

There is a lesson to be learned from this existential truth, namely, that whatever habits we develop in what we do and the way we do things, they exist because we learn the dynamics that constitute them, whether by trial and error, by assiduous practice, by resting and taking up the challenge again at a later time, or whatever. The mode of one's learning may vary, but the formation of a habit in each instance is basically an enlargement of one's kinetic repertoire, which is to say that one can form a habit only by learning a new dynamic pattern of movement. In the beginning, the formation is ordinarily a spontaneous developmental given, i.e. infants are not told how to do such and such nor are they told they must learn to do such and such in the first place—they would not understand anyway if they were *told*, for infants are precisely "without speech." Infants indeed initiate their own learning by first of all learning their bodies and learning to move themselves (Sheets-Johnstone 1999a/expanded 2nd ed. 2011). They do so without an owner's manual as well as without instructions from others, a manual that would state, for example, "lift and move your right foot forward, then gradually take weight on it as you peel off your left foot—the foot that is now behind you—from heel to toe," and so on, and so on. Infants learn quite by themselves to reach effectively, to grasp objects effectively, to walk, to feed themselves, and ultimately, to talk and thereby exceed their classification as infants. Habits of mind proceed in concert with these habit-formed and -informed accomplishments, most basically in expectations, i.e. in if/then relationships, of which more presently.

The formation of habits proceeds in just the opposite manner of the practice of phenomenology. In doing phenomenology, that is, in following its methodology, we not only make the familiar strange, but do so in part by disenfranchising our habits, i.e. by bracketing, by "renounc[ing] all erudition, in a lower or higher sense" (Husserl 1989, p. 96). Across the spectrum of human cultures, that is, in the most basic ontological sense that includes every human, habits are indeed a matter of *having made the strange familiar*. That familiarity becomes ingrained in what Husserl terms the psychophysical unity of animate organisms and their ways of living in the world. In more precise terms, habits develop by bringing what was out of reach and/or beyond understanding effectively and efficiently into the realm of the familiar and into what are basically synergies of meaningful movement that run off by themselves. Habits are indeed grounded from the beginning in movement, that is, in the primal animation of animate organisms that gives rise to sensings and sense-makings that evolve into synergies of meaningful movement and habits of mind. It is hardly any wonder, then, that foundational understandings of habit, its origin, nature, and genesis, are rooted in a "regressive inquiry" (Husserl 1970, p. 354) into ontogenetic life, or what Fink terms a "constructive phenomenology" (Fink 1995, p. 63).

In the course of their learning their bodies and learning to move themselves effectively and efficiently, infants form certain ways of "doing" that generate an ever-expanding repertoire of "I cans" (Sheets-Johnstone 1999a/ expanded 2nd ed. 2011, Chapter 5). We might recall in this context Husserl's and Landgrebe's emphasis on the fact that "I move" precedes "I do" and "I can" (Husserl 1989, p. 273; Landgrebe 1977, pp. 107–8). Certain ways of "doing" are indeed constituted in and by certain qualitatively inflected movement dynamics that inform an infant's "I cans," dynamics that create particular spatio-temporal-energic patterns. Just as infants nurse in distinctive ways and kick their legs in distinctive ways, so they ultimately learn to walk in distinctive ways, which is to say that the qualitative dynamics of one infant's movements are different from that of another. Ways of moving are indeed individualized. Moreover qualitatively inflected movement dynamics feed into a certain *style*, of which more later. What is of immediate moment here is that self-generated dynamics are the foundation of developmentally achieved habits.

Developmentally achieved habits are to be distinguished from non-developmentally achieved habits, that is, habits that are not cultivated from the beginning through learnings of one kind and another. The distinction between walking and smiling or laughing is one such distinction. One does not learn to smile or laugh: smiling and laughter, like crying, are spontaneous movement patterns that arise on their own. Such spontaneous human movement patterns are in fact quite remarkable. As Darwin succinctly observed, "Seeing a Baby (like Hensleigh's) smile & frown, who can doubt these are instinctive—child does not sneer" (Darwin 1987, Notebook M, No. 96, p. 542). Darwin's observation is in fact of moment: the relationship between instincts—what is "instinctive"—and habits warrants attention.

Instincts, like habits, are distinctive qualitatively inflected dynamic patterns. Those patterns, however, arise on different grounds. As specified and discussed in detail elsewhere with respect to infants and animate forms of life more generally (Sheets-Johnstone 2008, pp. 349–67), what Merleau-Ponty terms "natural signs," including "the realm of instinct," are part of the heritage of humans, Merleau-Ponty's dismissal of them to the contrary. As noted in that discussion, "when Merleau-Ponty writes that 'in man there is no natural sign'", and that "[i]t would be legitimate to speak of 'natural signs' only if the anatomical organization of our body produced a correspondence between specific gestures and given 'states of mind'" (Merleau-Ponty 1962, pp. 188–9), he is surprisingly oblivious of the dynamic congruity that binds movement and emotions, the kinetic and the affective (Sheets-Johnstone 1999b/2009). A nervous laugh might simply burst forth, for example, when one feels less than full assurance about what one is doing or how one is to answer to a question, just as a free lower leg might begin swinging or jiggling when one is seated and feeling bored or eager to get up and leave a lecture or meeting of some kind. While such bodily happenings might not be countenanced as instincts, they are without doubt natural signs, instances of spontaneous, involuntarily produced movements—"specific gestures"—tied to affective feelings—"given 'states of mind'." Adult instances aside, with respect to infant life, smiling, laughing, and crying are clearly the spontaneous expression of human nature: they are natural signs. They are, as Darwin indicates, instinctive beginning forms of sociality that are spontaneously generated; they are neither self-taught nor other-taught. They may certainly be honed, however, and in habitual intentional ways, as when an infant cries because it has learned all by itself that crying brings its mother or caretaker to it, or, when as a child in later years, it learns to feign a smile when greeting a certain adult person it does not like, or, when as an adult in still later years, it learns to restrain a laugh at a child's continuing awkwardness in order not to dissuade him or her from trying to do something. As is evident by such cries, feignings, and restrainings, humans can and do develop certain habits by choice on the basis of what was originally instinctive. Instincts may thus be the generating ground of habits, precisely as in crying to bring someone to you, in feigning a smile at someone you actually dislike, or in restraining a laugh in deference to embarrassing another. Moreover somatic responses (Johnstone 2012, 2013) such as shivering from cold are natural signs that may generate a habitual running to get a sweater or slippers, or to close a window or turn up the thermostat, or in other words, to do something rather than nothing in fear that one might be catching a cold. In short, what is basically instinctive and thus involuntary becomes open to modulations in later years, that is, to voluntary implementations that may and often do become habitual in certain circumstances.

Wholly voluntary learnings have no such roots in instincts or instinctive dispositions. Indeed, when children and adults voluntarily take up a new skill and in the process form new qualitatively inflected dynamic patterns that become habitual—when they learn to write, to type, to jump rope, to play the clarinet, to drive, to make a surgical incision, and so on—their learnings have no underlying "natural signs." In actual practice, however, their learned patterns are also modulated according to circumstance; they are open to variation depending on the particular situation of the moment and altered accordingly, as in making an abdominal incision or a spinal incision, or as in writing one's name with a piece of chalk on a blackboard or signing one's name with a pen on a house purchase contract.

There is a basic dimension of instincts, however, that warrants attention. In their pristine mode, i.e. before being possibly transformed by learnings of one kind and another, instincts are properly analyzed as self-organizing dynamics that flow forth experientially in spontaneous movement dispositions, thus basically, not just the spontaneous movement disposition of a fetus to move its thumb toward its mouth and not toward its ear or navel, for example, but *the spontaneous disposition to move in and of itself in the first place*, including movement of the neuromuscular system itself as it forms in utero. Such movement is not "action" nor is it "behavior." It is the phenomenon of movement *pure and simple*—a phenomenon that in truth is not so simple when analyzed phenomenologically in descriptive experiential terms, that is, as a phenomenon in its own right. Indeed, this pure and simple phenomenon is incredibly complex, far more complex than the terms "action" or "behavior" suggest when they are implicitly and largely unwittingly used in its place, as in talk and writings of "action in perception" (Noë 2004). Along similar lines, neither does "embodied movement" come close to a recognition of the phenomenological complexity of movement, even as in an attempt to abbreviate Husserl's consistent specification of the two-fold articulation of perception and movement (Husserl 1989) by stating, "Our embodied movement participates in seeing, touching, hearing, etc., thereby informing our perceptual grasp on the world" (Gallagher and Zahavi 2012, p. 109).

Husserl did not plumb the dynamic depths and complexities of movement, understandably so, however. His central though certainly not exclusive concern was cognition and the build-up of our knowledge of the world. He certainly did realize the complexity of what he consistently termed "affect and action" and the fact that he did not explicate them fully, terming them at one point simply "the root soil," "*the background that is prior to all comportment*" (Husserl 1989, pp. 292, 291, respectively). Moreover however briefly, he certainly did grasp the centrality of body movement to soul, to performance, to production, and to style. With respect to the integral connection of body movement and soul, he writes, "Each movement of the Body is full of soul, the coming and going, the standing and sitting, the walking and dancing, etc. Likewise, so is every human performance, every human production." In a Supplement to this section of *Ideas II*, he observes that "products and works" such as wielding a stick or writing a book "take on the spirituality of the Body," that products and works are "psycho-physical unities; they have their physical and their spiritual aspects, they are physical things that are 'animated'" (Husserl 1989, pp. 252, 333, respectively). Psychophysical unity and animation indeed go hand in hand (Sheets-Johnstone 2014/ this volume, Chapter II).

Precisely in his emphasis on *animation* and in his not just consistent but pivotal concern with *animate organisms* throughout his writings, Husserl's observations are clearly a beginning entry into the complex phenomenology of movement and its relation to instinct and habit, and this both in recognition of, and in going beyond the fact that "I move" precedes "I do" and "I can." In particular, Husserl notes that, "In original genesis, the personal Ego is constituted not only as a person determined by *drives*, from the very outset and incessantly driven by *original 'instincts'* and passively submitting to them, but *also as a higher, autonomous, freely acting* Ego, in particular one guided by rational motives, and not one that is merely dragged along and unfree. Habits are necessarily formed, just as much with regard to originally instinctive behavior (in such a way that the power of the force of habit is connected with the instinctive drives) as with regard to free behavior" (Husserl 1989, p. 267). In short, to yield to a drive establishes a habit just as "to let oneself be determined by a value-motive and to resist a drive establishes a tendency [...] to let oneself be determined once again by such a value-motive (and perhaps by value-motives in general) and to resist these drives" (ibid.). He points out explicitly that "Here *habit and free motivation intertwine*. Now, if I act freely, then I am indeed obeying habit too" (ibid., pp. 267–8). In effect, what I freely choose to do and do again that leaves a natural disposition or instinct behind is itself a habit: my freely-formed movement itself in virtue of its repeated patterning is in a basic sense habitual.

This existential reality is of moment for it indicates a substantively significant cognitive dimension in the formation of habits and in habits themselves. In more explicit terms, the intertwining of habit and free motivation and movement implicitly suggests habitual patterns of mind — habitual ways of valuing and of thinking. Given the fact that "consciousness of the world [...] is in constant motion" (Husserl 1970, p. 109), these habitual ways can hardly be ignored. Habits of mind are surely spurred by expectations, for example, most basically by what Husserl terms "if-then" relationships (Husserl, e.g., 1989, p. 63), and correlatively by what infant psychiatrist and clinical psychologist Daniel Stern terms "consequential relationships" (Stern 1985, pp. 80–1) and what child psychologist Lois Bloom terms "relational concepts" (Bloom 1993, pp. 50–2). Insofar as these relationships are foundational — "if I close my eyes, it is dark"; "if I move my lips and tongue in certain ways, I make and hear certain sounds" — it is not surprising that the relationships are foundational to everyday human habits, such as closing one's eyes to go to sleep or when a light is too bright, and saying the words "No" and "Yes." Just such kinesthetically felt and cognized experiences ground the faculty that Husserl identifies as the "*I-can* of the subject" (Husserl 1989, p. 13), a faculty that engenders a repertoire of abilities and possibilities that are indeed in many everyday instances habitual. More finely put in phenomenological terms, tactile-kinesthetic awarenesses and their invariants are realized in basic if/then relationships that we spontaneously discover in infancy in learning our bodies and learning to move ourselves. Tactile-kinesthetic awarenesses are thus a central aspect of animation, a tactile-kinesthetic built-in of life, a vital dimension in the formation of habits.

That expectations are indeed basic to animate forms of life can hardly be doubted, not only in such ordinary realities that if I turn my head and twist my torso, then a different profile of the object at which I am looking comes into view, and not only in such commonly passed over realities that "if I close my eyes, it is dark," but in hearing a strange rustling in the midst of silence or in smelling smoke. In other words, habits of mind are also spurred by happenings and by particular valuings and thoughts that follow in response to those happenings that become standard. Though they are open to possible variations according to circumstance, they retain their basic dynamic: the bodily-felt dynamic of apprehension, for example, or of suspicion, and so on. In this regard they might evolve in the form of "wondering if," for example, or "thinking that," precisely as when one hears a strange rustling in the midst of silence and straightaway "wonders if…" or smells smoke and straightaway "thinks that…" moreover habits of mind may be defensive as well as expectant. Ernest Becker, a cultural anthropologist who elaborated on Otto Rank's conception of truth-seeking as an immortality ideology—Rank was a one-time disciple of Freud—captured this defensive habit of mind in a striking way when he wrote about "the life-and-death viciousness of all ideological disputes": "Each person nourishes his immortality in the ideology of self-perpetuation to which he gives his allegiance; this gives his life the only abiding significance it can have. No wonder men go into a rage over the fine points of belief: if your adversary wins the argument about truth, *you die*. Your immortality system has been shown to be fallible, your life becomes fallible" (Becker 1975, p. 64). It is of interest to note that Husserl at one point gives voice to how what Becker terms an "allegiance" can be an obstacle to one's vision and understanding. He does so with respect to a "zoologist and naturalistic psychologist," each of whom is so wedded to the "*scientific* attitude" or to "'Objective' reality" that "[h]e wears the blinders of habit" (Husserl 1989, p. 193; italics and quote marks in original). The blinders of habit are clearly not limited to scientists, but include those whose "allegiance" deters them from considering findings, perspectives, or ideas different from, or inimical to their own.

As the above examples suggest, through investigations of habits of mind with full phenomenological rigor, one might come to a description of mental tendencies and dispositions in valuing and thinking. Yet such an investigation might be met with skepticism since it is possible that, even with the practice of free variation, mental tendencies and dispositions exist beyond one's individual phenomenological capacities. In essence, one might thus skeptically claim that there is no valuing and thinking "morphology" of humans akin to the real-life flesh and bone morphology of humans.[2] Insofar as phenomenological inquiries are open to verification, however, elaborations, amendments, corrections, and so on, are certainly possible and in fact to be cultivated if phenomenology is to prosper. Furthermore habits of mind fruitfully investigated phenomenologically might be authenticated and possibly even refined through Buddhist Theravada meditation practice. Such practice has basic methodological and experiential similarities with phenomenology (Sheets-Johnstone 2011a). It might thus be affirmed that whatever an individual's limitations might be with respect to encompassing a full-scale phenomenological description of habits of mind, that investigation is open both to verification by other phenomenologists and to habits of mind discovered through a different method of inquiry and study that has the possibility of complementing a phenomenological investigation and possibly even expanding its insights.

Concerns about a morphology of mind notwithstanding, the above discussion and examples indicate that habits of mind may be and commonly are formed coincident with kinetic habits, and from the beginning in learning one's body and learning to move oneself. The full-scale realities of habit are indeed psycho-physical in nature and develop in concert with experience. They are at once cognitively, affectively, and kinetically dynamic: they flow forth with varying intensities, amplitudes, and perseverations in each of these dimensions of animate life and at the same time as a singular whole in the habit itself. That Husserl writes often of the "intertwining" of body and soul is revealing in this respect, perhaps most decisively when he affirms that "the unity of man encompasses these two components not as two realities externally linked with one another but instead as most intimately interwoven and in a certain way mutually penetrating (as is in fact established)" (Husserl 1989, p. 100).

In sum, what comes to mind may be and not uncommonly is habitual in some degree, as the above examples indicate and as psychological renditions of associations might furthermore show. The idea that habits of mind exist, however, might pose conundrum. Such habits seem both to affirm and to contradict the fact that thoughts simply arise. Aficionados of the *brain* might claim that the affirmation and contradiction attest to the hegemonic nature of the brain; that is, they might latch on to the conun-drum as a validation of the monarchical status of the *brain* and its right to experiential ascriptions such as "If you see the back of a person's head, the brain infers that there is a face on the front of it" (Crick and Koch 1992, p. 153). The habit of inferring arises and the thought "a face on the front of it" arises because the brain infers and says as much. This rather comically

---

2   For perhaps similar reasons, some might claim that there is no "emotions morphology" of humans *en par* with the real-life flesh and bone morphology of humans.

eccentric not to say preposterously homuncular metaphysics is clearly at odds with experience.[3] However much thoughts may and do simply arise, we are able to concentrate attention on a text, on a report, on a paper we are writing, on a puzzle we are trying to solve, on a fugue or nocturne we are trying to learn, and so on. We are at the same time, however, something akin to passengers with respect to what turns up in the process of our concentrated attention—a wayward concern about an upcoming meeting, a recurring concern about how a sick child is doing, a resurging regret about not having done something earlier. Yet though thoughts outside our concentration may and do arise, we surely control "turning toward," as Husserl emphasizes, just as he emphasizes that we control our attention to something, that is, our interest (or disinterest) in something, and we of course control what we choose to do or not to do. We are indeed *freely-motivated* and *freely-moving* (e.g. Husserl 2001, p. 283). These dual facts of human life are obviously of pivotal importance to our understandings of habit. Supposing we are sufficiently attuned to our affective/tactile-kinesthetic bodies, we can, for example, choose to change our habit of turning only toward certain things and not others, or of finding interest in only certain things and not others, or of doing only certain things and not others. These dual facts of human life are of pivotal importance as well to understandings of habit and its relation to *style*. Husserl deftly and succinctly captures the relation of habit to style when he writes, "Every man has his character, we can say, his style of life in affection and action, with regard to the way he has of being motivated by such and such circumstances. And it is not that he merely had this up to now; the style is rather something permanent, at least relatively so in the various stages of life, and then, when it changes, it does so again, in general, in characteristic way such that, consequent upon these changes, a unitary style manifests itself once more" (1989, p. 283). That habits are breakable, so to speak, and that any particular habit can be replaced by a different habit means that one's style of life is precisely changeable with respect to what Husserl terms *"affection and action."* Husserl's common meaning of affection is tethered to "allure" and motivations (Husserl 2001, p. 196), that is, to "turning toward" and "interest." He writes, for example, of receiving

---

[3] Statements of neurobiologist Semir Zeki and neurologists Antonio and Hanna Damasio engender a similarly quirky metaphysics: "an object's image varies with distance, yet the brain can ascertain its true size" (Zeki 1992, p. 69); "To obtain its knowledge of what is visible, the brain [...] must actively construct a visual world" (Zeki 1992, p. 69); "When stimulated from within the brain, these systems [neural systems in the left cerebral hemisphere that 'represent phonemes, phoneme combinations and syntactic rules for combining words'] assemble word-forms and generate sentences to be spoken or written" (Damasio and Damasio 1992, p. 89).

"some joyful tiding and liv[ing] in the joy," pointing out that "Within the joy, we are 'intentionally' (with feeling intentions) turned toward the joy-Object as such in the mode of affective 'interest'" (Husserl 1989, p. 14).

Such investigations and findings conflict with present-day phenomenological studies that pass over kinetic and affective realities, and this in part because they unwittingly pass over ontogenetic realities of human life, choosing instead a perspective that is in truth adultist. Gallagher and Zahavi, for example, affirm that "[T]he sense of agency is not reducible to awareness of bodily movement or to sensory feedback from bodily movement. Consistent with the phenomenology of embodiment, in everyday engaged action afferent or sensory-feedback signals are attenuated, implying a recessive consciousness of our body." They cite Merleau-Ponty (1962) as a reference and conclude, "I do not attend to my bodily movements in most actions. I do not stare at my hands as I decide to use them; I do not look at my feet as I walk." Their apparent unwitting appeal to vision and neglect of kinesthesia is both telling and puzzling. Why would one stare at his or her hands in deciding "to use them" any more than one would look as one's feet as one walks unless there was a pathological condition of some kind.[4] In short, when phenomenologists write as knowledgeable adults without ever stopping to ask themselves how they came to be the knowledgeable adults they are—using their hands to grasp a cup or towel, walking along a trail or down the street—and in turn, offer fine-grained phenomenological descriptions of same, they pass over the need for a full-scale constructive phenomenology, a phenomenology that might indeed at times embrace a genetic phenomenology, the latter in the sense of determining how we come to the meanings and values we do.

A full-scale constructive phenomenology necessarily addresses the question of familiarity, in particular, the nature of that familiarity that undergirds habits having to do with using my hands, for example, and walking.

How indeed is it that reaching for a glass or throwing a ball, or walking or skipping, or moving in all the myriad habitual ways we move in our everyday lives, run off as what famed neurologist Aleksandr Romanovich Luria termed "kinesthetic melodies" (Luria 1966, 1973)? How is it that these melodies, with all their variations with respect to particular situations and circumstance, become ingrained in kinesthetic memory? How indeed —except on the basis of *familiar qualitative dynamic patterns*, particularly

---

4   One might be inclined to think that Gallagher and Cole's study of Ian Waterman, a person who "does not know, without visual perception, where his limbs are or what posture he maintains" (Gallagher 2005, p. 44), has unwittingly influenced phenomenological practice and in this instance compromised it.

inflected patterns of movement that run off in a way not dissimilar from the way that Husserl describes internal time consciousness "running off"? Movement, like time, is a "temporal object," and temporal objects "appear" in a wholly different way from "appearing objects": they are precisely "running-off phenomena" (Husserl 1964, p. 48; see also Sheets-Johnstone 2003, 2012, 2014/this volume, Chapter II). Familiar qualitative dynamic patterns are just such phenomena. We may thus ask how, other than as learned patterns of movement, patterns learned in infancy and early childhood, such familiar qualitative dynamic patterns come to be? As pointed out earlier, infants and young children learn their bodies and learn to move themselves in myriad ways in the course of growing. In effect, when present-day phenomenologists overlook ontogeny, they overlook the very ground of that adult knowledge that allows them to claim "a recessive consciousness of our body" and to state, "I do not attend to my bodily movements in most actions." Indeed, an adultist stance seems generally to allow a distanced stance with respect to the body: "The body tries to stay out of our way so that we can get on with our task" (Gallagher and Zahavi 2012, p. 163)[5]

A veritable phenomenological analysis of what is going on "in most actions" shows something quite different. It shows that, whether a matter of walking or eating or dressing ourselves or drying ourselves after a shower, or whether a matter of myriad other everyday "actions," the dexterity, the precision, the fluidity, and so on, that are necessary to the "action" running off are ingrained in kinesthetic memory in the form of an ongoing qualitative dynamic that is spontaneously inflected and modulated according to circumstance, an ongoing qualitative dynamic that was learned and cultivated in earlier years and is now so dynamically familiar that it runs off by itself. In short, whatever the everyday adult actions, their dynamic familiarity is anchored in the tactile-kinesthetic body and thus in kinesthetic memory. Their formal reality is in part related quite precisely to Husserl distinction between an appearing Object and a running off Object: staring at one's hands in deciding to use them or looking at one's feet in walking are not equivalent to everyday synergies of meaningful movement, synergies that were honed from infancy and early childhood on and that adult humans reap in the form of "getting on with our task." It is indeed not that the body "tries to stay out of our way," but that in learning our bodies and learning to move ourselves, we have amassed an incredibly

---

5   We might in fact ask whether it is "the body" that "tries to stay out of our way," or "we" who try to keep the body out of our way, or what "our way" would be had we not learned our bodies and learned to move ourselves and in the process forged those myriad familiar dynamic patterns that inform our everyday lives and that run off so effectively without our having to monitor them.

varied and vast repertoire of I-cans. To overlook ontogeny is thus to fail to ask oneself basic questions concerning one's adult knowledge and in turn foil foundational elucidations of habit. It should be added that neither does Merleau-Ponty ask himself ontogenetic questions, basically *genetic phenomenology* questions, nor does he, in his discussion of habit, provide answers to the question of how habits come to be formed. On the contrary, Merleau-Ponty declares simply that habit is "knowledge in the hands" (1962, p. 144) even though in the previous sentence he declares that "habit is neither a form of knowledge nor an involuntary action" (ibid.).

Gallagher and Zahavi's reliance on Merleau-Ponty is in fact disconcerting, and this because, again, quite to the contrary, movement "pure and simple" does not surface with phenomenological clarity and depth in Merleau-Ponty's writings. Without this surfacing, genuine phenomenological understandings of habit are kept at bay. In a long footnote, for example, in which he tries to explain how motion, "which acts as a background to every act of consciousness, comes to be constituted," Merleau-Ponty writes, "The consciousness of my gesture, if it is truly a state of undivided consciousness, is no longer consciousness of movement at all, but an incommunicable quality which can tell us nothing about movement" (Merleau-Ponty 1962, p. 276). Moreover his earlier appeal to "the bird which flies across my garden" (ibid., p. 275) actually confuses movement with objects in motion (for a phenomenological clarification of the distinction between movement and objects in motion, see Sheets-Johnstone 1979) and leads him simply to posit "[p]re-objective being." In short, Merleau-Ponty too passes over *the qualitative dynamics inherent in kinesthetic experience*, which indeed are "incommunicable" only if one disregards them. Merleau-Ponty in fact dismisses kinesthesia outright when he affirms that "As a mass of tactile, labyrinthine and kinaesthetic data, the body has no more definite orientation than the other contents of experience" (Merleau-Ponty 1962, pp. 287–8) and when, in his attempt to fathom the complexities of movement in relation to learning, he simply states, "a movement is learned when the body has understood it" (ibid., [1945], p. 139). His statement is in fact an unacknowledged near quotation from Henri Bergson who wrote almost fifty years earlier, "A movement is learned when the body has been made to understand it" (Bergson 1896/ 1991, p. 112). His continuing statement that a movement is learned when the body "has incorporated it into its 'world'," and that "to move one's body is to aim at things through it" is taken up explicitly by Gallagher and Zahavi. They declare, "[W]e are normally prepared to describe our habitual or practised movements as actions. I would say that 'I hit the ball' or 'I played one of Beethoven's sonatas', rather than 'the arm (or fingers) changed position in space'. But in this case the movements are at some level conscious. They are *teleological* actions which contain a reference to the objects at which they aim (Merleau-Ponty 1962, p. 139)" (Gallagher and Zahavi, p. 174).

A description of our "habitual or practiced movements" does not of course have to be, or even "normally" is, in the past tense any more than it has to be described "normally" in terms of action. Phenomenological descriptions hew fairly consistently to the present tense of the experience they are describing, taking into account its temporal flow and how the experience comes to be constituted. Furthermore, if "habitual or practiced movements" are to be elucidated phenomenologically, they warrant bona fide phenomenological descriptions that, rather than packaging them in *actions*, do justice to their particular and unique qualitative dynamics — whether a matter of hitting a ball, hammering a nail, playing one of Beethoven's sonatas, or playing Liszt's Liebestraum No. 3. Further still, doing phenomenological justice to "habitual or practiced movements" means realizing that *movement is not a matter of body parts having "changed position in space."* By its very nature, movement is neither positional nor is it simply spatial. Movement is a phenomenon in its own right, a spatio-temporal-energic phenomenon that is clearly distinguishable in essential ways from objects in motion, which do change position in space. To do phenomenological justice to the phenomenon of movement requires opening one's eyes not to positional awarenesses but to the dynamics of change (for a phenomenological analysis of movement, see Sheets-Johnstone 1966/1979 and 1980; Sheets-Johnstone 1999a/expanded 2nd ed. 2011).

The underlying problem in all these purported phenomenological descriptions of movement is a basic ignorance of movement "pure and simple," meaning that complex qualitatively dynamic phenomenon that is opaquely subsumed in various and sundry ways in action, behavior, and embodiment, and that is furthermore mistakenly described as an object in motion and thus relegated to what amounts to no more than positional information of one kind and another. Habits, both general human ones and highly personal human ones, are not reducible to changes of position unless, of course, one is referring to an attempt to change one's habit of slouch-sitting to erect-sitting, for example. Even then, kinesthesia cannot be ignored: that pan-human sense modality is integral to the change, not only to felt changed tensions but to changes in body line, i.e. changes in the linear design of one's body that, as experienced, are dependent in part on one's imaginative consciousness (on this latter topic, see Sheets-Johnstone 2011b). Moreover kinesthesia can hardly be ignored since it, along with tactility, is the first sensory modality to develop neurologically in utero (Windle 1971) and, barring accidents, is there for life. *Indeed it is an insuppressible sensory modality.* As well-revered and internationally-known neuroscientist Marc Jeannerod concluded in the context of examining "conscious knowledge about one's actions" and experimental research that might address the question of such knowledge, including experimental research dealing with pathologically afflicted individuals, "There are no reliable methods for suppressing kinesthetic information arising during the execution of a movement" (Jeannerod 2006, p. 56).

"Information" terminology aside, especially in the context not of position or posture but of movement, Jeannerod's declarative finding speaks reams about the foundational ongoing reality and significance of kinesthesia, reams that should certainly lead phenomenologists to take kinesthesia seriously and the challenge of elucidating its *insuppressible living dynamics* of signal importance. Puzzlingly enough, Gallagher bypasses this very foundational reality. When he writes (Gallagher 2005, p. 83), "The phenomenon of newborn imitation suggests that much earlier [before later forms of imitation and the "mirror stage"] there is a primary notion of self, what we might call a proprioceptive self—a sense of self that involves a sense of one's motor possibilities, body postures, and body powers, rather than one's visual features"—he clearly affirms that "a primary notion of self" is not a visual recognition of oneself. At the same time, however, he bypasses the foundational reality that is the tactile-kinesthetic body, its neurological formation, as noted above, encompassing the first sensory modalities to develop.[6] He bypasses as well findings such as those of infant psychiatrist and clinical psychologist Daniel N. Stern whose studies led him to the description of a "core self" identifiable in terms of four "self-invariants": self-agency, self-coherence, self-affectivity,

---

[6]   Proprioception, as first described by Sir Charles Sherrington and as taken up by many present-day academics (e.g. Bermúdez 2003; Thompson 2007; Gallagher 2005; Gallagher and Cole 1998), is basically a postural rather than kinetic sense. Indeed, Sir Charles Sherrington's original coinage of the term and his focal emphasis define proprioception as "the perception of where the limb is" (Sherrington 1953, p. 249). Proprioception provides us postural awarenesses and, in addition, a sense of balance through vestibular mechanisms. Gallagher and Cole uphold Sherrington's postural specification when they explicitly state, "Proprioceptive awareness is a felt experience of bodily position" (Gallagher and Cole 1998, p. 137). Gallagher and Zahavi do likewise when they state, "Although I do not have observational access to my body in action, I can have non-observational proprioceptive and kinaesthetic awareness of my body in action. Proprioception is the innate and intrinsic position sense that I have with respect to my limbs and overall posture. It is the 'sixth sense' that allows me to know whether my legs are crossed, or not, without looking at them" (2012, p. 162). Whatever the meaning of "non-observational [...] awareness of my body in action"—does "non-observational awareness" mean simply "knowing without looking"?—Gallagher and Zahavi clearly bypass phenomenologically deepened understandings of the sense modality that is kinesthesia, which is to say the experience of movement and its qualitative dynamics.

and self-history. As Stern states, "in order for the infant to have any formed sense of self, there must ultimately be some organization that is sensed as a reference point. The first such organization concerns the body: its coherence, its actions, its inner feeling states, and the memory of all these" (Stern 1985, p. 46; see also Sheets-Johnstone 1999c). Though not specified as such, these invariants all rest on the tactile-kinesthetic body (Sheets-Johnstone 1999b/expanded 2nd ed. 2011). The description of each dimension indeed validates the primacy of movement and the tactile-kinesthetic body. Recognition of this body would obviate the need of Gallagher or any other researcher to "suggest" anything. On the contrary, recognition of the tactile-kinesthetic body straightaway gives empirical grounds for affirming that the phenomenon of newborn imitation is rooted in a kinetic bodily logos attuned to movement (see, for example, Spitz 1983 on what Husserl would term the "allure" of movement), and further, that as that body learns, it cultivates and forges an ever-expanding repertoire of I-cans, that habits are engendered in that repertoire, and that a certain style—or "character" as Husserl also terms it—is born and being shaped in the process, a style that others readily recognize.

The lapses specified above indicate a call "to the things themselves." In heeding the call, one is led back to Husserl's phenomenological insights. They are indeed an imperative beginning to bona fide understandings of habit, a beginning that might proceed from, but is certainly not limited to his conclusion that "each free act has its comet's tail of nature" (Husserl 1989, p. 350). What Husserl meant by this metaphor is that, by way of earlier experiences, "[t]he Ego always lives in the medium of its 'history'," that "aftereffects" are present in "tendencies, sudden ideas, transforma-tions or assimilations" (ibid.). This insight in particular leads most decisively to an appreciation of the significance of ontogenetic studies. Pathological case studies may enhance phenomenological understandings, but they are not essential in the way that phenomenologically-informed ontogenetical studies are essential: a constructive phenomenology is indeed essential to understandings of habit, just as it is essential to under-standings of emotions and agency (on the latter topic, see e.g., Bruner 1990; Sheets-Johnstone 1999c; on the former topic, see Sheets-Johnstone1999b; Johnstone 2012, 2013). In fact, how "[t]he Ego always lives in the medium of its 'history'" is of sizeable import. Husserl implicitly indicates just how central that history is when he brings together habit and style, and habit and the freely-motivated, freely-moving subject. He states, "As subject of position-takings and of habitual convictions I have of course my style [...] I am dependent on my previous life and my former decisions [...] I depend on motives [...] I have a unique character [...] I behave according to that character in a regular way" (Husserl 1989, p. 343). While he is clearly at pains to distinguish "who I am" as natural being from "who I am" as "position-taking Ego," he is clearly at just as sharp pains to show their relationship, in other words, the relationship of what he terms the freely-acting Ego to "affect and action" (for a full discussion, see ibid., Supplement XI, pp. 340–3). His emphasis on the relationship of a foundational basis in nature—a lower psychic level—to a position-taking Ego is succinctly put when he states that, "with each position-taking, there develop 'tendencies' to take up the same position under similar circumstances, etc." (ibid., p. 293). The relationship is emphasized in different but related terms when, in describing "The spiritual Ego and its underlying basis," he points out that whatever is constituted naturally, i.e. in associations, tendencies, perseverations, and so on, permeates "all life of the spirit": spirit "is permeated by the 'blind' operation of associations, drives, feelings which are stimuli for drives and determining grounds for drives [...] All of which determine the subsequent course of consciousness according to 'blind' rules. To these laws correspond *habitual modes of behavior* on the part of the subject, acquired peculiarities (e.g. the habit of drinking a glass of wine in the evening)" (ibid., p. 289). It is in this context, several pages later (ibid., pp. 291–2) that Husserl writes of the *background that is prior to all comportment* and of what we find "in the obscure depths": "a root soil." In sum, habits, including habits of mind, particularly for Husserl in the form of motivations, are a basic dimension of a freely-moving subject, which is to say that the "medium of its history" is integral to the life of a subject.

Surely it is essential for phenomenologists to attempt a regressive inquiry, to take an ontogenetic perspective and carry out a constructive phenomenology. Habits are a fundamental dimension of human life. Indeed, we could not readily live without them. If everything were new at each turn, if all familiarity was erased and strangeness was ever-present, life as we know it would be impossible. A few final words about a dimension of habit make the point both incisively and decisively. That dimension has to do with style, specifically, our common dependence on style in our interchanges with others and our recognition of them as individuals to begin with. Husserl affirms, "One can to a certain extent expect how a man will behave in a given case if one has correctly apperceived him in his person, in his style" (Husserl 1989, p. 283). He offers many examples of style—not only in the way in which an individual judges, wills, "and values things aesthetically," but in the way "'sudden ideas' or 'inspirations' surge up [...] in the way metaphors come to him and [the way in which] his involuntary phantasy reigns," and even further, "in the way he perceives in perception [... and] "in the specific way his memory 'operates'." In short, Husserl affirms that style permeates to the core and does so on the basis of habit. What we notice in another person's style are precisely just such aspects of another person's comportment—the ways in which he or she typically relates to his or her surrounding world, thus not only the way in which a person "behaves," i.e. his or her typical kinetic qualitative dynamics, but the things the person typically values, his or her typical lines of thought, what he or she typically notices, and so on. Moreover Husserl includes in a person's style his or her "turning of attention," a turning that, Husserl states, "is also a 'comportment'," but is not a position-taking as are other aspects of the person's style. Yet here too, as Husserl observes, "the subject displays his 'peculiarity', i.e., in what it is that rivets his attention and how it does so [... how] [o]ne subject jumps easily from object to object, from theme to theme; another one remains attached for a long time to the same object, etc." (ibid., p. 291). In sum, Husserl's observations pertain to a social world. We indeed seem to be more aware of the habits of others than of our own habits. We do so to a sizeable extent on the basis of the movement of others, what we in a packaging way term their "behavior," but which we get a glimpse of in terms such as "jumping easily from object to object" in contrast to "remain[ing] attached for a long time to the same object." The qualitative dynamics of another are perceived. They are integral dimensions of his or her style. We can thus anticipate what another will likely do given such and such a situation. There is a certain familiarity about the person that is simply there, evidenced in the dynamics of his or her comportment across our history with them, hence dynamics that we have experienced before and have now come to expect. It should be noted that we do not anticipate ourselves in the way we anticipate others. As indicated above, we are commonly less aware of our own qualitative dynamics than we are of the qualitative dynamics of others — unless we have attuned ourselves to our own movement.

When we begin not with an adultist perspective and speculative entities to explain various phenomena, but with a veritable reconstructive or constructive phenomenology that allows one to "get back" to those non-linguistic days in which we learned our bodies and learned to move ourselves and in the process formed nonlinguistic corporeal concepts in concert with synergies of meaningful movement, we approach veritable understandings of mind. We find that those synergies of meaningful movement are orchestrated not by an embodied mind but by a mindful body, alive to and cognizant to its surrounding world and developing fundamental abilities to move effectively and efficiently within it from infancy and in fact from in utero onward.

References

Becker, E. (1975) *Escape from Evil*, New York: The Free Press.

Bergson, H. (1896/1991) *Matter and Memory*, Paul, N.M. & Palmer, W.S. (trans.), New York: Zone Books.

Bermúdez, J. (2003) The phenomenology of bodily perception, *Theoria et Historia Scientiarum*, VII (1), pp. 43–52.

Bloom, L. (1993) *The Transition from Infancy to Language: Acquiring the Power of Expression*, Cambridge: Cambridge University Press.

Bruner, J. (1990) *Acts of Meaning*, Cambridge, MA: Harvard University Press.

Crick, F. & Koch, C. (1992) The problem of consciousness, *Scientific American*, 267 (3), pp. 153–159.

Damasio, A.R. & Damasio, H. (1992) Brain and language, *Scientific American*, 267 (3), pp. 89–95.

Darwin, C. (1987) *Charles Darwin's Notebooks, 1836–1844*, Barrett, P.H., Gautrey, P.J., Herbert, S., Kohn, D. & Smith, S. (eds.), Ithaca, NY: Cornell University Press.

Fink, E. (1995) *Sixth Cartesian Meditation*, Bruzina, R. (trans.), Bloomington, IN: Indiana University Press.

Gallagher, S. (2005) *How the Body Shapes the Mind*, Oxford: Clarendon Press.

Gallagher, S. & Cole, J. (1995) Body image and body schema in a deafferented subject, *Journal of Mind and Behavior*, 16, pp. 369–390. Included in Welton, D. (ed.) (1998) *Body and Flesh: A Philosophical Reader*, pp. 131–147, Malden, MA: Blackwell Publishers.

Gallagher, S. & Zahavi, D. (2012) *The Phenomenological Mind*, 2nd ed., London and New York: Routledge.

Husserl, E. (1964) *The Phenomenology of Internal Time-Consciousness*, Heidegger, M. (ed.), Churchill, J.S. (trans.), Bloomington, IN: Indiana University Press.

Husserl, E. (1970) *The Crisis of European Sciences and Transcendental Phenomenology*, Carr, D. (trans.), Evanston, IL: Northwestern University Press.

Husserl, E. (1989) *Ideas Pertaining to a Pure Phenomenology and to a Phenomenological Philosophy*, Rojcewicz, R. & Schuwer, A. (trans.), Dordrecht: Kluwer Academic Publishers.

Husserl, E. (2001) *Analyses Concerning Passive and Active Synthesis*, Steinbock, A.J. (trans.), Dordrecht: Kluwer Academic Publishers.

Jeannerod, M. (2006) *Motor Cognition: What Actions Tell the Self*, Oxford: Oxford University Press.

Johnstone, A.A. (2012) The deep bodily roots of emotion, *Husserl Studies*, 28 (3), pp. 179–200.

Johnstone, A.A. (2013) Why emotion?, *Journal of Consciousness Studies*, 20 (9–10), pp. 15–38.

Landgrebe, L. (1977) Phenomenology as transcendental theory of history, in Elliston, F.A. & Mccormick, P. (eds.) *Husserl: Expositions and Appraisals*, pp. 101–113, Notre Dame, IN: University of Notre Dame Press.

Luria, A.R. (1966) *Human Brain and Psychological Processes*, Haigh, B. (trans.), New York: Harper & Row.

Luria, A.R. (1973) *The Working Brain: An Introduction to Neuropsychology*, Haigh, B. (trans.), Harmondsworth: Penguin Books.

Merleau-Ponty, M. (1962) *Phenomenology of Perception*, Smith, C. (trans.), London: Routledge & Kegan Paul.

Noë, A. (2004) *Action in Perception*, Cambridge, MA: MIT Press.

Sheets-Johnstone, M. (1966; 2nd eds. 1979/1980; 50th anniversary ed. 2015) *The Phenomenology of Dance*, Madison, WI: University of Wisconsin Press; Exeter: Dance Books Ltd; New York: Arno Press; Philadelphia, PA: Temple University Press.

Sheets-Johnstone, M. (1979) On movement and objects in motion: The phenomenology of the visible in dance, *Journal of Aesthetic Education*, 13 (2), pp. 33–46.

Sheets-Johnstone, M. (1999a/expanded 2nd ed. 2011) *The Primacy of Movement*, Amsterdam/Philadelphia, PA: John Benjamins Publishing.

Sheets-Johnstone, M. (1999b) Emotions and movement: A beginning empirical-phenomenological analysis of their relationship, *Journal of Consciousness Studies*, 6 (11–12), pp. 259–277. Included in Sheets-Johnstone, M. (2009) *The Corporeal Turn: An Interdisciplinary Reader*, Chapter VIII, Exeter: Imprint Academic.

Sheets-Johnstone, M. (1999c) Phenomenology and agency: Methodological and theoretical issues in Strawson's 'The Self', *Journal of Consciousness Studies*, 6 (4), pp. 48–69.

Sheets-Johnstone, M. (2003) Kinesthetic memory, *Theoria et Historia Scientiarum*, VII (1), pp. 69–92.

Sheets-Johnstone, M. (2008) *The Roots of Morality*, University Park, PA: Pennsylvania State University Press.

Sheets-Johnstone, M. (2011a/this volume, Chapter VIII) On the elusive nature of the human self: Divining the ontological dynamics of animate being, in van Huyssteen, J.W. & Wiebe, E.P. (eds.) *In Search of Self: Interdisciplinary Perspectives on Personhood*, pp. 198–219, Grand Rapids, MI: William B. Eerdmans Publishing Co.

Sheets-Johnstone, M. (2011b) The imaginative consciousness of movement: Linear quality, kinesthesia, language and life, in Ingold, T. (ed.) *Redrawing Anthropology: Materials, Movements, Lines*, pp. 115–128, Farnham: Ashgate Publishing.

Sheets-Johnstone, M. (2012) Kinesthetic memory: Further critical reflections and constructive analyses, in Koch, S.C., Fuchs, T., Summa, M. & Müller, C. (eds.) *Body Memory, Metaphor and Movement*, pp. 43–72, Amsterdam/Philadelphia, PA: John Benjamins Publishing.

Sheets-Johnstone, M. (2014/this volume, Chapter II) Animation: Analyses, elaborations, and implications, *Husserl Studies*, 30 (3), pp. 247–268.

Sherrington, Sir C. (1953) *Man on His Nature*, New York: Doubleday Anchor.

Spitz, R.A. (1983) *Dialogues from Infancy*, Emde, R.N. (ed.), New York: International Universities Press.

Stern, D.N. (1985) *The Interpersonal World of the Infant: A View from Psycho-analysis and Developmental Psychology*, New York: Basic Books.

Thompson, E. (2007) *Mind and Life: Biology, Phenomenology, and the Sciences of Mind*, Cambridge, MA: Belknap Press/Harvard University Press.

Windle, W.F. (1971) *Physiology of the Fetus*, Springfield, IL: Charles C. Thomas.

Zeki, S. (1992) The visual image in mind and brain, *Scientific American*, 267 (3), pp. 69–76.

Chapter IV

Getting to the Heart of Emotions and Consciousness[1]

I. Introduction:
Descriptive Foundations and Animation

The aim of this chapter is to open a path that penetrates to the core of affective experience — to the heart of emotion and consciousness. Opening such a path requires a consistent view of the integral wholeness of life; that is, it requires foundational experiential understandings of commonly separated aspects, precisely such aspects as emotion and consciousness, and more finely, empathy and altruism, for example, aggression and submission, disgust and joy. In light of this requirement, phylogeny and ontogeny are of signal importance as are phenomenological analyses. These facts and analyses provide the descriptive foundations necessary for foundational experiential understandings.

Common topics in investigations of social emotions such as empathy and altruism rarely provide descriptive foundations. Such topics thus fall outside the aim of this chapter as does a specific focus on a particular kind of behavior or emotion. Current theoretically fashionable perspectives that attempt to capture overlooked or essential features of life, namely, the enactive approach and embodiment theses, similarly fall outside the purview of this chapter. Phylogenetic and ontogenetic facts and phenomenological analyses will in fact ultimately suggest that these perspectives are lexical band-aids covering over long-lingering ignorances of the realities of life itself; they are descriptively as well as linguistically deflective.

The realities of life itself are of fundamental significance. Because they are, they warrant serious investigation and study from the beginning, the

---

[1] First published in *Handbook of Cognitive Science*, ed. Paco Calvo and Antoni Gomila (2008), Amsterdam: Elsevier: 453–465.

beginning in precisely a phylogenetic, ontogenetic, and phenomenological sense. To take phylogeny as an example, this clearly does not mean that present-day scientists and philosophers are responsible for concentrated investigations and studies *en par* with those of Darwin, approximating to the span of creatures he studied or to the years he devoted to their study. On the other hand, specializing in one animal or species of animal— including *Homo sapiens sapiens*—and generalizing phylogenetically in one way and another from there has its hazards. A striking instance is E.O. Wilson's monumentally thorough study of ants, which blossomed into the theoretical science known as sociobiology (Wilson 1975), which in turn blossomed into theoretical entities such as selfish genes and brain modules. When theory overtakes real-life observations, or when ready-made categories of behavior triumph over finely detailed descriptive accounts of the social interactions of wolves, chimpanzees, or humans, for example, or of beavers building dams or birds building nests, the basic realities of life itself are elided. To be noted too, however, is that descriptive accounts of the lives of nonhuman animals may be faulted for their anthropomorphism or for offering merely anecdotal rather than laboratory-controlled data. Jane Goodall's lifelong studies of chimpanzees (Goodall 1968, 1971, 1990) are testimonial to the impropriety of many such charges as are the studies of other researchers from a variety of perspectives (for a breadth of perspectives, see ethologists Mitchell et al. 1997; see also philosopher John Fisher 1996, and biologist Stephen Jay Gould 2000). Moreover the studies of Goodall, Strum (1987), Hall and DeVore (1972), and Schaller (1963), along with those of many other primate researchers, attest to the importance of recognizing descriptive foundations: descriptive foundations are the bed-rock of phylogenetic matters of fact, and thus, of evolutionary continuities (Sheets-Johnstone 2002; see also, Sheets-Johnstone 1986, 1994, 1996, 1999a/ exp. 2nd ed. 2011).

The realities of life itself are implicit in the original descriptive founda-tions set forth by Darwin. Indeed, the centerpin of Darwin's extensive as well as lifelong studies of animals was precisely living forms that move themselves. From his first studies as a biologist on The Beagle (Darwin 1839/1958) to his last studies of earthworms (Darwin 1881/1976), his morphological concerns were consistently tied to animation; that is, to how animate forms make a living, given the animate forms they are. His emphasis was thus not on a static morphology, but on what we might term a *morphology-in-motion*. A morphology-in-motion—animation—is first and foremost a subject–world relationship. Perception, emotion, cognition, and imagination all derive from the basic fact that whatever the animate form, it lives not in a vacuum but in a world particularized by its being the animate form it is. Precisely because it does not live in a vacuum, it is unnecessary to "embed" its perceptions, cognitions, or affective experiences in the world. Its interest, curiosity, hesitation, fright, and so on, its turning toward or turning away, and its approach or avoidance are emblematic of its affective motivations to move in distinctive ways with respect to the world in which it lives.

Animation is actually theoretically of a piece with the biological concept of "responsivity": "Plant seedlings bend toward light; meal-worms congergate in dampness; cats pounce on small moving objects; even certain bacteria move toward or away from certain chemicals [... T]the capacity to respond is a fundamental and almost universal characteristic of life" (Curtis 1975, p. 28). It is notable that we find just such observations throughout Darwin's writings, specifically with respect to emotions. He writes, for example, "Terror acts in the same manner on them [the lower animals] as on us, causing the muscles to tremble, the heart to palpitate, the sphincters to be relaxed, and the hair to stand on end" (Darwin 1871/1981, vol. 1, p. 39). He goes on to write of suspicion in "most wild animals," of courage and timidity being "variable qualities in [...] individuals of the same species," of some animals of a species being good-tempered and others ill-tempered, and of maternal affection in nonhuman animal life (ibid., pp. 39–40). In short, and even before he examines emotions at length in his well-known book *The Expression of the Emotions in Man and Animals* (Darwin 1872/1965), Darwin dwells at length on the responsivity of living creatures—on the primordial *animation* that is at the heart of life and across virtually the whole of the animal kingdom.

Precisely in this context, it is of moment to note Darwin's estimation of the vexing relationship of mind and body, of the challenge it presents, and of the proper mode of conceiving and approaching the challenge of understanding that relationship. He writes, "Experience shows the problem of the mind cannot be solved by attacking the citadel itself—the mind is function of body—we must bring some *stable* foundation to argue from" (Darwin 1838/1987, p. 564). While further comment will be made below on this insightful observation, the point of moment here is that *animation* is indeed the *stable* foundation from which to argue, for *animation* is inclusive of the whole of life, and for this reason is integral to all-inclusive and penetrating understandings of emotion and consciousness. In particular, animation tells us why distinguishing between behavior and movement is of vital significance; it tells us why concepts emanating from movement are of vital significance to animate life; it tells us why emotions too are descriptively declinable in terms of force, space, and time, why they too are manifestations of dynamic bodily feelings, in this instance, not just kinetic but affective dynamic bodily feelings; and finally, it tells us why emotions and movement are dynamically congruent. We will examine each of these four essentially enlightening aspects of animation in turn.

II. On the Distinction between Behavior and Movement

Descriptions of behavior rely first of all on pre-assigned categorical place-ments. An individual is eating, for example, or mating, fighting, or exploring; in other words, the individual is doing something that carries a ready-made label.

Identified within a ready-made category, the doing thereby falls also within a ready-made category of knowledge. The observer already knows what is involved on the basis of his or her own experience and applies that knowledge to his or her object of study. In short, the observer's first-person knowledge is the basis of his or her third-person behavioral ascriptions. What such ascriptions elide are the kinetic dynamics of any particular behavior. This fact was recognized by ethologists such as Ilan Golani who, by utilizing a movement notation system, was able to analyze the qualita-tive kinetic structure of movement, thereby coming to understand the actual dynamics of life itself. What these dynamics show is that "cognition is not separated from perception, perception is not separated from move-ment, and movement is not separated from an environment nor from a larger category designated as a behavior; on the contrary, the movement-perceptual system is behavior in the sense that it is the actual 'real-time', 'real-life' event as it unfolds" (Sheets-Johnstone 1999a/exp. 2nd ed. 2011, p. 218). Ethologist John Fentress's intricate studies of "how mice scratch their faces" (Fentress 1989, pp. 45–6) and his and other's combined study of ritualized fighting in wolves (Moran et al. 1981) demonstrate the significance of analyzing and understanding the kinetic dynamics of life itself. In his early explorations with automatons, neuroscientist Gerald Edelman arrived at similar conclusions. He found that *movement* was instrumental in gaining knowledge of the world, that the automaton Darwin III, for example, "categorizes only on the basis of experience" (Edelman 1992, p. 93); Darwin III could "decide," for example, "that some-thing is an object, that the object is striped, and that the object is bumpy" (ibid.) only on the basis of freely varied movement. Edelman's findings testify to the fact that animation is first and foremost a subject–world relationship and that life is grounded in animation: animals are impelled to move on the basis of their interest or aversion to what they perceive, what they recognize, and so on.

Though they have been largely overtaken by an attentive fixation on *the brain*, the above-mentioned studies should not be dismissed; they are not passé but curatively topical to the ills that plague a reductionist-leaning neuroscience. The point is succinctly made by Foolen et al. (2009) when they rightfully question whether mirror neurons are cause or effect of experience. If the latter, then morphology-in-motion—animation—is the core phenomenon of life, the core from which animal faculties and capacities arise. In other words, movement is our mother tongue (Sheets-Johnstone 1999a/exp. 2nd ed. 2011). Behavior is no match for this core phenomenon. Moreover certain methodological correspondences are evident between the above-mentioned studies and the studies of Edmund Husserl, the founder of phenomenology, and Hermann von Helmholtz, the noted 19th-century physicist-physiologist. Both Husserl and von Helmholtz emphasized the centrality of movement to perception and both made use of the free variation of movement in their epistemologically tethered research pursuits. For example, in the context of describing aspects of infant-child play with objects, von Helmholtz concludes that "the child learns to recognize the different views which the same object can afford in correlation with the movements which he is constantly giving it" (von Helmholtz 1878/1971, p. 214). In another text, he states that "our body's movement sets us in varying spatial relations to the objects we perceive, so that the impressions which these objects make upon us change as we move (von Helmholtz 1868/1971, p. 373). He furthermore devises not thought experiments but real-life *movement* experiments such as the following in quest of understanding what he calls "judgment[s] of relief in the floor-plane":

> [This judgment] can be tested by standing in a level meadow and first observing the relief of the ground in the ordinary way. There may be little irregularities here and there, but still the surface appears to be distinctly horizontal for a long way off. Then bend the head over and look at it from underneath the arm; or stand on a stump or a little elevation in the ground, and stoop down and look between the legs, without changing much the vertical distance of the head above the level ground. The farther portions of the meadow will then cease to appear level and will look more like a wall painted on the sky. I have frequently made observations of this kind as I was walking along the road between Heidelberg and Mannheim. (von Helmholtz 1910/1962, pp. 433–4)

Clearly, when experience is meticulously examined and meticulously varied, we can make self-evident the fact that movement quintessentially informs perception. The practice of phenomenology rigorously testifies to this fact. As Husserl states, "We constantly find here [in moving and per-ceiving] this two-fold articulation: kinesthetic sensations on the one side, the motivating; and the sensations of features on the other, the motivated" (Husserl 1989, p. 63). He furthermore underscores the consequential nature of the articulation, stating not only that "[I]f the eye turns in a certain way, *then* so does the 'image'" (ibid.); but more broadly that "'exhibitings' of are related back to correlative multiplicities of kinesthetic processes having the peculiar character of the 'I do', 'I move' (to which even the 'I hold still' must be added) [… A] hidden intentional 'if-then' relation is at work here" (Husserl 1970, p. 161).

It is of prime importance to recognize that these movement-perceptual relationships—in reality, movement-perceptual-cognitional relationships—are informed by and articulated within an affective experience of some kind. *Animate beings are moved to move.* To be moved by and move with interest toward something is different from being moved by and move with apprehension toward it; to be moved by and move with delight toward something is different from being moved by and move with disgust away from it. Animation opens the path toward just such holistic understandings of life. Behavior as it is commonly spoken of and written about does not approximate to the deeper and more complex facets of movement that are at the heart of animation. It does not uncover the consequential dynamic relationship of perception to movement, the significance of freely varied movement, or the integral role of emotion in perception and cognition. Indeed, from the viewpoint of affective experience, if I draw close to something or run away from it, if I am determined to solve a problem, convinced of the truth of my findings, or dumbstruck, for example, my experience is clearly not simply perceptual or cognitional but affective and as such, a testimonial to the reality of my being an animate being, a being that is moved to move, whether to explore, avoid, persist in my efforts, stand my ground, or, as Husserl points out, even to hold still. In sum, recognition of, and attention to movement opens our eyes to the complex reality that is animation, a reality that defines the multiple facets of a subject–world relationship.

III. Concepts Emanating from Movement

As indicated earlier, and as suggested by Darwin's observation that "the mind is function of body," primary attention to movement is the key to understanding the complex realities of animation, whether a matter of tigers, bats, humans, lizards, langurs, bees, or even bacteria. With respect to humans, we may first note that movement is the primary object of attention of human infants (Spitz 1983); it is the primary mode of social communication in infancy (Stern 1985); and it is the primary source of nonlinguistic concepts (Sheets-Johnstone 1990). The latter concepts are not poor relatives of later linguistic concepts; quite the reverse in that naming where something is—*inside* or *far away*, for example—or naming the temporal span of something—*sudden* or *prolonged*, for example—is rooted not in the words themselves but in experience. In short, nonlinguistic kinetic concepts ground fundamental concepts of space, time, and force. This fact is validated by a diversity of research reports and conclusions about infants and young children: for example, by Clark's finding that *in* is the first locative to be learned (Clark 1979; see also Grieve et al. 1977; Cook 1978; see too Piaget 1967, 1968, and Bower 1974 on "being inside"; see also Sheets-Johnstone 1990 for a phenomenological explication of an infant's experiences of *in* and *being inside*); by Bower's observations that not only is an infant fascinated by the opening and closing of its hand, but that it is fascinated by putting something inside someone else's hand, then closing it, then opening it, and so on (Bower 1979); and by Stern's observation that an infant's *hunger storm* is not a sensation but an ongoing dynamic (Stern 1990). We indeed begin life by thinking in movement (Sheets-Johnstone 1999a/exp. 2nd ed. 2011; see also Bruner 1991; Bloom 1993). This form of thinking does not disappear, but remains at the core of our capacities in the world, including our capacity to think in language, that is, in words. Infants are indeed not *prelinguistic*; language is *post-kinetic* (Sheets-Johnstone 1999a/exp. 2nd ed. 2011). Not only this but movement forms the I that moves before the I that moves forms movement (ibid.). In other words, movement is there from birth and before (Furuhjelm et al. 1976), feeding the faculties and concepts that mature precisely in the course of moving oneself.

To appreciate the concepts generated by movement, consider the experience of walking. The qualitative character of our experience depends on the inherently qualitative nature of movement. Our walk may be jaunty, for example, or slow and labored, determined, hesitant, rushed, or relaxed, and so on. Moreover we may follow a straight path across a parking lot, zig-zag erratically in walking down a street to avoid collisions with others, or follow regular cut-backs along a mountain trail, our movement in each instance creating a distinctive linear pattern. If it is windy, we may be tilted forward or if in pain, we may be twisted, our body in each instance having a distinctive linear design. Movement indeed has four fundamental qualities: tensional, linear, areal, and projectional quality. These qualities are of a piece in any movement sequence, that is, not simply in walking, but in reaching for a glass, kicking a ball, marching out of a room, drawing figure-eights in the air, and so on. They are inherent in any movement, but they can be analyzed phenomenologically, meaning that the nature of each quality can be spelled out. As intimated earlier, the intensity of our walk may vary and change, as when we realize that we are late and must hurry, a shift that increases our originally relaxed gait. Also, our body has a certain linear design and creates certain linear patterns in walking, its design and pattern being directional lines. Consider too that our body creates areal designs and patterns as well as linear ones. In walking, our body may be anywhere from contracted to expanded, depending, for example, on whether we are trying to hide our presence as we walk into or out of a room or whether we are walking open-armed to greet a friend; the movement itself may be anywhere from intensive to extensive, depending upon the spatial amplitude of our walk. We might, for example, stop short in an otherwise extensive walk through a forest, hunch over, slowly rise up to look ahead at what we thought was a bear, then take quite small steps backward in retreat. As with all qualities of movement, areal design and pattern too may vary and thus change the character of our walk. Consider finally the projectional quality of our walk, that is, whether our movement is abrupt, sustained, ballistic, or a combination of these qualities: a goose-stepping walk is notably different from a smooth, ongoing, relatively unaccented gait, for example. To be noted is that any particular projectional designation is actually inclusive of infinite degrees of shading and that any particular movement may be a combination of basic projectional qualities, as when, for example, we turn our head abruptly to the side while con-tinuing in our even-footed gait, or when we begin swinging our arms back and forth, giving them an initial impulse upward, then letting them follow through on their own momentum and gravitational pulls.

However brief the above analysis, it should be evident that kinesthesia is at the source of fundamental concepts of force, time, and space—of intensity, direction, amplitude, duration, and so on—and at the source as well of the originally qualitative character of these concepts, that is, not only of what is experienced as strong, moderate, or weak in the course of self-movement, for example, but also of what is fading and what is growing in intensity, what is sudden and what is attenuated, what is continuing to move on the basis of an initial impulse or powerfully driven at every moment, what is moving resolutely forward or diverging erratically onto different paths, what is loose and open-ended or tight and constricted, and so on. These qualitatively-laden concepts are integral to our understandings of emotion as well as movement. In particular, recog-nition of these concepts as deriving from our earliest experiences of move-ment onward is integral not only to our understanding of the subtle and intricate complexities of movement and thus of our capacity to learn to move ourselves efficiently and effectively in the world in the first place, but also of our understanding of affective feelings and thus ultimately of the dynamic congruency of movement and emotion.

IV. Affective Feelings

Emotions too are declinable in terms of space, time, and force. To appre-ciate this fact at its core, we need to look closely again at infancy and acknowledge what it teaches us about our humanness. Adult thoughts and theories about our human ways risk validity by dismissing—or denigrating (Dennett 1983, p. 384)—that period of our lives we all lived through as infants. We clearly see the truth of this claim in the fact that, for an infant, an emotional experience is a *whole-body experience*; an infant does not feel distress simply in its abdomen or pleasure only on its face. Accordingly, why is whole-body affective experience transformed into partial-body affective experience in many adult estimations of emotion? More finely put, why is misery or joy or sadness or anger conceived as felt only in one's head or face, or hand or belly? An adult example well illustrates the point at issue.

When one has missed attending a meeting and wants to catch up on happenings by reading the minutes, one may feel by turns interested, indifferent, doubtful, surprised, disappointed, and angered in the course of reading. The feelings are likely fleeting as well as in the background in relation to the reading itself. Yet they inform one's experience of reading the minutes and may in fact come strongly to the fore depending on their intensity. If they do, one finds oneself immersed in an affective dynamics, feeling them not only here and there, as if anger were simply a matter of clenched teeth and fists, or surprise simply a matter of a gasp and a pounding heart—though one may certainly feel specifically located tensions, a rush of air in one's throat, or sudden hammering heartbeats. One is, on the contrary, immersed throughout; the affective dynamics envelop one in a whole-body sense.

Infant psychiatrist and clinical psychologist George Downing asks, "When we think about emotion, should our focus be on the face or on the body as a whole?" (Downing 2005, p. 429). When he attempts to show how "[r]esearch strategies limited to the face," while having had "considerable success [...] may marginalize phenomena that, in fact, are deserving of more attention," he surely points us in the direction of reconsidering not just a partialized-body view of emotion but a view that is developmentally disjoint. That is, if, as Downing notes, "Affectively speaking, infants would seem to be full-body creatures from the start" (ibid.), how is it that adult humans commonly lose not sight but the *felt bodily sense* of their full-body affectivity? Having lost touch with their emotions in this experiential sense, adult humans thereby commonly fail to recognize the dynamics of emotion, conceiving emotions as *states* of being or as nothing more than discrete bodily *sensations*.

Affective dynamics are finely delineated by infant psychiatrist and clinical psychologist Daniel Stern in his illustrations of "affect attunement," situations in which a mother creates a qualitatively felt dynamic with her infant. Consider the following examples.

> A nine-month-old girl becomes very excited about a toy and reaches for it. As she grabs it, she lets out an exuberant "aaaah!" and looks at her mother. Her mother looks back, scrunches up her shoulders, and performs a terrific shimmy with her upper body, like a go-go dancer. The shimmy lasts only about as long as her daughter's "aaaah!" but is equally excited, joyful, and intense. (Stern 1985, p. 140)

> A nine-month-old boy is sitting facing his mother. He has a rattle in his hand and is shaking it up and down with a display of interest and mild amusement. As mother watches, she begins to nod her head up and down, keeping a tight beat with her son's arm motions. (ibid., p. 141)

Stern analyzes such instances of affect attunement in terms closely analogous to the qualities of movement specified in the previous sections, namely, in terms of *intensity*, *timing*, and *shape*. He breaks these dimensions down in greater detail, describing how a mother matches the "absolute intensity," "intensity contour," "temporal beat," "rhythm," "duration," and "shape" of her infant's dynamics (ibid., p. 146). The immediate point of note here is that whatever the mode of attunement, whether aural or kinetic, it is not a question of imitation but of dynamics, dynamics created by infant and mother together through some mode of bodily movement. The further point is that although the dynamics are clearly created through distinct bodily movements, including voice-producing movements, they are *whole-body experiences*, and this because they are experienced not objectively as an arm moving or a head nodding, or as someone shaking a rattle or banging on a toy (ibid., pp. 140–1), but as a wholly qualitative phenomenon having a certain spatio-temporal-energic character, such as when a mother matches her infant's kinetic dynamics with a vocalized "kaaaaa-*bam*, kaaaaa-*bam*" (ibid., p. 140).

In sum, affects, like movement, are whole-body spatio-temporal-energic phenomena; precisely as Stern indicates, they have distinct spatial contours, intensities, and temporalities. When we explode in anger, burst into song, begin to doubt, nurse a grudge, hesitate to speak out, continue to grieve, turn away in disgust, are seized by fear, and so on, it is *experientially* evident not only that emotions are manifestations of feelings but that emotions are distinctive in both a bodily-felt and bodily-observable sense and are therefore descriptively declinable.

V. Dynamic Congruency

In his article "Action and Emotion in Development of Cultural Intelligence: Why Infants Have Feelings Like Ours," infant psychologist Colwyn Trevarthen defines emotions "as manners of moving, and of responding to movement" (Trevarthen 2005, p. 63). He emphasizes the sensitivity of infants to "animacy" (ibid., p. 80), and more broadly, the way in which animal bodies are "motivated with intrinsic rhythm and intensity in the 'vitality' or 'sentic forms' of emotions," stressing in this context the dynamic temporal dimension of emotion and movement (ibid., p. 64).

Trevarthen's conception of emotion and his emphasis on animacy substantively echo Darwin's observation of "the intimate relation which exists between almost all the emotions and their outward manifestations." It is puzzling as well as notable that many present-day scientists and philosophers investigating emotions seem oblivious not only of Darwin's original insight into the intimate relation between emotion and movement but of ontogenetical studies of emotion such as those of Trevarthen and Stern. Their thinking is instead tied to behavior or action. In effect, they fail to realize that, to paraphrase anthropologist Claude Levi-Strauss, "movement is good to think." As previous sections of this chapter have shown, movement opens paths to multiple dimensions of animation. A discussional comment in a recent book on emotion suggests that a sense of the import of movement hovers at the edge of awareness. Answering a question about dynamics with respect to the ability of chimpanzees to recognize the facial expressions of conspecifics, ethologist Lisa Parr states, "Normally, chimpanzees don't really see facial expressions in a static way [...] Maybe movement in and of itself produces a lot of information about individual identity and maybe even about the type of expression that's being made" (Parr 2003, p. 80). Earlier, in her article in the book, she comments, "When facial expressions were presented as dynamic stimuli using video, subjects showed no preference for trials in which distinctive features were present. Therefore, the addition of movement, vocalizations and context significantly changed the manner by which chimpanzees discriminated some facial expressions" (ibid., p. 73). Most interestingly too, she notes, "The perception of facial expressions [...] produces a low-level motor mimicry in the perceiver that can be measured using electromyo-graphic recordings. These subtle movements correlate to the self-perception of emotion, suggesting an integral link between facial action and emotional experience" (ibid., p. 72).

Clearly, thinking in terms of *action*—like thinking in terms of *behavior*—deflects us from recognizing the rich and subtle spatio-temporal-energic dynamics of movement, and in turn from recognizing the rich and subtle dynamics of emotions and the intimate relation between movement and emotions. In short, once we realize that movement is indeed good to think, we begin thinking in terms of *dynamics*. Not only are Stern's studies of affect attunement testimony to these dynamics but so also is his identification of "vitality affects," which he describes precisely in kinetic terms such as "'surging', 'fading away', 'fleeting', 'explosive', 'crescendo', 'decrescendo', 'bursting', 'drawn out', and so on" (Stern 1985, p. 54). What ontogenetical studies of emotion clearly point to and elucidate through "vitality affects," "animacy," "affect attunement," and the like, is precisely movement and the intimate relation between emotion and movement.

The term *dynamic congruency* was introduced and the phenomenon of affective/kinetic concordance was originally analyzed in a 1999 article that combined an empirical approach with a phenomenological one (Sheets-Johnstone 1999b). The empirical analysis is based not on ontogenetical research but on a variety of studies of emotions, studies that, in a different but no less trenchant way, carry forward Darwin's basic insight that move-ment and emotion go hand in hand (Sheets-Johnstone 1999b). In particular, the article begins by showing how the research of medical doctor and neuropsychiatrist Edmund Jacobson grounds emotions in a neuromuscular dynamic; how that of neuropsychiatrist Nina Bull grounds emotions in "motor attitudes," that is, in bodily postures and in a readiness to move; and how that of psychologist Joseph de Rivera grounds emotions in our experience of being literally "moved" by emotions. The article proceeds to demonstrate the phenomenological import of these studies, precisely by identifying the *formal* congruency of emotion and movement, that is, their concordantly experienced qualitative dynamic. The *concept* of dynamic congruency is thus rooted in experience and is descriptively analyzable in terms of experience. To be noted is that a prime and in fact sterling value of actually *doing phenomenology* is to describe experience, which is to say, to meet the challenge of languaging experience. A careful, exacting, and evidentially supportable vocabulary is indeed essential to the attainment of veritable descriptive foundations. We can readily appreciate this fact by noting that it is the *natural* dynamic congruity of emotions and movement that allows us successfully both to mime feelings we do not actually feel and to inhibit the expression of those that we do. Indeed, the natural dynamic congruency of emotions and movement attests to the rationality of animation. If animals — human ones included — were not moved to move in ways they actually move or if they did not move in ways they were moved to move, there would be no possibility of moving efficiently and effectively in the world. Animation would literally have no inherent rhyme or reason.

In sum, animation is the "*stable* foundation" for understandings of consciousness in its entire multiple and varied forms. No more than any other animals do human animals need to be "embodied" or "embedded" in order to be fully accounted for and understood. To comprehend their foundational animation requires meeting the challenge of examining and describing experience in a rigorous and methodologically enlightened way, finding in the process a language commensurate with the realities of animation.

References

Bloom, L. (1993) *The Transition from Infancy to Language: Acquiring the Power of Expression*, New York: Cambridge University Press.

Bower, T.G.R. (1974) *Development in Infancy*, San Francisco, CA: W.H. Freeman.

Bower, T.G.R. (1979) *Human Development*, San Francisco, CA: W.H. Freeman and Co.

Bruner, J. (1991) *Acts of Meaning*, Cambridge, MA: Harvard University Press.

Clark, E.V. (1979) Building a vocabulary: Words for objects, actions and relations, in Fletcher, P. & Garman, M. (eds.) *Language Acquisition*, pp. 149–160, Cambridge: Cambridge University Press.

Cook, N. (1978) In, on and under revisited again, *Papers and Reports on Child Language Development 15*, pp. 38–45, Stanford, CA: Stanford University Press.

Curtis, H. (1975) *Biology*, 2nd ed., New York: Worth Publishers.

Darwin, C. (1838/1987) *Charles Darwin's Notebooks, 1836–1844*, Barrett, P.H., Gautrey, P.J., Herbert, S., Kohn, D. & Smith, S. (eds.), Ithaca, NY: Cornell University Press.

Darwin, C. (1839/1958) *The Voyage of the Beagle*, New York: Bantam Books.

Darwin, C. (1871/1981) *The Descent of Man and Selection in Relation to Sex*, Princeton, NJ: Princeton University Press.

Darwin, C. (1872/1965) *The Expression of the Emotions in Man and Animals*, Chicago, IL: University of Chicago Press.

Darwin, C. (1881/1976) *The Formation of Vegetable Mould Through the Action of Worms with Observations on Their Habits*, Ontario: Bookworm Publishing Co.

Dennett, D. (1983) Intentional systems in cognitive ethology: The "Panglossian" paradigm defended, *The Behavioral and Brain Sciences*, 6, pp. 343–390.

Downing, G. (2005) Discussion: Emotion, body, and parent-infant interaction, in Nadel, J. & Muir, D. (eds.) *Emotional Development*, pp. 429–449, Oxford: Oxford University Press.

Edelman, G.M. (1992) *Bright Air, Brilliant Fire: On the Matter of the Mind*, New York: Basic Books.

Fentress, J.C. (1989) Developmental roots of behavioral order: Systemic approaches to the examination of core developmental issues, in Gunnar, M.R. & Thelen, E. (eds.) *Systems and Development*, pp. 35–76, Hillsdale, NJ: Lawrence Erlbaum Associates.

Fisher, J.A. (1996) The myth of anthropomorphism, in Bekoff, M. & Jamieson, D. (eds.) *Readings in Animal Cognition*, pp. 3–16, Cambridge, MA: Bradford Book/MIT Press.

Foolen, A., Lüdtke, U., Zlatev, J. & Racine, T. (2009) *Moving Ourselves, Moving Others: The Role of E(motion) for Intersubjectivity, Consciousness and Language*, Amsterdam: John Benjamins.

Furuhjelm, M., Ingelman-Sundbert, A. & Wirsén, C. (1976) *A Child Is Born*, rev. ed., New York: Delacourte Press.

Golani, I. (1976) Homeostatic motor processes in mammalian interactions: A choreography of display, in Bateson, P.G. & Klopfer, P.H. (eds.) *Perspectives in Ethology*, vol. 2, pp. 69–134, New York: Plenum Publishing.

Goodall, J. (1968) The behaviour of free-living chimpanzees in the Gombe Stream Area, *Animal Behaviour Monographs*, I (Part 3), pp. 161–311.

Goodall, J. (1971) *In the Shadow of Man*, New York: Dell Publishing.

Goodall, J (1990) *Through a Window: My Thirty Years with the Chimpanzees of Gombe*, Boston, MA: Houghton Mifflin Company.

Gould, S.J. (2000) Foreword: A lover's quarrel, in Bekoff, M. (ed.) *The Smile of a Dolphin: Remarkable Accounts of Animal Emotions*, pp. 13–17, New York: Discovery Books.

Grieve, R., Hoogenraad, R. & Murray, D. (1977) On the young child's use of lexis and syntax in understanding locative instructions, *Cognition*, 5, pp. 235–250.

Hall, K.R.L. & DeVore, I. (1972) Baboon social behavior, in Dolhinow, P. (ed.) *Primate Patterns*, pp. 125–180, New York: Holt, Rinehart and Winston.

Husserl, E. (1970) *The Crisis of European Sciences and Transcendental Phenomenology*, Carr, D. (trans.), Evanston, IL: Northwestern University Press.

Husserl, E. (1989) *Ideas Pertaining to a Pure Phenomenology and to a Phenomenological Philosophy: Book 2 (Ideas II)*, Rojcewicz, R. & Schuwer, A. (trans.), Boston, MA: Kluwer Academic.

Mitchell, R.W., Nicholas, T.S. & Miles, H.L. (eds.) (1997) *Anthropomorphism, Anecdotes, and Animals*, New York: State University of New York Press.

Moran, G., Fentress, J.C. & Golani, I. (1981) A description of relational patterns of movement during ritualized fighting in wolves, *Animal Behavior*, 29, pp. 1146–1165.

Parr, L.A. (2003) The discrimination of faces and their emotional content by chimpanzees (Pan troglodytes), in Ekman, P., Campos, J.J., Davidson, R.J. & de Waal, F.B.M. (eds.) *Emotions Inside Out: 130 Years after Darwin's Expression of the Emotions in Man and Animals*, pp. 56–78, New York: New York Academy of Sciences.

Piaget, J. (1967) *La construction du réel chez l'enfant*, Neuchatel: Delachaux et Niestlé.

Piaget, J. (1968) *La naissance de l'intelligence chez l'enfant*, 6th ed., Neuchatel: Delachaux et Niestlé.

Schaller, G.B. (1963) *The Mountain Gorilla: Ecology and Behavior*, Chicago, IL: University of Chicago Press.

Sheets-Johnstone, M. (1986) Existential fit and evolutionary continuities, *Synthese*, 66, pp. 219–248.

Sheets-Johnstone, M. (1990) *The Roots of Thinking*, Philadelphia, PA: Temple University Press.

Sheets-Johnstone, M. (1994) *The Roots of Power: Animate Form and Gendered Bodies*, Chicago, IL: Open Court Publishing.

Sheets-Johnstone, M. (1996) Taking evolution seriously: A matter of primate intelligence, *Etica & Animali*, 8, pp. 115–130.

Sheets-Johnstone, M. (1999a/exp. 2nd ed. 2011) *The Primacy of Movement*, Amsterdam/Philadelphia, PA: John Benjamins Publishing.

Sheets-Johnstone, M. (1999b) Emotions and movement: A beginning empirical-phenomenological analysis of their relationship, *Journal of Consciousness Studies*, 6 (11–12), pp. 259–277.

Sheets-Johnstone, M. (2002/this volume, Chapter X) Descriptive foundations, *Interdisciplinary Studies in Literature and Environment*, 9 (1), pp. 165–179.

Spitz, R.A. (1983) *Dialogues from Infancy*, Emde, R.M. (ed.), New York: International Universities Press.

Stern, D.N. (1985) *The Interpersonal World of the Infant: A View from Psychoanalysis and Developmental Psychology*, New York: Basic Books.

Stern, D.N. (1990) *Diary of a Baby*, New York: Basic Books.

Strum, S.C. (1987) *Almost Human: A Journey into the World of Baboons*, New York: W.W. Norton.

Trevarthen, C. (2005) Action and emotion in development of cultural intelligence: Why infants have feelings like ours, in Nadel, J. & Muir, D. (eds.) *Emotional Development*, pp. 61–91, Oxford: Oxford University Press.

von Helmholtz, H. (1868/1971) Recent progress in the theory of vision, in Kahl, R. (ed. & trans.) *Selected Writings of Hermann von Helmholtz*, pp. 144–222, Middletown, CT: Wesleyan University Press.

von Helmholtz, H. (1878/1971) The facts of perception, in Kahl, R. (ed. & trans.) *Selected Writings of Hermann von Helmholtz*, pp. 366–408, Middletown, CT: Wesleyan University Press.

von Helmholtz, H. (1910/1962) *Physiological Optics*, vol. III, Southall, J.P.C. (ed. & trans.), New York: Dover Publications.

Wilson, E.O. (1975) *Sociobiology: The New Synthesis*, Cambridge, MA: Harvard University Press.

Chapter V

Schizophrenia and "the Comet's Tale of Nature"
A Case Study in Phenomenology and Human Psychopathology[1]

In the context of fleshing out his concept of primal sensibility, Husserl turns attention to the development of the ego, specifically its actions and affections, stating that "the Ego always lives in the medium of its 'history'" (Husserl 1989, p. 350). His ensuing descriptive account of primal sensibility, summed in his notion of the comet's tail of Nature, is doubly significant: it provides a broad and direct phenomenological base from which to present a new and veritably rich historical perspective on schizophrenia and at the same time opens phenomenology itself to the task of setting forth a bona fide phenomenology of nature. I should note that the new perspective is not meant as an ultimate key to schizophrenia but as a penetrating new vista from which to view the pathology. The new vista grounds abnormalities of the psyche in foundational understandings of nature, understandings that complement in exacting ways the notable expositions and analyses of schizophrenia set forth by Sass, specifically in the continuities he describes between the normal and abnormal by way of modern artists and schizophrenics (1992); by Ciompi, specifically in his integration of affect and cognition and in the specific kind of atmosphere he cultivates at his Soteria treatment center (1988, 2003, 2004); by Depraz, specifically in her attempt to elucidate affect in light of the unexpected (1998); by Parnas, specifically in his delineation of the immobilizing perplexity and incertitude typical of pre-psychotic individuals and their

---

1   First published in *Philoctetes* (journal co-sponsored by NY Psychoanalytic Institute), (2007), Vol. 1, No. 2: 5–45 (target article with commentaries and response). Several additions were made to the article following its original presentation as a guest lecture at the Center for Subjectivity Research, University of Copenhagen, 12 June 2006.

feelings of anxiety and "imminent disaster" (2000, p. 130); and by Gallagher, specifically in his sustained emphasis on the "disruption of pro-tention" in the temporal flow of experience in schizophrenia (2005, e.g. pp. 195, 200, 201). The new vista furthermore offers substantive empirical grounds for bridging a fundamental dichotomy in present-day neuro-scientific research, notably, the chasm between experience and the brain. Indeed, phylogenetic and ontogenetic facts of life provide neuroscientific researchers with what dynamic systems theorists term "real-time" phenomena and thus with bona fide empirical bases on which to ground otherwise speculative forays into neurological patternings in *the brain*.[2] These same phylogenetic and ontogenetic facts of life are seminal to classical psychoanalysis, i.e. to Freud's deep belief in the biological founda-tions of the psyche—e.g. "in the psychical field the biological factor is really the rock-bottom" (1937, p. 357)—and in this biological sense to his dis-owned *Project* (1966) that attempted a neurological grounding of psychic functioning.

I. Introduction: Primal Sensibility

Husserl specifies "primal sensibility" as the "underlying basis" of the "*intellectus agens*," the psychic foundation of the reasoning subject who actively makes sense of the world by his or her judgements, inferences, calculations, and so on (1989, pp. 344–7; see also pp. 288–93). He observes early on, for example, "the subject of spiritual acts"—the reasoning sub-ject—"finds itself dependent on an *obscure underlying basis* of traits of character, original and latent dispositions, and thereby dependent on nature" (p. 289). He speaks specifically in this context of "the ancient distinction" between reason and sensibility, sensibility being "a stratum of *hidden reason*," a stratum he elsewhere specifies as "instinct" (1970, p. 52; see also 1989, p. 346). He points out that the stratum of hidden reason "first of all at least extends as far as the constitution of nature […] since indeed all complicated relations of the 'if-then,' all causalities, can become guiding lines for theoretical, thus spiritual, explications" (1989, p. 289), and later likens the stratum to a "root soil" (p. 292), "*a background that is prior to all comportment* and [that] is […] presupposed by all comportment" (p. 291). Clearly, Husserl not only recognizes that "Nature is there from the first day," as Merleau- Ponty later declares but without precise elaboration (Merleau-Ponty 1988, p. 133; 1968, p. 267; see Sheets-Johnstone 1999a, pp. 306–8/2011, pp. 266–8 for a discussion), but he is at pains to specify as far as possible in the context of his analysis of the person as "free Ego" (Husserl 1989, p. 269) just how "Nature is there from the first day," that is,

---

2   See note 20 for further specifications of the relationship between "real-time" phenomena and neurological investigations of the brain.

how nature is the primal epistemological ground of the human epistemological subject. He finds, for example, that "all life of the spirit is permeated
by the 'blind' operation of associations, drives, feelings which are stimuli
for drives and determining grounds for drives, tendencies which emerge in
obscurity, et cetera, all of which determine the subsequent course of consciousness according to 'blind' rules" (p. 289). In a supplemental writing,
he explains the "blindness" of the rules by the fact that "[p]rimal
sensibility, sensation, et cetera *does not arise out of immanent grounds*, out of
psychic tendencies; it is simply there, it emerges" (p. 346). In other words,
feelings, underlying tendencies, unintentional associations, instincts, and
the like, are not constituted but factical aspects of the subject that, within
the context of Husserl's analysis, are observed simply to arise. In sum,
primal sensibilities as described by Husserl are spontaneous sensibilities
that are present naturally "from the first day" — from the birth of the
animate organism.[3] In and of themselves, they constitute the natural
ground of all motivated acts of the organism.

It bears emphasis that what is primal is not only the outwardly
sensuous — the world of colors, sounds, and so on. As Husserl explicitly
states, primal sensibility encompasses feelings, dispositions in the form of
"determining tendencies" such as patience or temper, instincts, and so on
(pp. 288–9), all of which enter into the receptivity of the organism and the
act of "turning toward" (p. 346). It is notable that these fundamental
aspects of sensibility dovetail existentially as well as conceptually with the
evolutionary specification of responsivity as a primary "sign of life" (Curtis
1975, p. 27). Primal sensibility and responsivity are complementary
descriptions of the animated livingness of animate forms generated by
nature. Moreover, Husserl's recognition of "determining tendencies" that
derive from nature and that generate differences among individuals corresponds empirically to Darwin's elemental observation formulated in his first
central tenet of evolution, namely, that there is *natural* variation among
individuals in any given species, one individual being more alert than
another, one more pugnacious than another, and so on (Darwin 1859/1968,
1871/1981).

The confluence of primal sensibility with biological responsivity and
variation among individuals is of singular moment. It signals a complementary acknowledgement of and attention to history, a *natural* history
and the significance of that history. Husserl himself points out, "The Ego
always lives in the medium of its 'history'; all its earlier lived experiences
have sunk down, but they have aftereffects in tendencies, sudden ideas,

---

3   Indeed, primal sensibilities are there before 'the first day'; they are there in
     the developing life of the fetus (see Furuhjelm, Inselman-Sundberg and
     Wirsén 1977).

transformations or assimilations of earlier lived experiences, and from such assimilations new formations are merged together, et cetera—just as in the sphere of primal sensibility, whose formations also pertain to the medium of the Ego" (1989, p. 350). Though clearly not including evolutionary history within the scope of his remark, Husserl nonetheless recognizes the essential role of nature in the history of the ego, including, implicitly, by the very nature of primal sensibility itself, an ontogenetic history. In fact, he sums up his recognition of the ego's history by saying, "All this has its natural course, thus even each free act [i.e. an act involving reason] has its comet's tail of Nature."[4] In effect, living meanings are phenomenologically *historically complex phenomena.* They have a natural history that, in its fullest sense, is bound not just ontogenetically but phylogenetically. Like living forms, living meanings hold—and have held—possibilities of further development, which is to say that they have evolved over time and that investigations of their origin and historical development tell us something fundamental about life in general and human life, including individual human lives, in particular.

II. The Comet's Tail of Nature and a Harmonious World

As Husserl implies, the comet's tail of Nature is a built-in dimension of humanness, informing human history at all levels, that is, across the whole of a human life as across the life of the species, because it is a built-in dimension of living meanings. Indeed, primal sensibilities are present in human nature in its totality, interwoven in perceptions, cognitions, feelings, movements, memories, expectations, and so on. Enfolded in the comet's tail of Nature, they are a dimension of humanness that in spite of its "hiddenness" can be phenomenologically elucidated. Precisely because they inform the subject totally—the subject at any age and in any state of

---

[4] Given Husserl's striking and unusual metaphor of a "comet's tail" to describe the foundational and perduring connection of spirit and nature, and thus to describe *an ontological* as well as epistemological dimension of personhood, it is curious that Merleau-Ponty finds different uses for the same metaphor, taking it up for quite other purposes. He uses the comet's tail first as a descriptive simile when he writes, "I stand in front of my desk and lean on it with both hands, only my hands are stressed and the whole of my body trails behind them like the tail of a comet" (1962, p. 100), and subsequently uses it as an explanatory device to resolve his puzzlement about movement, notably movement and objects in motion vis-à-vis the sight of a bird in flight: "It is not I who recognize, in each of the points and instants passed through, the same bird defined by explicit characteristics, it is the bird in flight which constitutes the unity of its movement, which changes its place [...] like the comet with its tail" (p. 275). (For a critique of the not uncommon notion of movement as a change of position, see Sheets-Johnstone 1999a/exp. 2nd ed. 2011, 2003.)

health—they demand assiduous investigation and examination in depth; while not transparent, they are not inimical to phenomenology. Moreover hints of their importance with respect to psychiatric pathologies are readily apparent in Husserl's constitutional analysis of the subject, in particular, his specification of the fundamental hand of Nature in the ego's elemental predisposition toward a harmoniously ordered world. "[W]e have in the sphere of lived experience," Husserl writes, "the immense field of primary sensibility with its network of tendentious nexuses, with its Objective constitutions, and with its rules, which are expressed in the theme: There appears an Objective world that is to be maintained concordantly" (1989, p. 347). A concordant or harmonious world is in fact a consistent thematic in Husserl's phenomenology, a thematic that is of foundational and resounding significance and that he ties basically to primal sensibility.[5]

Now to affirm that the rules of primal sensibility operate in the service of harmonizing the subject's experiences of the world is to say that maintaining a harmonious world is a *natural* foundational human predisposition, indeed, a *natural* foundational human priority. A harmonious or concordant world is one in which one can move comfortably and knowledgeably, one in which, when anxieties and fears arise—for example, when dangers and challenges arise—one is secure in one's ability to rise to the occasion in whatever ways desirable or required. To use R.D. Laing's apt term (1965), one's "primary ontological security" is a counterpoint to the existential vulnerabilities of being alive and finding oneself in a discordant world.

Yet if the rules of primal sensibility are "blind," as Husserl claims, that is, if the underlying natural basis of our lives is "obscure," and, indeed, if the rules operating with respect to dimensions of what he calls our "facticity" are "beyond our comprehension," as he explicitly states (1989, p. 288), then how are we to explain in a full phenomenological manner how harmony is achieved, and achieved not just cognitively through free acts of the ego but affectively through the comet's tail of Nature that is the foundation of free acts of the ego, and further, how the foundational predisposition to a harmonious world is precisely disrupted in psychological pathologies? In short, while the comet's tail of Nature is an essential aspect of humanness in theory, what experiential dimensions of human life reveal it in fact?

Husserl comes obliquely to our aid in answering the question when he states first that "[t]he underlying bases upon which is built the comprehensively motivated spiritual life of the other [...] present themselves [...] as 'variations' of my own"—or in other words, as possible human

---

5   Concordance—or harmony—is indeed a consistent theme in Husserl's writings (see Sheets-Johnstone 1999b).

sensibilities—and then states that we necessarily uncover these bases when we seek an understanding of the other's development (p. 288). He subsequently observes that in the process of examining another person's developmental life, we come to an understanding of how the person comes to be the way he or she typically is, that is, how the person's life as a socio-cultural historical phenomenon has conditioned his or her motivations and development. Yet as indicated above, such understanding is limited: Factical aspects are "beyond our comprehension." In his ongoing discussion of the problem, however, in a section titled "The spiritual Ego and its underlying basis," Husserl comes to our aid more directly, showing how he conceives both the impasse and a possible way through it. In particular after noting that the underlying bases of the other "present themselves [...] as 'variations' of my own," and that "I come across these [underlying] bases when I want to *understand someone's development*," he sets forth the procedure to be followed to gain such understanding and in the process confronts the seemingly impenetrable problem of facticity. With respect to the other, he states:

> I have then to describe, going from stage to stage, the surrounding world in which he grew up and how he was motivated by the things and people of his environment just as they appeared to him and as he saw them. Here we touch upon facticity, in itself beyond our comprehension. This child takes an original joy in sounds, that child does not. The one is inclined toward temper, the other toward patience. Natural causality enters in as well. Because of a serious fall, someone might become cripple, and that has consequences for his spiritual life: Certain groups of motivations are defunct from then on. We are not interested here in a real-causal analysis of these consequences. But medical knowledge can be of service toward an integration, in the correct way, of the psychic effects that are relevant for subjective development and consequently toward giving an account of them in the attempt to clarify subjective motivations and development. Here the physical is serving as an indication of what is to be integrated.

Clearly, the key to breaking through the impasse is to identify "psychic effects that are relevant for subjective development." *Relevant* psychic effects must, in other words, be identified before they can be integrated into subjective understandings, specifically, understandings of *motivations and development*. The basic question, of course, is, what constitutes a *relevant* psychic effect? Only if a determination is made of what constitutes a relevant psychic effect can something "physical" be justly taken as "an indication of what is to be integrated." Most importantly, a further phenomenological step can be taken on this basis. Something "physical" together with its relevant psychic effect can be taken not only as "an indication of what is to be integrated," but as a bona fide transcendental clue. In other words, the trick with respect to delineating the comet's tail of

Nature in experiential terms is precisely to identify something "physical," pinpointing its relevancy as a psychic effect and, in turn, to take it as a transcendental clue. Before turning in depth to one of two such physical aspects, pinpointing its relevant psychic effect, and then taking it as a transcendental clue, we must turn attention to an assumption about nature and offer a series of clarifications.

III. Nature

Nature is not simply physical reality. She shows herself spiritually — spiritually in Husserl's sense of "spirit" — in animate ways, which means in motivational proclivities and possibilities of every kind, cognitional and affective, and in self-generated capacities of every kind, that is, in what Husserl terms "I cans" as both practical and theoretical powers. Aristotle rightly observed (Aristotle *Physics*), "Nature is a principle of motion and change," foundationally dynamic rather than *object*-ive in a strictly material sense. It follows that if we want to grasp the comet's tail of Nature, we need to turn attention to the dynamics of life itself and attempt to clarify Husserl's strongly distinguished "lower" and "higher" levels, that is, sensibility and reason, and take clarifying exception to his remark that "Ego and nature stand in contrast" (1989, p. 350). The starkness of the line Husserl draws between ego and nature is conceptually tethered to his central and abiding concern with freedom, with the *"higher, autonomous, freely acting Ego"* (p. 267), with "the life of free acts" (p. 282), with "the Ego of freedom" (p. 349; see also, p. 224), with active ego-motivations (see e.g. p. 269), that is, with position-taking acts of judging, deciding, comparing, choosing, and so on. What he wants to point up by means of the stark contrast is that a free act, though it has its comet's tail of Nature, does not itself derive from nature; it derives not from "mere natural lawfulness" but from the ego (p. 350). The contrast, however, is less absolute than it appears. Husserl qualifies it, for example, when he observes that affection is "the means of the bond between Ego and nature," qualifies it only to an extent, however, because though affection "bonds" ego and nature, affection, as he has earlier stated, "belongs quite certainly in the sphere of nature" (p. 349). He qualifies the starkness of the contrast less ambiguously when he observes, "I can decide freely, and at the same time I am following my habitual inclination" (p. 350), and when he elsewhere describes how, in certain instances, *"habit and free motivation intertwine"* (p. 267). He qualifies it less ambiguously, too, when he observes that "all activity of the Ego presupposes affection, even if — in the developed subject — it is not exactly the one of primal sensibility" (p. 349), i.e. even if affection stems from secondary sensibility, a sensibility into which reason has entered and thereby becomes "degraded" reason (p. 345). On the other hand, qualifications are unequivocally absent in categorical statements that pit sensibility against reason, as when, for example, Husserl states, "I am entirely free if I am not motivated passively, that is, if I do not carry out the consequence through affection but through 'rational motives'" (p. 350), or when, in emphasizing that the free ego is not a product of experience, he states, "I precisely am the one I am, not as nature, but as a position-taking Ego" (p. 343). In short, when one takes both qualifications and categorical statements into account, the putatively clear phenomenological terrain on which the contrast is at times drawn turns swampy. It turns swampy precisely because Husserl's qualifications consistently show a shaded and complex ground rather than a stark and absolute division.

Now certainly Husserl is just in maintaining that affections are passive; that is, feelings, dispositions, and impulsions simply arise. We do not choose our feelings, for example, but only how and if we act on them. As Jung succinctly points out, "Affects are not 'made' or willfully produced; they simply happen" (1968, pp. 278–9). The critical question concerns our actions in light of our affections: we can react on the basis of our feelings and "do" without thinking — without any position-takings, as Husserl would say — or we can choose in a deliberate and reflective sense to do or not to do (see Johnstone 1986). In this sense, surely it is true that free acts can be contrasted with reactive ones. What needs clarification in this context is the concept of nature. If nature is the all-inclusive term used to denote that which is deterministic and/or that which arises passively without active involvement in the form of position-takings, then nature is being narrowly defined, that is, defined in such a way that fundamental aspects of what is human, i.e. free will and reason, are conceived to transcend nature; they are not natural phenomena but originate and exist outside nature.

The question is whether this understanding of nature is tenable and properly justifiable or whether it restricts and even hobbles a properly phenomenological understanding of humanness. Is it not precisely part of the nature of humans to be able to think before they act, for example? Is it not precisely part of the nature of humans to be able to justify what they do on the basis of reasoned judgements? The problem the questions enfold is not a matter of linguistics but a matter of Nature herself, and not only with respect to giving Nature her living due in a broad sense, but with respect to understanding the nature of humans and the nature of that human nature within the total compass of Nature. Where, after all, does humanness have its roots, *all* its roots, if not in nature? Two mundane empirical observations, homely in their simplicity, put the issue in brief but telling perspective. They show that what is in question is indeed *humanness*, specifically, natural dimensions of humanness.

On the basis of his extensive first-person studies of the natural world, Darwin wrote, "Animals may constantly be seen to pause, deliberate, and resolve. It is a significant fact, that the more the habits of any particular animal are studied by a naturalist, the more he attributes to reason and the less to unlearnt instincts" (1871/1981, p. 46). On the basis of the same extensive first-person studies of the natural world, Darwin wrote, "The fact that the lower animals are excited by the same emotions as ourselves is so well established, that it will not be necessary to weary the reader by many details. Terror acts in the same manner on them as on us, causing the muscles to tremble, the heart to palpitate, the sphincters to be relaxed, and the hair to stand on end" (p. 39).

What these observations tell us and tell us unequivocally is that reason and emotion are facets of the living world and indeed *interwoven* facets. Both derive from nature. At the simplest level, then, clarification turns not on qualifying the sharp contrast between ego and nature but on elucidating the complex relationship between the free-acting ego and the reactive or passive ego, precisely as Husserl is at pains to do with respect to nature's being the primal epistemological ground of the epistemological subject "from the first day." Clarification indeed turns on a full and veridical elucidation of nature, an elucidation that puts in relief the error of conceiving nature as merely physical. Such a conception is in fact contradicted by the very description Husserl gives of primal sensibility: feelings are not purely physical; temper and patience as dispositional tendencies are not purely physical; instincts are not purely physical. Each is a cognitively—in Husserl's sense, doxically—resonant dimension of living creatures, animate forms of one kind and another that make sense of the world in their own way and that have made sense in their own way such that they are alive and well in the present world.[6] Reason and the free acts of a reasoning subject are neither outside nature nor opposed to nature but bona fide expressions of a natural capacity, as Darwin's observations readily indicate. Moreover, a second clarification presents itself on these very grounds. Reason is itself by nature affectively motivated—by feelings of curiosity, self-interest, conviction, or uncertainty, for example. Reason and affect are indeed separable aspects of lived experience only after the fact. In the natural flow of everyday life, they are of a piece, as, for example, when one is taken aback by surprise or struck by feelings of doubt and, in turn, naturally begins weighing possible understandings of the situation and possible courses of action. Finally, clarification turns on a full and veridical elucidation of history. If the ego lives in the medium of its history, its

---

[6] Jung's concept of instinct and symbolic thought is relevant to this very point. His description of the confluence of instinct and symbol follows Husserl in its layered or stratified notion of the subject, but a notion in which Jung sees continuity rather than discontinuity with respect to nature (see Jung 1968, pp. 172–3).

history in the full sense must be taken into account since that history necessarily conditions its present acts and abstentions from acting. Two particularly penetrating psychoanalytic observations are of moment in this context and in fact cast a psychoanalytic light on the earlier cited observations of Darwin. Jung points out, "'Thinking' existed long before man was able to say: 'I am conscious of thinking'" (1968, p. 280). He furthermore points out that "Just as the human body is a museum, so to speak, of its phylogenetic history, so too is the psyche. We have no reason to suppose that the specific structure of the psyche is the only thing in the world that has no history outside its individual manifestations" (p. 287). As will be apparent, the three clarifications together with the observations of Darwin and Jung are of singular moment in a determination of the nature of schizophrenia on the basis of transcendental clues, themselves based on psychic effects relevant to motivation and development.

IV. On the Way to Schizophrenia

It is important to emphasize from the beginning that, contrary to traditional phenomenological practice in both a methodological and theoretical sense, what is natural is in this instance being taken as a clue to the pathological, and not the reverse. In other words, with respect to traditional phenomenological practice, we are not taking the pathological as a clue to understanding the normal, but are taking the normal as a clue to understanding the pathological. The import of this procedure is to show that the pathological has definitive roots in the normal, that there is a continuity rather than discontinuity, and that the pathological is a radical intensification of the normal.

The flow of experiences in normal everyday life is anchored in the natural continuity of affect and reason and is primarily experienced as a seamless flow that itself unfolds naturally on behalf of maintaining a harmonious world. Indeed, it is because it is anchored in the natural continuity of affect and reason that the flow is primarily experienced as seamless and as harmonious. A particular moment within the flow, however, warrants keen and sustained attention. When one is surprised or struck by feelings of doubt, when one meets with the unexpected or feels something is wrong or strange, one spontaneously draws back from the flow. This *wholly natural response*, the singular product of both affect and reason, is a relevant psychic effect and constitutes a core phenomenon to be investigated. The response signals a fundamental discordancy, a break in the otherwise seamless flow and ongoing harmony of the world. The experienced discordancy is existentially epitomized in the startle reflex, a phenomenon grounded both ontogenetically and phylogenetically in animate life, that is, in the natural and spontaneous affective-cognitive-kinetic reaction of individuals to a sudden and unexpected change in their experience of the world. Taking the reflex as a transcendental clue to the comet's tail of Nature provides entrée into a nonharmonious world. It allows one to examine the experience of discordancy, what amounts to a break in the familiar flow of everyday life, and thereby gain insight into fundamental aspects of the pathology of schizophrenia.

In their classic study of the startle reflex, psychologists Carney Landis and William Hunt, supported by, and affiliated respectively with, the New York Psychiatric Institute and Hospital and Connecticut College, observed and filmed the responses of an extraordinarily broad range of subjects to the unexpected sound of a pistol shot: they filmed subjects from human infants to human adults, from nonhuman primates and other mammals to reptiles and amphibia, and from officers of the New York City Police Department to schizophrenics, manic-depressives, feebleminded persons, epileptics, and other afflicted hospitalized persons. They found "the most prominent feature" of the startle reflex to be a general bodily flexion, a posture "which resembles a protective contraction or 'shrinking' of the individual" (1939, p. 23).[7] They note that while the English word "startle"

---

[7] It is important to note that, with respect to ontogeny, Landis and Hunt distinguish specifically and at length between the Moro reflex and the startle reflex. On the basis of existing research, they state that, "The startle pattern is primarily a flexion response, while the Moro reflex is primarily an extension response" (1939, p. 60). They comment, "Following the primary extension in the Moro reflex there is a secondary flexion response which has been described as a 'clasping' response, but it is doubtful whether this is a true clasping response or merely a slow return to normal posture" (pp. 60–1). In their own investigations involving many infants, they found that infants "not more than one month old showed the Moro reflex in response to the [pistol] shot," that in the second month, "the response began to show signs of deteriorating," that the reflex was "seldom clear and unequivocal and sometimes failed to appear" during the third and fourth months, and that "No Moro reflexes were found after the first four months" (p. 63). Most significantly, they found that "Those infants who did not show the Moro reflex responded with the startle pattern," and that this pattern "was first seen during the second month of life, and from then on it was found in all infants, each of whom showed some element of the pattern in response to the shot" (p. 64).

Landis and Hunt's detailed distinction between the two responses and their preferred interpretation of the relationship between the two—the Moro, being "the grosser, more noticeable" pattern, may conceal the startle reflex (pp. 66–7)—merit close attention, as does their conclusion that both patterns may exist in infants from the age of six weeks and that the Moro does not necessarily have to disappear before the startle response appears. Their finely thought-out distinction, interpretation, and conclusion notwithstanding, the different kinetic dynamics of the two responses merit equally close attention with respect to fear and vulnerability. (For a discussion of the different kinetic dynamics see Sheets-Johnstone 2008.)

adequately captures the suddenness of the movement reaction—the individual who is startled jumps or starts—the German word *zusammenfahren* "shows the true flexion nature of the startle pattern by its meaning of 'going together' in the sense of shriveling or shrinking" (p. 10). In conjunction with this linguistic distinction, one might note that Landis and Hunt's detailed verbal description of the pattern—"blinking of the eyes, head movement forward, a characteristic facial expression, raising and drawing forward of the shoulders, abduction of the upper arms, bending of the elbows, pronation of the lower arms, flexion of the fingers, forward movement of the trunk, contraction of the abdomen, and bending of the knees" (p. 21)[8]—is far less revealing of the shriveling or shrinking, i.e. "the true flexion nature of the startle pattern," than their schematic representation of the bodily and facial pattern, which leaves not only no doubt about shriveling or shrinking, but no doubt that the shriveling or shrinking is in the service of protecting oneself from possible harm. That "[t]he response is very rapid and follows sudden, intense stimulation" further testifies to the protective nature of the response. That the response "is a basic reaction, not amenable to voluntary control, [and] is universal" underscores the panhuman and in fact pananimate protective significance of the response.

In their discussion of what they term "conscious correlates," in which they draw on earlier research in which subjects were asked to describe their experience of startle, Landis and Hunt point out certain "phenomenological" resemblances and differences between startle and two emotions—fear and anger (pp. 132–3).[9] In their later discussion of possible emotions within the experience of startle itself—such emotions being what they term "secondary behavior" with respect to "the immediate, involuntary, general flexion" that is the startle pattern (p. 135)—they specify "a four-point division of [possible] responses": curiosity, fear, annoyance, and overflow effects (pp. 138ff). They give brief indications of corresponding behaviors with respect to the first three responses—e.g. "Fear would include actual flight behavior as well as mere defensive gestures."[10] They give a somewhat fuller descriptive account of "overflow effects," an account that,

---

8 Landis and Hunt state that the eye blink "always occurs" (1939, p. 23), and later note that the general bodily flexion pattern notwithstanding, the eye blink is "the most reliable element" of the startle pattern (p. 64).

9 After noting that "[a]ll three are usually unpleasant," Landis and Hunt state, "Fear shows more tension and strain than startle and less excitement; anger shows less of excitement and tension and about the same amount of strain. Where startle is primarily characterized by excitement and tension, fear is characterized by tension and strain, and anger by lesser amounts of all three" (1939, p. 133).

10 See also Nina Bull (1951), a psychiatrist who gives a comprehensive analysis of the difference between startle and fear.

together with fear behavior, has certain affinities with descriptions of schizophrenic spectrum disorders. They write:

> The final category of overflow effect would include all those cases where the behavior does not seem to be rational and directed toward the stimulus but rather to be an overflow effect at some neural level, perhaps because the primary response is not sufficient to resolve all the motor tensions aroused by the discharge of the revolver. Changes in posture, nervous giggles, smiling, inconsequential remarks to the experimenter, and the like, are typical of this behavior. The verbal responses are particularly interesting and worthy of study. Here the secondary behavior takes place on a symbolic level rather than on the direct level of manual or bodily expression, but it seems fully as satisfactory to the individual as the more direct bodily expressions. (p. 139)

It is significant with respect to schizophrenia that certain aspects of the overflow effects also resemble what ethologist Michael Chance identifies as prolonged startle (1980). Chance describes an instance of the latter in his study of long-tailed macaques. He writes that when an infant is temporarily rejected by its mother because she is elsewhere engaged, the infant "releases its grasp of her body and drops off, but then dashes wildly about" (p. 98). Videotape studies show that "the apparently wild movements consist of a highly coordinated series of erratic twists and turns, with as many as nine separate positions being taken up" (ibid.). They show too that, "At the same time that the infant is dashing wildly about, it is also attending to its mother, ready to take the first opportunity to return to her, which the mother indicates by stretching out her arm" (ibid.). Chance's appraisal of the infant's behavior as a prolonged startle rests on his previous examination of startle reactions, particularly with respect to their heightened arousal value. He states that the apparently wild movements are in fact "nothing less than a protracted startle reaction of the infant, whose attention is rigidly fixed on its mother; the erratic zigzag movements of its behavior express an equilibratory set of movements controlled by a conflict between tendencies to approach and to withdraw. This set of movements provides evidence that the excitement of the initial startle reaction is sustained over at least several seconds and probably throughout the time the infant is separated from its mother, providing it with a defensive escape strategy while it is obliged to be away from her" (ibid.).[11] He specifies such a "sustained state of arousal" as being a "*form of response to persistent threat together with the threat itself encapsulated within the society*" (p. 99). What he means by saying that "the threat itself [is] encapsulated

---

11   Chance concludes, "Startle is universally regarded as a sudden instantaneous reaction, but that it can be prolonged in a defensive attitude is shown by the behavior of the young long-tailed macaque" (1980, pp. 98–9).

within the society" is that the threat comes not from outside predators, for example, but from within the individual's own social world.

Overflow effects and prolonged startle are clearly signals of protracted discordancy, an ongoing intensely felt jarring that perturbs an individual's feelings, thoughts, and movements. A familiar harmonious world is, after all, eclipsed and not just for a fleeting moment; the experienced discordancy is a perseverating discordancy. That a perseverating discordancy can give rise to perseverating fear or to a perseverating state of anxiety, to wild thoughts, to irrational speech, or to aberrant behaviors is hardly surprising. Infant and child psychologist Mildred Robeck's explanation of the core experience of startle is pointedly illuminating in this regard. She writes, "The infant is startled because the flow of sensations to which she or he has habituated are disrupted" (1978, p. 127).[12] Surely if a sudden cessation in the flow of *familiar* sensations (what is more aptly termed familiar dynamics since it is not a question of discrete stimuli; see Sheets-Johnstone 2006 for a full discussion of the difference between sensations and dynamics) is startling, a continuing cessation understandably makes the initial experience all the more intense. Overflow effects, erratic movements, a defensive attitude and strategy, and so on, are natural responses of an individual to a suddenly and perseveratingly unfamiliar world. Such responses might be ways of holding on, of relieving fear-laden tensions, of seeking support from new sources, and so on. To live in an inharmonious world is, after all, to live not only in a world one cannot trust, but a world one does not understand, a world to which one has lost the key. From this perspective, a perseverating discordancy may give rise not just to perseverating fear and a perseverating state of anxiety, for example, but, in turn, to a world of one's own making.

Landis and Hunt's description of two secondary behaviors that fall outside their four-point division of possible emotions are suggestive of this very possibility. They state that the secondary behaviors are reactions "in which the primary response either persists while the individual remains immobile, and which are apparently due to a sort of tonic perseveration of the response, or in which the primary response is continued and heightened into a secondary behavior which appears to be voluntary in nature. This continuation of the startle pattern usually introduces changes and distortions in the response" (1939, pp. 139–140). The perseverating response on the one hand, and the continuing and heightened voluntary response on the other hand, are clearly suggestive of a catatonic state on the one hand and of other more variable schizophrenic pathologies on the other. Several additional observations of "secondary behavior" are

---

12   Robeck actually conflates the Moro and startle reflex, but her observation with respect to a habituated "flow of sensations" is keenly accurate.

pointedly related to schizophrenics and significant in this respect. Landis and Hunt state that in response to the pistol shot, "catatonic patients exhibited much more extreme and elaborate secondary responses than did other groups. There were always fear responses, and often there was actual flight" (p. 142). They state, "A peculiar, stylized form of secondary behavior of the fear variety appeared in some psychopathological patients, particularly among the schizophrenics. This was a protective gesture in which the hands were placed over the genital organs" (p. 143). Finally, they state that, "There was another protective gesture noticed in some of our female schizophrenic, manic-depressive, and encephalitic patients: The hands would be raised to cover the throat" (p. 144). Clearly, their classic study illuminates affective, cognitive, and kinetic aspects of a suddenly discordant world, a world that for some individuals, does not end with startle or even prolonged startle, but perseverates in open-ended fashion, following, in Luc Ciompi's terms, a distinctive if highly variable affect-kinetic-logic.

V. Archetypes within the Comet's Tail of Nature

The startle reflex is quite clearly not merely a physical phenomenon like a rain shower. It is an experience that not only has relevant psychic effects, but may, as the above account shows, have intense and ongoing relevant psychic effects. Seen in this initial phenomenological light, the startle reflex reveals itself as an affective corporeal archetype, an elemental animate dynamic having inherent "affective force," a descriptive term Husserl consistently uses in describing the phenomenon of attention, specifically, those experiences in which an individual is focally awakened and drawn in varying degrees of interest toward an intentional object (e.g. 1973a, p. 81; 2001, e.g. pp. 200, 219). It is phenomenologically significant that the kinetics of the affective force of the startle reflex is the antithesis of the kinetics of the affective force of interest that Husserl describes, i.e. a drawing back in fear rather than a drawing toward in interest. The affective differential is indeed the motivating ground of the kinetic differential, turning toward and approaching or turning away and escaping, or in more dramatic terms, of investigating an unknown but still harmonious world or of fleeing a discordant one. An elucidation of the kinetic antithesis is taken up in a further piece of research since it properly follows an elucidation of the archetypal dynamics of the grounding phenomenon, i.e. the startle reflex and its relationship to the initial psychic dynamics of schizophrenia.[13] It bears notice, however, that turning away is of as foundational import as the phenomenologically recognized movement of turning toward, and that

---

[13] We might note that the drawing back that is in the beginning in the service of protection is later in the service of escape in turning away.

its omission from phenomenological investigations is telling at many levels, beginning with affectivity and the integral relationship of affectivity to movement.

Scientific literature on the startle reflex implicitly identifies startle as an affective corporeal archetype, one that is kinetically anchored in a shrinking protective move in face of a suddenly discordant and possibly harmful world. To be noted and emphasized is the fact that the tense pulling back is not a movement away from something in particular but a general bodily attitude toward the world, an *en garde* attitude toward one's surrounding world *in toto*, and this because the surrounding world *in toto* has been qualitatively condensed: It has been spontaneously compressed into an unknown totally enveloping here-and-now that has a threatening and possibly dangerous character. As Landis and Hunt emphasize, "When we speak of the startle pattern as a general flexion response it should not be considered a directional response involving movement *away from* the stimulus. The response is quite independent of the sound source [i.e. the revolver shot], and the flexion is in no way changed by the direction from which the stimulus comes [...] The gun may be fired above the subject's head, in the median plane, or below his knees; it may be in front of him, behind him, or at either side, but the startle pattern remains unchanged" (1939, p. 31).

It bears emphasis too that, though Landis and Hunt initially say virtually nothing of the affective charge integral to the startle pattern itself other than by the adjectives "shriveling or shrinking" and by the specification a "protective contraction," the heightened and intense state of arousal that initially defines startle is clearly one of fear, precisely as evidenced in the shrinking or shriveling protective bodily response, fear that may in certain individuals and certain circumstances give way to kinetically erratic, non-serviceable, involuntary, and/or bizarre dynamics, as Landis and Hunt specify in their description of "overflow effects" and in their itemization of other secondary behaviors. In short, the startle pattern articulates a protective dynamic in face of a discordant world, a dynamic that articulates the affective corporeal archetype of fear. In an existential sense, the initial stage of schizophrenia is continuous with the affective corporeal archetype. It is a psychic instantiation of the archetype, a psychic shriveling or shrinking in face of a frighteningly discordant world. From this perspective, it is with clear insight that Laing describes *primary ontological insecurity* as an existential condition in which anxieties and dangers reign supreme (1965, p. 39). To live in a continual state of alertness to danger is to feel an unrelenting vulnerability that does not just hover over one but, in Laing's terms, engulfs, implodes, or petrifies one (pp. 43–9), in each instance enveloping one in an ever-present existential insecurity. An extraordinarily explicit acknowledgement of this aura of insecurity is voiced by a patient in one of Laing's family case studies. After quoting the patient's statement, "I haven't any deep feelings. I'm just not made that way," Laing notes, "But she certainly knew what fear was. For instance, when an aunt shouted at her recently, she said, 'I felt just—I've often seen the cat shrink and it felt like that inside me'" (Laing and Esterson, 1971, pp. 29–30).

Shrinking is in fact the very term Parnas uses to describe the nature of ipseity in schizophrenia (2000; see also Parnas, Bovet & Zahavi 2002 on ipseity). The concordance between corporeal and psychic archetype is not a linguistic coincidence but a phenomenological congruity: the nature of the corporeal archetype that defines the startle reflex is of a piece with the nature of the psychic archetype that defines the self in schizophrenia. The archetypes are cut of the same vulnerable and protective cloth. Their concordance is moreover implicit in Sass's description of the "aura" preceding "schizophrenic breaks" as moments in which "the patient will be suspicious and restless, often filled with anticipation or dread" (1992, pp. 43, 44), and in his later observation that sums up clinical reports on the "subtle symptoms, which often dominate the incipient phases of a psychotic break" (p. 45). "Even the most articulate schizophrenics," he writes, "are usually reduced to helplessly repeating the same, horribly inadequate phrase: Everything is strange, or everything is somehow different" (p. 46). Indeed, a *psychotic break* is, like the startle reflex, a break in the flow of familiar sensations or dynamics: in both instances, the surrounding world is no longer harmonious. Gallagher indicates just such disharmony in his focal emphasis on a *disruption* in the normal temporal flow of experience in schizophrenia, i.e. a *disruption* of protentions, which he links specifically to a loss of a sense of agency but which basically constitutes precisely a break in the flow of harmonious experience (2005). The temporal disruption is concomitant with a loss of everyday familiarity and the experience of a discordant world. Indeed, strangeness is existentially linked to an existential vulnerability and fear. Their tight relationship is dramatically evident in the aura often preceding a schizophrenic break. The aura is limned in German as stage fright (*Trema*), an affective condition already congruent with the apprehension intrinsic to the startle reflex. In this condition, Sass writes, "the person has a sense of having lost contact with things [... and] often stares intently at the world" in what has been labeled "the truth-taking stare" (1992, p. 44). In a later discussion, he pointedly calls attention to the fact that emotional and perceptual experiences accompanying the stare "*interrupt the natural flow* of physical or mental activity" (p. 68; italics added). Not only this, but he comments, too, that a schizophrenic might make the emotional and perceptual experiences —the *Stimmung*, as he terms them (p. 45)—"diminish or disappear by stepping out of his contemplative stance and taking up some familiar activity" and that in fact, "Many schizophrenic patients [...] report that they will throw themselves into some kind of familiar activity as a way of diminishing their symptoms" (p. 73).[14] Clearly, a flow of *familiar* sensations −familiar dynamics−is of paramount affective import: familiarity diminishes vulnerability, fear, anxiety, terror.[15]

Examples of the kinship of strangeness, vulnerability, and fear in fact abound in Sass's descriptions of what he describes as three aspects of the *Stimmung*: unreality, mere being, and fragmentation. Moreover, in a fourth aspect, the apophany, though fear goes unnamed, "a profound and almost unbearable tension" does not, nor does the feeling of being "gripped" by an urge to escape it (p. 60). *Primary ontological insecurity* is again of singular import in this context, for the pathological heightening of strangeness, vulnerability, fear, anxiety, and terror is tied to just such insecurity. Indeed, the relationship between the affective mode of self-consciousness characterized as stage fright in schizophrenia and the affective impact of a dangerous world is adumbrated in Laing's observation that, "In a world full of danger, to be a potentially seeable object is to be constantly exposed to danger. Self-consciousness, then, may be the apprehensive awareness of oneself as potentially exposed to danger by the simple fact of being visible to others. The obvious defence against such a danger is to make oneself invisible in one way or another" (1965, p. 109). Notable, too, from this heightened affective perspective is the fact that, a characteristic dampening of emotions or "flattening of affect" (Sass 1992, e.g. pp. 23-4) notwith-standing, fear and terror are common descriptive terms in case studies of schizophrenics, case studies that, in addressing the dual nature of schizo-phrenia, require a fuller elucidation of the comet's tail of Nature than that given here but nonetheless testify to the primary affects of fear and terror. Laing, for example, observes, "Despite his longing to be loved for his 'real self' the schizophrenic is terrified of love. Any form of understanding *threatens* his whole defensive system" (1965, p. 163). Similarly, writing of the dual nature of schizophrenics to feel themselves both grandiose and

---

14 Sass also warns, however, that "in more extreme cases schizophrenic hyper-awareness can be so intense as to *prevent* engagement in [...] everyday actions" (1992, p. 73).

15 I might note that if the *Stimmung* "seems to occupy a kind of anxious twilight zone somewhere between act and affliction," as Sass states (1992, p. 74), that is, somewhere between something voluntary and involuntary, and correlatively, between a harmonious and inharmonious world, then anxiety −the "anxious twilight zone"−hangs in the balance between what one can control in the form of bringing back the familiar and not control in the form of the strange. When affliction prevails, what Husserl would identify as the freely acting ego is stilled by the experience of strangeness; exaggerated and intensified awarenesses rivet its attention.

powerless, Sass remarks that the individual "can as easily feel constrained or paralyzed by a sense of awesome responsibility and apocalyptic terror as reassured by feelings of power and security" (1992, p. 303). At a later point, in considering the paradox of a grandiose or solipsistic self and a loss of self, he addresses the question of "how the sense of awesome ontological power can devolve into a kind of abject metaphysical terror" (p. 325). Moreover, a direct quotation from a patient leaves no doubt of the extremities of fear that are present in schizophrenia. "You can't imagine how terrifying it is," the patient says, "to realize that you're in a world of organic machines with the intuitions that enable you to create truths [...] What really terrified me was when I realized that I could conceive of wrenching the world from its axis" (pp. 334–5).

Given such heightened feelings of vulnerability, fear, and terror, it is hardly surprising that a sense of death-in-life resonates at a depth equal to that of primary ontological insecurity (Laing 1965, p. 138). "The desire to be dead," Laing writes, "is probably the most extreme defensive posture that can be adopted. One no longer fears being crushed, engulfed, overwhelmed by realness and aliveness [...] since one is already dead." He notes, in turn, "The anxieties attendant on the schizophrenic's phantastic omnipotence are undercut by living in a condition of phantastic impotence" (1965, p. 176). Sass analyzes the hybrid schizophrenic mode of being in terms of solipsism and a loss of self as indicated above, but he also early on aptly capsulates the "death-in-life" ontological condition Laing describes as "a sort of corpse with insomnia" (Sass 1962, p. 8).

In sum, the kinship of strangeness, vulnerability, and fear underlies the primary ontological insecurity and death-in-life feelings at the heart of schizophrenia and in essence structures the elemental affective parallel between the startle reflex and both the *Trema* and the *Stimmung*. In these affective experiences, the everyday world comes to a halt, in the one instance in a palpably shrinking bodily attitude, in the other in a palpably shrinking psychic attitude. The key to understanding their relationship is essentially affective, but an affective not devoid of reason or cognition. On the contrary, the primordial experience of strangeness has a definitive cognitive as well as affective character. Gallagher's identification of a schizophrenic's loss of protentions with a "prenoetic" affective response (2005, e.g. pp. 190, 200, 204) is misleading in this respect, for it dissociates affect from cognition or intellect proper.[16] The dissociation is in fact as misleading

---

16 Gallagher has affirmed (pers. comm.) that by the term prenoetic, he means primal sensibility, but the term clearly falls short of that mark: it fails to do phenomenological justice to the complexity and richness of primal sensibility or to the complexity and richness of the "noetic." Indeed, from an ontogenetic perspective, one could rightly argue that the term "prenoetic" can only refer to a time before birth. Studies of infants show clearly that

with respect to the startle reflex as with respect to the *Trema* and *Stimmung*. Feelings of fear, terror, or anxiety that arise in face of a loss of familiarity have a built-in cognitive aspect; they are all rightly characterized as cognitive affects in the same way that doubt, conviction, wonder, and incredulity are cognitive affects (Johnstone 2011, p. 174; included in work-in-progress, Chapter III). We see cognitive affects indisputably when vulnerability and fear come to the fore in face of a strange world that presents itself. The experienced strangeness is to begin with a cognitively charged affective experience and it reverberates in ongoing cognitively charged affects. Indeed, aspects that Sass describes as features of the truth-taking stare—unreality, mere being, fragmentation—pinpoint basic ways in which the experience of strangeness generates a break in the flow of familiar sensations constituting normal everyday life. The experience is clearly one in which affect and cognition are intertwined.

VI. Conclusions

To understand schizophrenia through the prism of the startle reflex is clearly not to view it through an arbitrarily chosen vantage point in nature but through the primal sensibility that is a compound of strangeness, vulnerability, and fear. Taking the psychic effects of the startle reflex seriously, that is, as a transcendental clue to the comet's tail of Nature, we are led first to recognize the primal sensibility that is the startle reflex itself and the import of what Husserl describes as one's own "bare sensuous-ness" (1973b, p. 145), a sensuousness that here conclusively transcends individual differences insofar as what is uncovered is a fundamental animate sensibility of human nature and of animate nature generally. What

---

intelligence is alive from the beginning. One might also note in this context the error of aligning a schizophrenic's experience of "inserted thoughts" with a loss of a sense of ownership. The locution "my thoughts" is a grammatical identification, not an ontological statement. The loss of a sense of personal connection to passing thoughts is a matter of affectivity: familiarity, interest, doubt, curiosity, wonderment, and so on. Affectivity roots thoughts in a felt hereness. In fact, "ownership" is not a phenomeno-logically found datum in the experience of thoughts but a linguistic deduction (see Sheets-Johnstone 2006 for a further elucidation of this topic). It might also be noted that, notwithstanding the fact that we may give concentrated thoughtful attention to some particular matter, thoughts arise on their own. We have far less control of them than we ordinarily think we do. Our feelings and affective proclivities and the immediate activities in which we are engaged normally rivet our thoughts in the sense of con-trolling them, tethering them to what Gallagher and others might term a "personal I," though here, too, our minds can and certainly do wander on their own, as when the thought of a meeting at noon interrupts our relaxed and interested reading of the morning newspaper.

we are led to recognize in turn is how schizophrenic spectrum disorders play out initially along the lines of this primal sensibility, or in other words, how the comet's tail of Nature in schizophrenia reveals itself in the form of an archetype, an archetype that is the psychic correlate of the corporeal archetype of the startle reflex.

Seen through the natural prism of the reflex, schizophrenia is initially a protective reaction, a spontaneous pulling back as a way of coping with vulnerability. What the startle reflex highlights in terms of its protective nature is in fact *vulnerability*, a foundational existential condition of all life (see Zubin and Spring 1977). Indeed, vulnerability is an affectively laden "existentiale" in Heidegger's sense. It is conditioned by fear; that is, to be aware of one's vulnerability and to feel that vulnerability in the flesh is to be aware of, and to feel open to, possible harm. To be continuously aware and open in this way is to live in a continuous state of uncertainty, a state of possible or impending doom, a state in which fear is rife and in which harmony precisely does not prevail. In such a state, the familiar and harmonious everyday world disappears in a way akin to the world Sartre describes in the context of the look and the existence of others, a world that "has a kind of drain hole in the middle of its being and that is perpetually flowing off through this hole" (1956, p. 256). A schizophrenic breaks spontaneously with this discordant world, shriveling or shrinking in face of it.

That the loss of an everyday familiarity can be fearsome is surely understandable. That relentless feelings of uncertainty and insecurity can be unbearably frightening should be equally so. The conception and effectiveness of a Soteria care center is of moment in this respect.[17] Why, we may

---

17 With respect to neuroleptic drug treatment, Ciompi's Soteria Berne adheres to "low-dose psychotic strategies" and differs in this respect from Mosher's Soteria California at which no antipsychotic drugs are used. Ciompi specifies the low-dose strategies, stating that they are "focused on the reduction of otherwise not controllable states of tension, [and] are used in close collaboration with patient and family, with the final aim of controlled self-medication" (Ciompi & Hoffmann 2004, p. 142). It is notable that in the context of comparing the two Soteria, Mosher states, "What must be emphasized is the fact that Soteria Bern [sic] and Soteria California were both able to achieve very good results during the acute phase of psychosis with interpersonal methods and no or low-dose neuroleptic drug treatment. In addition, the two social environments were similar (at least on the Moos Scale), giving credence to the notion that these caring, supportive, humane, protective, interpersonally focused non-hospital environments can reduce or eliminate the need for antipsychotic drug treatment during the most disorganized period of psychosis. This aspect of the Bern [sic] replication provides support for our contention that a properly organized social

ask, would such a care center be conceived and why would it be effective if not that it cultivates a familiar and harmonious world? In such a setting, there is no too jarring a noise, too harsh a rebuke, too uncertain a situation, too feared a certain presence, and so on. The affective felt sense of "too" in these instances—the experience of "too jarring," "too harsh," "too uncertain," "too feared"—is equivalent to what D.H. Lawrence in other contexts knew as a world that is "too much with us" (see literary critic Daniel Stern's Wordsworthian attribution to Lawrence in Stern 1971, p. 29; see also Sheets-Johnstone 1979). The world that is "too much" for a schizophrenic is a world of unendurable tensions, unbearable assaults, overwhelming anxieties, a threatening or dangerous world that is clearly the antithesis of a harmonious one. A protective psychic contraction in face of this world, a contraction that is the archetypal psychic correlate of the startle reflex, is a natural response. The protective psychic response is in fact isomorphic with, and existentially homologous to, the protective corporeal response: in each instance, one pulls back from what is discordant and possibly harmful. Like the protective corporeal response, however, the protective psychic response does not provide affective closure. On the contrary, it leaves one on the brink of a puzzling, unfamiliar, foreboding world, hence on the brink of some form of movement to resolve the threatening discordancy, movement that essentially turns either toward or away from it.[18] As indicated earlier, an elucidation of this further dimension with respect to schizophrenia entails further elucidations of the comet's tail of Nature, beginning with the movement of turning away.

Insofar as the ontogenetic and phylogenetic credentials of the startle reflex condition its psychic correlate as well, it is not surprising that early infant and child experiences can predispose an individual toward schizophrenia. The ego does indeed live in the medium of its history, as Husserl affirmed. Moreover, studies of nonhuman animals—studies that, however scientific their aim, are in actuality hideous with respect to the human torture of nonhuman animals—attest to schizophrenia in dogs and nonhuman primates (Newton & Gantt 1979; Lyon & Nielsen 1979; see also

---

environment can virtually eliminate the need for the rapid introduction of drugs into the treatment of acute psychosis" (Mosher 2004, p. 358).

[18] In effect, one approaches the discordancy with interest and curiosity or flees it in panic and terror, but in a qualitatively significant kinetic as well as affective manner: hesitantly, for example, or swiftly, circuitously or straightforwardly, and so on. While movement in face of a discordancy might appear as either an immediately reactive or thoughtfully measured response, that is, as a product of either sensibility or reason, a study of motivation consistently discloses that neither sensibility nor reason operates in a vacuum but that the two constitute a complex and subtle whole, Husserl's notion of "degraded" reason notwithstanding.

Keehn 1979a, 1979b; Carr 1979). Given its ontogenetic and phylogenetic credentials, schizophrenia is clearly not a disaster happening in a brain but a *natural* response to a break in the normal everyday flow of familiar sensations, a *natural* response to a discordant world that is psychically threatening and dangerous. Moreover, affectivity is central to this natural response just as it is central to the startle reflex and to responsivity in everyday life generally. Landis and Hunt's classification of affects as *secondary* behavior is misguided in this respect. The protective shriveling that constitutes the startle reflex is incontrovertibly laced with fear: one draws back not deferentially, for example, or as a precaution, but in alarm and possibly even panic. Clearly, from this perspective, schizophrenia is in every way, and in Jung's sense, a *psychogenic* illness (1960, p. 226), not a brain disease.[19] It is first and foremost the illness of a subject in face of a world. To affirm as much is not to exclude the integral significance of the brain but to recognize the immediately experienced and observable phenomenon itself with a view to understanding it in person.[20]

In sum, the comet's tail of Nature taken as a transcendental clue leads us to those lower levels of which Husserl writes. Those levels give us deep insights into the foundations of human psychopathologies and the continuities of those pathologies with fundamental everyday realities of normal human life. Parnas and Zahavi (2000, p. 12) state, "Phenomenology will have to overcome its phobic tendencies and enter into a critical dialogue with analytical philosophy, cognitive science, and the behavioral sciences." Evolutionary biology should definitely be added to their list, both in terms of the ego "living in the medium of its own history" and in terms of "the comet's tail of Nature." Evolutionary biology is phenomeno-

---

19 "'Psychogenesis' means that the essential cause of a neurosis, or the condition under which it arises, is of a psychic nature. It may, for instance, be a psychic shock, a grueling conflict, a wrong kind of psychic adaptation, a fatal illusion, and so on" (Jung 1960, p. 226). But see also Jung's discussion on pp. 245ff. and his final conclusion, "Let us discuss the question of psychogenesis once more when the psychic side of schizophrenia has had a square deal" (p. 249).

20 Short of first-person experiential understandings, one could hardly begin to map the brain functionally, much less know what to look for in the way of abnormal neurological functions. First-person experiential understandings are furthermore the *sine qua non* of valid correlations between inner and outer, that is, between scientifically differentiated neurological and behavioral studies. Further still, real-life bodily ways of being in and toward the world are the centerpin on which any possible "future success of mind-brain-body docking" (Panksepp 2002, p. 51) rests. Indeed, an essential conceptual as well as lexical shift is required with respect to such docking: In animate forms of life, it is not the brain that mediates between mind and body but the living, animate body that mediates between mind and brain.

logically expressed in both our phylogenetic and ontogenetic histories. It informs our lives and is the point of departure for illuminating the comet's tail of Nature at the heart of our humanness.

References

Aristotle (1984) *Physics*, in Barnes, J. (ed.) *The Complete Works of Aristotle*, Hardie, R.P. & Gaye, R.K. (trans.), pp. 315–446, Bollingen Series LXXI.2, Princeton, NJ: Princeton University Press.

Bull, N. (1951) *The Attitude Theory of Emotion*, New York: Nervous and Mental Disease Monographs (Coolidge Foundation).

Carr, A.T. (1979) The psychopathology of fear, in Sluckin, W. (ed.) *Fear in Animals and Man*, pp. 199–235, New York: Van Nostrand Reinhold.

Chance, M.R.A. (1980) An ethological assessment of emotion, in Plutchik, R. & Kellerman, H. (eds.) *Emotion: Theory, Research, and Experience: Vol. 1. Theories of Emotion*, pp. 81–111, New York: Academic Press.

Ciompi, L. (1988) *The Psyche and Schizophrenia: The Bond between Affect and Logic*, Schneider, D.L. (trans.), Cambridge, MA: Harvard University Press.

Ciompi, L. (2003) Reflections on the role of emotions in consciousness and subjectivity, from the perspective of affect-logic, *Consciousness and Emotions*, 4 (2), pp. 181–196.

Ciompi, L. & Hoffmann, H. (2004) Soteria Berne: An innovative milieu therapeutic approach to acute schizophrenia based on the concept of affect-logic, *World Psychiatry*, 3 (3), pp. 140–146.

Curtis, H. (1975) *Biology*, 2nd ed., New York: Worth Publishers.

Darwin, C. (1859/1968) *The Origin of Species*, Burrow, J.W. (ed.), Harmondsworth: Penguin Books.

Darwin, C. (1871/1981) *The Descent ff Man, and Selection in Relation to Sex*, Princeton, NJ: Princeton University Press.

Depraz, N. (1998) Can I anticipate myself? Self-affection and temporality, in Zahavi, D. (ed.) *Self-Awareness, Temporality, and Alterity*, pp. 83–97, Dordrecht: Kluwer Academic.

Freud, S. (1937) Analysis terminable and interminable, in Strachey, J. (ed.) *Standard Edition of the Complete Psychological Works of Sigmund Freud*, vol. 5, pp. 316–357, Riviere, J. (trans.), London: The Hogarth Press.

Freud, S. (1966) Project for a scientific psychology, in Strachey, J. (ed. & trans.) *Standard Edition of the Complete Psychological Works of Sigmund Freud*, vol. 1, pp. 283–397, London: The Hogarth Press.

Gallagher, S. (2005) *How the Body Shapes the Mind*, New York: Clarendon Press.

Husserl, E. (1970) *The Crisis of European Sciences and Transcendental Phenomenology*, Carr, D. (trans.), Evanston, IL: Northwestern University Press.

Husserl, E. (1973a) *Experience and Judgment*, Landgrebe, L. (ed.), Churchill, J.S. & Ameriks, K. (trans.), Evanston, IL: Northwestern University Press.

Husserl, E. (1973b) *Cartesian Meditations*, Cairns, D. (trans.), The Hague: Martinus Nijhoff.

Husserl, E. (1989) *Ideas Pertaining to a Pure Phenomenology and to a Phenomenological Philosophy: Book 2 (Ideas II)*, Rojcewicz, R. & Schuwer, A. (trans.), Dordrecht: Kluwer Academic.

Husserl, E. (2001) *Analyses Concerning Passive and Active Synthesis: Lectures on Transcendental Logic*, Steinbock, A.J. (trans.), Dordrecht: Kluwer Academic.

Johnstone, A.A. (1986) The role of "Ich Kann" in Husserl's answer to Human skepticism, *Philosophy and Phenomenological Research*, 46 (4), pp. 577–595.

Johnstone, A.A. (2011) The basic seld and its doubles, *Journal of Consciousness Studies*, 18 (7–8), pp. 169–195. Included in *The Pan-Cultural Human*, work-in-progress, Chapter III.

Jung, C.G. (1960) The psychogenesis of mental disease, Hull, R.F.C. (trans.), *Bollingen Series 20, Collected Works*, vol. 3, New York: Pantheon Books.

Jung, C.G. (1968) The archetypes and the collective unconscious, Hull, R.F.C. (trans.), 2nd ed., *Bollingen Series 20, Collected Works*, vol. 9, part 1, Princeton, NJ: Princeton University Press.

Keehn, J.D. (ed.) (1979a) *Psychopathology in Animals: Research and Clinical Implications*, New York: Academic Press.

Keehn, J.D. (1979b) *Origins of Madness: Psychopathology in Animal Life*, New York: Pergamon Press.

Laing, R.D. (1965) *The Divided Self*, Harmondsworth: Penguin Books.

Laing, R.D. & Esterson A. (1971) *Sanity, Madness, and the Family: Families of Schizophrenics*, 2nd ed., New York: Basic Books.

Landis, C. & Hunt, W.A. (1939) *The Startle Pattern*, New York: Farrar & Rinehart.

Lyon, M. & Nielsen, E.B. (1979) Psychosis and drug-induced stereotypies, in Keehn, J.D. (ed.) *Psychopathology in Animals: Research and Clinical Implications*, pp. 103–142, New York: Academic Press.

Merleau-Ponty, M. (1962) *Phenomenology of Perception*, Smith, C. (trans.), London: Routledge & Kegan Paul.

Merleau-Ponty, M. (1968) *The Visible and the Invisible*, Lefort, C. (ed.), Lingis, A. (trans.), Evanston, IL: Northwestern University Press.

Merleau-Ponty, M. (1988) *In Praise of Philosophy and Other Essays*, Wild, J., Edie, J. & O'Neill, J. (trans.), Evanston, IL: Northwestern University Press.

Mosher, L.R. (2004) Non-hospital, non-drug intervention with first-episode psychosis, in Read, J., Mosher, L.R. & Bentall, R.P. (eds.) *Models of Madness: Psychological, Social and Biological Approaches to Schizophrenia*, pp. 349–364, London: Routledge.

Newton, J.E.O. & Gantt, W.H. (1979) The history of a catatonic dog, in Keehn, J.D. (ed.) *Origins of Madness: Psychopathology in Animal Life*, pp. 145–157, New York: Pergamon Press.

Panksepp, J. (2002) The self and "its" vicissitudes: Critique of the commentaries, *Neuropsychoanalysis*, 4 (1–2), pp. 44–61.

Parnas, J. (2000) The self and intentionality in the pre-psychotic stages of schizophrenia: A phenomenological study, in Zahavi, D. (ed.) *Exploring the Self*, pp. 115–147, Amsterdam/Philadelphia, PA: John Benjamins.

Parnas, J. & Zahavi, D. (2000) The link: Philosophy—psychopathology—phenomenology, in Zahavi, D. (ed.) *Exploring the Self*, pp. 1–16, Amsterdam/Philadelphia, PA: John Benjamins.

Parnas, J., Bovet, P. & Zahavi, D. (2002) Schizophrenic autism: clinical phenomenology and pathogenetic implications, *World Psychiatry*, 1 (3), pp. 131–136.

Robeck, M.C. (1978) *Infants and Children: Their Development and Learning*, New York: McGraw-Hill Book.

Sartre, J.-P. (1956) *Being and Nothingness*, Barnes, H. (trans.), New York: Basic Books.

Sass, L.A. (1992) *Madness and Modernism: Insanity in the Light of Modern Art, Literature, and Thought*, New York: Basic Books.

Sheets-Johnstone, M. (1979) Can the body ransom us?, *Contact Quarterly*, 41 (3–4), pp. 14–20.

Sheets-Johnstone, M. (1999a/exp. 2nd ed. 2011) *The Primacy of Movement*, Amsterdam/Philadelphia, PA: John Benjamins.

Sheets-Johnstone, M. (1999b) Rethinking Husserl's fifth meditation, *Philosophy Today*, 43 (Supplement), pp. 99–106.

Sheets-Johnstone, M. (2003) Kinesthetic memory, in Gallagher, S. & Depraz, N. (eds.) Embodiment and Awareness [Special issue], *Theoria et Historia Scientiarum*, 7 (1), pp. 69–92.

Sheets-Johnstone, M. (2006) Essential clarifications of 'self-affection' and Husserl's 'sphere of ownness': First steps toward a pure phenomenology of (human) nature, *Continental Philosophy Review*, 39, pp. 361–391.

Sheets-Johnstone, M. (2008) *The Roots of Morality*, Philadelphia, PA: Pennsylvania State University Press.

Stern, D. (1971) The mysterious new novel, in Hassan I. (ed.) *Liberation: New Essays in the Humanities*, pp. 22–37, Middletown, CT: Wesleyan University Press.

Zubin, J. & Spring, B. (1977) Vulnerability—A new view of schizophrenia, *Journal of Abnormal Psychology*, 86 (2), pp. 103–126.

Chapter VI

The Descent of Man, *Human Nature, and the Nature/Culture Divide*[1]

Abstract: *How does human nature, especially as typically construed within an imposed nature/culture divide, fit into Darwin's keen and detailed descriptions of animate life? My answer will point out omissions on each side of the nature/ culture divide, a divide academically evident in the division between "the humanities" on the one side and "the sciences" on the other. It will proceed to concentrate attention pre-eminently on an incredible lacuna in today's scientific research, and in research generally over the 138 years since* The Descent of Man and Selection in Relation to Sex *was published, namely, on the lack of recognition of, and in turn the lack of penetrating and self-enlightening research on, "the law of battle" as a real human phenomenon. As described by Darwin, "the law of battle" is a biological matrix, natural to humans as to other animals, though tempered by "civilization." As I will show, variously aided and abetted, the matrix has not only been reduced to a cellular phenomenon, i.e. sperm competition, but has been culturally elaborated — culturally "exapted," to borrow Gould and Vrba's term — to subserve strictly cultural ends far beyond the original, ends having to do with the pursuit of various forms of "cultural fitness," and this from the beginnings of recorded human history.*

Introduction

Darwin's great legacy rests on descriptive foundations. Throughout his three major books we have descriptions of myriad forms of life, both flora and fauna. Following their focal morphological descriptions in *The Origin of Species*, we find in *The Descent of Man and Selection in Relation to Sex* and in *The Expression of Emotions in Man and Animals* — and in Darwin's last book on worms as well, *The Formation of Vegetable Mould Through the Action of Worms with Observations on Their Habits* — more concentrated descriptions of

---

1   First published in *Anthropological Theory* (2010), Vol. 10, No. 4: 343–360.

fauna as morphologies-in-motion. Indeed, in these books we are given detailed descriptions of animate forms, forms engaged in the affective-cognitive-kinetic living realities of life itself, and moreover in ways that strikingly demonstrate commonalities and relationships within an evolutionary heritage. In short, as Darwin's writings so strikingly show, descriptive foundations are the cornerstone of theory building. Without descriptive foundations, there would be no evolutionary theory. There would be no basis for claiming an inherent and ongoing relationship among all forms of life, present and past. Those relationships are grounded in evolutionary facts gleaned from first-hand studies of life. That they are so grounded brings to the fore the fact that facts of life are grounded in experience, first-person experiences of life itself. Descriptive accounts of these experiences are the foundation of human knowledge about the worlds of nonhuman animals. They are—or should be—the foundation of human knowledge about the human animal itself.

Yet how does the human animal as typically construed within the prism of a nature/culture divide fit into Darwin's keen and detailed descriptions of animate life? My answer is that in a quite crucial sense it does not, and this because of an incredible lacuna in today's scientific research, and in research generally over the 138 years since *The Descent of Man and Selection in Relation to Sex* was published, namely, on the lack of recognition of, and in turn the lack of penetrating and self-enlightening research on, "the law of battle" as a *real* human phenomenon. As described by Darwin, "the law of battle" is a biological matrix, natural to humans as to other animals, though tempered in humans according to Darwin, but without elaboration, by "civilized people" (Darwin 1871/1981, p. 326). By "civilized people" indeed. As I will show, "the law of battle" in humans has been "civilized" beyond recognition. It has been hidden under the aegis of aggressive behavior and/or reduced to a cellular phenomenon, "civilized" practices that only further shroud the central fact that the matrix has been culturally elaborated—culturally "exapted," to borrow Gould and Vrba's term (1982) —to subserve strictly cultural ends far beyond the original, ends having to do with the pursuit of various forms of "cultural fitness," and this from the beginnings of recorded human history.

Its exaptation has been aided and abetted on both sides of the nature/culture divide. On the one side is an over-fawning attention on *the brain* in present-day neuroscience and cognitive science that deflects attention precisely from a Darwinian view of life, that is, that elides close-up study of the living nature of human nature and thus, most importantly, deflects attention from a recognition of evolution. On the other side are elevations of culture over nature by social constructionist dogma and the like, elevations on the side of the humanities that have the consequence not simply of deflecting attention from evolution but of ignoring or denying its significance altogether. The fault lines on each side of the nature/culture divide obviously embody the academic division between "the sciences" on the one hand and "the humanities" on the other. The lines warrant elaboration as a preamble to an elucidation of the culturally exapted or co-opted human "law of battle."

I.

Present-day human neuroscience and cognitive science display an unprece-dented admiration—one might even say idolatry—of *the brain*. Their riveted and to my mind thoroughly blinkered attention to *the brain*—the human one—virtually eclipses proper ongoing attention to evolution and its foundational import to understandings of human nature. The blinkered attention of these sciences seeps into the humanities, as when language, art, and empathy, for example, are deemed a function of mirror neurons via the fashionable culturally-spawned magical lexical band-aid of "embodiment": Vittorio Gallese and George Lakoff, in their "neural theory of language," write that *concepts*—concepts such as *grasping*—are "*embodied* in the sensory-motor system" (Gallese and Lakoff 2005, p. 19; emphasis added); David Freedberg and Vittorio Gallese write that "*embodied* mechanisms" underlying human responses to images and to visual works of art are "universal" (Freedberg and Gallese 2007; emphasis added); Vittorio Gallese, Morris Eagle and Paolo Migone write that "*embodied* simulation" is "a mandatory, nonconscious, and prereflexive [brain] mechanism" that "generates representational content" allowing one person immediate understanding of another person's intentional goal, emotion, or "sensa-tion" (Gallese et al. 2007, pp. 143–4; emphasis added). It is of moment to note that, to date, mirror neurons have never been shown to exist in human brains. As one neuroscientist himself recently noted: "A flood of theories regarding what mirror neurons do in humans came out before anyone proved whether they exist or not [...] A lot more groundwork needs to be done before people can talk about these theories of simulation, language and so forth" (Ilan Dinstein, quoted by Tina Hesman Saey 2009, p. 11). While people in the humanities not infrequently buy a piece of the brain to fortify their claims, as in George Lakoff and Mark Johnson's *Philosophy in the Flesh* (1999), the major fault lies clearly with those scientists who are mesmerized by *the brain* as if it were the oracle at Delphi, the shrine to which all questions concerning humans are addressed and from which all bona fide explanations of humans will emanate. An advertisement of a course offered by The Teaching Company in the bimonthly journal *Science News* (175 (13), p. 3) succinctly validates *the brain* as oracle. The course, titled "How Your Brain Works," is taught by a neuroscience professor at Vanderbilt University and is described as follows: "Everything you hear, feel, see, and think is controlled by your brain. It allows you to cope masterfully with your everyday environment and is capable of producing breathtaking athletic feats, sublime works of art, and profound scientific insights. But its most amazing achievement may be that it can understand itself."

Of course, the idea of controlling and predicting is an enduring scientific precept, so interest in an ordained controller—whatever the ordained controller is deemed to be—is not unusual nor, presumably, is the desire to teach people how a particular controller controls. The problem comes with outlandish claims, such as the brain controls "[e]verything you hear, feel, see, and think," as if brains thought of reading this article or feel now like having a chocolate bar. Such outlandish claims obviously make brains rather than people the subject of experience, a practice not in the least uncommon in neuroscience. Francis Crick and Christof Koch, for example, declare: "If you see the back of a person's head, the brain infers that there is a face on the front of it" (1992, p. 153). Antonio Damasio, Patricia Churchland and Terence Sejnowski, Semir Zeki and hosts of others make and have made similar experiential ascriptions. An older ascription made by a primatologist is in fact also notable. In 1975 Robert Harding wrote: "Nonhuman primates have brains capable of cooperative hunting" (1975, p. 255), as if when summoned by hunger, brains roll forth to do battle on the savannah.

Whether a matter of control or of experiential ascriptions, *the brain* is a product of pure and simple reductionism, and pure and simple reductionism works patently against descriptive foundations (for more on the incontestable need for and value of descriptive foundations, see Sheets-Johnstone 2002). In pure and simple reductionist thought, there is, in the original words of 19th-century sea captain Frederick Marryat—and the later words of Mary Beeton in her 1861 book *The Book of Household Management* and Samuel Smiles in his 1875 book *Thrift*—"a place for everything and everything in its place" (Marryat 1842; Beeton 1861; Smiles 1875). Indeed, reductionism decrees that humans are properly describable only in point-by-point, localized ways. The living, dynamic world of animate beings is virtually off-limits: *that* world is precisely *un*predictable, *un*certain. Who knows in exactly which direction a whale will turn or when it will sound? Who knows when a baby will wake or cry or a crow fly off to another perch? Such knowledge would be akin to knowing the exact patterns and shifting shapes in which clouds will form and re-form. Unpredictability aside, an ordered and orderly world in which there is a place for everything and everything in its place is a material world that leaves out meaning or makes meaning a pure and simple neurological phenomenon, a world that not only present-day cognitive scientists conjure but that philosopher Evan Thompson straightforwardly instantiates when he states, "[t]he nervous system [...] creates meaning" (Thompson 2007, p. 13).

In sum, reductionism compresses life into a neurological caricature of life. With not a full-bodied living animal in sight, neither fine and pain-staking observations and descriptions of life itself can be made nor, in consequence, can the topic of evolution rise to its proper prominence as the ground floor of human self-understandings.

On the humanities side, humans are typically construed from the view-point of culture and culture is typically conceived honorifically not only as the spawning ground of all that is sweetness and light about humans but as the venerated ground separating humans from animals. From culture comes language, art, libraries, homes, beds, chairs, tables, cooking, temples, cemeteries, and so on. Moreover, technical ingenuity figures also on the cultural side in the form of film, television, computers, cell phones, and so on. On all these counts and more, a sizeable number of humans count themselves a significant cut above animals. An odd fact, however, remains. Experiments on animals have benefited humans and continue to benefit them or are promised to benefit them in the future. Nonhuman animals are used to test a variety of substances, infected with this or that disease or chemical, sent off as proxies into space and investigated as neurological proxies, captured and caged to procure certain substances and liquids humans use to provide themselves with greater vitality or sex appeal, and so on. The question, of course, is: "if humans are un-related to animals, how is it that animals are clinical, experimental, neurological, and chemical stand-ins for humans?" Clearly, to consider themselves *un*-related pro-duces not just an illogical state of affairs, but a thoroughly immoral and unenlightened one. In other words, inconsistent valuations of nonhuman animals, that is, flighty, self-contradictory, and thoroughly capricious atti-tudinal changes that lack reasoned reflection, are one thing; an underlying insistence on evolutionary discontinuities together with an espousal of con-tinuities for human convenience whenever needed or deemed necessary is quite another. Indeed, to claim evolutionary continuities on self-serving pragmatic grounds and discontinuities on axiological/ontological ones is incontrovertible evidence of both a failed morality and a failed intelligence. In such circumstances and practices, *Homo sapiens sapiens* fails to live up to its doubly vaunted status in the world.

The idea that, in virtue of culture, humans transcend nature is clearly open to question. When we look at human civilizations across history in a broad sense, two features stand out with special salience: war and art. The remains of the former are treasured in cemeteries and prominently housed in monuments and memorials; the remains of the latter are treasured in stage and concert performances and prominently housed in museums. Indeed, humans look back proudly to burial sites and cave art in the

Paleolithic. Cultural emblems that allow humans to marvel at their laudable and ingenious past are treasured and cared for. The emblems are consistently taken to mark the transcendence of humans over nature. This self-serving pure and simple rendition of nature, however, like any self-serving pure and simple reductionism, overlooks fundamental realities of human nature. Traditional wisdom about bipedality readily substantiates the critical oversight. Traditional wisdom teaches that the advent of *consistent* or 100 percent bipedality—in comparison with an estimated 55 percent terrestrial bipedality in australopithecines and a 10 percent terrestrial bipedality in their ancestors (Pilbeam 1986)—brought with it two notably distinct capacities: the capacity to see to further distances and thereby the capacity to plan ahead, and the capacity to make tools by freeing the hands. The capacity to see to further distances and thereby plan ahead clearly extols human intelligence, but what of present-day foot-dragging on climate change and what of a runaway global human population, to mention only two prominent current examples? We are still bipedal, but where is the capacity to see to further distances and to plan ahead? The capacity to make tools by freeing the hands extols a creative intelligence, but what of the unmonitored proliferation and use of guns and assault weapons in the US and of the ongoing development of nuclear weapons? Our hands are indeed free, but what have we done and what do we continue to do with them? Have humans truly transcended nature or have they, on the contrary, *taken what is evolutionarily given and in untold instances shaped or reworked it culturally*—precisely, *culturally*—in various deleterious ways by elaborating, suppressing, neglecting, or exaggerating what is evolutionarily given? (For a thoroughgoing analysis of this claim in relation to power and power relations see Sheets-Johnstone 1994.) Clearly in declaring that culture separates humans from animals, in essence, insisting that humans in the form of *Homo sapiens sapiens* are a species apart, humans are in truth myopically aggrandizing what they prize in themselves and turning a blind eye to what is in fact unprizable.

In sum, with either a riveted attention on *the brain* or an elevation of culture over nature, humans effectively cut themselves off from the animal kingdom and the natural world. In consequence, Darwin's descriptive foundations go by the boards, their import utterly unetched onto the consciousness of humans. It is not just that evolution fades from view but that humans remain ignorant, unenlightened in critical ways about their own history, their evolutionary heritage as animate forms, one among what may be close to 10 million other morphologies-in-motion within the kingdom Animalia (Curtis 1976, p. 1002).

II.

The criticality of human ignorance is nowhere better exemplified than by the benighted state of awareness of "the law of battle." I begin with a number of successive passages from Darwin's descriptive accounts of the law as laid out in his 14 chapters stretching over some 575 pages in *The Descent of Man and Selection in Relation to Sex*. The passages lead us from general observations about the evolutionary phenomenon of male–male competition to specific ones about human male–male competition.

> There are [...] sexual differences quite disconnected with the primary organs [...] such as the greater size, strength, and pugnacity of the male, his weapons of offence or means of defence against rivals. (vol. 1, p. 254)

> [S]exual selection has played an important part in the history of the organic world. It is certain that with almost all animals there is a struggle between the males for the possession of the female. (vol. 1, p. 259)

> Our diffculty in regard to sexual selection lies in understanding how it is that the males which conquer other males, or those which prove the most attractive to the females, leave a greater number of offspring to inherit their superiority than the beaten and less attractive males. Unless this result followed, the characters which gave to certain males an advantage over others, could not be perfected and augmented through sexual selection. (vol. 1, pp. 260–1)

> In almost all the Orders [of insects], the males of some species, even of weak and delicate kinds, are known to be highly pugnacious; and some few are furnished with special weapons for fighting with their rivals. But the law of battle does not prevail nearly so widely with insects as with higher animals. (vol. 1, p. 418)

> [M]any male birds are highly pugnacious, and some are furnished with special weapons for fighting with their rivals. (vol. 1, p. 422)

> Male stickleback fish are extraordinarily bold and pugnacious [...] Their battles are at times desperate; for these puny combatants fasten tight on each other for several seconds, tumbling over and over again, until their strength appears completely exhausted. (vol. 2, p. 2)

> Almost all male birds are extremely pugnacious, using their beaks, wings, and legs for fighting together. We see this every spring with our robins and sparrows. The smallest of all birds, namely the humming-bird, is one of the most quarrelsome. (vol. 2, p. 40)

> Most male birds are highly pugnacious during the breeding-season, and some possess weapons especially adapted for fighting with their rivals. But the most pugnacious and the best-armed males rarely or never depend for success solely on their power to drive away or kill their rivals, but have special means for charming the female. With some it is the power of song, or of emitting strange cries, or of producing instru-mental music [...] Many birds endeavour to charm the females by love-

dances or antics, performed on the ground or in the air, and sometimes at prepared places. (vol. 2, pp. 232–3)

With mammals the male appears to win the female much more through the law of battle than through the display of his charms. (vol. 2, p. 239)

All male animals which are furnished with special weapons for fighting, are well known to engage in fierce battles (vol. 2, p. 240) [...] When the males are provided with weapons which the females do not possess, there can hardly be a doubt that they are used for fighting with other males, and that they have been acquired through sexual selection. (p. 242)

[M]ale monkeys, like men, are bolder and fiercer than the females. They lead the troop, and when there is danger, come to the front. We thus see how close is the parallelism between the sexual differences of man and the Quadrumana. (vol. 2, p. 320)

There can be little doubt that the greater size and strength of man, in comparison with woman, together with his broader shoulders, more developed muscles, rugged outline of body, his greater courage and pugnacity, are all due in chief part to inheritance from some early male progenitor, who, like the existing anthropoid apes, was thus characterised. (vol. 2, p. 325)

Man is the rival of other men; he delights in competition, and this leads to ambition which passes too easily into selfishness. These latter qualities seem to be his natural and unfortunate birthright. (vol. 2, p. 326)

The foregoing quotations leading up to the reality of human male–male competition can be elaborated initially by calling attention to a passing reference of Darwin, the place at which he mentions that in some bird species, males endeavor to charm the females at "prepared places." *Leks*—a Swedish term—is the name given to special grounds on which male–male competition takes place, grounds that are returned to year after year at mating season, males enacting what is justly termed their ritual competitive practice. Leks are not peculiar to avian males, as is commonly thought, but to species of insects, flies, lizards, butterflies, antelope, wildebeest, deer, fish, frogs, and bats (Attenborough 1990; Höglund and Alatalo 1995).

Though he is definitely neither concerned with leks nor writing about leks, just such "prepared places" enter into cultural historian Johan Huizinga's description and discussion of war in a chapter of his book *Homo ludens*. Huizinga provides examples of how in the Middle Ages, for example, and in early Greece, battles in the form of duels, community clashes and national conflicts were fought according to certain rules, including where the battle was to take place and how long it was to last. He writes of the difference between such true or civilized contests—*agons*, where combatants are equals—and uncivilized contests—non-agonistic forms of fighting as in "the surprise, the ambush, the raid, the punitive expedition and wholesale extermination," virtually decrying such forms of fighting as outside culture and, interestingly enough, waged by "lesser breeds without the law" (Huizinga 1955, pp. 90, 89–90, respectively). The point is not that the formal, rule-governed human male–male competitions that Huizinga describes qualify as leks but that they are of the same character as leks; that is, they are archetypal examples of ritual male–male competition, derivative from the ancestral form. In finer terms, when culturally co-opted by humans, agonistic male–male competition no longer serves its original sexual purpose, i.e. it is no longer a matter of winning fights with other males in order to win females. It is, as Huizinga describes it, a matter of upholding one's honor or of administering justice, for example. Indeed, abilities (and perhaps even weaponry) that evolved originally and specifically for the purpose of sexual pursuit and conquest are utilized to a different end, a cultural end serving psycho-social, socio-political, or socio-economic supremacy of one male or group of males over another.[2]

---

2   At the Symposium, McShea commented on this paper in the form of what he called two "quibbles." The first questioned the claim that all "culturally-mediated expressions of male–male competition no longer serve their original purpose" (pers. comm.). He stated, "we don't really know that 'ambition', for example, or 'power' do not lead to greater reproductive success." In response, I would question whether it is really "reproductive success" that ambition and power achieve or whether it is not simply sexual success. The desire for children is, after all, not commonly reported to be the prime motivator in an ambitious or powerful male's bedding of a female. That child support has to be legally mandated further supports the priority of sexual success over reproductive success. The second "quibble" questioned whether the "co-opting of passions (associated with male–male competition)" may have beneficial results in that co-opting keeps "these very dangerous animals" (i.e. males) "busy in a relatively harmless way" via sports, politics, money-making, and so on. My beginning response would be that sports may indeed constitute a "relatively harmless" outlet for competition, as Konrad Lorenz claimed, though in the context of aggression, not male–male competition (Lorenz 1966). My continuing response, however, would be that while in a general comparative sense the co-opting of passions may indeed be "relatively harmless" — compared, that is, to outright killing, massacring, and so on — money-making and politics can have physically and/or psychologically devastating effects, effects that are overwhelmingly harmful. *Greed*, for example, can deprive others to the point of penury and starvation, just as *power* and *territorial pursuits*, for example, can oppress others, degrading and humiliating them to the point of psychologically destroying their lives.

      The above responses to McShea's comments were written after the Symposium in the course of our follow-up correspondence and prior to my original submission of this article for publication. In light of McShea's

Put in biological perspective, Huizinga's writings about war and "trials by battle" give us an initial sense of how cultures elaborate the biological phenomenon of male–male competition, that is, of how "the law of battle" is and has been co-opted from its evolutionary moorings and elaborated on the cultural stage of human societies and civilizations. His writings thereby provide an initial sense of how Darwin's succinct description of human males—"Man is the rival of other men; he delights in competition, and this leads to ambition which passes too easily into selfishness"—is the point of departure for understanding what is played out culturally in myriad ways, not only in the fundamental, seemingly indelible, and ever-present human practice of war, but in the radically non-agonistic practices of genocidal massacres, territorial takeovers, resource plunderings, and more, including the ever-present wholesale raping of women and even children.

Darwin's description can in fact be elaborated along psychologically inflected cultural lines. Rivalry and competition leading to ambition and selfishness can be played out in the form of ideas, ultimately, in life and death psychological struggles over ideas. In his masterful critique of psychology and its abandonment of a concern with *psyche*—with soul—

---

further thoughtful and challenging comments in his gracious review of this article for the journal, I would like to amplify my responses briefly along two further interrelated lines of thought concerning the possibility of keeping "these very dangerous animals" "busy in a relatively harmless way" via the activities of sports, politics, and money-making.

Competitive sports are a cultural elaboration of a natural phenomenon: play. When prematurely introduced and intensely promoted, as in some Little League programs in the US, they can suppress natural dispositions to play and foreground aggression in its place: "Where competition drowns out play, in particular, the bodily play originating in infancy and typical of young children, it undermines its own foundations, foundations that are phylogenetic as well as ontogenetic. In so doing, it transforms its otherwise low-profile place in early life and gives rise to an altogether other social activity. [...] The name of the game is win, and win at all costs" (Sheets-Johnstone 2003, p. 409; 2008, p. 242). Not surprisingly, the imperative perdures into adult competitive sports, as witness the 2010 World Cup (see Parks 2010). Wars, of course, are competitive and equally tied to winning at all costs, hence, tied to politics and business as well as to sports. Wars are furthermore exciting for the actual combatants, not simply in a competitive win or lose sense but in a competitive life or death sense. Recent books on war, i.e. Evan Thomas's *The War Lovers* and Sebastian Junger's *War* (in addition to his film *Restrepo* made with Tim Hetherington), are topical to the point as are several chapters in *The Roots of Morality* (Sheets-Johnstone 2008). The books and chapters tie in with my dialogue with McShea and spur hopes for an ongoing substantive discussion of the biological reality of male–male competition and its cultural elaborations, and for a thoughtful public awareness of the phenomenon beyond the halls of academia.

psychoanalyst Otto Rank shows how soul-belief was first attached to woman, who through procreation brought to life the souls of the dead, and how it was later attached to the hero whose courageous conquests were heralded in mythic tales, thus how, in the beginning, soul-belief was tied to notions of immortality. Rank proceeds then to show how soul-belief and attendant notions of immortality eventually lost all relationship to animate life and became attached instead to "scientific intellectualism," an intellectualism embodied in the "new god" of *truth*. Every conflict over truth, he remarks, "is in the end the old struggle for the soul's existence and its immortality" (Rank 1998, pp. 59, 60, respectively). In taking up Rank's theme of truth-seeking, cultural anthropologist Ernest Becker vividly and strikingly points out:

> If anyone doubts [that the conflict over truth is a struggle over immortality], let him try to explain in any other way the life-and-death viciousness of all ideological disputes. Each person nourishes his immortality in the ideology of self-perpetuation to which he gives his allegiance; this gives his life the only abiding significance it can have. No wonder men go into a rage over fine points of belief. If your adversary wins the argument about truth, *you die*. Your immortality system has been shown to be fallible, your life becomes fallible. History, then, can be understood as the succession of ideologies that console for death. (Becker 1975, p. 64)

Male–male rivalry and competition are indeed culturally elaborated in complex ways, ways that become ingrained as much in individual psyches as in nationalist and religious ones. That ambition and selfishness are generated from the rivalry and competition is hardly surprising. Darwin's brief observation is in fact supported from multiple other perspectives. Affirming male–male competition on the basis of his own research studies as well as those of Darwin, anatomist and anthropologist Sir Arthur Keith states that: "at the base of man's 'competitive complex' is [his] desire for place and power—ambition" (Keith 1968, p. 58). Sir Arthur in fact considers ambition to be "the most compelling of human passions" (Keith 1946, p. 145). Three hundred years earlier, Thomas Hobbes wrote of man's selfishness. His well-known observation that life is "solitary, poor, nasty, brutish, and short" and his descriptions of the difficulties such life presents run along different but no less compelling lines with respect to the ease with which selfishness is generated (Hobbes 1651/1930). That Hitler's ambition was to found a thousand-year Reich and that Stalin's was to found the first-ever socialist state are further support of Darwin's observation. Their personal ambitions are supportive as well of Rank's seminal claims about human immortality ideologies, as are de Gaulle's proclamation of "la France eternelle" and of US Army Third Infantry Division Major Morris T. Goins's pronouncement to soldiers before the push to Baghdad on 13 April 2003: "Thirty-six hours, then we'll be in the history books forever" (*New York Times* "Quotation of the Day"). Studies of our primate relatives lend further support to Darwin's observation. Consider the following description:

> There is no mistaking a dominant male macaque. These are superbly muscled monkeys. Their hair is sleek and carefully groomed, their walk calm, assured and majestic. They move in apparent disregard of the lesser monkeys who scatter at their approach. For to obstruct the path of a dominant male or even to venture, when unwelcome, too near to him is an act of defiance, and macaques learn young that such a challenge will draw a heavy punishment. (Eimerl and DeVore 1965, p. 106)

Clearly, as Darwin observed, there is a "close parallelism" between "man and the Quadrumana," i.e. nonhuman primates. Jane Goodall provides further evidence of the close parallelism in her description of a chimpanzee, Mike, and of just how "Mike's rise to the number one or top-tanking position in the chimpanzee community was both interesting and spectacular":

> A group of five adult males, including top-ranking Goliath, David Graybeard, and the huge Rodolf, were grooming each other. The session had been going on for some twenty minutes. Mike was sitting about thirty yards apart from them, frequently staring toward the group, occasionally idly grooming himself. All at once Mike calmly walked over to our tent and took hold of an empty kerosene can by the handle. Then he picked up a second can and, walking upright, returned to the place where he had been sitting. Armed with his two cans Mike continued to stare toward the other males. After a few minutes he began to rock from side to side. [...] Gradually he rocked more vigorously, his hair slowly began to stand erect, and then, softly at first, he started a series of pant-hoots. As he called, Mike got to his feet and suddenly he was off, charging toward the group of males, hitting the two cans ahead of him. The cans, together with Mike's crescendo of hooting, made the most appalling racket: no wonder the erstwhile peaceful males rushed out of the way. Mike and his cans vanished down a track, and after a few moments there was silence. [...] After a short interval that low-pitched hooting began again, followed almost immediately by the appearance of the two rackety cans with Mike close behind them. Straight for the other males he charged, and once more they fled. [...] Rodolf was the first of the males to approach Mike, uttering soft pant-grunts of submission, crouching low and pressing his lips to Mike's thigh. Next he began to groom Mike, and two other males approached, pant-grunting, and also began to groom him. (Goodall 1971, pp. 112-3)

In *The Roots of Morality*, I commented on Goodall's description as follows:

> Though on an infinitesimally smaller scale than the scale of possible human attempts at dominance, Mike's bid for dominance is readily comparable to human male bids for dominance, and not only individual

male bids but national bids, bids in the form of displays that break into
otherwise peaceful relations, that utilize immediate attention getting
objects, that provoke fear, and by provoking fear, aim to subdue or sub-
jugate others. Piercing through ordinary activities of everyday life, such
human displays of power can and do generate unendurable tensions
that readily leave vengeful, rancorous figures in their wake as well as
cringing, submissive ones. (Sheets-Johnstone 2008, p. 106)

The foregoing exposition of male–male rivalry and competition notwithstanding, what Darwin specifies as the "natural and unfortunate birthright" of human males is not indelibly scripted, any more than it is
indelibly scripted in other animals. *All* males are not equally driven to
compete, to dominate, and so on. The first tenet of evolution is variation.
There is indeed *variation* among males with respect to quarrelsomeness,
bellicosity, and combativeness, what Darwin frequently describes as
"pugnacity." The point of moment here, however, is to acknowledge
straightforwardly what I term *real* male–male competition (Sheets-
Johnstone 2008) or, in other words, to acknowledge the evolutionary
realities of our humanness in the form of male–male competition and to
shed light on the ways in which "the law of battle," which phylogenetically
serves strictly reproductive ends, has over eons of human time been
culturally co-opted to serve quite other ends, ends having to do with
ambition, power, dominance, greed, territorial pursuits, immortality
ideologies, and so on, and this by squelching the life and livelihood of
those who stand in the way or by outright killing.

III.

Two notable and thriving present-day academic research programs are
obstacles to the straightforward recognition of *real* human male–male competition. The biological matrix of *real* male–male competition is either
hidden under the aegis of aggressive behavior or reduced to a cellular
phenomenon. Each obstacle warrants attention.

   In light of his popular 1966 book *On Aggression*, Konrad Lorenz might
be cited as the forerunner of academic research on the topic. In that book,
Lorenz writes of "the aggressive instinct" (p. x), of the "survival value of
aggression" (p. 39), of the "survival value of the rival fight [… that] leads to
useful selection where it breeds fighters fitted for combat with extra-
specific enemies as well as for intra-specific duels" (p. 39), and of the fact
that "present-day civilized man suffers from insufficient discharge of his
aggressive drive" (p. 235). He furthermore writes at some length of "a
powerful phylogenetically evolved behavior which," he says, "I propose to
call that of militant enthusiasm" (p. 259). He speaks of how phylogenetically evolved behavioral patterns can "interact" with "culturally
ritualized social norms and rites" (p. 259), but oddly enough never

mentions *real* male–male competition and its human cultural subduction into war.

War is indeed a cultivated human taste, the cultural magnification of the biological archetype of *real* male–male competition, co-opted from its original sexual context and put in the service of dominance *über alles* and all that dominance *über alles* brings with it. It is of considerable interest to note in this context that, with the neglect of attention to *real* male–male competition, there is a correlative unwitting leap from talk of humans to talk of "man," not as a commonly used synonym for "human" but with pointed reference to "man's destructiveness," man's "innate aggression," man's propensity to war, and so on, as in Carthy and Ebling's edited book *The Natural History of Aggression* (1964, p. 4). In short, that it is not a question of humans generally but of males in particular is everywhere evident but nowhere acknowledged. Moreover, in neglecting any mention of the biological phenomenon of *real* male–male competition in discussions of aggression, whether its "natural history" or its psychological aspects, writings on the subject testify to an absorption in what is derivative rather than what is original: from a biological perspective, *male–male competition motivates aggression, and not the reverse.*

"Aggression" is a label put upon a certain kind of behavior — unprovoked offensive action upon another, as the *OED* indicates; male–male competition is, in contrast, a bona fide biological phenomenon. How any particular competition plays out depends on just those biological variables Darwin discusses in his explanation of sexual selection; that is, some males are more pugnacious than others, some more energized, some more vocal, and so on. Though unmentioned as such, a propensity toward unprovoked offensive action upon another is just such a biological variable, precisely as Mike's behavior indicates. Aggression exists along an affective psycho-sociological gradient. The biological matrix of male–male competition exists in humans along a decidedly *cultural* gradient, a gradient readily exemplified in the degree to which, and the ways in which, cultures can and do promote competition in the pursuit of power, fame, territory, glory, and so on, and in the correlative honing of heroes and prominencing of warriors. As Lorenz astutely observed: "Virtues such as heroism and courage are regarded as being 'manly' and are traditionally associated with waging war. Conversely, the avoidance of war or the pursuit of peace are generally regarded as 'effeminate', passive, cowardly, weak, dishonorable or subversive" (Lorenz 1966, p. 275).

Lorenz wrote more than 40 years ago, but today's writings on aggression are virtually no different except in their reductionist treatment of aggression. In the Preface to his book *Biology of Aggression* — a gathering of 18 articles by people at the National Institute of Mental Health and in departments of psychopharmacology, psychology, biology, neurobiology, psychiatry, and zoology—editor Randy J. Nelson writes:

> For years, the roles of learning and environmental influences, both social and nonsocial factors, were prominent in discussions of the etiology of human aggression. Biological factors were not thought likely to be important candidates for dealing with human aggression or violence. With recent advances in pharmacology and genetic manipulation techniques, new interests in the biological mechanisms of human aggression have been pursued. Certainly, aggression is a complex social behavior with multiple causes, but pursuit of molecular biological causes may lead to interventions to prevent excess aggressive behaviors.

Following a brief paragraph that defines aggression as "overt behavior with the intention of inflicting physical damage upon another individual" and that provides a sentence or two about territorial aggression in pursuit of resources and the possibility of an animal averting combat by a sub-missive gesture, Nelson begins his next paragraph with the statement: "Because most aggressive encounters among humans and nonhuman animals represent a male proclivity, studies using the most appropriate murine model (such as testosterone-dependent offensive intermale aggression, which is typically measured in resident-intruder or isolation-induced aggression tests) are discussed" (Nelson 2006, p. v). In short, reductionism holds sway. There is no entry in the index for male–male competition; there is no entry for Darwin; and in fact neither is there an entry for evolution. Indeed, the preponderance of articles are rooted in experimental or laboratory research on nonhuman animals; those dealing with humans are rooted in neurobiology, psychopharmacology, or psycho-physiology. The biological matrix of male–male competition across the kingdom Animalia and its cultural exaptation by humans are indeed nowhere on the map.

The cultural honing of heroes and the cultural adulation of warriors have been staples of human civilization for centuries and even millennia. Surely it should be astonishing rather than merely surprising that *real* male–male competition has been an ignored dimension of human history. Inattention to human history aside, what is singularly remarkable in today's world of biological sciences is how real male–male competition has vanished in a reductive sleight of hand into sperm competition. A 2006 book titled *Sperm Competition in Humans: Classic and Contemporary Readings* gives ample evidence of the subversion of the real-life phenomenon into a near parody of what Darwin aptly recognized as "the law of battle," even to the point of a proposing a "kamikaze" sperm hypothesis (Baker and Bellis 1988/2006, 1989/2006). As Geoffrey A. Parker, the 1970 "discoverer" of sperm competition in insects, defines it, sperm competition is the

"competition between the sperm from two or more males over the fertilization of ova" (Parker 2006, p. 33). Parker "suggests" sperm competition as
an explanation of why sperm are "so small and so numerous" (p. 33). As
one of the contributors to the book remarks, however, in a paper titled
"Human Sperm Competition," "Data on the incidence of human sperm
competition are meager" (Smith 1984/2006, p. 110). He adds that "Most
come from forensic genetics studies conducted to exclude paternity, and
very few from human population genetics studies" (pp. 110–1). It is
relevant in this context of human sperm competition and "paternity" to
quote an outlandish claim by sociobiologists Martin Daly and Margo
Wilson that epitomizes the blatant omission of *real* male–male competition.
Daly and Wilson state: "If a marriage contract provided a man with a
magical guarantee of paternity, the world would be a more peaceable
place!" (Daly and Wilson 1983, p. 285). Does paternal uncertainty foment
war, genocide, an *über alles* mentality, and other forms of *real* male–male
competition, whether national or religious? Or does war, genocide, an *über
alles* mentality, and other forms of *real* male–male competition rather open
the door to rape, unwanted pregnancies, and fatherless children, the latter
in spite of the fact that, as one contributor with seemingly molecular
anthropomorphic candor states, "The human vaginal environment is considered generally hostile toward sperm" (Smith 1984/2006, p. 105).[3]

In sum, there is no doubt but that "the law of battle" of which Darwin
wrote at length and in meticulous descriptive detail across both invertebrate and vertebrate species in *The Descent of Man* has been submerged in
aggression, subverted into sperm competition, and in general disregarded
—all, I would add, to the detriment of humans knowing themselves as they
really are. As phenomenological philosopher Edmund Husserl would
admonish, "to the things themselves"—in other words, to the realities of
life itself and to understandings of that lifeworld. To win one's freedom
from ignorance, whatever its culturally inculcated source, requires recognition of human evolution, the basic phenomenon of male–male competition, and of the ways in which that biological matrix is and has been
culturally elaborated. It requires what might be called an expansion of
ordinary consciousness, not only the ability to reflect on experience, but the
sagacity to acknowledge experience as the ground floor of any objective
study—precisely as Darwin's investigations of animate life teach us: his
questionings of himself and others about that life, and his sojournings

---

3 Smith goes on to remark: "Evidence for this is partially circumstantial in
that only a very small fraction of ejaculated sperm ever reach the uterine
tubes where fertilization usually occurs. Of the hundreds of millions of
sperm contained in each ejaculate, only about 2,000 arrive in the vicinity of
the descending ovum" (Smith 2006, p. 105).

onward through scrupulous observations and descriptions toward a solidification into theory. To win one's freedom thus means what I once described as practicing one's chosen profession "close-up," that is, immersing oneself in the living, experiential foundations on which any empirical study of individuals is based. In close-up study of *real* male–male competition, one indeed discovers options. A brief story, however anecdotal, makes the point:

A Native American grandfather was talking to his grandson about how he felt about the tragedy on 11 September. He said: "I feel as if I have two wolves fighting in my heart. One wolf is vengeful, angry, violent. The other wolf is loving, forgiving, compassionate." The grandson asks him: "Which wolf will win the fight in your heart?" The grandfather answers: "The one I feed."[4]

Humans—male humans in this particular instance—are free to choose what they affectively cultivate. Realizing their affective freedom—in effect, that cultural offsprings of biology are nondeterministic—means realizing they are not locked in. Their natural power to reflect gives them other options as does their knowledge of the possible range of human experience. Ignoring or turning away from these other options, they compromise their self-glorifying intelligence, the doubly sapiential wisdom of *Homo sapiens sapiens*. The descent of man can in turn be literally read as a moral rather than evolutionary descent, a descent that runs from the self-ennobling heights of *Homo sapiens sapiens* to the gutters of *Homo nescius et barbarus*—*nescius* meaning precisely ignorant, lacking knowledge. The dangers of a moral descent can be countered only by a moral education grounded in an evolutionary history that humans undertake about themselves. We are, after all, together in this onrunning flow of life in which we find ourselves. The legacy of Charles Darwin is rich and extends beyond *The Origin of Species*. What we learn from his writings is a measure of the depths of our humanity. What we in turn open ourselves to examining and what we contribute in our own time is a measure of our individual integrity and sapience.

---

4   It is worth noting from a specifically cultural perspective that the grandfather is a Native American Indian, someone who has a *de facto* spiritual nature. Not that all Native American Indians were docile, non-warring peoples, but that there is a whole history of "the white man" usurping lands cultivated and lived on by Native American Indians. In short, would the conversation, however anecdotal, have the credibility and impact it has if the grandfather had been just a grandfather—or, say, an Hispanic grandfather or a German grandfather or an Israeli grandfather or a Northern Irish grandfather, not to say a plain old American grandfather?

Acknowledgement

It is with great pleasure that I acknowledge Ian Baucom, Director of the John Hope Franklin Center at Duke University, who invited me to be one of four guest speakers at the Darwin Anniversary Symposium, "Darwin Across the Disciplines," in November 2009. Each guest speaker had a commentator from the Genomic Institute at Duke. It is with equally great pleasure that I acknowledge Daniel McShea, Professor of Biology at Duke, who was my interlocutor. The original version of this article was presented at the Symposium.

References

Attenborough, D. (1990) *The Trials of Life: A Natural History of Animal Behavior*, Boston, MA: Little, Brown.

Baker, R.R. & Bellis, M.A. (1988/2006a) "Kamikaze" sperm in mammals?, in Shackelford, T.K. & Nicholas, P. (eds.) *Sperm Competition in Humans: Classic and Contemporary Readings*, pp. 119–122, New York: Springer.

Baker, R.R. & Bellis, M.A. (1989/2006) Elaboration of the kamikaze sperm hypothesis: A reply to Harcourt, in Shackelford, T.K. & Nicholas, P. (eds.) *Sperm Competition in Humans: Classic and Contemporary Readings*, pp. 127–129, New York: Springer.

Becker, E. (1975) *Escape from Evil*, New York: The Free Press.

Beeton, I.M. (1861) *The Book of Household Management*, London: S.O. Beeton.

Carthy, J.D. & Ebling, F.J. (1964) *The Natural History of Aggression*, New York: Academic Press.

Crick, F. & Koch, C. (1992) The problem of consciousness, *Scientific American*, (September), pp. 153–159.

Curtis, H. (1976) *Biology*, 2nd ed., New York: Worth Publishers.

Daly, M. & Wilson, M. (1983) *Sex, Evolution, and Behavior*, 2nd ed., Belmont, CA: Wadsworth Publishing.

Darwin, C. (1871/1981) *The Descent of Man and Selection in Relation to Sex*, 2 vols., Princeton, NJ: Princeton University Press.

Eimerl, S. & DeVore, I. (1965) *The Primates*, New York: Times, Inc.

Freedberg, D. & Gallese, V. (2007) Motion, emotion and empathy in esthetic experience, *Trends in Cognitive Sciences*, 11 (5), pp. 197–203.

Gallese, V., Eagle, M.N. & Migone, P. (2007) Intentional attunement: Mirror neurons and the neural underpinnings of interpersonal relations, *Journal of the American Psychoanalytic Association*, 55, pp. 131–176.

Gallese, V. & Lakoff, G. (2005) The brain's concepts: The role of the sensory-motor system in conceptual knowledge, *Cognitive Neuropsychology*, 21, pp. 1–25.

Goins, M.M.T. (2003) "Quotation of the Day", *New York Times*, 13 April, [Online], http://www.nytimes.com/2003/04/13/international/worldspecial/13INFA.html?t.

Goodall, J. (1971) *In the Shadow of Man*, New York: Dell.

Gould, S.J. & Vrba, E.S. (1982) Exaptation—a missing term in the science of form, *Paleobiology*, 8, pp. 4–15.

Harding, R.S.O. (1975) Meat-eating and hunting in baboons, in Russell, H.T. (ed.) *Socioecology and Psychology of Primates*, pp. 245–257, The Hague: Mouton.

Hobbes, T. (1651/1930) *Hobbes: Selections*, Woodbridge, F.J.E. (ed.), New York: Charles Scribner's Sons.

Höglund, J. & Alatalo, R.V. (1995) *Leks*, Princeton, NJ: Princeton University Press.

Huizinga, J. (1955) *Homo ludens: A Study of the Play Element in Culture*, Boston, MA: Beacon Press.

Keith, Sir A. (1946) *Essays on Human Evolution*, London: Watts.

Keith, Sir A. (1968) *A New Theory of Human Evolution*, Gloucester, MA: Peter Smith.

Lakoff, G. & Johnson, M. (1999) *Philosophy in the Flesh: The Embodied Mind and Its Challenge to Western Thought*, New York: Basic Books.

Lorenz, K. (1966) *On Aggression*, Wilson, M.K. (trans.), New York: Bantam Books.

Marryatt, F. (1842) *Masterman Ready*, London: Blackie & Son Ltd.

Nelson, R.J. (2006) Preface, in Randy, J.N. (ed.) *Biology of Aggression*, pp. v–ix, Oxford: Oxford University Press.

Parker, G.A. (2006) Why are there so many tiny sperm? Sperm competition and the maintenance of the two sexes, in Shackelford, T.K. & Nicholas, P. (eds.) *Sperm Competition in Humans: Classic and Contemporary Readings*, pp. 33–46, New York: Springer.

Parks, T. (2010) The shame of the World Cup, *New York Review of Books*, LVII (13), pp. 44–49.

Pilbeam, D.R. (1986) Distinguished lecture: Hominoid evolution and hominoid origins, *American Anthropologist*, 88, pp. 295–312.

Rank, O. (1998) *Psychology and the Soul: A Study of the Origin, Conceptual Evolution, and Nature of the Soul*, Richter, G.C. & Lieberman, E.J. (trans.), Baltimore, MD: Johns Hopkins University Press.

Saey, T.H. (2009) Human cells play simon says, too, *Science News*, 176 (6) (12 September), p. 11.

Science News (2009) The teaching company advertisement, *Science News*, 175 (13) (20 June), p. 3.

Sheets-Johnstone, M. (1994) *The Roots of Power: Animate Form and Gendered Bodies*, Chicago, IL: Open Court Publishing.

Sheets-Johnstone, M. (1998) Consciousness: A natural history, *Journal of Consciousness Studies*, 5 (3), pp. 260–294.

Sheets-Johnstone, M. (1999a) Emotions and movement: A beginning empirical-phenomenological analysis of their relationship, *Journal of Consciousness Studies*, 6 (11–12), pp. 259–277. (Also in Sheets-Johnstone, M. (2009) *The Corporeal Turn: An Interdisciplinary Reader*, ch. VIII, pp. 195–218, Exeter: Imprint Academic.)

Sheets-Johnstone, M. (1999b/exp. 2nd ed. 2011) *The Primacy of Movement*, Amsterdam/Philadelphia, PA: John Benjamins Publishing.

Sheets-Johnstone, M. (2002/this volume, Chapter X) Descriptive foundations, *Interdisciplinary Studies in Literature and Environment*, 9 (1), pp. 165–179.

Sheets-Johnstone, M. (2003) Child's play: A multidisciplinary perspective, *Human Studies*, 26, pp. 409–430.

Sheets-Johnstone, M. (2008) *The Roots of Morality*, University Park, PA: Pennsylvania State University Press.

Smiles, S. (1875) *Thrift*, New York: Harper & Brothers.

Smith, R.L. (1984/2006) Human sperm competition, in Shackelford, T.K. & Nicholas, P. (eds.) *Sperm Competition in Humans: Classic and Contemporary Readings*, pp. 67–118, New York: Springer.

Thompson, E. (2007) *Mind in Life: Biology, Phenomenology, and the Sciences of Mind*, Cambridge, MA: Belknap Press/Harvard University Press.

Chapter VII

On the Hazards of Being a Stranger to Oneself[1]

Abstract: *This chapter traces out the socio-political consequences of self-ignorance and self-deception. These consequences were clearly recognized more than 2,000 years ago by early Greek philosophers, in part along the lines of "a conceit of wisdom." The consequences were more recently spelled out in striking ways by Carl Jung in his psychoanalytic analyses of "mass-minded man" who, through self-ignorance and self-deception, wreaks havoc and cruelty on others. The chapter also points up the challenge of attaining self-knowledge and possible paths to its attainment that bolster or augment classic psychotherapeutic approaches.[2]*

I. Three Personal Modes of the Stranger

We come into the world as strangers. By being attentive to and learning the ways of the world, especially the ways of creatures like ourselves, we make our way knowledgeably, efficiently, and effectively within it. Such a successful apprenticeship depends on our being attentive to our bodies, learning their animate possibilities and limitations, building on and expanding the dynamics of our kinesthetically-felt bodies. In engaging in more and more complex ways with the everyday world, we correlatively expand the horizons of our awareness and transform the initial strangeness of the world into an everyday familiarity. The everyday world thereby becomes a relatively safe and predictable haven, but one not inimical to strangeness. Indeed, what we come to know individually as the familiar everyday world is not the limit of the world. By the same token, what we come to know individually as our familiar everyday selves is not the limit

---

[1]   First published in *Psychotherapy and Politics International* (2008), Vol. 6, No. 1: 17–29.

[2]   This chapter was originally presented as a public lecture held at St Marys College on 29 May 2007 and sponsored by the Institute of Advanced Study at Durham University, Durham, UK. The public lecture was one of a series of presentations as a Distinguished Fellow at the Institute in the spring of 2007.

of ourselves, at least not if we are open to the challenge of examining what Jung called our shadow side or "undiscovered self" — of which more presently.

We come into the world as strangers. Western bible-based religions exalt this fact, although in a notably different way. Their attention is riveted not on the developmental phenomenon known as human ontogeny but on a heavenly God and on fidelity to that God. From their perspective, we are strangers here on Earth who will find our real home only in heaven, in God's domain. Our status as strangers is thus mitigated if not alleviated by religious allegiance and practice. So also may be the fearful pangs of death that afflict us as earthlings. Specific deistic fidelity is required, however, insofar as each religion has its own god, its own theology or ideology of god, and its own way of providing support to its followers in the way of salvation, of eternal life, or of being God's chosen people. Given our vulnerable status as strangers here on Earth together with the knowledge and fear of our ultimate death, religions may indeed be conceived as Jung in a totally noncritical way conceived them: "psychotherapeutic systems in the truest sense of the word, and on the grandest scale" (Jung 1970, p. 172).[3] They assuage our earthly fears, most prominently our fear of death, not by cultivating familiarity with the world, but by making the unknown palatable as it were, that is, by cultivating hope and the promise of a better life to come or by elevating us in status with respect to others.

Both the ontogenetic stranger and the theological stranger warrant consideration, and not only as separate formulations with essential differences that distinguish them, but conjointly in terms of certain conceptual affinities. The prenatal womb of the one, for example, is conceptually akin to the postmortal heaven of the other; a blissful paradise obtains at either end. Similarly the protecting, nurturing mother of the one is conceptually akin to the protecting, nurturing Father of the other; a parental figure watches over one in each instance, safeguarding one's life. One might say in view of these affinities that theology recapitulates ontogeny. A third personal mode of the stranger, however, warrants more pressing consideration, not least because it is commonly overlooked. That it is commonly overlooked is ironic because this stranger affects us profoundly, penetrating to the core of both our individual and socio-political lives. This stranger is the psychological stranger that Jung identifies as the shadow. We come into the world as strangers to this stranger and many of us go out of the world as strangers to this stranger as well — strangers in the psychological sense of being deficient in self-knowledge. In our typically busy relationship to the

---

3 Jung (1970) adds that religions "express the whole range of the psychic problem in mighty images; they are the avowal and recognition of the soul, and at the same time the revelation of the soul's nature."

world, we leave *self*-knowledge largely out of the equation. Our eyes and ears are typically focused outward and while we make and have made the world familiar, we remain a stranger to ourselves. In a word, we are knowers of the world but remain opaque to the knower.

The irony of our self-opacity is compounded when viewed in the light of the historical significance and priority of self-knowledge in Western thought. "Know thyself" is not just a well-known marker of Western civilization anchored in ancient Greek thought, but a highly esteemed marker. Socrates epitomized the dictum in his own life and emphasized its fundamental import in many ways in many dialogs. Speaking to Phaedrus, for example, he states, "I must first know myself, as the Delphian inscription says; to be curious about that which is not my concern, while I am still in ignorance of my own self, would be ridiculous" (*Phaedrus* 230). To Protarchus, he points out that ignorance of the self is evident in three domains: wealth, beauty, and wisdom. He specifies each domain in turn in the following words: "the ignorant [person] may fancy himself richer than he is [... a]nd still more often he will fancy that he is taller or fairer than he is, or that he has some other advantage of person which he really has not [... a]nd yet surely by far the greatest number [of people] err about the goods of the mind; they imagine themselves to be much better men than they are" (*Philebus* 48–9).

In such passages, Socrates adumbrated what Jung more than 2,000 years later described as the shadow side of the human psyche. Indeed, in the *Charmides*, Socrates speaks of an *unconscious* disposition to dissemble with respect to actual knowledge. In answer to a criticism of Critias, he first asks, "How can you think that I have any other motive in refuting you but what I should have in examining into myself?" and then specifies his motive as "a fear of my unconsciously fancying that I knew something of which I was ignorant." Moreover he goes on to broaden the human significance of self-knowledge, asking whether "the discovery of things *as they truly are*, [is not] a good common to all mankind" (*Charmides* 166; italics added). In effect, he testifies to the socio-political benefits of self-knowledge. Resemblances thus obtain not only between Socrates' notion of the human psyche and Jung's twentieth-century formulation of the human psyche, that is, of the human penchant to "err about the goods of the mind" but, as we shall see more fully, in their common recognition of the socio-political price of both self-ignorance and self-deception.

When we consult Plato directly, we find further notable resemblances between ancient Greek thought and Jung's psychoanalytic. To imagine oneself a better human being than one actually is, is to take on what the Athenian Stranger in Plato's *Laws* describes as the "conceit of wisdom" (*Laws* IX 863). The Athenian Stranger—an ironically named character in terms of this chapter since the Stranger is Plato himself—is the protagonist, the foreign "Other" who, in dialog with Clinias, the Cretan, and Megillus, the Spartan, is the conceptual source of knowledge for the formulation of laws that produce what he deems "the good society" (see Zeitlin 1993 for a detailed analysis of Plato's quest to delineate "the good society"). To take on the "conceit of wisdom," says the Athenian Stranger, is to fall short of the highest virtue: one does not accurately assess one's knowledge but professes to know what one in fact knows not. As he goes on to point out, this form of ignorance can have dire socio-political consequences. In particular, the Athenian Stranger affirms that when "conceit of wisdom" is "possessed of power and strength, [it] will be held by the legislator to be the source of great and monstrous crimes" (ibid.). In finer terms, when ignorance is not simple, resulting in only "lighter offences" but is accompanied by a "conceit of wisdom," ignorance doubles (ibid.). When "doubled ignorance" combines with power and strength, criminal action results. Present-day testimony to the trenchancy of this observation is readily available. We have only to open our eyes to the "great and monstrous crimes" that are today committed by certain leaders, among whom a certain pre-eminent leader in whom the embodiment of the conceit of wisdom combines with unparalleled power and strength.

That the socio-political consequences of self-ignorance and self-deception were clearly recognized early on in Western civilization, and that the consequences let alone the fact itself of self-ignorance and self-deception have gone virtually unnoticed for more than two thousand years — or if duly noticed in such classic texts as Hannah Arendt's *Eichmann in Jerusalem* (Arendt 1977), have eventuated in essence in no more than pro forma hand-wringings rather than in intense investigations into the nature of human nature — is a sharp and telling comment on *Homo sapiens sapiens*. In finer terms, that "know-thyself" is today nothing more than a sweet and sentimental idea, paling before such putatively more critical present-day concerns as self-esteem and self-image, is surely testimony to the staunchly obdurate self-opacity of *Homo sapiens sapiens*. Clearly, self-knowledge affects not just one's individual life but the larger socio-political arena in which one lives one's life. This basic fact of human life warrants attention in itself. But it furthermore warrants investigations into the nature of human nature, and in light of insights gained into that nature, into educative processes that, as Plato urged, best promote the attainment of "the good society." In sum, the third stranger is of critical moment. The hazards of being a stranger to oneself leech out socio-politically in deleterious directions.

II. Further Historical Connections:
On the Way to Jung's Psychoanalytic of Mass-Minded Man

Jung's clinical work and extended delvings into his own psyche taught him that self-knowledge is the key both to an honest and psychologically healthful life and to a fully meaningful and even enriched life. The illness of a patient, he states, "is not a gratuitous and therefore meaningless burden; it is *his own self*, the 'other' whom, from childish laziness or fear, or for some other reason, he was always seeking to exclude from his life" (Jung 1970, pp. 169–70; italics in original). Commenting more fully at a later point, he affirms: "We should not try to 'get rid' of a neurosis, but rather to experience what it means, what it has to teach, what its purpose is. We should even learn to be thankful for it, otherwise we pass it by and miss the opportunity of getting to know ourselves as we really are" (Jung 1970, p. 170). In short, Jung affirms that what we keep from ourselves as we habitually and egoistically plump ourselves up in one way and another is an obstacle "to know[ing] ourselves as we really are."

Jung's analytical words resonate conceptually not only with the 2,000-year-old words of Socrates and Plato but with the 2,000-year-old words of the Buddha, which themselves parallel in precise ways those of Socrates and Plato. For Buddhists generally, self-knowledge is foundational to understanding "things as they truly are"; it is foundational to wisdom. In his introduction to *The Middle Length Discourses of the Buddha*, Bhikkhu Bodhi writes that "The task of insight meditation is to sever our attachments by enabling us to pierce through [the] net of conceptual projections in order to see things as they really are" (Bodhi 1995, p. 40). "[T]o see things as they really are" and "[to discover] things as they truly are" are patently coincident with "knowing ourselves as we really are." The path in each instance leads to seminal truths about ourselves. These truths are not, of course, all sweetness and light. As the internationally renowned Vietnamese monk Thich Nhât Hanh notes, "Mahayana teachers sometimes identify the Dharma treasure with the good and beautiful [...] The true face of our essential nature is also the mud—the greed, hatred, ignorance—the suffering and the killing between human beings" (Nhât Hanh 1985, pp. 28–9). He amplifies this "other side" of human nature explicitly at a later point when he states—obviously from first-hand experiences of the Vietnamese war—"The bombs, the hunger, the pursuit of wealth and power—these are not separate from your nature" (Nhât Hanh 1985, p. 30). Such truths about ourselves naturally take work—and time—to discover. Moreover as long as we are living and awake, the flow of our feelings, thoughts, dispositions, fantasies, motivations, images, and so on—everything that structures both our spontaneous movements and gestures and our deliberations and actions—is limitless. Our potential knowledge of the flow is correlatively limitless. Examining the full and multifaceted spectrum of the flow as it arises, noticing what is present and not shrinking from the awareness of what is present—even taking time in the first place to notice what is present—takes courage, energy, perseverance. Perhaps most basically it takes interest, interest in what it is to be human and in the complex density of being human. Self-knowledge is indeed limited only by our individual selves. That Jung considers self-knowledge a lifelong enterprise and that Buddhists similarly consider meditation a lifelong enterprise attests to the fact that, however habitual, individual human experience is inwardly complex and ongoing and what is complex and ongoing inwardly is always open to examination.

Jung's psychoanalytic project is related methodologically as well as conceptually to distinguished ancient Greek philosophers and to Buddhism; that is, it is methodologically akin to the maieutics practiced by Socrates and Plato, and to Buddhist meditational practice. It is furthermore akin to phenomenological practice, a practice colloquially described as "making the familiar strange." Undoing what phenomenologists term "constitution" —undoing everyday sense-making through the phenomenological procedure of bracketing and descriptive analysis—goes against the grain insofar as it means unraveling the familiar meanings and values of our lives and tracing them back to their origins. Undoing the process of constitution testifies eloquently to the complexity of the task with which we are faced from the beginning of our lives: making sense of ourselves and the animate and inanimate world about us. From the very beginning we are moved to move. We are naturally inclined to explore and to make sense. We are instinctively motivated to open ourselves toward the world and its wonders. Moreover, smiling comes naturally to us. We are indiscriminate in our openness toward others. Of specific moment here is that, in contrast to our natural curiosity in face of the animate and inanimate world and our spontaneous initial outward openness toward it, the energy and motivation toward self-knowledge comes not from nature directly but from a desire to make transparent the nature of our humanness. In contrast, then, to our spontaneous outward openness toward the world, self-knowledge requires a diligent effort toward *inward* openness. When we unravel ourselves phenomenologically, we open a particular path toward "the goods of the mind," showing us how, in our sensemakings, we take for granted and assume that we already know, perhaps sometimes even shaping or reshaping experience so that experience fits our comforts as well as our theories. Unraveling ourselves phenomenologically may thus show us that "the goods of the mind" are at times counterfeit.[4]

---

[4] It is also notable that verification by others guards against phenomenological omissions, errors, and so on. Phenomenological analyses are indeed

With respect to both meditational and phenomenological practice, being present to what is, *as it is,* is challenging. In meditational practice, however, it is not a matter of building down what has been built up, that is, of going against the epistemological grain as in phenomenology. The Buddhist challenge testifies to a different kind of complexity: the complexity not of making sense of ourselves in the process of making sense of the world but the complexity of mind pure and simple, in a worldly unencumbered mode as it were. To begin with, one finds oneself far less in control than one ordinarily thinks oneself to be or even perhaps cares to admit. Serious meditational practice can indeed expose an unbending "conceit of wisdom." When we stop filling mind with the stuff of the sensory world and encounter it on its own ground, we find that, left to its own devices, it capriciously brings forth its own objects—feelings, thoughts, images, desires, and so on—zinging here and there wholly on its own and at seeming random. As Buddhist monk Joseph Goldstein succinctly put it, "The mind wanders" (Goldstein, undated cassette recording, JG215). We find, in effect, that we do not control our minds; we control only what, in light of our thoughts, feelings, fantasies, images, and so on, we actually do—or choose not to do. While we can direct our attention to our breath or some other object as in meditational practice, or to thoughts and feelings with respect to such and such a subject, topic of investigation, or problem in our everyday lives, and certainly find it possible to succeed in concentrating on it, that we do so is not testimony to our power to control our mind; it is testimony only to our potential capacity to concentrate, and in particular, to our success in concentrating in this particular here and now such that we are uninterrupted by other concerns, unimpeded by distractions, and the like. Our potential capacity to concentrate is in fact put to a bare-bones test in meditational practice, for ordinarily, we neither find the mind—*our* mind—so engrossing that we want to attend to it, nor do we ordinarily attend to it in the process of its focusings and wanderings in the first place. We are, indeed, ordinarily strangers to it.

Were a neutral observer—a stranger, if you will—to judge the degree to which humans were strangers to themselves, or in positive terms, self-observant to the end of gaining self-knowledge, he or she would find little indication of a continuing and consolidated interest in the pursuit of self-knowledge, let alone a concern with its value to education. In fact, apart from the general observation that the pursuit of self-interest rather than the pursuit of self-knowledge fuels and has fueled human life—recognizably so, we might note, in the dominant forms of consumerism and entertain-

---

not mere idiosyncratic reports about experience but follow a precise methodology through which verification by others is possible.

ment in today's everyday Western world—the stranger might well judge that twentieth- and twenty-first-century Western humans pursue an aberrant, even thick-headed route to knowledge of themselves. They devote their study to *the brain* as to the Temple at Delphi, exalting the dictum "know thyself" as if it pertained to neural tissue. The critical judgement would rightly recognize that the ancient call "know thyself" is a call to the living individual him/herself, hence to serious first-person introspective and reflective labours, a call, in short, to "thyself" in immediate and direct experience, an experience not of *the brain* but of one's individual human being from start to finish.

III. From the Shadow to Mass-Minded Man

Jung expressed his view of the shadow trenchantly and succinctly when he wrote, "One does not become enlightened by imagining figures of light but by making the darkness conscious." He went on to remark, "The procedure, however, is disagreeable and therefore not popular" (Jung 1983, pp. 265-6). Indeed, when we open to the shadow side of ourselves, we have the possibility of illuminating the darker corners of our humanity and seeing their ever more disastrous socio-political consequences. The consequences do not await us in a distant future but present themselves to us straightforwardly—and relentlessly—in human history and in today's globalized world. They lead us to pose the following questions: What is the nature of a being who cannot live in peace with others of its own kind, who is obsessed with power and who has the power in equal measure to create and to destroy, and to destroy not simply his own kind but other kinds as well and indeed the whole Earth? More finely, what is the nature of a being who cannot live without killing, not in order that he may eat but in order that others, whether termed the enemy or the devil, the intruder or the insurgent, but singularly epitomized as *the stranger*, are obliterated?

Jung did not write of the stranger but nevertheless gave powerful clues regarding answers to these questions. He did so in terms of the shadow, that is, of the "undiscovered self" and the need for its discovery. That his insights have not been culled by people in the humanities and human sciences and in turn brought to bear on "the human condition" and studied as such is initially puzzling. Puzzlement readily fades, however, on recognition of a commonplace but by no means inconsequential fact. The humanities and soft human sciences are notably unlike the hard sciences—physics, chemistry, microbiology, neurology, physiology, metallurgy, astronomy and so on—areas of study in which there is conceptual and practical continuity. In the humanities and soft human sciences—psychology, sociology, philosophy, history, and so on—there is no such continuity, or so little or so short-lived that insights and findings disappear, remembered only as passing moments in the ongoing stream of human thought. In effect, there are no truths in the annals of the humanities and soft human sciences as in the annals of the hard sciences, or at least nothing recognized as truths. For example, there is nothing equivalent to the law of gravity or to factual knowledge of the circulation of the blood. In the hard sciences, one generation not only learns from another but builds upon that learning, weeding out what is not empirically sustainable and building on what is; in the humanities and soft human sciences, there is no such learning, weeding, and building. Studies in the humanities and soft human sciences tend toward fads—fads such as cultural relativism, behavior modification, critical theory, positivism, and postmodernism. This is not to say there are not fads in the hard sciences—fads in the sense of proposing near absolute answers in the way, for example, that some strands of present-day neuroscience do by segmenting *the brain* into functional modules. All fads aside, when it comes to studying themselves in humanistic and soft human scientific terms and learning from such study, learning in the sense of applying the findings of empirically and phenomenologically carried out investigations, humans seem at a loss. Whatever the findings, life commonly proceeds in its habitual ways; fundamental changes in practice or thought are hardly initiated much less sustained. In effect, neither the human obsession with power nor the human disposition to obliterate the stranger is brought into the light, confronted straightforwardly, and questioned. However noxious, nefarious, or barbarous, age-old patterns of thinking and behaving remain as entrenched as ever.

Yet surely it is time that "great and monstrous crimes" were tracked down to their psychic motivations, that conceptual and practical continuities began to emerge in the humanities and soft human sciences, and in particular, that the disposition to gloat on power and the dispositional fervor to kill were brought out from their dark corners within the human psyche. Jung's insights into "the undiscovered self" provide solid grounds for embarking on this challenging task. His conception of the shadow in human affairs might even be formulated as the human law of psychic gravity, or better, the human law of psychic anti-gravity: "do not dive into the depths to search the murky psychic waters that constitute your shadow; better to project its contents unwittingly onto others." In essence, the law constitutes an injunction against self-knowledge. The socio-political consequences of obeying the law, of perpetuating self-ignorance and self-deception, are deftly spelled out in the tenth volume of Jung's collected works, a volume containing essays written or presented in lecture form between 1918 and 1959, a period spanning the First and Second World Wars. The title of the volume, *Civilization in Transition*, readily signals a comprehensive vision of humanity as being at a critical crossroad and of having the possibility of moving toward self-knowledge and an enlightened humanity. The essays are described on the inside jacket cover as being concerned with "the contemporary scene and, in particular, [with] the relation of the individual to society," but a fitting epigraph of the book might well read, in Jung's own words, that "for man to regard himself 'harmless' is to add 'stupidity to iniquity'" (Jung 1970, p. 296).

Jung indeed emphasizes over and over the need for self-knowledge in the very real terms of an examination of the psyche in full: not just its conscious contents but its latent feelings and dispositions that lie hidden away in the unconscious, whether repressed or whether forgotten remnants of the past. He terms such feelings and dispositions "incompatible contents" —contents that are not simply incompatible with social behaviour, with law and morality but incompatible with the individual's notion of him or herself, that is, with the conscious contents that *to his or her mind* make up the whole of his or her life. Clearly, "incompatible contents" echo just the kinds of ignorance Socrates and Plato identified in their conversations with fellow citizens and foreigners more than 2,000 years ago. That the echo spans 2,000 and more years surely testifies to the fact that self-ignorance and self-deception are not the idiosyncratic tendency and practice of just a few individuals scattered across human history but are rooted in the empirical realities of human nature. Moreover self-ignorant and self-deceptive people do not simply disown disagreeable aspects of themselves. They do indeed project those aspects onto others: it is others who are contemptible, poor, lazy, dishonest, frivolous, aggressive, stupid, and so on.

Avoidance of the shadow is a xenophobic avoidance: the shadow is the instantiation of the stranger *within*. It is odd that, in his identification and analyses of archetypes, Jung did not single out the stranger as an archetypal figure, that is, a figure that, whether within or without, is formally symbolic of a certain kind of person or situation, namely, one that is basically feared or threatening. Indeed, the archetype of the stranger *without* is fundamentally lodged not only in the human psyche but phylogenetically in the nonhuman animal psyche; human and nonhuman animals alike are basically wary of strangers, a wariness explained or explainable in evolutionary terms as adaptive. While gradations of xenophobia exist across the animal kingdom and while both human and nonhuman animals can display an openness toward strangers, a basic apprehension and closure is nevertheless commonly evident, and not only toward those who are unfamiliar, but those who are unlike oneself. Chimpanzees keep their distance from a conspecific whose behavior changes, who now moves about strangely because afflicted with polio, for example (Goodall 1971, pp. 221–2). Human apprehension and distancing has a much wider compass, commonly centering on a dissimilarity in language, skin color, and beliefs, as well as behaviors, and so on. The psychoanalytic stranger—the stranger *within*—elicits similar feelings and behavior: apprehension and distancing are indeed themselves archetypal responses to the archetypal stranger. In addition to apprehension and distancing, however, the stranger within elicits a further reactive response; one not only fears and distances oneself from the psychoanalytic stranger but turns a blind eye and deaf ear to any resemblance to the stranger within. As noted earlier, being opinionated, rapacious, dishonest, and unreasonable are characteristic of others, not oneself. The stranger within is indeed, precisely as Jung observes, "the 'other' whom [... one is] always seeking to exclude from [one's] life."

The problem is that self-ignorant, self-deceptive people are not self-contained modules of stupidity; they jeopardize the very society of which they are a part, and, by extension, the wider world in which their society exists and with which it interacts. Human history substantiates this claim: nations are xenophobic and reactively projective in just the way that individuals are. Though not mentioning xenophobia or projection outright, the noted British writer Julian Barnes, for example, in highlighting the historically distrustful relationship between England and France, writes that "the fundamental character traits each nation deplores in the other are the same: arrogance, cruelty, and a desire for dominance; selfishness, duplicity, hypocrisy; cowardice and betrayal." He asks: "Are these authentically observed defects, or merely a reflection of the viewing country's own faults? Or both at the same time? And are they specifically Anglo-French, or does the catalogue apply to any striving nation-state?" (Barnes 2007, p. 6). Without speaking of a lack of self-knowledge, he elaborates further on the Anglo-French relationship, remarking that "each supposed fact and understanding about our conjoined cross-Channel history has an equal and opposite counter-fact and counter-understanding" (ibid.). "Both sides," he says, "are monocular when it comes to joint history. Each celebrates its victories and ignores its defeats [...] unless that defeat—like Dunkirk or Waterloo—has something in it which can supply a sustaining myth" (ibid.).

The sustaining myths nations tell themselves—in contemporary times, the sustaining myth that "progress is being made," for instance, or that "this nation does not engage in torture"—are an amplified version of the sustaining myths individuals tell themselves and obviously emanate from those myths. Because the myths can reverberate with deadly ferocity, self-knowledge is crucial and the self-knowledge of each individual is crucial. Passages in Jung's essays bring this relationship to the fore vividly and with an unflinching eye. In the Terry Lectures given at Yale University in 1937, he exclaimed:

> Look at all the incredible savagery going on in our so-called civilized world: it all comes from human beings and their mental condition! Look at the devilish engines of destruction! They are invented by completely

innocuous gentlemen, reasonable, respectable citizens who are every-thing we could wish. And when the whole thing blows up and an indescribable hell of devastation is let loose, nobody seems to be responsible. It simply happens, and yet it is all man-made. But since everybody is blindly convinced that he is nothing more than his own extremely unassuming and insignificant conscious self, which performs its duties decently and earns a moderate living, nobody is aware that this whole rationalistically organized conglomeration we call a state of a nation is driven on by a seemingly impersonal but terrifying power which nobody and nothing can check. (Jung 1970, pp. 231–2)

It is notable that Hannah Arendt's 1977 characterization of Adolph Eichmann in terms of "the banality of evil" accords perfectly with Jung's more general 1937 characterization of people: "everybody is blindly con-vinced that he is nothing more than his own extremely unassuming and insignificant conscious self, which performs its duties decently and earns a modest living." Indeed, though Jung was speaking implicitly of Germans, it was not just Germans who were "blindly convinced" but Nazi collabora-tors resembling in some respect Maurice Papon, for instance. In its obituary of Papon of 24 February 2007, *The Economist* begins by noting (p. 99) that, "Among the ranks of the French civil service, it would be hard to find a more perfect example [of rectitude. ... He carried out] instructions ... to the letter and correct form was followed. *Un fonctionnaire*, as the tag went, *est fait pour fonctionner*: the purpose of a bureaucrat is simply to do his job." The obituary ends in fact by emphasizing the role of *un fonctionnaire*: "In court, assured as ever, [Papon] played the scapegoat. He felt no remorse, had no regrets. He had done his job."

The self-opacity of the "blindly convinced" is reminiscent of the vapid-ness of Heidegger's "*they*" the "everybodys" who fail to live authentically, who are cowards to confront their own fears, in particular, the fear of their own death, and are instead consumed in "idle talk" (Heidegger 1962). The Jungian-Heideggerian kinship is actually ironic in light of Heidegger's support of, and allegiance to, the Nazis, for Heidegger's *they* are precisely those who can and do follow orders unquestioningly to kill others; *they* are simply "performing their duties decently", doing their job. The self-opacity of the "blindly convinced" and of the *they* may also be linked directly to the motivations of those who take pleasure in the high excitement and bravado of killing others, who thrive on manly competition. Darwin rightly identi-fied male–male competition as "the law of battle," an evolutionary fact of male life. He described what we might call enactments of the law in 12 chapters, upwards of 460 pages, detailing the competitive behavior of males in species across the animal kingdom. What hardly needs saying is that the law has been culturally elaborated in infinitely barbarous and violent ways by humans, notably male humans. What in a phylogenetic sense began as male–male competition in the service of mating has mushroomed into an ever larger cloud that threatens to efface not just humanity, as noted earlier, but the 99 million other species inhabiting this planet and the planet itself. Male–male competition is in fact an overlooked and indeed ignored topic of study (for more on this issue, see Sheets-Johnstone 2003, 2008). Its neglect in terms of human history and our present barbarously violent world is indeed astounding. *Real* male–male competition is nowhere on the academic map, let alone on laymen's or politician's lips even though its real-life presence is all about us. It will not do to distract our attention with studies of sperm competition (Birkhead 2000; Birkhead and Moller 1998; Parker 1998; Simmons 2001). Sperm are, after all, rightly doing their job in a quite laudable biological sense, a sense totally unlike the savagery to which *real* male–male competition is devoted and for which it is culturally honed. Neither should we be distracted by discourses on aggression. Aggression is a cultural euphemism for the essentially biological phenomenon of male–male competition, something akin to *les préciosités* in earlier French literature where authors, rather than speaking of teeth, for example, spoke of "the furniture of the mouth." Aggression deflects our attention from the basic evolutionary phenomenon in just such ways. Indeed, those humans who are "blindly convinced" that they are just doing their job include those whose motivation lies in the pleasure of killing others, in the sheer excitement and bravado of war. To reverse Jung's words, they are adding iniquity to stupidity. If the present scientific surge toward reductionism were really a credible pursuit, then surely the most significant study a geneticist could pursue would be a search for the gene that drives male–male competition and expresses itself culturally in war. If the idea sounds ludicrous, consider the following report concerning the role of hormones in the service of cooperation and trust.

Following up her summation of primatologist Robert Sussman's book *Man the Hunted* in her extended *Newsweek* article titled "Beyond Stones and Bones," science writer Sharon Begley states that "Being hunted brought evolutionary pressure on our ancestors to cooperate and live in cohesive groups." She then states that "more than aggression and warfare," coopera-tion and living in cohesive groups "is our evolutionary legacy" (Begley 2007, p. 56). Subsequent to this sweepingly bald statement, she goes on to affirm that "Both genetics and paleoneurology back [up] that [evolution-ary] legacy [of cooperation and living in cohesive groups]. A hormone called oxytocin, best-known for inducing labour and lactation in women, also operates in the brain (of both sexes). There, it promotes trust during interactions with other people, and thus the cooperative behaviour that lets groups of people live together for the common good" (Begley 2007, pp. 56–7). If such a claim were true, why is not the hormone oxytocin made avail-able and clinically administered worldwide? To affirm that a hormone promotes trust is in reality an outlandish and irresponsible claim, let alone piece of journalism. Were it plausible, it follows that if a hormone can promote cooperation and trust, then surely a hormone can promote male–male competition and war. Again, if this were so, then surely the hormonal treatment of male–male competition in the cultural service of war should receive immediate medical attention and be treated accordingly.

In sum, nothing can compete with self-knowledge. But clearly, nothing either can compete with the challenge of attaining self-knowledge. Ignoring the challenge, however, comes at a socio-political-ecological price. Mass-minded man is a menace precisely because of his ignorance. He has never looked within. He has never made the effort to know himself as he truly his. His "conceit of wisdom" protects him from exploring "the goods of his mind," which, if exposed to the light, would show him to be at times unfair, hypocritical, fearful, stubborn, vindictive, deceptive, haughty, full of vengeance, and more. Mass-minded man produces what Jung terms "psychic epidemics" (Jung 1970), a term that exquisitely captures the real-life affective import and social infectiousness of mass political movements. The following quotations from Jung are eloquent testimonials to the insights and truths that a soft human science can offer, insights and truths that surely stand as beacons of light from the past that illuminate the present.

In 1916, Jung described the First World War in a way uncannily descriptive of America's action in Iraq and in its present "war on terror." He began by asking, "Is the present war supposed to be a war of economics?" And answered "That is a neutral American business-like standpoint, that does not take the blood, tears, unprecedented deeds of infamy and great distress into account, and which completely ignores the fact that this war is really an epidemic of madness" (ibid., p. 233). In 1932, lecturing in Vienna, he stated, "To a quite terrifying degree we are threatened by wars and revolutions which are nothing other than psychic epidemics. At any moment several millions of human beings may be smitten with a new madness, and then we shall have another world war or devastating revolution. Instead of being at the mercy of wild beasts, earthquakes, landslides, and inundations, modern man is battered by the elemental forces of his own psyche" (ibid., p. 235). In 1933, lecturing in Cologne and Essen, he observed that

> The collective man threatens to stifle the individual man, on whose sense of responsibility everything valuable in mankind ultimately depends [...] So-called leaders are the inevitable symptoms of a mass movement. The true leaders of mankind are always those who are capable of self-reflection [...] Small and hidden is the door that leads inward, and the entrance is barred by countless prejudices, mistaken assumptions, and fears. Always one wishes to hear of grand political

and economic schemes, the very things that have landed every nation in a morass [...] But I speak not to nations, only to the individual few, for whom it goes without saying that cultural values do not drop down like manna from heaven, but are created by the hands of individuals. If things go wrong in the world, this is because something is wrong with the individual, because something is wrong with me. Therefore, if I am sensible, I shall put myself right first. For this I need [...] a knowledge of the innermost foundations of my being. (ibid., p. 230)

In these challenging and overwhelmingly militaristic and technology-driven times in which we live, we would do well to consider the age-old dictum and the age-old practices of maieutics and meditation and to consider as well the virtues of—dare I mention the word?—introspection and, further still, the phenomenological virtue of making the familiar strange. In a word, paths toward self-knowledge exist. In these challenging and overwhelmingly militaristic and technology-driven times in which we live, we would do well to consider too the events that others before us lived through and the insights they gained through their experiences and reflections. Given the vaunted intelligence of humans, is it not stupid of us *not* to learn from their insights, their practices, their experiences, their reflections? Why indeed not be—as eighteenth-century British philosopher George Berkeley would say (Berkeley 1709/1929, p. 85, see also pp. 72-3)— "at the pains of a little thought" about what history can teach us? Why indeed not see how the power-driven destructive side of human history repeats itself over and over, only with more and more sophisticated technologies whose sole aim is to kill other humans and to destroy their way of life. Rather than genuflecting to militaristic and technological traditions and to passing fads, in effect rather than repeating history, we would do well to consider the history of psychic epidemics produced by mass-minded man and acknowledge that the present one in which we live is of such proportions never reached before, that the time is short, that there is no quick fix. There is only the necessity of an ongoing dedication to the pursuit of self-knowledge such that the conceit of wisdom coupled with power and strength is vanquished, that those so afflicted with ignorance no longer flourish, going forth and multiplying as they do today, that *Homo sapiens sapiens* finally redeems itself and lives up to its own billing, that it is no longer the dangerous species that endangers all others and the Earth itself. Surely we need a worldwide educational system that encourages and even inculcates the courage to look within.

"Our modern education is morbidly one-sided," Jung remarked. He went on to say,

No doubt we are right to open the eyes and ears of our young people to the wide world, but it is the maddest of delusions to think that this really equips them for the task of living. It is the kind of training that enables a young person to adapt himself outwardly to the world and reality, but no one gives a thought to the necessity of adapting to the self, to the powers of the psyche, which are far mightier than all the Great Powers of the earth. (Jung 1970, p. 153)

"[…] than all the Great Powers of the earth." Is this a hyperbolic claim? If we look with courageous honesty at the simmering anger of the oppressed, at the unadulterated violence of the powerful and the ambitiously powerful, at the all-engulfing fear that saturates so many people's lives, at the relentless desire for excitement and bravado that saturates so many *other* people's lives, at the unquenchable thirst for vengeance that, culturally inculcated, lasts for centuries, then the Great Powers of the psyche that drive people to power and to fight and to kill can hardly be denied. Surely, then, we need an educational system in which self-knowledge figures prominently, in which children and young people learn about the disposition of humans to project their own shortcomings, their own foibles, their own stupidities, their own harmful practices onto others — an education system in which the concern is to see human nature as it truly is. If it is true that "[n]o one who does not know himself can know others" and that "in each of us there is another whom we do not know" (Jung 1970, p. 153), then surely we should ask: do we each of us have the courage to open ourselves to "the goods of the mind," to be sensible and "put myself right first," to rise to the challenge of knowing ourselves as we truly are?

References

Arendt, H. (1977) *Eichmann in Jerusalem: A Report on the Banality of Evil*, New York: Penguin Books.

Barnes, J. (2007) The odd couple, *New York Review of Books*, 54 (5), pp. 4–9.

Begley, S. (2007) Beyond stones and bones, *Newsweek*, (19 March), pp. 53–58.

Berkeley, G. (1709/1929) An essay toward a new theory of vision, in Calkins, M.W. (ed.) *Berkeley Selections*, New York: Charles Scribner's Sons.

Bhikkhu Bodhi (1995) Introduction, in Bhikkhu Bodhi (ed.) *The Middle Length Discourses of the Buddha*, pp. 19–60, Boston, MA: Wisdom Publications.

Birkhead, T.R. (2000) *Promiscuity: An Evolutionary History of Sperm Competition*, Cambridge, MA: Harvard University Press.

Birkhead, T.R. & Moller, A.P. (1998) *Sperm Competition and Sexual Selection*, San Diego, CA: Academic Press.

Goldstein, J. (undated) *The Nature of Mind*, (undated cassette tape), Wendall Depot, MA: Dharma Seed Archival Center.

Goodall, J. (1971) *In the Shadow of Man*, New York: Dell Publishing/Delta Books.

Heidegger, M. (1962) *Being and Time*, New York: Harper & Row.

Jung, C.G. (1970) *Civilization in Transition, 2nd edn. Collected Works Vol. 10*, Bollingen Series XX, Princeton, NJ: Princeton University Press.

Jung, C.G. (1983) *Alchemical Studies, Collected Works, Vol. 13,* Bollingen series XX, Princeton, NJ: Princeton University Press.

Nhât Hanh, T. (1985) *A Guide to Walking Meditation,* Nyack, NY: Fellowship Publications.

Parker, G. (1998) Sperm competition and the evolution of ejaculates: Towards a theory base, in Birkhead, T.R. & Moller, A.P. (eds.) *Sperm Competition and Sexual Selection,* San Diego, CA: Academic Press.

Sheets-Johnstone, M. (2003) Real male–male competition, Keynote address, *Society for Women in Philosophy, Pacific Division,* University of Oregon.

Sheets-Johnstone, M. (2008) *The Roots of Morality,* University Park, PA: Pennsylvania State University Press.

Simmons, L.W. (2001) *Sperm Competition and Its Evolutionary Consequences in the Insects,* Princeton, NJ: Princeton University Press.

Zeitlin, I.M. (1993) *Plato's Vision: The Classical Origins of Social and Political Thought,* Englewood Cliffs, NJ: Prentice Hall.

Chapter VIII

On the Elusive Nature of the Human Self
Divining the Ontological Dynamics of Animate Being[1]

I. Introduction

Notable methodological and experiential similarities exist between Husserl's phenomenology and vipassana (Buddhist) meditation[2] that have sizeable import in themselves and sizeable import for divining the nature of the self, divining not in the sense of prophesying or conjecturing—or of endowing with a divine spirit—but in the sense of experiencing outside the natural attitude, hence in the methodologically nuanced sense of following along lines of the "supernatural." Divining rods are thus in this instance empirically proven rods, i.e. bona fide methodologies. Methodological and experiential similarities between a Western philosophy and an Eastern

---

1   First published in *Interdisciplinary Perspectives on Personhood*, ed. Wentzel van Huyssteen and Erik P. Wiebe (2011), Grand Rapids, MI: William B. Eerdmans Publishing: 198–219.

2   Vipassana (insight) is the oldest form of Theravāda Buddhism, "the Buddhist heart of the Theravāda meditational discipline" (King 1992, p. 82). Bhikkhu Bodhi points out in his introduction to *The Middle Length Discourses of the Buddha* that "[i]n the Buddha's system of mental training the role of serenity [samatha] is subordinated to that of insight because the latter is the crucial instrument needed to uproot the ignorance at the bottom of samsāric bondage" (Bhikkhu Bodhi 1995, p. 38). King echoes this placement of vipassana when he observes that "it is implied in sacred scripture that vipassanā alone *could* be a discipline sufficient for salvation." He suggests further that "a kind of consensus exists that the modern age and modern people are best suited to vipassanā as an independent spiritual technique for achieving enlightenment, largely bypassing jhānic-style practice" (King 1992, p. 116), i.e. bypassing yogic practices, and cultivating "bare insight" alone.

practice indeed provide mutually validating evidence of a consciousness beyond the natural attitude—a "supernatural" consciousness. The mutually validating evidence might well intensify present-day interests of scientists in phenomenology and correlatively motivate them to study meditational practices to the point they approach the study of these areas of experience with the same vigor and zeal they study deficits such as blindsight, for example, and conditioned "motor" responses such as eye-blinking. The mutually validating evidence would in fact ordinarily count as experimental replication, cross-cultural replication at that, of a scientifically arrived-at ontological truth about humans, a fact testifying to the importance of understanding consciousness or mind from what we might call the cultivated end of the cognitional spectrum. Such under-standing ultimately involves not merely an acknowledgement but an illumination of "the subjective." With that illumination comes the possi-bility of insight into the nature of "the self." The self is not equated to con-sciousness but is understood in the context of the lived and living temporal dynamics of consciousness.

I begin with a general comparison of phenomenological and Buddhist understandings of mind and proceed from there to examine four features relative to phenomenological and vipassana practice: the reduction, the attentive onlooker, content, and the stream of experience. The general com-parison and the ensuing exposition of features are of course interrelated; they are considered separately only at an analytical level and for analytical purposes. Once the foundational reduction is achieved, each feature is in fact a methodological and experiential stage or stratum contingent on the previous one. The inherent interrelationships will become evident in the course of analysis and summary conclusion.

II. General Comparison:
Everything Comes from the Mind

In the beginning verse of *The Dhammapada*, the Buddha says, "All phenomena are preceded by the mind, issue forth from the mind, and con-sist of the mind" (Wallace 1999, p. 176, n. 1). He says something similar, but with a teleo-epistemological rather than ontological emphasis, in the *Ratnameghasutra*: "All phenomena are preceded by the mind. When the mind is comprehended, all phenomena are comprehended" (Wallace 1999, p. 176).[3] While subjective idealism might be read into the Buddha's sayings, it is rather a question of the active nature of the mind. In other words, the sayings are not statements of philosophical positions taken by the Buddha,

---

3   Multiple statements of the Buddha underscore the same observation: "Con-sciousness leads, rules, makes all modes of mind [...] By mind the world is led, by mind is drawn" (Bhadantacariya Buddhaghosa 1976, p. 91).

but conclusions drawn from and about meditative experience. In meditating, we can experience the nature of the mind and how it works by cultivating mindfulness, which means being mindful of bodily sensations; of feelings of pleasantness, unpleasantness, or neutrality; of thoughts—as when we plan, judge, or remember, for example; of emotions—as when we feel joyful, fearful, or bored, for example; and of the continually changing nature of sensations, feelings, thoughts, and emotions. These "mental factors," as they are called, flow from the mind. They are phenomena that arise in the form of expectations, desires, aversions, memories, smells, sounds, preferences, pains, and so on. Through diligent meditational practice we come to experience the nature of the mind, and in and through this experience to understand how the mind shapes and colors experience, and in habitual ways. In brief, the nature of the mind is revealed and so also is the way in which habits of mind—reactive patterns, repeated thoughts, recurrent aversive feelings, and so on—determine experience, motivating us to certain preferences, acts, and so on.

The meditational journey thus has both epistemological and ontological dimensions. By practicing meditation, one develops and cultivates a capacity for mindfulness and gains insight into the ways in which one conditions one's own experiences. Practice is challenging precisely because the mind is by nature active; sensations, feelings, thoughts, emotions arise by themselves in an ongoing, ever-changing stream. Jack Kornfield, a Buddhist monk and teacher trained and ordained in Asia and a psychotherapist as well, captures the challenge of practice when he likens the mind to a puppy:

> [M]editation is very much like training a puppy. You put the puppy down and say, "Stay" Does the puppy listen? It gets up and it runs away. You sit the puppy back down again. "Stay." And the puppy runs away over and over again. Sometimes the puppy jumps up, runs over, and pees in the corner or makes some other mess. Our minds are much the same as the puppy, only they create even bigger messes. In training the mind, or the puppy, we have to start over and over again. (Kornfield 1993, p. 59)[4]

---

4   See also Goldstein & Kornfield (1987, p. 48). It should be noted that far from being popularized Western versions of Vipassana Buddhism, Western sources used in this essay are the work of Westerners trained and ordained as monks in Asia. Of the writings of Goldstein and Kornfield, the Dalai Lama wrote, "It is encouraging to find Westerners who have sufficiently assimilated traditions of the East to be able to share them with others" (in Goldstein & Kornfield 1987, unpaginated). He wrote a similarly praising foreword to Mark Epstein's first book, calling attention to his "twenty years experience in both Western psychotherapy and Buddhist meditation" (in Epstein 1995, p. x).

As progress comes in meditation, the nature of the mind and of everyday habits of mind become epistemologically revealing: "[W]e are able to go from the level of 'My back hurts,' which is a concept, to the level of what is really happening, which are certain sensations, arising and passing" (Goldstein & Kornfield 1987, p. 18). In this way, meditators "awaken" to the way things really are.[5]

"Mind" is a rarely used term in phenomenology where, if anything, it has a psycho-ontological rather than epistemological meaning (Husserl 1980, p. 22). The comparable or correlative term in phenomenology is "consciousness," in some instances, "psyche" or "subjectivity" and in a special sense, "transcendental ego" or "transcendental subjectivity." To facilitate comparison, but also in light of the close resemblance in meaning between the phenomenological term(s) and the term "mind" as used in Buddhist texts, "mind" will be used in what follows.

In *The Crisis of European Sciences*, Husserl makes several statements that underscore the fact that everything comes from the mind. He remarks, for example, that "during the consistently carried-out epoché, it [the world] is under our gaze purely as the correlate of the subjectivity which gives it ontic meaning, through whose validities the world 'is' at all" (Husserl 1970, p. 152). In *Cartesian Meditations*, he states that "this world, with all its Objects, [...] derives its whole sense and its existential status, which it has for me, from me myself, *from me as the transcendental Ego*" (Husserl 1973a, p. 26). "Mind" is not named as such, but it is clearly at the core of the phenomenological theme of constitution. There is furthermore in *Cartesian Meditations* a remarkable passage that repeats in phenomenological terms the initial statement made by the Buddha in the two passages quoted above, namely, that everything not only comes from the mind but that "[a]ll phenomena are preceded by the mind." The passage occurs in the context of Husserl's explaining the nature of bracketing and its effect, that is, the "'putting out of play' of all positions taken toward the already-given Objective world" and the consequent revelation of the ego alone as source of all meanings and validities (ibid., pp. 20–1). Husserl writes, "Thus the being of the pure ego and his *cogitationes*, as a being that is prior in itself, is antecedent to the natural being of the world — the world of which I always speak, the one of which I *can* speak" (ibid., p. 21). Husserl's "prior" like the Buddha's "preceding" is not a temporal-ontological priority but a logical-existential priority.[6]

---

5   To awaken to the way things really are is to follow the experiential path of the Buddha, whose name means "one who is awake."

6   A temporal, ontological priority might perhaps not be altogether excluded insofar as the transcendental ego is a universal form or "absolute" (see, e.g., Husserl 1989, pp. 420–1). Something similar might be said for Nibbāna (Sanskrit, Nirvāna), which at various places the Buddha links with that

The phenomenological journey is an epistemological one through and through. For example, in the context of explicating "the total transformation of attitude" of the phenomenologist, Husserl speaks of how horizons are in "constant motion," surrounding our everyday actions in the world and feeding into our constitution of the world:

> [T]he particular object of our active consciousness, and correlatively the active, conscious having of it, being directed toward it, and dealing with it—all this is forever surrounded by an atmosphere of mute, concealed, but cofunctioning validities, a *vital horizon* into which the active ego can also direct itself voluntarily, reactivating old acquisitions, consciously grasping new apperceptive ideas, transforming them into intuitions. Because of this constantly flowing *horizonal character*, then, straightforwardly performed validity in natural world-life always presupposes validities extending back, immediately or mediately, into a necessary subsoil of obscure but occasionally available reactivatable validities, all of which together, including the present acts, make up a single indivisible interrelated complex of life. (Husserl 1970, p. 149)

The phenomenologist's task is to uncover what is horizonally hidden as well as what has been taken for granted or assumed in "natural, normal life" (ibid.), i.e. everyday experience. Uncovering sedimentations of meaning and validities leads back to *origins*, thus to elucidations of the way in which meaning and value are constituted. Through the practice of phenomenology, an "*inner structure of meaning*" is revealed (Husserl 1970, "The Origin of Geometry", p. 371), and with it, "subjective origins" (Husserl 1973a, p. 49), i.e. understandings of consciousness and object, intending and sense, or, in other words, understandings of "mind." As we will see in progressively greater detail over the following four sections, the meditator's concern with *what*—what is actually present—is corollary to the phenomenologist's concern with *how*—how what is actually present comes to have the meaning and value it has.

III. The Reduction

The aim of reduction is different in phenomenology and vipassana meditational practice, but the act of reducing is comparable and the consequence of reduction is similar: quite simply, reduction reduces the everyday living world, allowing us to investigate it at bare minimum. In phenomenology,

---

which is not born and does not become or die. Bhikkhu Bodhi makes brief but pointed references to these passages when he discusses Nibbāna—e.g. "there is an unborn, unbecome, unmade, unconditioned, the existence of which makes possible 'escape from the born, become, made, and conditioned,'" or again, "[Nibbāna is] the unborn, unageing, unailing, deathless, sorrowless, undefiled supreme security from bondage" (Bodhi 1995, pp. 31–2).

the reduction literally reduces our customary attitude toward the world by suspending everyday beliefs and judgements (in strict phenomenological terms, by performing the *epoché*): we now take everything as a "mere phenomenon" (ibid., p. 20). In vipassana, the reduction reduces our customary bodily attitude toward the world: we sit still, we close our eyes. In notably different ways, but in both instances equally, *the reduction takes the individual out of the natural attitude.* The world is still present, but the meditator and the phenomenologist suspend or withdraw from their everyday ways of being in it: everyday ways of engaging it, everyday involvements with it, and most important, everyday ways of being present to it and knowing it. In each case, the initial act of reduction makes the familiar strange. The quest, in turn, is to make the strange familiar, i.e. to come to know the bare truths of experience.

In phenomenology, the act of reduction is effected by "bracketing": "[E]verything transcendent that is involved must be bracketed, or be assigned the index of indifference, of epistemological nullity, an index which indicates: the existence of all these transcendencies, whether I believe in them or not, is not here my concern; this is not the place to make judgments about them; they are entirely irrelevant" (Husserl 1973b, p. 31).

Though there is no mention of "bracketing" in vipassana, the practice institutes a comparable "index of indifference." It is effected by what Buddhist monk Achaan Chah describes as "taking the one seat," an act by which "[w]e create the compassionate space that allows for the arising of all things" (Kornfield 1993, p. 31). Quoting Achaan Chah (his teacher), Kornfield writes, "'You will see it all arise and pass, and out of this, wisdom and understanding will come'" (ibid.). By taking the one seat, as by bracketing, we come to see everything that we add to experience. Through meditative practice, we see what is actually present—how things really are[7]—and how we embellish what is actually present with concepts, habits of thought and feeling, judgements, and so on, in a way similar to the way in which, through phenomenological practice, we come to understand how the object *as meant* goes beyond the sensuously present object. In each instance, the reduction leads to deepened understandings of both what is actually present and how we go beyond what is actually present.

---

[7] In his Introduction to *The Middle Length Discourses of the Buddha*, Bhikkhu Bodhi writes, "The task of insight meditation is to sever our attachments by enabling us to pierce through [the] net of conceptual projections in order to see things as they really are" (Bodhi 1995, p. 40). The purpose of the task set by vipassana meditation—"to see things as they really are"—will surface thematically in many ways in the course of this chapter.

IV. The Attentive Onlooker

Noticing is at the core of vipassana meditational practice. Mindfulness is cultivated through the practice of attention. A description by Buddhaghosa, a monk who lived nearly a thousand years after the Buddha's death (c. 500 BC), vividly captures the rigor demanded by mindful attention:

> Now suppose a cowherd wanted to tame a wild calf that had been reared on a wild cow's milk, he would take it away from the cow and tie it up apart with a rope to a stout post dug into the ground [...] [S]o too, when a bhikkhu [a monk] wants to tame his own mind which has long been spoilt by being reared on visible data, etc., as object [...] he should take it away from visible data, etc., [...] and bring it into the forest or to the root of a tree or to an empty place and tie it there to the post of in-breaths and out-breaths with the rope of mindfulness. (Bhadantacariya Buddhaghosa 1964, pp. 288–9; VIII.153)

A beginning meditator is instructed to concentrate on breathing, and in concentrating, to notice movement of the abdomen rising and falling, or the sensation of breath in and out at the nostrils, and to notice as well thoughts, feelings, a sense of pleasantness or unpleasantness, and so on, as these experiences arise in the course of concentrating on the breath. The meditator maybe surprised to find that neither concentration nor noticing comes easily. Concentration on breathing, a singular object, wavers and may disappear altogether many times in the course of a sitting; similarly, mindfulness of the flow of consciousness—the stream of sensations, thoughts, feelings, and so on—lapses: there are gaps in noticing all that arises and passes away. Some teachers of vipassana liken the disappearance of concentration and lapses in mindfulness to riding on a train. One boards a train; one notices where one gets on and the first changes in scenery; but then some time later, one finds oneself in totally different scenic surrounds and with not the slightest idea of how one arrived there or what one missed along the way. Not only has concentration of one's attention vanished but one has no idea at what point noticing disappeared. Thus Goldstein and Kornfield remark of beginning meditators: "At first in meditation our moments of awareness are far apart and we may only notice thoughts in the middle or even at their end, after many cars of the train have passed and we've taken a long ride" (Goldstein & Kornfield 1987, p. 55). In short, the mind wanders quite on its own, which is why it can be likened to a puppy that will not stay put.

There is no phenomenological equivalent to training the puppy, though there is certainly an apprenticeship necessary to dedicated phenomenological practice. The lack of an equivalent is due not to divergent conceptions of everyday mind (consciousness) in phenomenology and vipassana, but to the fact that the practice of phenomenology and the practice of vipassana meditation utilize different though not unrelated methodologies, and correlatively, have different though not unrelated ends. To put the point concisely, *turning toward* and *turning inward* are fundamentally different epistemological orientations and pursuits, but both entail a radical attitudinal shift that is not altogether unique in its results. A transcendental attention characterizes phenomenological methodology; bare attention characterizes vipassana methodology. We will consider each in turn.

Phenomenological methodology involves what Husserl at one point terms "the splitting of the ego" (Husserl 1973a, p. 35):

> If the Ego, as naturally immersed in the world, experiencingly and otherwise, is called *"interested"* in the world, then the phenomenologically altered—and, as so altered, continually maintained—attitude consists in a *splitting of the Ego*: in that the phenomenological Ego establishes himself as *"disinterested onlooker"* above the naïvely interested Ego. That this takes place is then itself accessible by means of a new reflection, which, as transcendental, likewise demands the very same attitude of looking on "disinterestedly"—the Ego's sole remaining interest being to see and to describe adequately what he sees, purely as seen, as what is seen and seen in such and such a manner. (ibid.)

The "disinterested onlooker" is the "nonparticipating" reflective ego (ibid., pp. 34-5), the phenomenological ego who takes what is seen, for example, "purely as seen." Because in the phenomenological attitude the ego abstains from predicating, valuing, believing, and so on, phenomenological reflection is attentively, and in turn, substantively different from natural reflection:

> In the *"natural reflection"* of everyday life [...] we stand on the footing of the world already given as existing—as when, in everyday life, we assert: "I see a house there" or "I remember having heard this melody." In *transcendental-phenomenological reflection* we deliver ourselves from this footing, by universal epoché with respect to the being or nonbeing of the world. The experience as thus modified, the *transcendental experience*, consists then, we can say, in our *looking at* and describing the particular transcendentally reduced *cogito*, but without participating, as reflective subjects, in the natural existence positing that the originally straightforward perception [...] contains or that the Ego, as immersing himself straightforwardly in the world, actually executed. (ibid., p. 34)

Reflection in both the natural and transcendental attitude makes possible "an experiential knowing" (ibid.), but a knowing that, as is evident, is radically different in the two instances. Transcendental reflection discloses ongoing cognitional processes undergirding a subject's natural experiential knowing of the world, and indeed, his or her experiential having of such a world in the first place. In effect, the transcendental *epoché* opens up con*stitutional* dimensions of natural experience: horizons of meaning, unifications, sedimentations, and syntheses that are the formative backbone of everyday experience. As Husserl remarks, "[a]s an Ego in the natural attitude, I am likewise and at all times a transcendental Ego, but [...] I know about this only by executing phenomenological reduction" (ibid., p. 37). The transcendental ego is thus not a new arrival on the scene, but a discovered dimension of consciousness made possible by a radical shift in attitude. With the shift in attitude an attentive onlooker comes to the fore in a particular mode of reflection: the attentive onlooker looks at natural everyday experience through the prism of transcendental subjectivity: *constituting consciousness*.

Now in phenomenology, the attentive onlooker is consistently described as *above* the flow of everyday experience:[8] "[D]uring the consistently carried-out epoché, it [the world] is *under* our gaze purely as the correlate of the subjectivity which gives it ontic meaning" (Husserl 1970, p. 152); "[T]hrough the epoché a new way of experiencing, of thinking, of theorizing, is opened to the philosopher; here, situated *above* his own natural being and *above* the natural world, he loses nothing of their being and their objective truths and likewise nothing at all of the spiritual acquisitions of his world-life or those of the historical communal life" (ibid.; italics in original); "Our epoché [...] denied us all natural world-life and its worldly interests. It gave us a position *above* these" (ibid., p. 175; italics added); "This is not a 'view', an 'interpretation' bestowed upon the world. Every view about [...], every opinion about 'the' world has its ground in the pregiven world. It is from this very ground that I have freed myself through the epoché. I stand *above* the world, which has now become for me, in a quite peculiar sense, a *phenomenon*" (ibid., p. 152; italics in original).

In contrast to the phenomenologist's position as *above* the flow of everyday consciousness, the attentive meditative onlooker notices—one might even aptly say *listens to*—the flow of experience just as it happens, taking it all in just as it is, without interfering with it. The attentive meditative onlooker is in this sense *alongside* experience rather than looking on it from above. This *alongside presence* specifies a capacity to be with what is scary, for instance, and to be attentively present to the experience, however long it might last, as Kornfield's experience attests:

> When I was a young monk I traveled with my teacher Achaan Chah to a branch monastery on the Cambodian border eighty miles away from our main temple. We were offered a ride in a rickety old Toyota with doors that didn't close fully. Our village driver was really speeding that day, recklessly passing water buffalo, buses, bicycles, and cars alike around blind curves on a mountainous dirt road. As this continued I felt

---

[8]   A *transcendental* shift is, etymologically, a shift that basically involves *climbing* (from Latin *transcendere*; *trans*, "across, over", *scandere*, "to climb").

sure I would die that day, so for the whole time I gripped the seat-back and silently prepared myself. I followed my breath and recited my monks' prayers. At one point I looked over and saw my teacher's hands were also white from gripping the seat. This reassured me somehow, even though I also believed him to be quite unafraid of dying. When we finally arrived safely, he laughed and said simply, "Scary, wasn't it?" In that moment he named the demon and helped me make friends with it. (Kornfield 1993, p. 92)

Other passages in vipassana texts are similarly instructive. Consider the following meditational instructions, for example:

Pain is a good object of meditation. When there's a strong pain in the body, the concentration becomes strong. The mind stays on it easily, without wandering very much. Whenever sensations in the body are predominant make them objects of meditation. When they are no longer predominant, return to the breath. The awareness should be rhythmic, not jumping or clutching at objects, just watching "rising-falling," "pain," "itching," "heat," "cold," "rising-falling." When you find yourself tensing because of pain, carefully examine the quality of unpleasantness, the quality of painfulness. Become mindful of that feeling. (Goldstein 1976, p. 18)

The term "bare attention" — a Burmese phrase used to describe the practice of noticing "the arrival and departure of all self-activities from the grossest physical motion to the most subtle emotional nuance or half-thought" (King 1992, p. 72) — captures the alongside attitude of the attentive onlooker:

Bare Attention is a clear and single-minded awareness of what actually happens *to* us and *in* us, at the successive moments of perception. It is called "bare", because it attends just to the bare facts of a perception [...] [It is] a bare registering of the facts, without reacting to them by deed, speech, or by mental comment which may be one of self-reference (like, dislike, etc.), judgment or reflection. (Thera 1969, p. 30)

Bare attention means observing things as they are, without choosing, without comparing, without evaluating, without laying our projections and expectations onto what is happening; cultivating instead a choice-less and non-interfering awareness. (Goldstein 1976, p. 20)

In sum, the attentive onlooker in vipassana focuses on what is present, examining it closely, monitoring its changes, watching it heighten or fade, and finally vanish. What comes with this practice is an "opening of what is closed," a "balancing of what is reactive", and an "exploration of what is hidden" (Goldstein & Kornfield 1987, p. 15–24). By hewing to direct experience, by staying present to what is present and only what is present, one discovers flowing subjective processes — sensations, cravings, aversions, judgings, restlessness, contentment, and so on. Staying present requires being mindful, and cultivating mindfulness requires an attentive onlooker who is at the same time both inside and alongside experiences of everyday life, who is thereby attentive to his or her own subjective processes as they unfold in the course of experience, and who is thus able to open to pain, for example, and to examine it instead of immediately or simply reacting to it. In just this sense, the attentive onlooker in vipassana observes *alongside* rather than looks down from above. We see this attitude from an intensified inward perspective in a description of meditation on "the dynamic body-self", the end phrase of which was quoted above:

> [T]he meditative center of attention proceeds ever more inward until the feeler and thinker contemplates his own feeling and thinking processes, catching them on the wing, as it were. The general picture of the meditator in this type of meditation is that of a person sitting slightly aside from "himself" in all his activities, physical and mental, and coolly, detachedly watching them go on, as though completely outside himself in another person. Sometimes with respect to breaths, the illustration used is that of a city watchman who counts the carts, cattle, chariots, and people of all sorts going in and out of the city gate. The same observational attitude can be extended to thoughts and emotions as well as breaths. Thus, with the detachment of a watchman, the meditator just registers the arrival and departure of all self-activities from the grossest physical motion to the most subtle emotional nuance or half-thought. (King 1992, p. 71)

The positional difference between the attentive onlooker in phenomenology and in vipassana meditation corresponds to a difference in methodologies. What is accomplished by an active suspension of beliefs and judgements in phenomenology is accomplished in vipassana by an active attention to the bare facts of experience. The attentive onlooker's aim, however, is in each case fundamentally the same: *to be true to the truths of experience.* Through bare attention, the meditator comes to know what is present as it is and for as long as it is. Attention may come and go in the process of meditating, but what is being cultivated is the ability "to see things as they truly are" (King 1992, p. 92). Husserl's call "to the things themselves" echoes this aim. Husserl would indeed have no quarrel with "Bare Attention":

> After the practice of Bare Attention has resulted in a certain width and depth of experience in its dealings with mental events, it will become an immediate certainty to the meditator that *mind is nothing beyond its cognizing function.* (Thera 1969, p. 38)[9]

---

[9] In this passage on Bare Attention, Thera is actually concerned with showing that no "I" is to be found in experience. The quoted passage continues as follows: "Nowhere, behind or within that [cognizing] function, can any individual agent or abiding entity be detected. By way of one's own direct experience, one will thus have arrived at the great truth of No-soul or

V. Content

However different their positional attitudes and methodologies, both phenomenologist and vipassana meditator are disinterested spectators of experience and are thus uninvolved in the actual content of experience — what will henceforth be designated *content as such*. In seeing a house, for example, the phenomenologist is not concerned with whether its address is visible, whether it has a good foundation, or whether its color has faded. The phenomenologist's concern is only with the perception of the house, how this particular thing seen — this object of visual perception — is recognized as a house, with all the judgements, memories, and values that recognition entails. In effect, to elucidate the intentional structure of "seeing a house" is to be uninvolved with the house in any everyday sense — as something to buy, something to admire, or something that one regularly passes on the way home. The phenomenologist's attention is directed toward *constitution* — toward the "how" of experience, as in *how* we come to see a house.

In vipassana meditation, there is equally a lack of concern with content *as such* and an attention instead to the processes of mind ongoing in experience. The meditator's attention is directed not toward understanding how things come to have the meaning and value they do, but toward something closely related: how things "truly are," and by contrast, how we embellish experience with habitual judgements, reactive feelings, future plans, and so on. The content of experience — being anxious about being caught in a traffic jam, for example — becomes grist for the meditator's mill; the meditator notices simply what is there, without getting caught up in the feelings, thoughts, and situation *as such*, that is, without allowing the feelings, thoughts, and situation to spill over and, in effect, take over the experience of what is actually present. Thus, the meditator may simply feel sensations of heat and a tightness in the chest, for example, to name two among many possible bodily sensations he or she might feel. In noticing only what is present, the meditator may softly label or name it — for example, with respect to sensations, heat, "heat"; tightness, "tightness"; with respect to thoughts, trapped, "trapped"; hours, "hours"; with respect to feelings, anxious, "anxious"; worry, "worry"; with respect to perceptions, cars, "cars"; noise, "noise"; and so on, following the mind wherever it goes, or until, as Goldstein suggests with respect to mindfulness of pain, "the mind

---

Impersonality [...], showing that all existence is void of an abiding personality (self, soul, over-self, etc.) or an abiding substance of any description" (p. 38). This culminating truth of Vipassana Buddhism — the realization of no-self — is different from, but not incompatible with, Husserl's phenomenological understandings of transcendental consciousness, even as seemingly personified in and by a transcendental Ego.

[...] naturally come[s] to a state of balance" (Goldstein 1976, p. 18). In effect, the meditator notices an unfolding process of sensations, thoughts, and feelings as they come and go, arise and disappear. Goldstein and Kornfield at one point briefly characterize nonattention to content *as such* as an uninvolvement with *story*. They remark, "You can actually observe the thought process with mindfulness, noticing the arising of thought without getting lost in each story. It is a powerful and freeing realization to see that you are not your thoughts, to observe the stream of inner thought and be aware of it without being identified and caught up in it" (Goldstein & Kornfield 1987, p. 58).

One might say that, rather than being carried along by the content of experience, one follows *the form* of experience in both vipassana meditation and phenomenology. Formal tethering is most clearly exemplified in phenomenology by Husserl's elucidation of the constitutive structures of meaning, the formal elements giving rise to experience and making experience possible. Foremost among these formal structures are internal time consciousness with its protentions (experienced as expectations) and retentions (experienced as recollections), unifying syntheses that draw on both passive synthesis and sedimentations of past experience, and horizons or surrounding spheres of meaning that enter experience as complex synchronic and diachronic fields of awareness. All of these formal structures of mind contribute to and condition habitual modes of cognition. "[T]endencies of consciousness" that translate into "doxic" habits are present in habitual modes of feeling and moving as well (Husserl 1989, pp. 268–9); "unnoticed, 'hidden' motivations, which are to be found in habit, in the events of the stream of consciousness" (ibid., pp. 235–6), are part and parcel of all facets of experience. In the practice of phenomenology, the *form* of experience takes precedence over the content *as such*, content that would otherwise impel one to do certain things, for example, or to react in certain ways. In the practice of phenomenology too, one is caught up not in *a story*—whether a story told by thoughts, judgements, feelings, memories, or whatever—but in the process of "meaning-bestowing" of constitution.

A similar formal concern structures vipassana meditation but to a different end. The aim here is not to elucidate *how* experience is constituted, but to awaken to the elemental realities of everyday experience. When we experience things as they really are, we awaken to what is actually present but, as noted, we also awaken to the many ways in which we embellish the present with plans, memories, worries, and desires. In this sense, we might say that we catch ourselves in acts of meaning-bestowing, "meaning bestowings" we see through because we have left content *as such* behind. But in this sense, we might also say that we experience content at *its* level, i.e. simply as a *phenomenon*. Kornfield exemplifies the phenomenal character of content in his instructions on noticing the breath, though he does not label the experience in this way:

> [A]wareness of breathing does not come right away. At first we must sit quietly, letting our body be relaxed and alert, and simply practice finding the breath in the body. Where do we actually feel it—as a coolness in the nose, a tingling in the back of the throat, as a movement in the chest, as a rise and fall of the belly? [...] As we feel each breath we can sense how it moves in our body. Do not try to control the breath, only notice its natural movement, as a gatekeeper notices what passes by. What are its rhythms? Is it shallow or long and deep? Does it become fast or slow? Is there a temperature to the breath? (Kornfield 1993, pp. 60–1)

Kornfield's questions about the breath and the earlier example of seeing a house demonstrate a restricted attention; the intent in each instance is to grasp the object purely as a phenomenon. One might thus say that attention is directed to a particular object without its usual baggage. But, as we have seen, one may also say that both phenomenologist and meditator are in different ways attentive to the particular object precisely *with* its baggage, baggage in the phenomenal sense of disclosing the subject. In other words, in their restricted or concentrated attention, phenomenologist and meditator become aware both of the phenomenal object and of what they are bringing to experience over and above the phenomenal object, what they are importing conceptually, imagistically, and linguistically; what they are presuming or taking for granted; and so on. Phenomenologists penetrate to the core structures of sense-making; meditators penetrate to the core nature of the mind. In each instance, it is a question of holding fast to experience, examining and awakening to what is there. From this perspective, both practices may be characterized as a *turning inward* to elucidate the subject of experience.

VI. The Stream of Lived Experiences

The passing nature of all experience, of things in the world, and of life itself is a fundamental insight of Buddhist meditation and basically structures Buddhist thought. In this sense, ontology rather than epistemology might be thought to be at the core of Buddhist meditational practices and systems of thought. But in fact the fundamental ontological truth—the bare experiential fact of impermanence—is rooted epistemologically, and as so rooted, has psychological implications. Brief consideration of these implications will bring basic experiential and theoretical aspects of vipassana meditation to light.

Impermanence causes suffering, or *dukkha*: "From the fact of the impermanence of the world, it follows that all things are unsatisfactory [...] The word *dukkha* is rendered variously as 'ill', 'suffering', 'pain', and so on, [...] [b]ut in other contexts, [...] the term is used in the wider sense of 'unsatisfactory'" (Kalupahana 1976, p. 37). Buddhist scholar David Kalupahana explains the reason "the impermanence of the world" causes suffering; "The nature of man is such that he craves for eternal or permanent happiness. But the things from which he hopes to derive such happiness are themselves impermanent [...] Hence his *suffering*. The things from which he tries to derive satisfaction may therefore, in the ultimate analysis, be *unsatisfactory*" (Kalupahana 1976, p. 37). The fact that things come and go, arise and pass away, are born and die is a fact of life; experience demonstrates and bears out impermanence. In the practice of vipassana meditation, impermanence is experienced directly in the very character of mind or consciousness itself. Goldstein gives a concise experiential account of impermanence when he says that in turning attention inward, we at first find only "self" or "I" but that "slowly this self is revealed as a mass of changing elements, thoughts, feelings, emotions, and images, all illuminated simply by listening, by paying attention" (Goldstein 1976, p. 22–3). In another text, he and Kornfield ask, "What do we see when we look at the mind?" They answer, "Constant change [...] It is like a flywheel of spinning thoughts, emotions, images, stories, likes, dislikes, and so forth. There is ceaseless movement, filled with plans, ideas, and memories. Seeing this previously unconscious stream of inner dialogue is for many people the first insight into practice" (Goldstein & Kornfield 1987, p. 47).

Nyanaponika Thera, a Ceylonese monk, presents a more everyday account of impermanence when he writes that "Bare Attention brings order into the untidy corners of the mind. It shows up the numerous vague and fragmentary perceptions, unfinished lines of thought, confused ideas, stifled emotions, etc., which are daily passing through the mind" (Thera 1969, p. 41). Mark Epstein, a practicing Western psychiatrist who trained as a monk in Asia, presents a similarly familiar account of "constant change" when he writes of meditation vis-à-vis the "everyday mind":

> Meditation is ruthless in the way it reveals the stark reality of our day-to-day mind. We are constantly murmuring, muttering, scheming, or wondering to ourselves under our breath: comforting ourselves, in a perverse fashion, with our own silent voices. Much of our interior life is characterized by this kind of primary process, almost infantile, way of thinking: "I like this. I don't like that. She hurt me. How can I get that? More of this, no more of that." (Epstein 1995, p. 109)

The meditator's attention is tethered to the experienced fact that sensations, thoughts, and so on, arise and perish. She does not become caught up in their "story," but is attentive only to the sensations and thoughts as phenomenal objects. In this way, the meditator comes to know only "whatever arises, as it arises, when it arises, in the bare fact of its arising" — and when it vanishes (King 1992, p. 144). Meditative attention to the breath is of central moment in this regard. The breath is a mirror of the mind that

meditators seek to comprehend. However much one's breath may be interrupted by thinking, wishing, liking, and so on, when one returns consistently to the breath, one finds there the paradigm of impermanence: in-
breath, out-breath, pause; in-breath, out-breath, pause—each phase and the
sequence as a whole arising and passing away. The phenomenon of
breathing makes self-evident the basic truth of impermanence; it demonstrates experientially the fact that impermanence is literally built into our
lives. With the practice of bare attention on the breath, "the moment-to-
moment nature of mind and self" is experienced, and with this experience
"comes a shift from a spatially based experience of self to a temporal one"
(Epstein 1995, p. 142).

How is a meditator's changing field of sensations, thoughts, and
emotions related to phenomenology, or more concretely, how is impermanence—a specifically temporal awareness—related to Husserl's investigations and analyses of time consciousness? The relationship lies in a joint
recognition of and attention to the ongoing stream of experience. What a
meditator discovers and follows diligently is the transitoriness of experience, the vagaries of the mind that arise and pass away within the stream,
to the end that the nature of the stream itself—the mind—is comprehended. What a phenomenologist discovers and follows diligently are the
undercurrents constituting temporal objects within the stream—e.g. perceptions, images, memories—and the temporal nature of the stream itself—
transcendental subjectivity in the form of internal time consciousness. The
stream of experiences in meditating is a streaming present in the same way
that the stream of experiences in phenomenologizing is a streaming
present: for meditator and for phenomenologist alike, it is an ongoing,
ever-changing now. The stream is in fact the same stream experienced and
examined from a different perspective. To crystallize the underlying
similarity requires a closer look at Husserl's internal time consciousness.

Husserl characterizes the initial moment of any experience as a primal
impression that is constantly changing: "This consciousness is engaged in
continuous alteration. The actual tonal now [Husserl is using a melody as
an example] is constantly changed into something that has been; constantly, an ever fresh tonal now, which passes over into modification, peels
off" (Husserl 1966, p. 50). In the internal consciousness of time, primal
impressions recede; they flow into the past, and in so doing, are altered:
"The now-phases of perception constantly undergo a modification. They
are not preserved simply as they are" (ibid., p. 88). Husserl goes on to show
specifically how retentions and protentions—intentionalities with respect
to past and future—are modes of internal time consciousness. Though not
characterized as such, the experience of impermanence is clearly "the transcendental clue" (see, for example, Husserl 1973a) for phenomenological
understandings of temporal constitution. In other words, how we hold

onto sounds in such a way as to hear a melody, for example, or how we hold onto various perceptions of a flower or perspectives on a statue in such a way as to grasp a unitary object are questions whose point of departure is the experience of impermanence: the sounds die away, the flower blossoms and withers;[10] the view of the statue changes as I approach it from the front. The central question Husserl seeks to answer—"how temporal Objectivity [...] can be constituted in subjective time-consciousness" (Husserl 1966, p. 22)—is clearly tied to the experience of impermanence. Taken purely at a descriptive level, primal impression and recession testify over and over to impermanence: what is present con-tinually passes away, recedes, or as Husserl also says, "sinks back, with-draws" (ibid., e.g. p. 94). Constitution is thus indeed an accomplishment: without the "open and implicit intentionalities [of constitution]." Husserl writes, "objects [...] would not be there for us"; they are "subjective *accomplishments*" (Husserl 1970, p. 160). From this perspective, temporal constitution is a subjective victory over impermanence. What Husserl terms "continuous flux" is obviously, even if not explicitly, characterized by continuous change—impermanence.

It is of interest to note, too, that Husserl qualifies the word "flux" as metaphorical, and indeed says with respect to "the primal source-point and a continuity of moments of reverberation," that "[f]or all this, names are lacking" (Husserl 1966, p. 100). The Buddha says something similar about Nibbāna (Nirvana) when he describes it as "profound, hard to see and hard to understand, [...] unattainable by mere reasoning" (Bodhi 1995, p. 31).[11] Bhikkhu Bodhi in fact writes that "[N]o conception in the Buddha's teaching has proved so refractory to conceptual pinning down as this one" (Bodhi 1995, p. 31). Yet however refractory or lacking in names, the flux of internal time consciousness and Nibbāna are experiential realities. We can thus *not* depend wholly on language but must consult experience, in particular, consult experience within the transcendental *epoché* or within vipassana meditational practice for verification. The appeal to experience

---

10 This example is given in order to indicate Husserl's concern with memory as well as with retention and his specific differentiation of the two in his analysis of internal time consciousness.

11 The complete statement in *The Middle Length Discourses of the Buddha* is as follows: "This Dhamma that I have attained is profound, hard to see and hard to understand, peaceful and sublime, unattainable by mere reasoning, subtle, to be experienced by the wise. But this generation delights in worldliness, takes delight in worldliness, rejoices in worldliness. It is hard for such a generation to see this truth, namely, specific conditionality, dependent origination. And it is hard to see this truth, namely, the stilling of all formations, the relinquishing of all attachments, the destruction of craving, dispassion, cessation, Nibbana" (p. 260, Sutta 26.19).

and the limits of language aside, the essential core of the epistemological relationship between constitution and impermanence becomes apparent in just this context. A "continuity of moments of reverberation" adumbrates how, from a temporal perspective, constitution is the reverse of impermanence: constitution is a matter of *putting together — unifying, making continuous — what is impermanent*. The "continuity of moments of reverberation" refers to the temporal structures of sense-making with their retentional and protentional modes. Temporal constitution is thus the phenomenological-epistemological corollary of impermanence; it unifies what arises and passes away into a singular object *as meant*.

In sum, what Husserl consistently describes in *The Phenomenology of Internal Time-Consciousness* as a "continua of running-off phenomena" (Husserl 1966, p. 48) and elsewhere as a "streaming psychic life" (Husserl 1977, p. 107), "lived experience streaming away" (ibid., p. 108), "subjective time [...] existing in the mode of 'streaming', existing as lived experience in the streaming" (ibid., p. 130), is in essence a description of impermamence, but impermanence transcended through the unifying structures of internal time consciousness. We might thus justly conclude that "[t]he marvelous time-structure of the streaming transformation" (ibid., p. 107) is indeed the phenomenological equivalent of "the movement of mind" (Goldstein & Kornfield 1987, p. 54). Both attest to the impermanent temporal structure of the mind. Thus, in strictly theoretical terms, *how* we constitute is the phenomenological equivalent of *what* we constitute, and *what* we constitute is the Buddhist equivalent of *how* we constitute. Buddhism validates phenomenological findings regarding constitution, and phenomenology validates Buddhist findings regarding impermanence.

VII. Conclusion

The empirically sound methodological divining rods offered by vipassana meditation and phenomenology tell us why the nature of the self is elusive: the self is nowhere to be found in experience. What is found in experience are cognitive-affective-kinetic habitualities that are experientially evident in preferences, dispositions, styles of movement, ways of feelings, and patterns of thinking. The self is, in short, a construct. The construct is based on animate realities, but has no reality in and of itself. The construct is obviously fortified by language: by "myself," "oneself," "yourself," "ourselves," and so on, all of which reify a "self." What the empirically sound methodological divining rods essentially reveal and illuminate is the living temporal dynamics of being: the impermanent nature of all that is. The "self" is no exception. It is no more than the sum of habitualities evident in what Husserl describes at one point as "personal character" (Husserl 1973a, p. 67) and that vipassana monks describe as "habits of mind."

References

Bhikkhu Bodhi (1995) Introduction, in *The Middle Length Discourses of the Buddha*, Bhikkhu Ñyānamoli & Bhikkhu Bodhi (trans.), Boston, MA: Wisdom Publications.

Bhadantacariya Buddhaghosa (1964) *The Path of Purification*, Bhikkhu Ñyānamoli (trans.), Colombo, Ceylon: A. Semage.

Bhadantacariya Buddhaghosa (1976) *The Expositor: Buddhaghosa's Commentary on the Dhammasangani*, vols. 1 & 2, Pe Maung Tin (trans.), Mrs. Rhys Davids (ed. & rev.), Pali Text Society/London: Routledge & Kegan Paul.

Epstein, M. (1995) *Thoughts without a Thinker*, New York; Basic Books.

Goldstein, J. (1976) *The Experience of Insight*, Boston, MA: Shambhala.

Goldstein, J. & Kornfield, J. (1987) *Seeking the Heart of Wisdom: The Path of Insight Meditation*, Boston, MA: Shambhala.

Husserl, E. (1966) *The Phenomenology of Internal Time Consciousness*, Heidegger, M. (ed.), Churchill, J.S. (trans.), Bloomington, IN: Indiana University Press.

Husserl, E. (1970) *The Crisis of European Sciences and Transcendental Phenomenology*, Carr, D. (trans.), Evanston, IL: Northwestern University Press.

Husserl, E. (1973a) *Cartesian Meditations*, Cairns, D. (trans.), The Hague: Martinus Nijhoff.

Husserl, E. (1973b) *The Idea of Phenomenology*, Alston, W.P. & Nakhnikian, G. (trans.), The Hague: Martinus Nijhoff.

Husserl, E. (1977) *Phenomenological Psychology*, Scanlon, J. (trans.), The Hague: Martinus Nijhoff.

Husserl, E. (1980) *Ideas Pertaining to a Pure Phenomenology and to a Phenomenological Philosophy (Ideas III)*, Klein, T.E. & Pohl, W.E. (trans.), The Hague: Martinus Nijhoff.

Husserl, E. (1989) *Ideas Pertaining to a Pure Phenomenology and to a Phenomenological Philosophy [Ideas II]*, Rojcewicz, R. & Schuwer, A. (trans.), Dordrecht: Kluwer Academic.

Kalupahana, D.J. (1976) *Buddhist Philosophy*, Honolulu, HI: University of Hawaii Press.

King, W.L. (1992) *Theravada Meditation: The Buddhist Transformation of Yoga*, Delhi: Motilal Banarsidass Publishers.

Kornfield, J. (1993) *A Path with Heart*, New York: Bantam Books.

Thera, N. (1969) *The Heart of Buddhist Meditation*, Newburyport, MA: Weiser.

Wallace, A.B. (1999) The Buddhist tradition of samatha: Methods for refining and examining consciousness, *Journal of Consciousness Studies*, 6 (2–3), pp. 175–187.

Chapter IX

The Body as Cultural Object/ The Body as Pan-Cultural Universal[1]

Abstract: *In addition to implicitly carrying forward a Cartesian-inspired depreciative assessment of the body, many cultural disciplines (including philosophy) have been heavily influenced by postmodern dogma which basically regards the body as little more than a cultural artifact. Received wisdom and dogma together preclude an appreciation of the body as pan-cultural universal. A consideration of early stone tools in the light of phenomenological corporeal matters of fact shows how the body is the source of fundamental meanings, a semantic template. The analogy between the two major hominid tooth forms – molars and incisors – and the major early stone tools – core tools and flake tools – is in fact obvious once animate form and the tactile-kinesthetic body – the sensorily felt body – is recognized. A consideration of the experience of eyes as windows on two worlds exemplifies a further dimension of the body as pan-cultural universal. The experience of eyes as centers of light and dark is tied to an intercorporeal semantics that is rooted in morphological/visual relationships and attested to by biologist Adolf Portmann's notion of inwardness. The experience is furthermore shown to be the basis of cultural practices and beliefs related to the creation of circular forms such as the mandala. Phenomenological attention to corporeal matters of fact as exemplified by paleoanthropological artifacts, by the experience of inwardness, and by cultural drawings of circular forms underscores the desirability of a corporeal turn, an acknowledgement of animate form and of the tactile-kinesthetic experiences that consistently undergird hominid life.*

---

1 First published in *Phenomenology of the Cultural Disciplines*, ed. Lester Embree and Mano Daniel (1994), Boston, MA: Kluwer Academic Publishers: 85–114.

Many times in the course of thinking of ways in which I might begin this essay, my thoughts turned back to Paul Valéry. While it would have been appropriate to attempt to situate the essay in the context of Schutz's work, Valéry's provocative piece titled "The Problem of the Three Bodies"[2] proved in the end too magnetic. In this short piece, first published in 1943, Valéry proposes that each of us in our thoughts is not two but three bodies —"at least." That Valéry diverges numerically from phenomenological and existentialist accounts is precisely what is of moment.[3] He distinguishes not only the felt body from the physical body but the *seen* body from both. This "second" body comes after what Valéry terms "the privileged object" that is "My Body" and before the imaginatively unified but visually disjoint and fragmented body of science, the body which, as Valéry puts it, "has unity only in our thought, since we know it only for having dissected and dismembered it." In sharp distinction from the privileged object that is My Body, the second body, Valéry says, "knows no pain, for it reduces pain to a mere grimace."

Valéry's three-body schema invites us to consider the living body in what I call sensory-kinetic terms, and in turn to realize that the usual living body/physical body distinction can be more finely analyzed and understood, indeed, to realize that corporeal analyses can be generated on the basis of sensory-kinetic understandings. Valéry's first two bodies coincide actually with what I have elsewhere described as the tactile-kinesthetic body and the visual body (Sheets-Johnstone 1990; see also Sheets-Johnstone 1986), and his third body with what I have elsewhere described as the progressively materialized body of Western science (Sheets-Johnstone 1992a). The distinctions constitute a phenomenologically informed insight, an insight suggestive not only of the distinctive perceptual modes in which we are bodies for ourselves and for others, but of the epistemological ordering of those perceptual modes. There is to begin with a recognition of the tactile-kinesthetic mode in which I am first and foremost a body for myself. Second, there is a recognition of the visual mode in which I am a body for others and to a more limited degree, a body for myself. Third, there is a recognition of the fragmented object body of Western science.

Now the visual body that is perceptually distinct from both my tactile-kinesthetic body and the body that, with all its tubules, organs, nerve fibers, and so on, is an object of science, is a body that Valéry says "goes

---

2   The essay is actually an essay within an essay. See "Some Simple Reflections on the Body" (Valéry 1964, pp. 235–40).
3   One might well wonder whether Husserl's distinction between two bodies, and two bodies only, is a function of the German language. Having no such ostensibly complete and ready-made linguistic corporeal categories, Valéry's "thoughts" may have been open to the possibility of a range of bodies.

little farther than the view of a surface" (Valéry 1964, p. 37). As I shall hope to show, however, that surface is a complicated tapestry on and within which two principal modes of meaning are constituted. On the one hand, our social relations, like the relations of many social animals, are anchored in our visual bodies. Because our visual bodies are part of what we are as animate forms and because animate forms are evolutionary forms of life, our visual bodies are the ground of an intercorporeal semantics whose roots run both deep and wide. It is not surprising, then, that that intercorporeal semantics is foundationally describable in terms of corporeal archetypes; thus, with respect to humans and to other culture-bearing creatures, it is a semantics that in the most fundamental sense is not culturally relative. Moreover because visual bodies are animate forms and because animate forms are evolutionarily linked in distinctive ways, it is furthermore not surprising that the intercorporeal semantics that fundamentally defines our own human social relations defines the social relations of many extant primate species and, by the same token, necessarily defined the social relations of ancestral hominid species as well. On the other hand, our visual body is consistently related to our tactile-kinesthetic body, our first body. Indeed, the underside of the tapestry is interwoven in fundamental ways with meanings transferred from the tactile-kinesthetic body. The two bodies are thus coordinated and in myriad ways, as any close analysis of empathy or close observation of normally competent adults, growing infants, gymnasts, and choreographers attest. Tactile-kinesthetic concepts are in consequence open to visual elaboration; that is, concepts originally formed on the basis of the tactile-kinesthetic body are—or may be—the spawning ground of visual concepts—the concept of an edge giving rise to the concept of line, for example.

My essay deals with both of these principal modes of meaning of our "second body"—with conceptual offshoots as it were, and with an intercorporeal semantics. In both cases corporeal invariants, tactile-kinesthetic and visual, come into play. My first concern will be with conceptual offshoots. I will first describe how the tactile-kinesthetic body is a semantic template and then how, in an epistemological sense, vision learns from touch, that is, how the visual body, fashioning itself after the tactile-kinesthetic body, itself becomes a model upon which tactile-kinesthetic concepts are elaborated.[4] I will then describe how our own seen bodies are the ground of our social relations and how those relations are part of an intercorporeal semantics more ancient than we. I will interweave the two themes in the process of treating both of these phenomena: the theme of

---

4   This section of my essay is based on a section of "The Hermeneutics of Tool-Making: Corporeal and Topological Concepts," chapter 2 of *The Roots of Thinking* (1990).

what philosophical reflection on a non-philosophical discipline might bring forth and the theme of "what the 'cultural disciplines' in general might be."

I.

Paleoanthropologists, archaeologists, and anthropologists have all consistently remarked on how ancestral hominids, in fashioning stone tools, made tools do the work of teeth. They speak consistently of how they were replaced by tools. For example, one archaeologist writes, "In an evolutionary perspective, the use of hands and tools, sticks, bones, and stones, to tear, cut, and to pound and grind foodstuffs is but a simple extension of the functions performed by the jaws" (Bordaz 1970, p. 8). He goes on to describe flaking techniques and the creation of edges. What he and other evolutionary scientists do not speak of, and what they do not even stop to question, is "the simple extension," that is, how the replacement came to be. Where did the notion of a tool come from? What similarity was conceived between teeth and stones? Where did the notion of an edge come from? Such questions never surface in paleoanthropology and related disciplines not simply because there is typically no interest in conceptual origins, but because there is no explicit acknowledgement of a tactile-kinesthetic body. In the world of paleoanthropology, the body is reduced to an object in the same sensory-effacing way that pain is "reduced to a mere grimace." Unlike the surface that is no mere externality but that is undergirded by a tactile-kinesthetic life and in this sense has a living density about it, the visual body of the paleoanthropologist has insides only in the sense of an objectified anatomy and physiology. As for the surface itself, only what is visible counts—thus, behavior—and the behavioral surface with respect to tactility, for example, is all on the side of the object. Experience in the sense of the felt character of things is consistently discounted. It is ironic, then, that while ancient stone tools are spoken of precisely in terms of tactility—they are *retouched* or not (meaning they have been manually *worked* or not)—language never opens up a vista on the tactile-kinesthetic body. The touching/touched relationship is ignored. "My Body" is ignored. Because the artifactual evidence is never grounded in tactile-kinesthetic experience, the body ends up being consistently reduced to, and treated as, an object, indeed, a *cultural* object to the degree that although recognized as having evolved, it is understood only in the reflected light of its products—most notably, its stone tool-making, its cave drawings, its burial practices.[5]

---

5   This blindered understanding of the body is not unlike the postmodernist's blindered understanding of the body, for the postmodernist too sees the body only in a reflected light—the reflected light of language or of socio-political practices. Thus it too reduces the body to nothing more than a

There is actually a compound irony here in that paleoanthropology —
like other cultural disciplines — is itself a cultural object complete with, for
example, hunting males and gathering females, and gathering females who
being no longer periodically receptive are — in the memorable words of
several evolutionary scientists — "continuously copulable."[6] The striking
insight of postmodern thought — that 20th-century evolutionary biology in
its paleoanthropological understandings and reconstructions has been a
cultural construction — unfortunately stopped short of its full potential, and
this because the built-in opacity of postmodernist thought with respect to
the living body precludes realization of how and in fact why evolutionary
biology need not be so skewed.[7] An understanding of the human body as
first of all a hominid body, and as such engendering pan-hominid invariants by way of animate form and tactile-kinesthetic experience, is the basis
for an understanding of the body as pan-cultural universal. Moreover an
understanding of the human body as a social body, and as such engendering intercorporeal invariants — again by way of animate form and tactile-
kinesthetic experience — is a further basis for an understanding of the body
as pan-cultural universal. In other words, evolutionarily speaking, there
are corporeal matters of fact to be discovered. The hominid body, of which
humans are the latest variation, has in fundamental respects not changed
over the past three and a half million years. It has changed styles of living,
its brain has grown, and so also has its size, but it is still bipedal; it is still
weaponless; its developmental sensory scheme, beginning in tactility, has
not changed. What paleoanthropologists fail to recognize is the full import
of these corporeal invariants. To do so, they would need to begin asking
questions about origins beyond the single, typical question they already
ask, and they would furthermore need to take those other questions about
origins seriously in a methodological sense. Whereas their typical

---

cultural object — a linguistic entity or a cultural construction inscribed with
power relations. In both cases, fundamental meanings of animate form and
of tactile-kinesthetic experience are overlooked. The body that is coincident
with these fundamental meanings is precisely the body that is a semantic
template, the body that is not a mere semiotic conveyance but is rather the
very *source* of fundamental human concepts, indeed, *hominid* concepts — the
concept of power, the concept of a tool, the concept of drawing, the concept
of death, the concept of language itself. This body is nowhere to be found in
accounts which reduce the body to a cultural object.

6   The phrase comes originally from Beach (1974, p. 357). But see also Symons
    (1979, p. 106). For a critical discussion of the characterization, see Sheets-
    Johnstone (1992b). (The latter article is a version of chapter 3 of Sheets-
    Johnstone, 1994.)

7   For a critical analysis of how the living body is put *sous rature* by post-
    modernism, see Sheets-Johnstone (1992c). The paper is a version of chapter
    4 of Sheets-Johnstone (1994).

question—"What was it like?," i.e. what was it like to live two million years ago as *Homo habilis* or one million years ago as *Homo erectus*—sneaks wistfully into analyses of fossil evidence and not infrequently precipitates speculative scenarios, it could turn into a bona fide quest undergirded by a bona fide methodology that would elucidate the living meanings of animate form and tactile-kinesthetic experience—or in more general terms, that would elucidate what it means to be the bodies we are, and to have been the bodies from which we evolved.[8] What is needed to realize the full import of corporeal invariants is thus a shift in attitude both about animate form and tactile-kinesthetic experience and about method itself.

Through a sensory-kinetic examination of hominid stone tool-making, I will exemplify what that shift in attitude—and thus what a bona fide methodology—would provide in the way of knowledge.

---

[8] For a discussion of paleoanthropological methodology and its possibilities, see Sheets-Johnstone (1990, chapters 13 and 14, "Methodology: The Hermeneutical Strand" and "Methodology: The Genetic Phenomenology Strand").

It is pertinent to point out that paleoanthropologists are not above self-admonishments and -criticisms with respect to engaging in what they commonly call "story-telling," but what one well-known authority more dramatically and derisively called "theatre." See Zuckerman (1973, p. 451).

It is pertinent to point out too that a lack of recognition of the experiential dimensions of hominid corporeal invariants and a concentration instead on the body as mere featured surface can egregiously skew interpretations of the fossil evidence. One need only consider the status of Neanderthals. Until recent times, when multicultural awareness and pluralism have become *de rigueur* and new theories have begun to upset the long protected and privileged applecart of *Homo sapiens sapiens*, Neanderthals were paleoanthropological outcasts. With their prognathous features, strongly recessive chins, prominent brow ridges, and bulky frames, they were not appealing creatures, at least not to most white European male evolutionary scientists. No matter that their cranial capacity was larger than ours—that fact was either brushed quickly aside or explained away; no matter that they buried their dead—not only the first such known practice, but a practice carried out in extraordinary ways that necessarily signify a concept of caring as well as death—they were simply not comely. In view of the facts and non-facts of the matter, it is difficult not to interpret their long disinheritance as merely a felt repugnance: "We don't want to be related to *them!*" The abhorrence is similar to the reaction of people in Darwin's time who recoiled from the thought of being related to apes. One hundred-thirty and more years later, some people are still fussy. For discussions of recent re-evaluations of Neanderthals, see Bower (1989, p. 388; 1990, p. 235; 1991, pp. 360–1, 363). For an early discussion of the facts and non-facts of the matter, see Brace & Ashley Montagu (1965).

II.

Hominid teeth that mash and grind food have a specific tactile character; so too do hominid teeth that bite and scrape. If you run your tongue along the occlusal surface of your upper teeth starting at your molars and progress toward your front teeth (and I hope you, the reader, will do this, and several times over), you will discover a distinct tactile change: an irregular, bumpy surface ends and an even, thin edge begins. In very brief terms, a thick, grooved, and discontinuous array of edges gives way to a thin, even, single edge. Although not spoken of in biology as major hominid tooth forms, there is no doubt but that molars and incisors constitute fundamental hominid dental types. Actual experience shows further that these two dental types are connected with two basic kinds of eating acts: mashing and biting.

Consider now that there are two major forms of early stone tools recognized by paleoanthropologists: core tools and flake tools. Core tools are relatively thick pieces of stone. As testimonial to that thickness, they are usually held not between fingers and thumb but up against the palm of the hand. They have several protruding edges that commonly stand out in relief in the same way that the edges of molars stand out in relief a relative jaggedness with respect to functional surface is typical of each. Flake tools are in contrast relatively thin pieces of stone. As testimonial to their thinness, flake tools are commonly pinched between finger(s) and thumb—like a razor blade. A flake tool has a single manually traceable edge, and, unlike a core tool, it has more readily distinguishable sides as well as a single pronounced edge. Pinched between finger(s) and thumb, it is a lengthier, more vertically aligned object than the more squat and thick core tool. Its surfaces are moreover relatively flat like an incisor rather than rounded and irregular like a molar.

The analogy between the two major tooth forms and the two major tool forms is obvious once the tactile-kinesthetic body is recognized. The ground of the analogy is palpably evident in the tactile experience of the occlusal surface of teeth, of what is called the "dental arcade." As one well-known paleoanthropologist described the arcade—but *quite apart from any reference to tactile-kinesthetic inspection and quite apart from any reference to stone tools*—"a continuous anterior cutting blade" replaces a slicing and grinding instrument; in other words, starting at the back teeth as originally suggested, one readily observes that molars give way to incisors (Pilbeam 1972, p. 59).

Now edges either stand out in relief, as with molars and core tools, or they define contour, as with incisors and flake tools. In either case, however, whatever has an edge has power. Understandably, then, the critical character of a stone tool in the beginning was not that it have a definite, set shape but that it "have an edge." The beginnings of stone tool-making were in consequence not a matter of flaking stones in specific ways; rather, early hominids took whatever edges resulted from flaking. A concern with shape becomes evident at a later stage, namely, in Acheulian handaxes. (Acheulian handaxes were general purpose tools that were widely used in Africa, Southwest Asia, and Europe.) Where edges are not created as surface properties of an object but a single all-over edge dominates, the surfaces of the object are likely to be perceived as sides, and this because the same edge that defines simple contour *ipso facto* defines sides. Our hands are a paradigmatic instance of this relationship. In fact, where sides are not *accidents* of flaking but are created in their own right, the stone has been shaped by turning it over, the knapper working the edge first from what will ultimately be one face, then what will ultimately be the other face, then from the first, and so on. Rather than jagged edges, "evenly trimmed sides" result (Leroi-Gourhan 1957, p. 66). In effect, a three-dimensional act eventuates in a two-sided object. As with the Acheulian handaxes, the visual character of such a tool is prominent; shape in the form of an all-over contoured edge is a strikingly notable feature. Just so with our hands whose shape is perceived as an over contour and whose sides are readily in evidence by turning them over. Furthermore, just as the *entire* stone is a tool, so our entire hand is a tool as in gripping and striking. Analogical thinking is thus again clearly evident.[9] Acheulian handaxes are conceptually linked with hands in the same way that the earlier Oldowan tools are conceptually linked with teeth. Not that the tactile-kinesthetic character of stone tools disappeared in the course of the development of the handaxes. On the contrary, it was elaborated in visual terms as is evident from the fact that the contour of an Acheulian handaxe can be followed not only *manually*, but *visually*, that is, as a linear form. This shift toward rectilinearity added a new dimension to the tactile-kinesthetic foundations of stone tool-making. There are several points to be made in conjunction with the innovation.

---

[9] There is a single recent reference in the literature—by British anthropologist K.P. Oakley—to a correspondence between Acheulian handaxes and hominid hands. The correspondence was originally suggested by German archaeologist R.R. Schmidt (see his superimposed drawing of a hand on the outline of an Achuelian handaxe in his *The Dawn of the Human Mind*, 1936, pp. 96-7.) Oakley interestingly comments that "a bifacial hand axe was perhaps subconsciously visualized as representing a third hand, a hand that unlike the flesh-and-blood original had the capability to cut and skin the carcasses of the animals scavenged or hunted." He speaks of this representation as "symbolic thought," but offers no further analysis (Oakley 1981, p. 208).

To begin with and as indicated earlier, a stone made into a tool is first of all transformed by touch. The stone is given a new tactile character, one whose power is tested not by *looking* but by *feeling* along the edge created by flaking. Second, to understand the passage from an essentially tactile-kinesthetic object to an essentially tactile-kinesthetic visual one is to understand the way in which an edge, while losing nothing of its original tactile character, comes to be seen as a line. Where vision and tactility are confused rather than understood, an understanding of sensory differences is compromised. Lines are visual translations of tactile contour. They are a semantic advance, an advance in meaning. An Acheulian handaxe is not simply the result of more refined hand-eye coordinations, as some paleoanthropologists claim (see, for example, Wolpoff 1980, p. 186); it is the result of a sensory-kinetic development in perceptual meaning, a transfer of *sense* in the double sense of that term. Consideration of straight edges clarifies the nature of that transfer and exemplifies a third distinctive feature of stone tool-making as an evolving art. Straight edges are paradigmatic of synesthesia, straightness being a visual datum, edges being a tactile one. Tactility, in other words, determines the evenness of an edge, not its straightness, as any few moments with a blindfold will attest. Thus, with respect to straight edges, vision appropriates what is originally a tactile datum and makes it its own. In the process, a new meaning is forged. Straight edges produce straight lines, as both Euclidean constructions and projective sightings presuppose.

Viewing the evolution of stone tools from a sensory-kinetic perspective provides understandings of the way in which a hominid sensorium functions. It furthermore provides understandings of analogical thinking, the roots of which lie in a gnostic tactility-kinesthesia—"gnostic" in the original etymological sense of "knowing." Analogical thinking is both basic to hominid thinking and basically corporeal.

III.

The tactile-kinesthetic invariants I have described are pan-hominid corporeal invariants: what we each separately discover in our individual mouths is essentially the same. I would like now to consider how a pan-hominid corporeal invariant is linked to an *intercorporeal* invariant, or in both finer and broader terms, how fundamental tactile-kinesthetic experiences, being the ground of fundamental visual experiences, are in turn the ground of fundamental social experiences. I will in these terms progressively elucidate how a fundamental intercorporeal semantics informs our social lives. To begin with, I will describe a corporeal archetype within that semantics, perhaps the most basic corporeal archetype insofar as it both anchors and intensifies our sense of ourselves and anchors and intensifies our sense of others.

When we close our eyes, another world comes to the fore, and in a regular cycle every day of our lives. Though illuminated from time to time by flashes or dots of light, by images, and by dreams, this world is typically described as quintessentially dark. There is more in the experience of sightless eyes however than a quintessential darkness. When we close our eyes, we exit one sensory world and enter another. With the closing off of vision, a clear-cut boundary is established between an outer world and an inner world — or in more precise sensory-kinetic terms, between a *seen* world and the *felt* tactile-kinesthetic world of my body. The purely tactile boundary felt between myself and the outside world is in fact much less clear. Indeed, tactile boundaries between ourselves and what we touch are vague and in a way we cannot clarify. Moreover we cannot perform any tactile act which would nullify our surface tactility and thus possibly intensify sight in a way commensurate with the way a lack of vision intensifies the whole of our tactile-kinesthetic body.[10] We cannot either bracket our tactile-kinesthetic body. We cannot de-actualize its presence. We are always, in Valéry's words, "my body." No matter that we pass over or ignore our actual tactile-kinesthetic connections with things in the course of driving, eating, writing, walking, listening, or sitting; we are in perpetual contact with the world. In motion or at rest, being in touch is central to our aliveness. Indeed, as Aristotle long ago noted, "touch [...] is the essential mark of life"; without it, "it is impossible for an animal to be" (Aristotle, *On the Soul* 435b 16–17). What a lack of vision does in Aristotelian terms is illuminate the heart of our soul. In closing our eyes, we become aware of sightlessness as entrance to the primordial tactile-kinesthetic world which is "my body."

I would like to ask you, the reader, to close your eyes and open your eyes, alternating between the two acts and taking time in each case to experience what is there. I ask you to do this in order to verify by your own experience the brief description I will offer.

> Eyes are mystic circles, mystic not in an occult sense but in the sense of generating wonder, even of inspiring profound awe. Open them, and a dazzling, bustling world is present. Close them, and an opaque and dense but sparsely-populated landscape appears. Open them, and awareness not only meets with an expanse of objects but moves freely within it, springing from one focal node to another. Close them, and the field of possible attention contracts; wandering randomly within an unmarked terrain, attention illuminates only the place it happens to be. Open them, and the tactile-kinesthetic character of one's roving, active

---

10 Of course I can sleep, and in sleeping, dream. In this sense, I can nullify my tactile-kinesthetic body and intensify vision. The "I can" here is, however, illusory since any actual powers to enact sleep or dreams are fictional. The acts come or they do not come — by themselves.

glance is hardly felt. Close them, and one's eyes are transformed into a tactile-kinesthetic playground of sensations-pressures, pinchings, flutterings, squintings: sightless eyes caught short of an object.

Eyes are mystic circles that open on otherness and open on inwardness. They are windows onto two worlds. To the degree they stay open on inwardness, the initial darkness begins to dissipate. We begin seeing into the darkness. The space within becomes luminous. What was initially dark is no longer dark. It is as if the light that is normally cast upon the open eye continues inward to the point that the eye no longer either searches for one of its customary objects or illuminates after-images. The flutterings of the eye subside. The light within is felt rather than seen.

When our open eyes meet the open eyes of another, the experience of eyes as mystic circles is potentially as great. This is because the eyes of others are the locus of their mystery as persons. We know in a thoroughly intuitive way that we have the possibility of experiencing them as entrance to a tactile-kinesthetic world similar to our own, a world each of us calls "my body." What is the nature of this possible experience of another? Again, I ask you to verify a brief descriptive analysis, this time by actually meeting the eyes of another person with your own.

> The eye of the other is a circle, the *first* circle we experience. We endow the visual—the circle that we see—with a tactile-kinesthetic reality. We meet the eyes of another and immediately apprehend a rounded form leading to that inside space which is another person. Our own sense of inwardness that is immediate upon closing our eyes is the ground upon which the inwardness of the other is appresented. Correlatively, we see reflected in that same experience the nature of our own bodily being. Transferring onto our own body the visual form that we perceive before us, we apperceive the circular form as part of ourselves. We thus endow the tactile-kinesthetic with a visual reality. We appropriate *circles* as part of our own bodily being, circles not as mere geometric forms but as bodily forms resonant with the mystery of life. Our eyes, like the eyes of others, are apperceived as *circles* of light, *circles* leading to inside.
>
> Of course the eyes we see can also be in and of themselves semantically potent. The eyes of another can stop us in their tracks; they can pierce us; they can magnetize us; they can invite us. They can do all of these things because the mystic circle is itself alive. Indeed, that it *moves* and has *tactile values* is part of its mystery. It constricts, glistens, hardens, widens, turns vacant, flits about. Though I do not actually see the circles that are *my* eyes widen in curiosity, grow vacant in boredom, flit in discomfort, constrict in fright, glisten in rapture, harden in anger, I know the *feel* of all of these mystic circles. I know their dynamics. I have a felt bodily sense of their meaning. Thus, when I see the mystic circles which are the eyes of another, I intuitively recognize their expressive character.
>
> When I go beyond the intuited qualitative meaning of the mystic circles—their curiosity, apprehension, or boredom, for example—

toward the density which is the full bodily presence of the other, I allow my own seeing eyes a greater space of vision beyond me. To the degree that I begin to fathom the mysterious interior of the other, I let go of my own inwardness. I cannot, after all, be in two places at once: either I stay centered inside the circles of my own being or I expand the boundaries of those circles toward the other. To the degree I enter into the mystic circle of the other, there is an ebbing of my own felt bodily sense and a growing sense of the mystic inwardness of the other, an inwardness that remains dark, that is not illuminated by momentary flashes of light or by images, but that is pregnant with the rich, interminable, awesome density of another being.

Eyes are organs of sight; but they are also organs of social relationship. They are the privileged site of our contact with others. Fundamental aspects of our intercorporeal semantics are rooted in just such aspects of ourselves, in our being the bodies we are. Because we tend to forget that an intersubjectivity is first and foremost an intercorporeality, we tend to forget that meanings are articulated by living bodies. Common linguistic and conceptual focus is in fact wrongly placed: an intersubjectivity is more properly conceived and labeled an intercorporeality. We are there for each other first of all in the flesh. An understanding of intercorporeal archetypal meanings demands that we recognize this fact. It demands secondly that we recognize the seenness of each other and the communal somatic verities that go with that seenness. Third, it demands that we recognize not merely what we *do* as forms of life, but recognize ourselves as a form of life.

With further respect to an intercorporeal semantics, we tend to forget that the perceived world is already alive with significations, that it is not dead and inert until we christen things with names, or indeed, as if we christen things into *being* by giving them a name. As the previous experiences I hope show, animate form is already meaningful. Our own eyes are meaningful in and of themselves. They are archetypally meaningful as windows onto two worlds, as centers of light and dark, as entrances to a tactile-kinesthetic world, our own and that of others. They are archetypally meaningful as circles, as I will presently show in a more developed manner. These meanings can be and are reworked—amplified or suppressed—in diverse metaphysical and epistemological ways from culture to culture. Rather than directly setting forth these ways, I will attempt to demonstrate archetypal meanings of eyes in the context of actual disciplinary practices, including the disciplinary practice of philosophy. I will do this by pursuing the notion of animate form—first with reference to its general semantic import, and then with specific reference to its morphological/visual import.

IV.

Paleoanthropology (not to mention other disciplines closer to home—if not home itself) misses the semantic dimension of animate form because it fails to recognize the corporeality and intercorporeality of life as something other than mere anatomy on the one hand and mere behavior on the other, and fails as well to take seriously the actual ways in which anatomy is destiny.[11] Not dissimilar oversights are apparent in experimental primatological studies and in studies in the philosophy of mind. The consistent problem is, first, that bodies—animate forms—are not acknowledged and understood, and second, that descriptive analyses of what is actually there are passed over in favor of explanatory hypotheses of what is there. With respect to the latter problem—and to gloss on a comment of Joseph Campbell—"If you haven't had the experience, how can you explain what is going on?"[12] With respect to the first problem, it is clear not only that phenomenological studies are needed, but that what Husserl described in the name of "psychophysical organism" is directly related to descriptive renderings of animate form. Husserl himself consistently emphasizes the *animateness* of bodies, nonhuman as well as human, and even including works or products fashioned by bodies: they too are psychophysical unities that "have their physical and their spiritual aspects, they are physical things that are 'animated'" (1989, p. 333).

Now to realize this psychophysical unity is to realize that sense-making is a built-in feature of animate life. Making sense to others and making sense of others is, in the most fundamental sense, in our bones—in archetypal forms of sensing and moving. We are indeed *rational animals*: we make sense *of* our bodies—and the bodies of other creatures—and we make sense *with* our bodies. Fundamental human beliefs and practices are testimonial to this double form of sense-making. But *all* creatures are rational in this sense; they all make sense *of* their bodies and *with* their bodies, in manifold ways and to radically different degrees. They communicate with each other—not only social primates or mammals generally, for example, but social insects such as ants and bees. They care for themselves—by licking, by scratching, by preening, and by other bodily acts. They further-

---

[11] Freud is reputedly the source of this notion. It is ironic then that, credited with such a rich insight, he actually left the body behind and unattended: he developed the idea that anatomy is destiny only in terms of a single bodily organ. Indeed, he never mined his initial insight that, in his own words, "The ego is first and foremost a bodily ego" (1955, p. 26; the phrase is repeated on p. 27). The ontogenetical *corporeal* psychoanalytic ego is phenomenologically related to the phylogenetic heritage of the body as semantic template.

[12] Campbell (1988, p. 61): "If you haven't had the experience, how can you know what it is?"

more both sense and understand their own bodies and those of others: "If I do this, then I can reach the fruit"; "If I give chase, the other will run." In particular, *any creature that must learn to move itself discovers* — in the deepest Husserlian sense — *its own kinestheses*. From a paleontological viewpoint, we could indeed ask how otherwise such animals, including we humans, could possibly have evolved. Sense-making is a corporeal fact of life. Our own intercorporeal seenness is part and parcel of this corporeal fact. Social animals are "born to see and bound to behold" each other as animate forms.[13] More than this, creatures from butterflies to mountain sheep, from coral fish to humans are patterned in morphological ways that correlate with eyes that behold. Were paleoanthropologists to balance renditions of behavior with renditions of experience, that is, were they to eschew mere explanatory accounts of behavior in favor of both descriptive and explanatory renderings of experience, they would have the possibility of uncovering those fundamental morphological/visual relationships that are the corporeal foundation of our intercorporeality. In both broader and summary terms, attentiveness to what is actually there in corporeal experience would afford them the possibility of discovering those fundamental ties that bind animate form to animate sensibilities and that in so doing entwine creatures in an intercommunal life.

Though not described in quite such terms, a remarkable description of the intercorporeal import of morphological/visual relationships is presented by Swiss biologist Adolph Portmann in his book *Animal Forms and Patterns* (1971). Of particular moment is Portmann's description of *inwardness* as a basic biological character, a character common to all creatures who see one another and who mutually express what he calls "psychical processes," that is, moods and feelings by way of postures, colorations, and other bodily markers. Marjorie Grene, in an article on Portmann's biology, translated Portmann's phrase for inwardness — literally, "relation to the environment through inwardness" — by the word "centricity." "'Inwardness' alone," she said, "is too exclusively subjective and fails to convey the *relatedness* that Portmann's concept entails" (Grene 1974, pp. 272-3). Because important difficulties as well as insights are to be found in Grene's essay, I will briefly indicate them and consider their adverse effect upon an understanding of corporeal archetypes and an intercorporeal semantics. I hope in this way to exemplify the hazards as well as the benefits of reflecting philosophically on a non-philosophical discipline and to show that philosophical reflections must themselves be validated.

Grene notes that Portmann's concept acknowledges a quality of life that is itself acknowledged only "at the boundary of science" (ibid., p. 273), that is, it acknowledges a *subject* of existence. Her general point in the beginning

---

[13]   I borrow the phrase from Erwin W. Straus (1970).

is that "Portmann's reflections about living things cannot be contained within the frame of Galilean science" (ibid., p. 275). In her initial discussion of centricity, she considers a possibly strong objection to Portmann's thesis, namely, that while we humans experience centricity, and unquestionably so, how can Portmann extrapolate on the basis of our experience "to the whole living world?" (ibid., p. 274). In answering to this objection, she glosses Portmann's concept in three ways. She first states that Portmann's concept, while embracing a notion of consciousness, is not claiming that consciousness may be predicated of *all* creatures, but rather that it is "one style [...] of centricity," and that "sentience" may be more generally extended to all animals (ibid.). She then states that sentience is "the inner expression of centricity as such" and that in "reaching out toward an environment and taking in from it," a creature is a dynamic *individual* — a subject — thus altogether different from something inorganic (ibid.). Finally, she states that in claiming centricity is a basic character of living things, she, like Portmann, is not "extrapolating [...] to a vast and remote past, but only trying to pin down with a fitting phrase a description of a common quality of our present experienced world." In other words, "Portmann's extrapolation," she says, "is descriptive and contemporary, rather than explanatory of an inaccessible past" (ibid., p. 275).

Now in conjunction with the rather odd notion that Portmann's biological descriptions have no historical significance, Portmann merely describing what is before us here and now, Grene makes the further peculiar, even cryptic, comment that in *describing* "the living forms we see before us and around us here and now," that we at the same time "try in imagination to lessen the intensity of centricity in its aspect of inwardness" (ibid.). What is queer is to find both a denial of historical interest in what is actually before us and an attempt to minimize it. Indeed, the denial and the attempt together appear backward steps among the forward ones that Portmann seems to be taking; they are a perplexing refusal of what Portmann as an evolutionary biologist would seem clearly to be affirming. What is at stake such that it is necessary to rein in experience in this way? Further, why is an attempt to lessen what we experience tied to the attempt to detach ourselves from the past? A reticence to extrapolate, most particularly a reticence to aver something of those hominids who were our ancestors, who invented stone tools, who conceived of death, who conceived of themselves as sound-makers, who, by artifactual evidence, likely conceived of numbers,[14] who drew replicas of animals and other artistic

---

14 Ashley Montagu's remark with respect to a two-sided Acheulian handaxe is noteworthy. He states that "It is clear that each flake has been removed in order to produce the cutting edges and point of the tool with the minimum number of strokes; for if one examines this tool carefully, one may readily

forms on the walls of caves, and who, to begin with, began walking in a consistently bipedal manner, thus radically changing the morphological/ visual relationship of their social bodies,[15] is a reticence to look ourselves in the eye. Either this or it means looking ourselves in the eye and seeing only gene pools. If we consider what is of central importance in paleoanthropology—that all humans are hominids but not all hominids are human— there is no justification for hedging with respect to extrapolation. Taking evolution seriously means taking our own historical past seriously, to the point that we realize that, short of avouching the truth of creationist doctrine, we humans did not arrive here *deus ex machina*; short of avouching the truth of related received wisdom, we humans did not invent all the cognitive wheels on which we run; short of avouching the truth of postmodern theory, we humans are not cultural artifacts. What is of moment beyond this historical obligation to embrace and comprehend our paleoanthropological past is that to temper what is actually there by trying to lessen its actual experienced impact is to invalidate the description. Indeed, *why not understand how the experience comes to be what it is by unbuilding inwardness and attempting to fathom its origin and impact*? Most importantly too, if *relatedness* is of seminal significance in Portmann's concept of inwardness, then certainly it is of moment in terms of *any* eyes that have the power to recognize inwardness in others, and this because *any* eyes that, in their relatedness to what is about them, can see centricity in others —and Portmann's examples are many—cannot be denied their intercorporeal understandings.

When we look at Portmann's work itself, we see that he emphasizes over and over again both visual powers and the morphological characters —what he calls the "organs"—that go with them. These "organs" may be patterns such as ocelli, they may be appendages, or, as suggested earlier, they may be postures or colorations, but regardless of their specific character, all of them act upon the eye of the beholder; they are "organs of social relationship" (Portmann 1971, p. 197).[16] Innumerable instances in the literature on nonhuman primates and other nonhuman social animals

---

perceive that no more flakes have been removed than were minimally necessary to produce the desired result" (1976, p. 271). For a phenomenological analysis of the origin of counting, see Sheets-Johnstone (1990, chapter 3).

[15] For a discussion of the import of these radical changes, see Sheets-Johnstone 1990, particularly chapters 3, 4, 5, and 7).

[16] It is important to note what Portmann himself emphasizes, namely, that his concentration on visual form should not make us forgetful of "how great the social importance of stimuli of touch may also be in animals; nor how powerfully scents and sounds may act on ourselves as well as on animals" Portmann 1971, p. 185).

support Portmann's insight; they clearly suggest intercorporeal experiences of inwardness, recognitions of another as an Other. The experiences are implicit in instances in which one creature understands what it is to be seen by another, for example, or what it is to be fixed by the gaze of another.[17] On the one hand, these recognitions underscore the fact that there are non-human animals who understand, just as we do, that vision itself has power, and indeed, that, in a Foucauldian sense, on the other side of any optics of power, there is *the power of optics* itself.[18] On the other hand, they indicate that there are nonhuman animals who understand, just as we do, that morphological aspects of animate form are expressive. Surely, then, given these understandings of morphology and vision, it is no great leap to acknowledge that, in the world of animate form, *morphological organs may be eyes themselves.* Indeed, what are the eyes of another for my beholding eye if not mystic circles leading to a body I do not feel but whose depths I can fathom as a density of being? Eyes are indeed morphological organs in exactly the sense Portmann specifies. They are doors opening onto an experience in which inwardness is adumbrated, an experience that is grounded in the sensory-kinetic nature and potentialities of vision itself. In precisely this sense, they are archetypal aspects of animate form. While we might have a shallow and momentary glimpse of the power of vision and its capacity to lead us to an experience of inwardness as we merely *watch* an animal carry on its activities—buzzing from flower to flower, building a dam, chasing a ball—that faint and fleeting experience of the power of vision is apprehended—arrested, as it were—when we actually meet the eyes of another animal with our own and dwell in those mystic circles which speak to us of the being of another. Inwardness is reflected back to us by those archetypal organs we call eyes, eyes that are not simply receptor organs but morphological aspects of animate form.

The eye indeed is a mystic circle. To put this biological fact of experience in much closer historical perspective, and to flesh it out further in the direction of a phenomenologically-informed philosophical anthropology, I would like to consider the eye as it has been cross-culturally understood at two extremes: the mystic circle which is the evil eye and the mystic circle which is the reverential or sacred eye. The former can be traced back to pre-Semitic Sumerian cuneiform texts.[19] The latter has been symbolized cross-

---

[17] Perhaps the most immediately telling examples are those in which one animal deceives another by enacting a behavior within the species' normal repertoire but for other than "normal" purposes; see Whiten & Byrne (1988).

[18] For a discussion of this relationship, see Sheets-Johnstone (1993, especially chapter 1).

[19] It can also be traced back to the Book of Proverbs in which one reads: "Eat thou not the bread of him that hath an evil eye" (Proverbs 23.6).

culturally for millennia and is readily exemplified by the mandala.[20] In fact, I have space here only to consider the mandala, and that briefly. I leave the evil eye for a future time.[21]

V.

Jung tells us that the Sanskrit word "mandala" means circle and that, where used in rituals, it is "an instrument of contemplation," an instrument that "is meant to aid concentration by narrowing down the psychic field of vision and restricting it to the centre." He goes on to say that the circles which describe the mandala "are meant to shut out the outside and hold the inside together" (Jung 1968, p. 356). The initial question is, how did mandalas originate? Where did the *concept* of a mandala come from? If we look to the body as a semantic template, then a spatio-teleological simi-larity is immediately apparent. The mystic circle that is the mandala is spatially patterned on that original mystic circle that is the eye. The teleo-logical correspondence is borne out in the fact that the eye is both the original "instrument of contemplation" and the instrument par excellence that aids our concentration by focusing our attention. In contemplation, the eye shuts out the outside and holds the inside together by literally closing

---

[20] Although in general, and as mandala scholars Jose and Miriam Arguelles point out, "literature concerning the Mandala is not extensive," cross-cultural evidence demonstrating the universality of the mandala is not lacking (Arguelles & Arguelles 1972, p. 20). Mandalas are circular drawings common to Navajo Indians, for example, as well as to Buddhists. Moreover the Aztec stone calendar was drawn in the form of a mandala. In addition, there are ancient architectural constructions that have a notably circular form. Stonehenge is a well-known example. The rounded barrows believed to have been constructed by King Sil (or Zel) in England during the Bronze Age are further cases in point. With respect to these burial or treasure barrows, the "Great Round" that is Silbury Hill is an extraordinary forma-tion. (Regarding "The Great Round," see Neumann 1955). The significance of its rounded form, as Michael Dames (1976) describes it, has striking parallels with the psychocosmological significance of mandalas as explained in the present text. Clearly what is lacking is not cross-cultural evidence demonstrating the universality of the mandala but a phenomeno-logically worked out concept of the mandala. The Arguelles's say as much when they write that "most of [the literature] deals with the Mandala as a sacred art form of the Orient, and although some thinkers—such as Eliade and Jung—have related the Mandala to other cultures and traditions, no one has developed a concept of its universality to any extent." As the present chapter will show, what is needed is a phenomenological analysis that recognizes and elucidates the psychophysical unity of the mandala.

[21] An initial analysis of the evil eye was given as part of a paper presented at a panel session titled "The Corporeal Turn," Society for Phenomenology and Existential Philosophy, Boston, MA, October 1992.

itself, for example, by intentionally avoiding other eyes or other objects, or by glazing itself, thus keeping the world of things at bay. Mandalas are circular forms morphologically and teleologically modeled on the image of eyes.

The similarity is thus not a mere surface similarity. Moreover the mandala is generally interpreted as a symbol of the self and of the cosmos. It is in fact an aesthetic instantiation of the *correspondence* between self and world, microcosm and macrocosm. It is, in effect, a "psychocosmogram" (Tucci 1961, p. 25). To understand how the circular form that is the mandala and that is patterned on the eye came to stand for the self and the world is first of all to experience eyes as channels through which a dual light is cast, that is, as windows on two worlds, as openings on a luminosity both within and without. What needs clarification is how those dual experiential possibilities of eye-light take on the specific symbolic import that they do in the mandala.

That the language in which the power of the eye is described is consistently anchored in images of light is readily tied to the original experience of the eye as an organ of light. From the fact that I open my eyes and it is light comes the possibility of my being enlightened. The archetypal power of the eye to inform and edify is thus linked to clarification, to elucidation, and so on. That the metaphoric language in which the powers of the mandala are described is also consistently anchored in images of light is an indication of a further symbolic extension from original experience. This further symbolic structuring is evident in the equation of light with consciousness. There is, in other words, a cognate relationship among light, consciousness, mandala, and eye, eye being the root form. Thus, the language of consciousness is also the language of light. Furthermore, like the center of the eye that reflects light and like a luminous consciousness that is a center of light, so also the center of the mandala radiates light. Of striking interest in this context is Husserl's language in describing the Ego. "It is the *center*," he writes, "whence all conscious life *emits rays and receives them*" (Husserl 1989, p.112; italics added). It is emphatically clear from Husserl's descriptive analyses that Objects as well as the Ego radiate light, and that the epistemological relationship between Ego and Object is similarly structured in images of light Husserl speaks, for example, of "twofold radiations, running ahead and running back: from the center outward, through the acts toward their Objects, and again returning rays, coming from the Objects back toward the center in manifold changing phenomenological characters" (ibid.). Over and over again, the original source of those two-fold radiations is described as a center, a center that Husserl says is analogous to the body as center of all sensory awareness (ibid.).

Now before continuing with the descriptive analysis of mandalas as a symbolic extension of the archetypal power of eyes, it is apposite at this juncture to raise some critical questions. Do we really experience rays, as Husserl says? Do we really experience the Ego, and as a center which emits and receives rays? If we do not, then we may ask, why use this language? Or perhaps better, why are we drawn to using this language? I would answer precisely in terms of the fundamental *but unelucidated* relationship of eyes to light and to consciousness. The archetypal power of eyes to shed light, to lead us to self- and other-understandings, is not the power of receptor organs. It is in fact a power realized in bracketing, for it is a power to see into the constitutive form or essence of a thing. Precisely insofar as it is structured in light, the relationship Husserl describes between Ego and Object is akin to seeing into the dark, to grasping the quintessential nature of things, to grasping "inwardness." Husserl's descriptive languaging of the experience of understanding another individual further exemplifies the correspondence. Of comprehending another, he writes, for example, "[I] look into his depths"; "I see deeply into his motivations" (ibid., pp. 310, 341). What Husserl is doing in his phenomenological analyses of the Ego and the Object is elucidating the light, that is, elucidating the archetypal power of eyes to illuminate the dark. In broader terms, the quest of phenomenology is to throw light on the light — to know knowing, to understand understanding. What this suggests is not only that the very idea of phenomenology is grounded in the experience of inwardness, in the experience of illuminating the dark, *but that the original of that experience has not yet been brought to light and described.* In other words, while the aim of phenomenology has been to arrive at and elucidate inwardness, it has done so without elucidating that original archetypal experience by which experiences of oneself and of the world are structured in images of light. In still other words, phenomenology itself is grounded in bodily experience. Though genetically unilluminated, inwardness is the eidos of the whole of Husserl's phenomenological undertaking.

Together with phenomenology itself, Husserl's languaging both of the relationship of Ego and Object and of the Ego itself as a center of light — a center of "conscious life" — sheds considerable light on why a mandala is a basically circular spatial form that cross-culturally symbolizes the psyche.[22]

---

22 See Jung (1968) and Campbell (1988) for drawings and graphic incorporations of mandalas. In light of the evidence — the drawings and the graphic incorporations — and of the extraordinary cognate relationships outlined in the present chapter, it is puzzling to find analyses of the corporeal origin of the mandala lacking and indeed to find the question of why the mandala is first and foremost a circle rather than a square or a cone, for example, entirely omitted. A pervasive cultural inattention to the body and to bodily experience would seem to explain the omissions. Tucci, for example, casts experience in the role of follower rather than leader in the generation of the concept of a mandala. He speaks of the mandala as a geometric projection

Circular forms made in the image of the eye circumscribe a symbolic Ego in terms of inwardness. But they also circumscribe within the whole of their compass a privileged place: *a center*, a unique point from which light emanates. Of the fact that mystics place themselves at the center of a mandala, a recognized authority on Indian mandalas writes that "Man places in the centre of himself the recondite principle of life, the divine seed, the mysterious essence. He has the vague intuition of a light that burns within him and which spreads out and is diffused. In this light his whole personality is concentrated and it develops around that light" (ibid., pp. 25–6). If man *places* the principle of life or mysterious essence at the center of his being, however, the principle or essence cannot have been *found* to be there, that is, it cannot have been actually experienced. On the other hand, if man *feels* a light within himself, a light that, while concentrated, diffuses itself throughout his being, animate essence must be a corporeally experienced fact of life. On this account, a centering of oneself inside the circle of a mandala is not the result of a seemingly gratuitous act. It is a symbolic elaboration of a bona fide felt experience, the experience of eyes as openings onto a world in which light is felt rather than seen. This experience and the experience of eyes as circles leading to inwardness together appear closely related to the dual dimensions Husserl singles out as descriptive of spirit or animate presence: "spirits are the subjects that accomplish *cogitationes*"; spirit is "the *fullness* of the person" (Husserl 1989, pp. 292, 293). Indeed, inwardness is to *subjecthood* and to the mystery of being at the center as a radiant center is to *fullness* and to the mystery of the center of being. Experiences of inwardness and of a radiant center are archetypal experiences of light as spirit — or psyche. Symbolically instantiated in the drawing of a mandala, they become an archetypal human act aimed at self-understanding.[23] *Drawing* the circular form is symbolic of wholeness.

---

of the world, and though he explicitly states that he is not concerned with its origin, he nevertheless emphasizes its "worldly" genesis, i.e. the mandala is a pictorial representation of cosmic processes. In fact, Tucci explicitly states that "experience […] suggested certain analogies" with the drawn figure after it was conceived and drawn. The mandala thus appears to be tied to experience only after the fact and only in the most general sense (Tucci 1961, pp. 23–6; quote from p. 25).

23   The act is dimly prefigured each time we close our eyes to sleep. As an actual journey inward, it is presaged in a psychological sense by the world we find awakened in the darkness of our fantasies and dreams. Like the eye itself, the eye that is the mandala leads to the I, to the self, to the subject; so also it leads to the *fullness* of myself as person, to my potential for wholeness, to the mandala that is my body (see Tucci 1961, specifically chapter 5: "The Mandala in the Human Body"). Note also that Jung's "self-reflections," carried out over seven years and forming the basis of his

Again, phenomenology itself as well as Husserl's languaging of the relationship between Ego and Object sheds considerable light on why a mandala is a basically circular form that cross-culturally symbolizes the cosmos as well as the self. To put oneself in the center of the mandalas to be at the very hub of the universe, centered rather than spinning along on the outer edge; to put oneself in the center is to be "at the still point of the turning world,"[24] at the unmoving eye of the storm, calm, quiet, unjostled, unperturbed by all that is whirling about one in three-dimensional space. Thus to be both *inside* and *at the center* of the mystic circle of the mandala is to have the potential of understanding at a cosmic level everything that is going on about one. No longer being whirled along at the spinning edge, one has the possibility of apperceiving the whole and with it, an illumination of the spirit—the animating essence—of the cosmos itself. Putting oneself at the center is thus akin to the phenomenological epoché—to bracketing the everyday fact-world the better to see clearly into its nature, to accomplishing those *cogitationes* that comprehend it. Eastern meditational practices bear out the kinship, "Just sitting" produces insight.[25]

Now this archetypal mode of self- and world-understanding is at odds with typical 20th-century Western modes of understanding, modes in which eyes have lost touch with their archetypal power to see into the dark. They have become merely observant eyes. They are eyes that are busy gathering information, measuring, quantifying, inspecting, surveying, looking, watching. They are eyes that are perpetually on the move, and on the edge rather than at the center. They are eyes of a piece with bodies that are mere culturally-inscribed surfaces. They are eyes that have lost sight of their potential to see into the nature of things. To see into the nature of things requires a sense of their inwardness. It requires a sense of the life of the thing that one is looking at. In the words of a long misunderstood but ultimately Nobel-recognized cytogeneticist (whose work was on a most lowly form of plant life—corn, the plant equivalent of fruit flies), it requires "a feeling for the organism" (see Fox Keller 1983). A feeling for the organism. A feeling for stone tools. A feeling for geometry. A feeling for perception. A feeling for the body. With particular respect to the object, the relationship Husserl describes between Ego and Object is precisely akin to "a feeling for the organism." Eyes that lack a feeling for the organism no

---

analytic psychology, document the symbolic connections between creative act and inwardness. Through "active imagination," Jung actively generated and entered into a fantasy world through which he charted the unconscious and its archetypal forms. See, for example, Jung (1968). In this illustrated work, Jung discusses mandalas and their significance.

24 The line is from T.S. Eliot's *Four Quartets* ("Burnt Norton," IV) (1943).

25 See Nagatomo (1987, pp. 227–42). See also his "An Eastern Concept of the Body: Yuasa's Body-Scheme," in Sheets-Johnstone (1992a, pp. 48–68).

longer bring with them a resonant and open sensibility. They are mere receptor organs. Poised in their sockets, they look at what is before them and duly record its properties; they watch what they see and duly record its reactions. All of those optics of power of which Foucault writes are generated on the basis of just such factual and fact-seeking eyes. Such eyes have all the living juice squeezed out of them and cannot fathom being inside. They cannot see into the nature of things; they cannot see into darkness,. neither their own nor that of the object before them.

The two distinct sets of eyes return us directly to the themes of the symposium. To work through the body as animate form, as psychophysical organism, attending to experience and providing corporeal analyses of same, is to come to deeper and fuller understandings of the ties that bind us in a common evolutionary heritage.[26] Facets of animate form have the potential of leading us to corporeal invariants, to pan-cultural universals, to archetypal meanings, to fundamental human self- and world-understandings. What philosophical reflection on non-philosophical disciplines has shown is that what is required is a corporeal turn, that is, an acknowledgement of animate form and of the tactile-kinesthetic experiences that

---

[26] Our common evolutionary heritage binds us primatologically as well as cross-culturally, and in ways strongly suggestive of the theme of inwardness. At least two chimpanzees, when given the experimental opportunity, placed objects *in* a container, in preference to placing them *on* something or *under* something. Moreover, after sniffing and licking a chalk-made circle, both put themselves *inside* it—the one chimpanzee at one moment sitting in it, and at another moment rolling about in it and making sweeping motions on the floor with her arms. The other chimpanzee "suddenly jump[ed] into the middle of the circle, rubbing all around herself (in a circle) with the back of her hands," then sat down, then rubbed again (Premack 1975, pp. 45–61; see in particular pp. 48–51).

The actions of the chimpanzees strongly recall evidence from developmental psycholinguistics. The first preposition a child learns as both locative state and locative act is the preposition "in" and its derivatives, "inside," and "being inside." This linguistic fact is related in substantive ways to an appreciation of the body as a semantic template. Bodily experiences dispose all of us as infants toward a knowledge of "in." From our first acts of suckling to being put in a crib or other container, from being enclosed inside arms to being inside houses or other shelters, from being put inside wrappings to putting our arms inside sleeves, we all have had (and we continue to have) multiple experiences of *in*, insides, and being inside. Moreover though we think of ourselves only as being born *into* the world, we all came from insides, miraculous insides that protected us by shutting out the outside and holding our insides together. In effect, all humans and in fact all gestated creatures were once inside the mandala which is the womb. In a Jungian psychoanalytic sense, that experience, though no longer remembered, may resonate within our collective unconscious as an archetypal experience of in, of being inside, of inwardness.

consistently undergird the lives of living creatures. What the cultural disciplines might be is foreshadowed in this turn. An appreciation of "my body" is not only rarely apparent in Western biology, anthropology, paleo-anthropology, and psychology. It is rarely apparent in Western philosophy. Were people in all of these disciplines disposed in the context of their investigations to consider kinesthesia, for example, they would discover the intimate connection between tactility and movement and with it, fundamental distinctions between the tactile-kinesthetic and visual body. But they would in turn discover too that these fundamental distinctions lead ultimately to convergences. The lithic elaboration of edges into lines and the archetypal power of eyes to see into the dark are exemplary instances of the rich and substantive conjunctions of the tactile-kinesthetic and visual bodies.

A corporeal turn would furthermore foster an appreciation of cultural *interdisciplinary* studies. When culturally oriented academicians view humans (or other creatures) simply on a behavioral level, in particular, as a visual specimen from which information is to be gathered and on which reports are to be made, they invariably begin by separating out their particular "interest," be it economic, anthropological, religious, socio-logical, or psychological. Thus, not only is experience neglected or trans-posed to what is measurable, but the near exclusive focus on behavior compartmentalizes knowledge. The problem is that we do not *live* in this parceled-out manner. Our sociology is not separate from our psychology; our anthropology is not separate from our medical practice. Disciplinary fragmentation exacerbates the neglect of experience. It reduces knowledge about living creatures to discrete pieces of information about them. Living creatures fail to be recognized as the "persistent wholes" that they are.[27] The mission of a philosophy of the cultural disciplines should thus be to "interdisciplinize" — to draw together — as well as to "universalize." The mission of a philosophy of the cultural disciplines should in this sense recall that original Socratic philosophy that knew no bounds, that persisted in its investigations and followed every query wherever it led.

Phenomenology is critically positioned to carry out just this philosophy. Phenomenologists who describe what is actually there in experience follow the paths of experience where they lead and in so doing have the possi-bility of relating their descriptive analyses to diverse fields of study, tying together fragments of disciplinary information into coherent under-standings. Particularly with respect to analyses of fundamental *bodily* experiences, a phenomenologist is critically positioned to show how funda-mental cultural practices and beliefs, even those stretching back to stone

---

[27] The phrase "persistent wholes" is J.S. Haldane's. See his *The Philosophical Basis of Biology* (1931, p. 13).

tool-making, are in fact founded upon the pan-cultural universal that is the living hominid body. Even further, and again, following the paths of experience where they lead, a phenomenologist is critically positioned to show how the living hominid body, being something more than a particular piece of anatomy or behavior, is, in its intercorporeal semantics, strikingly similar to the bodies of other primates. Through just such phenomenological studies of animate form, human nature would be properly anchored in a natural history. Husserl's writings call us consistently to the task of forging this natural understanding of human nature. They consistently invoke our continuity with nonhuman animals and thus our anchorage in the natural world. It is indeed ironic that paleoanthropology as presently practiced should consistently ignore this task and that precisely *a suspension of the natural attitude* should allow us the possibility of seeing with the clearest of eyes into the darkness of our own natural history.

References

Arguelles, J. & Arguelles, M. (1972) *Mandala*, Berkeley, CA: Shambala.

Ashley Montagu, M.F. (1976) Toolmaking, hunting, and the origin of language, in Harnad, S.R., Steklis, H.D. & Lancaster, J.B. (eds.) *Origins and Evolution of Language and Speech, Annals of the New York Academy of Sciences*, 280.

Beach, F.A. (1974) Human sexuality and evolution, in Montagna, W. & Sadler, W.A. (eds.) *Reproductive Behavior*, New York: Plenum Press.

Bordaz, J. (1970) *Tools of the Old and New Stone Age*, Garden City, MA: The Natural History Press.

Bower, B. (1989) New evidence ages modern Europeans, *Science News*, 136 (25).

Bower, B. (1990) Tracking Neanderthal hunters, *Science News*, 138 (15).

Bower, B. (1991) Neanderthals' disappearing act, *Science News*, 139 (23).

Brace, C.L. & Ashley Montagu, M.F. (1965) *Man's Evolution*, New York: Macmillan.

Campbell, J. (1988) *The Power of Myth*, New York: Doubleday.

Dames, M. (1976) *The Silbury Treasure*, London: Thames and Hudson.

Eliot, T.S. (1943) Burnt Norton, IV, in *Four Quartets*, New York: Harcourt, Brace and Co.

Fox Keller, E. (1983) *A Feeling for the Organism: The Life and Work of Barbara McClintock*, New York: W.H. Freeman & Co.

Freud, S. (1955) *Complete Works of Sigmund Freud, Standard Edition XIX*, Strachey, J. (trans.), London: Hogarth Press.

Grene, M. (1974) The characters of living things, 1, in *The Understanding of Nature: Essays in the Philosophy of Biology*, Dordrecht: D. Reidel.

Haldane, J.S. (1931) *The Philosophical Basis of Biology*, New York: Doubleday, Doran and Co.

Husserl, E. (1989) *Ideas Pertaining to a Pure Phenomenology and to a Phenomeno-logical Philosophy, Second Book (Ideas II)*, Rojcewicz, R. & Schuwer, A. (trans.), Dordrecht: Kluwer Academic.

Jung, C.G. (1968) *The Archetypes and the Collective Unconscious*, 2nd ed., Hull, R.F.C. (trans.), Bollingen Series XX, Princeton, NJ: Princeton University Press.

Leroi-Gourhan, A. (1957) *Prehistoric Man*, New York: Philosophical Library.

Nagatomo, S. (1987) An analysis of Dagen's "Casting Off Body and Mind", *International Philosophical Quarterly*, 27 (3), pp. 227–242.

Nagatomo, S. (1992) An Eastern concept of the body: Yuasa's body-scheme, in Sheets-Johnstone, M. (ed.) *Giving the Body Its Due*, pp. 48–68, Albany, NY: State University of New York Press.

Neumann, E. (1955) *The Great Mother*, Manheim, R. (trans.), Bollingen Series, vol. 47, New York: Pantheon Books.

Oakley, K.P. (1981) Emergence of higher thought 3.0–0.2 Ma B.P., *Philosophical Transactions of the Royal Society of London B, Biological Series*, 292, pp. 205–211.

Pilbeam, D. (1972) *The Ascent of Man*, New York: Macmillan.

Portmann, A. (1971) *Animal Forms and Patterns*, Czech, H. (trans.), New York: Schocken Books.

Premack, D. (1975) Symbols inside and outside of language, in Kavanagh, J.F. & Cutting, J.E. (eds.) *The Rok of Speech in Language*, pp. 45–61, Cambridge, MA: MIT Press.

Schmidt, R.R. (1936) *The Dawn of the Human Mind*, London: Sidgwick & Jackson.

Sheets-Johnstone, M. (1986) Existential fit and evolutionary continuities, *Synthese*, 66, pp. 219–248.

Sheets-Johnstone, M. (1990) *The Roots of Thinking*, Philadelphia, PA: Temple University Press.

Sheets-Johnstone, M. (1992a) The materialization of the body: A history of Western medicine, a history in process, in Sheets-Johnstone, M. (ed.) *Giving the Body Its Due*, pp. 132–158, Albany, NY: State University of New York Press.

Sheets-Johnstone, M. (1992b) Corporeal archetypes and power: Preliminary clarifications and considerations of sex, *Hypatia*, 7 (3), pp. 39–76.

Sheets-Johnstone, M. (1992c) Corporeal archetypes and postmodern theory, Paper delivered at the symposium *Philosophy of Bodymind*, American Philo-sophical Association Pacific Division Meeting, Portland, OR, March.

Sheets-Johnstone, M. (1994) *The Roots of Power: Animate Form and Gendered Bodies*, Chicago, IL: Open Court Publishing.

Straus, E.W. (1970) Born to see, bound to behold: Reflections on the function of upright posture in the esthetic attitude, in Spieker, S.F. (ed.) *The Philosophy of the Body*, pp. 334–361, Chicago, IL: Quadrangle Books.

Symons, D. (1979) *The Evolution of Human Sexuality*, New York: Oxford University Press.

Tucci, G. (1961) *The Theory and Practice of the Mandala*, Brodrick, A.H. (trans.), London: Rider & Company.

Valéry, P. (1964) Some simple reflections on the body, in *Aesthetics (Collected Works)*, vol. 13, Manheim, R. (trans.), pp. 35–40, New York: Pantheon.

Whiten, A. & Byrne, R.W. (1988) Tactical deception in primates, *Behavioral and Brain Sciences*, 11, pp. 233–273.

Wolpoff, M. (1980) *Paleoanthropology*, New York: Alfred A. Knopf.

Zuckerman, Lord S. (1973) Closing remarks to symposium, in Zuckerman, Lord S. (ed.) *The Concepts of Human Evolution, Symposia of the Zoological Society of London*, 33, New York: Academic Press.

Chapter X

Descriptive Foundations[1]

I.

"No foundation all the way down the line." These words are uttered several times over in the course of William Saroyan's play *The Time of Your Life* by an otherwise near-mute character. The words could be uttered with equal conviction by a social constructionist to a foundationalist or by a foundationalist to a social constructionist, the charge of the social constructionist being a denial of anything foundational, the charge of the foundationalist being a denial of anything foundational about the social constructionist's denial. From an evolutionary perspective, I believe the truth of the matter lies in the acknowledgement that what is evolutionarily given is culturally reworked in multiple and intricate ways, and in the corollary acknowledgement that our task as educators and as academic explorers is to inquire into both the foundations of our humanness and their cultural translations. I described this inquiry several years ago in *The Roots of Power* in the following way:

> [T]he difficult task that lies before us, perhaps particularly now, at the tag-end of a fractious and fractionating twentieth century, is to delineate the ways in which cultures differentially rework the heritage that is our common evolutionary heritage. The rewards of this difficult and patient work will be to understand in the most fundamental senses what is pan-cultural and what is idiosyncratically cultural, not in order to have the differences between the two identified as some abstract bits of knowledge to add to our lore, but to appreciate in our bones and behaviors what it is to be the particular animate form and gendered bodies that we are. (p. 2)

Let me begin by pinpointing a few foundational aspects of our pan-cultural human nature. Animation is foundational; bipedality is foundational; concepts deriving from the body—hunger, sleepiness, itchiness, hotness, coldness, thirst, pain, for example—are foundational; kinetic qualia-qualities of movement such as expansive, constricted, forceful, weak, straight, curved,

---

[1] First published in *Interdisciplinary Studies in Literature and Environment* (2002), Vol. 9, No. 1: 165–179.

diagonal, slow, fast, attenuated, abrupt, collapsing—are foundational; movement patterns developing in the course of infancy and childhood— both individual movements such as reaching, babbling, crying, and walk- ing, and socio-relational movements such as joint attention, imitation, smiling, and turn-taking are foundational. Foundational aspects of human nature derive from what is evolutionarily given. They testify to the fact that we are first and foremost Darwinian bodies, bodies that are at once the source of corporeal concepts and of an intercorporeal semantics.[2]

Nonhuman animals are no less Darwinian bodies than we human ones. Darwin described these bodies far more extensively than he described human bodies. He described them not in ways that diminished them, but as the living individuals they are, that is, as morphologically and behavior- ally distinct creatures—what might be called *animate forms*. His pain- staking, worldwide observations of nonhuman animals led him to con- clude that mental powers and emotions evolved no less than morphol- ogies. He thus described how nonhuman animals are attentive to things in their environment; how some are curious; how some have the capacity for language; how some imitate other members of their species; how some remember past happenings and modify their future behavior accordingly;[3] how many of them imagine, as is evident from movements and sounds made while sleeping, i.e. while dreaming; how some reason; how some individuals are more intelligent than other individuals within the same species; how some use weapons and tools. Darwin's writings are in fact studded with remarks about the acuity and feelings of nonhuman animals. His many detailed accounts include the following observations, the first paradigmatic of emotions, the second paradigmatic of reasoning:

> The fact that the lower animals are excited by the same emotions as our- selves is so well established, that it will not be necessary to weary the reader by many details. Terror acts in the same manner on them as on us, causing the muscles to tremble, the heart to palpitate, the sphincters to be relaxed, and the hair to stand on end. (Darwin 1871/1981, p. 39)

> Animals may constantly be seen to pause, deliberate, and resolve. (p. 46)

Moreover his detailed studies include reference to the whole of the animal kingdom, observations of invertebrates as well as vertebrates.

---

2   For more on Darwinian bodies, see Maxine Sheets-Johnstone, *The Roots of Thinking* (1990), *The Roots of Power: Animate Form and Gendered Bodies* (1994), and *The Primacy of Movement* (1999/exp. 2nd ed. 2011).

3   Many species of bird discriminate in just this way. After becoming sick from eating a noxious butterfly or mealworm, for example, bluejays and starlings (respectively) do not eat the species of butterfly or mealworm again. See biological texts under the heading of "Mimicry"; for example, Keeton and Gould's *Biological Science* (1986, pp. 875–7).

Speaking in a section on the development of mental faculties with respect to increasing brain size, he draws an analogy between the extraordinary size of the cerebral ganglia of ants and the extraordinary size of the human brain. "It is certain," he states,

> that there may be extraordinary mental activity with an extremely small absolute mass of nervous matter: thus the wonderfully diversified instincts, mental powers, and affections of ants are generally known, yet their cerebral ganglia are not so large as the quarter of a small pin's head [... T]he brain of an ant is one of the most marvellous atoms of matter in the world, perhaps more marvellous than the brain of man. (p. 145)

He furthermore observes what Swiss biologist Adolph Portmann in his book, *Animal Forms and Patterns*, terms "inwardness" (1967, pp. 183–201). Speaking of how dogs in general like to go walking and describing antithetical postures and feelings of his own dog depending upon the path chosen for a walk, he recounts how initially the dog "showed his pleasure by trotting gravely before me with high steps, head much raised, moderately erected ears, and a tail carried aloft but not stiffly," and then how, at a possible turning point in the walk, the dog's initial posture and feelings might change. "Not far from my house," he writes,

> a path branches off to the right, leading to the hot-house, which I used often to visit for a few moments, to look at my experimental plants. This was always a great disappointment to the dog, as he did not know whether I should continue my walk; and the instantaneous and complete change of expression which came over him as soon as my body swerved in the least towards the path [...] was laughable. His look of dejection was known to every member of the family, and was called his *hot-house face*. This consisted in the head drooping much, the whole body sinking a little and remaining motionless; the ears and tail falling suddenly down, but the tail was by no means wagged. With the falling of the ears and of his great chaps, the eyes became much changed in appearance, and I fancied that they looked less bright. His aspect was that of piteous, hopeless dejection [...] Every detail in his attitude was in complete opposition to his former joyful yet dignified bearing. (Darwin 1872/1965, pp 57–60)

These various descriptive accounts of nonhuman animals leave no doubt but that Darwinian bodies are no mere automatons. Further, they leave no doubt but that Darwin was a keen observer of nature—actually, of plants as well as animals. Further still, it is clear from these various descriptive accounts that Darwin's *experience* of nature was neither anthropocentrically biased nor anthropomorphically inclined. His experience was objective in the best and even proper sense: it was unsullied by pretensions; it was unfettered by theory, most specifically, theory in advance of evidence; it was genuinely inquisitive; it was motivated by a genuine respect for all forms of life.

Now while it is common to speak laudingly of the keenness and scope of Darwin's observations, it is not commonly recognized, certainly not explicitly, that his observations, as written, *describe his experiences.* His written observations are in fact equivalent to his experiences in the sense that they detail what he saw, felt, heard, smelled, and even tasted.[4] Though focal attention is consistently — one might even say, exclusively — riveted on his theory of natural selection, Darwin's *descriptive* writings are of fundamental significance, for it is these descriptive writings that ground his theory, that are its foundation. More broadly, all evolutionary understandings and explanations of Nature are in the end tethered to this experientially-derived descriptive literature. In other words, Nature is explained — the basic theory of natural selection arises — only in light of observable evidence, evidence Darwin lays out in detailed *descriptive* terms for the reader. Reading this literature, we learn a good deal about nonhuman animals. We learn that they are perceptive, thoughtful, and affectively moved by creatures and things in their environment, and we learn further that their perceptive, affective, and thoughtful ways are intimately related to our own.

In sum, Darwin's descriptive accounts of the natural living world reveal something about the lives of others and in turn something about our own lives.

I highlight the *descriptive* foundations of evolutionary theory in part because these descriptive foundations have fallen by the wayside, particularly in the highly visible present-day writings on evolution by sociobiologists and cognitive scientists. When I noted earlier that Darwinian bodies are not automatons, I could have added "as per Descartes," and gone on to point out that neither are they robots lumbering about on behalf of selfish genes, as per latter-day scientists wedded to sociobiological theory[5] nor are they head-end neurological mechanisms, as per cognitivists of all stripe who collapse bodies into brains.[6] Darwinian bodies are out there in the world for all to see. We have only to open our eyes. Opening our eyes, we experience them and the whole of nature, the natural world. I highlight the descriptive foundations of evolutionary theory equally to call attention to experience, specifically to the fact that descriptive foundations

---

4   See Robert Grudin's account of Darwin's gustatory experience of beetles in *The Grace of Great Things: Creativity and Innovation* (1990).

5   See particularly Richard Dawkins's *The Selfish Gene* (1989) and *Unweaving the Rainbow* (1998); George C. Williams's "Mother Nature Is a Wicked Old Witch" (1993).

6   See, for example, Daniel Dennett's *Consciousness Explained* (1991); J.H. Barkow, Leda Cosmides and John Tooby's *The Adapted Mind* (1992); and Andy Clark's *Being There: Putting Brain, Body, and World Together Again* (1997).

are themselves grounded in experience. Descriptive foundations do not come by way of reducing the living world to genes, collapsing it into brains, or modeling it along the lines of a computer. Descriptive foundations are laid by way of direct experience of the living world. Only by hewing to experiences of that world have we the possibility of arriving at veridical descriptive accounts of nature, and in turn, arriving at explanations of nature, theoretical constructs, and the like.

In what follows, I would like to clarify and amplify these thoughts along two distinct lines. The first line concerns phenomenology and Darwinian evolutionary biology. I turn to phenomenology for three inter-related reasons: it is methodologically essential to understandings of human nature; like Darwinian evolutionary biology, it too is tethered to experience and is basically a descriptive project; and again, like Darwinian evolutionary biology, it too is concerned with origins.

I will very briefly characterize these aspects of phenomenology in preface to sketching focal concerns of an evolutionary semantics and to specifying how an evolutionary semantics exemplifies basic accords between Darwinian evolutionary biology and phenomenology. In this context I will also pinpoint more explicitly—by way of acknowledging the critical importance of descriptive foundations—how certain present-day versions of evolutionary theory compromise Darwin's original insights. I will then follow up on the second line of thought, elaborating the claim that ecocritical literature is basically of a piece with Darwin's writings, not just in terms of an obvious mutual focus on Nature, but more deeply in terms of offering descriptions of nature, and in so doing, answering to the challenge of languaging experience, a challenge common to both literatures but distinctive in each case. In essence, what I hope to do by pursuing these two lines of thought is to show how there are indeed foundations, all the way down the line, and that these foundations undergird what we otherwise think of and in fact separate academically as disparate fields of knowledge.

II.

Phenomenological analyses are descriptive analyses of experience. It is presumably for this reason that phenomenology has of late been accorded a small foot in the cognitivist's door. Formerly, all one found behind the door was a cerebral mall with assorted offerings: nervous systems or parts thereof—frontal lobes, for example, or selected neurons; algorithmic formulae; brain imaging programs of various kinds; hypothetical brain modules; hypothetical brains in vats; hypothetical entities like cognitive maps, feature analyzers, and autonomous response planners; and of course that perdurable hardcore item, the computer. Experience was nowhere around. To be more precise, the *behavior* of the cognitivist's hardware and software was investigated, fantasied, postulated, or programmed behind the door, but whatever the behavior, it was not equivalent to experience, first-person experience. Behavior is in fact a category of experience and in that conceptual sense is parasitic on experience.

Now in order to do justice to the complexity of first-person experience, phenomenology requires that a certain methodology be followed, a methodology that in the first place requires bracketing, or putting out of gear everyday assumptions, beliefs, and the like that epistemically color and shape what is actually there, sensuously present in experience. The first step is thus something of a cleansing procedure, akin perhaps to washing one's hands and putting on special gloves prior to surgery. The purpose is to decontaminate oneself of bugs—doxic in the phenomenological case, toxic in the surgical case—that have taken up home in or on us and that we easily transfer to any objects with which we interact. The result for the phenomenologist is to make the familiar strange, to greet it as for the first time, in order retrospectively to understand how what was once strange came to be familiar, that is, meaningful in the ways it now is. Phenomenological analyses and descriptions thus take us back to origins; we come to understand how, in Husserl's words, things come to have the meaning and value they do. Analyses disclose processes of sense-making at the core of experience. Descriptions of how we make sense of the world— how we put it together—elucidate a process of constitution: we do not *create* the world; we *constitute* it in the course of our experiences of it. In the most fundamental sense, we constitute it via our bodies (Sheets-Johnstone 1990, 1994, 1999/exp. 2nd ed. 2011). Our bodies are semantic templates. Hence it is not surprising that fundamental human concepts are corporeal concepts, and that concepts in the nonhuman animal world are equally corporeal concepts.

However different their methodologies, phenomenology and Darwinian evolutionary biology are both concerned with origins. I documented the convergent concern initially in *The Roots of Thinking* (1990) by presenting eight paleoanthropological case studies ranging from an analysis of the origin of stone tool-making and the origin of counting, to the origin of hominid sexual signaling behavior, the origin of language, the origin of the concept of death, and the origin and significance of Paleolithic cave art, showing in each instance how the body was the source of concepts central to the invention, discovery, or practice. Understandings of origins are crucial to understandings of human nature, to human self-under-standings. On the one hand, however much attention is given to answering two of the three basic questions of biology—"how does it work?" and "what is its survival value?"—it cannot make up for a failure to address the third question, the question of origins: "how did it come to be?" On the other hand, however many socio-historical specifics are amassed, they can never make up for an ignorance of origins, and thus can never illuminate the foundations of human nature. Socio-historical specifics indeed take for granted the very things to be explained as fundamental to humankind: language, counting, and drawing, for instance, unless, of course, one takes these human capacities not as hominid inventions or discoveries but as *deus ex machina* creations.

A neglect of origins is particularly telling with respect to the invention of verbal language. Consider, for example, that one of the conditions of possibility of verbal language rests on an awareness of oneself as a sound-maker. Corresponding to this awareness, and hence condition, are certain lingual powers, both tactile and articulatory. Short of the awareness and of the corresponding powers, an articulated verbal language could hardly have been invented. In other words, a voice must be discovered and with it a world of possible lingual and sublingual movements and positions that create a world of possible sonances of varying pitches, textures, amplitudes, and so on. Clearly, ancestral hominids would have had to have made such tactile-kinesthetic/aural discoveries before a verbal language could be invented. Moreover their invention was necessarily contingent on tactile-kinesthetic invariants. If verbal language was to have a fixed place in an individual's world, and if it was in fact part of a shared world, a *social* phenomenon, then a common body of experience was requisite, a common body of movement possibilities and capacities, precisely in the form of species-specific tactile-kinesthetic invariants.

Phenomenologically-informed findings such as these about the origin of language are properly part of an evolutionary semantics, a semantics that, in elucidating how meanings are corporeally created and generated across the whole of the animal kingdom, takes into account an extraordinarily diverse range of phenomena. An evolutionary semantics includes form values (morphological patternings, colorations, and so on) and animate values (postural, gestural, or otherwise kinetic patterns that articulate particular kinds of social relationships such as invitations, threats, and reassurances, or which are affectively expressive of feelings such as fright, sadness, surprise, and so on); it includes signaling behaviors (sexual and otherwise) and what ethologists commonly call "displays"; it includes the symbolic structure of primordial verbal language, the symbolic structure of gestural languages, the relationship between speech perception and production, and more.[7] In effect, an evolutionary semantics exemplifies how,

---

[7] I initially outlined an evolutionary semantics in *The Roots of Thinking* (1990) and subsequently fleshed it out along further lines in *The Roots of Power* (1994) and in *The Primacy of Movement* (1999/exp. 2nd ed. 2011). In these books, I drew in a central way on one or more of the following topics in conjunction with one or more of the following sources: "form values" in Adolph Portmann's *Animal Forms and Patterns* (1967); "the symbolic

in addition to being mutually concerned with origins, phenomenology and Darwinian evolutionary biology can be mutually concerned with producing descriptions of how meaning is corporeally represented across the animal kingdom. It exemplifies furthermore how, being concerned with descriptions of life as it is lived, both phenomenology and Darwinian evolutionary biology are necessarily rooted in experience, in highly distinctive ways, quite obviously, but rooted in experience all the same. In sum, insofar as meaning is integral to experience and a constant across the whole of animate nature, an evolutionary semantics is an open field calling for interdisciplinary investigations into forms of meaning as they are corporeally created and experientially sensed by animate forms of life.

The points of convergence between phenomenology and Darwinian evolutionary biology testify to the foundational significance of *attending to Darwinian bodies*, what the eminent biologist J.S. Haldane referred to in *The Philosophical Basis of Biology* as "manifestations of persistent wholes" (1931, p. 13), that is, intact living creatures in the throes and pleasures of their everyday lives. Only by attending to such bodies do we come to veritable understandings of Nature, understandings that are truly ecological, that spell out for us in living terms the singular integrity and interconnectedness of all living forms. From this perspective, one can readily appreciate why selfish genes are not ecologically meaningful: they are divorced from the living bodies they purportedly inhabit. Indeed, selfish genes do not, properly speaking, have environments or bodies. They have only an aim: to be passed on and thus represented in the next generation. Brain modules and their kin are similarly ecologically meaningless because they too are divorced from the living bodies they purportedly inhabit and from the living world as well. In short, entities such as selfish genes and brain modules have no descriptive foundations because they are nowhere to be found in experience. They are pre-eminently explanatory constructs, hypothetical conjurations of life rather than the real thing. It is important to note that, because they have no factual existence, they cannot be refuted by science through standard experimental procedures, i.e. through bona fide scientific methodology. It is perhaps hazardous but relevant in this context

---

structure of primordial language" in a number of writings of Mary LeCron Foster, among which: "The Symbolic Structure of Primordial Language" (1978); "Meaning as Metaphor I" (1982); "Body Process in the Evolution of Language" (1992); "Language as Analogic Strategy: Suggestions for Evolutionary Research" (1994); "Reconstruction of the Evolution of Human Spoken Language" (1996); "gestural language" in David F. Armstrong, William C. Stokoe and Sherman E. Wilcox's, *Gesture and the Nature of Language* (1996); "the relationship between speech perception and speech production" in Alvin M. Liberman and Ignatius G. Mattingly's, "The Motor Theory of Speech Perception Revised" (1985).

to point out a comparable state of affairs with respect to postmodernism. As briefly shown earlier, the foundations of phenomenology are descriptive because what is foundational is experience. Description is fundamental both methodologically and substantively. In neither respect is it fundamental to postmodernism; language is not commonly a descriptive power for postmodernism but a rhetorical one. Hence, the distance of postmodern thought and methodology from Darwinian evolutionary biology and from an acknowledgement of Nature to begin with.

In sum, a fine and diligent attention to experience leads us to the possibility of fine and diligent descriptions of experience. Descriptive elucidations of experience, in turn, lead us to the possibility of elucidating origins. We can thus appreciate why descriptive foundations are the bedrock of both Darwinian evolutionary biology and phenomenology. In turn, given the grounding import of descriptive foundations, we can readily begin to appreciate the essential task of languaging experience in the formulation and production of knowledge and the fundamental challenge it presents.

III.

The task now is to show how ecocritical writings and Darwin's writings are of a piece, being grounded in descriptions of nature that answer to the challenge of languaging experience.

Theoretical issues aside, ecocritical writings are either writings of nature directly or writings about the writings of nature by others. The writing may focus on a place, a journey, an interaction with an animal, or it may flesh out a character's relationship to a garden or landscape, or it may examine certain cultural practices with respect to nature, but whatever the particular focus and whatever the particular form — an essay, for example, or a poem — the writing is pre-eminently descriptive or pre-eminently concerned with description. It is because the writing is at heart descriptively tethered that the challenge exists to language experience and that, correlatively, the impact of the piece is affective, stirring feelings, images, reflections.

To highlight the centrality of description to ecocritical literature, it might be instructive to distinguish briefly between describing nature and representing nature. The not uncommon idea that nature is *represented* — that what writers do is *represent* places, journeys, interactions with animals, relationships with the environment, and so on — belies the descriptive foundations of ecocriticism. What is descriptive hews to the *whole* of experience, that is, to the conjunction of subject and object, or, in phenomenological terms, to the conjunction of meaning — giver and object as meant. What is representative condenses experience solely to what-is-out-there. It leaves out the experiencer, measuring itself against certain objective, what-is-out-there features of experience, judging whether to render them more exactingly, for example, or in greater detail. It would be nice to say in this context that biological writings represent nature and that ecocritical writings describe nature, but unfortunately, the joints are not there to carve. We can straightaway acknowledge the lack of fit by recalling the earlier citations from Darwin's writings. It would be nice to say too that the difference between nature described and nature represented is nothing more than a matter of perspective; writing may be viewed as the labor of a subject, for example, or as an already accomplished act and may thus be said to describe nature from the writer's perspective and to represent it from the reader's perspective. Conceptually, however, the difference runs far deeper than these categoric distinctions, and the reason I believe it does is that the challenge facing an ecocritical writer is precisely not to *represent* nature—to portray it, depict it, or even symbolize it, and in so doing to linguistify what-is-out-there—but to language experience, and in justly languaging the experience of nature, to do justice to nature.

This experiential conceptualization of the ecocritical task coincides with a certain conceptualization of the value and purpose of ecocritical writings. Whether one is writing of one's own experiences of nature or, for example, analyzing and glossing the experiences of a character in a novel, inquiring into cultural attitudes toward nature, examining discourses of environmental degradation or of environmental transformations of human consciousness, reflecting on scientific texts as literary productions, or exploring the complex meanings of environmental change, what is wanted is not an objective veridicality but a resonating experiential veridicality. The ecocritical task, then, is clearly one of languaging experience since the only way one attains to a resonating experiential veridicality is by meeting the challenge of languaging experience.

I pointed up a basic distinction between nature represented and nature described, and in turn am distinguishing between an objective and a resonating experiential veridicality, in order to accentuate the fact that the foundations of ecocritical literature, like the foundations of Darwinian evolutionary biology—and phenomenology—are descriptive. What, then, is the descriptive difference between Darwin's writings and ecocritical writings—or do Darwin's writings also resonate with an experiential veridicality? We might note to begin with that just as Darwin's descriptive accounts of the natural living world reveal something about the lives of others and in turn reflect something about our own lives, so also do ecocritical writings. One might thus justifiably be led to answer that the descriptive difference between the two writings is a difference in degree rather than in kind. I say "*justifiably* be led to answer" because the difference in degree can in fact be spelled out more exactingly, and precisely by way of a consideration of language and the challenge of languaging experience. By justifying the answer in this way, I will hope to clarify my insistent claim that ecocritical literature is fundamentally a matter of languaging the experience of nature.

To begin with, language is not experience and experience is not language. Language comes not only after in a phylogenetic and ontogenetic sense; it comes after experience in the more specific sense that we move, see, hear, feel, imagine, hope, think, cry, smile, understand, judge, and so on, quite without language. We experience ourselves, other animate beings, inanimate things, and spatio-temporal happenings in meaningful everyday ways that are wordless. Words not only often but regularly come after-wards. We language what we have heard, seen, felt, and so on. We relate — verbally or in writing — what happened at a meeting, for example, or how a slight cold turned into the flu. And not only do we read stories, articles, messages, and so on, that tell us of the experience of others, but we relate what we have read: verbally or in writing, we share with others our excite-ment over a new book or our dismay in reading new assaults on English by our President. In brief, experience is what we talk about, write about, read about. The trick, then, is to have — or to imagine — the experience.

Realizing the trick in the course of everyday Western life is itself a trick, and this because everyday Western life is crammed with television, answering machines, cell phones, the internet, e-mail, books, newspapers, magazines, postal messages, friendly conversations, tête-à-têtes, family gatherings, and so on. The unceasing din of our techno-cultural para-phernalia and the ever-present hum of our social communications can readily lead us to think that language is an omnipresent condition, even a fated incessancy of being human, and as such, is *constitutive of experience to the core*. When we closely examine experience, however, we find that we are sensuously present to something — the smell of an orange, the sound of a voice, the feel of a breeze — and at the same time that we go beyond that sensuous presence toward meaning. Humans are not alone in this respect. All living beings find the world portentous in some way: inviting, threaten-ing, reassuring, pleasant, noxious, and so on. A complex of judgements, expectations, and feelings enters into meaning, and while for humans the complex may include verbal snatches or litanies of thought, just as it may include fleeting or recurrent images, it is not wholly constituted by them. When we are immersed in experience, we are immersed affectively, reflectively, sensuously, cognitively in meaning, not language. Language from this perspective is an *ex post facto* phenomenon, and is thus far less something to be taken for granted as constitutive of experience than as a challenge to one's experiential acuity and one's imagination.

The *place* of language in everyday Western human life in fact presents an interesting perspective on, and extension of, ecocritical concerns with *place* at the same time that it provides a compelling example of how we are deflected from realizing the *ex post facto* nature of language with respect to experience. Consider, for example, the extent to which urban and suburban landscapes are linguistically cluttered places: grocery stores, banks, shopping malls, bars, restaurants, government offices—all are overrun with language, saturated with it: words are written and said everywhere, though we should perhaps note that, in comparative terms, in no place are they written and said more than in academia. Consider in contrast how wilderness is singularly pristine. It is fresh, untainted by language, untouched by human tongues. It is simply there, complete in itself; it has no need of linguistification. Its contrast with the everyday human world is stark, striking. One is reminded of Paul Claudel's *théâtre du silence* (e.g. *L'Annonce faite à Marie*, 1940). Experience resonates in a silence replete with meaning. The trick is indeed to have the experience.

The trick, however, should not blind us to the formidable powers of language. The power to construct a reality, to retell a life, to detail an encounter, to flesh out an intimation, a suspicion, or an anticipation, all these powers testify to the complexities and subtleties that language can engender. To approximate to these powers, one must delve into language; one must explore, experiment, invert, transpose, search and even sound out words to find *les mots justes*, words that not just adequately, but quintessentially capture a reality, a life, an encounter, and so on. At the same time, one must attend to experience, listen to it, return to it, reflect on it. Only then can one judge whether what one is saying resonates experientially, and with an essential veridicality. In effect, the power of language to capture experience is not a ready-made power but a cultivated one, cultivated not in the sense of being something *recherché* but in the sense of requiring painstaking, diligent effort. Ecocritical writings are distinctive in this respect. A ready-made language is not there to appropriate. In contrast, a ready-made language was there for Darwin to appropriate, just as it is there for any present-day biologist to appropriate. A ready-made language conforms to the central descriptive task of a biologist: namely, to be in the service of observation. Yet, as we have seen from citations of Darwin's writings, a biologist's observations *can* resonate experientially. When they do, they readily evoke an experientially-resonant response—an appreciation, for example, as of the marvelous cerebral ganglia of ants; or an empathic recognition, as of the bodily feel of terror; or simple laughter, as at the piteous, hopeless dejection of a disappointed dog. An otherwise objective veridicality can thus pass over into a resonating experiential veridicality. Hence, while language is a ready-made for a biologist, it is not thereby of necessity devoid of experiential resonance. When present-day writings in ethology strike experiential chords, they testify precisely to a difference in degree: everyday language is not just in the service of observation, giving us the facts, but is descriptive of life as it is lived from the inside out.

If I were to characterize more finely the realization of a resonating experiential veridicality, I would say that it stems from writing that is qualitatively alive, that aims at evoking the dynamic livingness of nature, that implicitly senses a full-bodied reader at the other end, and that throughout, heeds the tacit injunction to be true to the truths of experience. Hewing to experience leads to a vast terrain that present-day scientists customarily banish, all the while, however, taking it for granted and utilizing it naïvely in their own observations, and clandestinely in what they call "verbal reports." If ecocriticism emulates the spirit of scientific methodology, as Glen Love urges (1999, p. 71), then it emulates it not directly but by wrestling with the challenge of languaging experience and of being true to the truths of experience. In this respect, methodology is important, and a phenomenological perspective in particular becomes significant. Phenomenology *completes* science by grounding its assumptions, presuppositions, and most crucially, its basic concepts—concepts such as space, world, culture—in experience. Toward the very end of his *Cartesian Meditations*, Husserl writes of phenomenology as "*the beginning of a radical clarification of the sense and origin* (or of the sense in consequence of the origin) *of the concepts: world, Nature, space, time, psychophysical being, man, psyche, animate organism, social community, culture,* and so forth" (1973, p. 154). Clearly, in banishing experience, scientists cut themselves off from the foundations of their knowledge. In contrast, however diverse their perspectives, and whether explicitly or implicitly, phenomenology, Darwinian evolutionary biology, and ecocriticism all insistently refuse a world without experience. They thereby insistently authenticate a world of living subjects—a world of Darwinian bodies.

Their joint anchorage in experience is suggestive; that is, their common foundation in experience suggests that, in fundamental ways, everything academic is interconnected. The common foundation thus adumbrates an ecological academy, an academy that would ultimately flesh out those interdisciplinary ties that bind us in a common pursuit of knowledge, in a common humanity, in a common creaturehood, and in a common natural world, and that would indeed, through such fleshing out, illuminate foundations all the way down the line. The encompassing ecological perspective would not only recognize but celebrate differences in all their richness and complexity, yet as variations upon the common themes they embody, not as themselves foundational truths. An ecological academy might thus come to redefine human nature and in ways that resonate with D.H. Lawrence's apocalyptic vision: "We ought to dance with rapture that we should be alive and in the flesh, and part of the living, incarnate cosmos. I am part of the sun as my eye is part of me. That I am part of the earth my feet know perfectly, and my blood is part of the sea" (1932, p. 200).

References

Armstrong, D.F., Stokoe, W.C. & Wilcox, S.E. (1996) *Gesture and the Nature of Language*, Cambridge: Cambridge University Press.

Barkow, J.H., Cosmides, L. & Tooby, J. (eds.) (1992) *The Adapted Mind*, New York: Oxford University Press.

Clark, A. (1997) *Being There: Putting Brain, Body, and World Together Again*, Cambridge, MA: MIT Press.

Claudel, P. (1940) *L'Annonce faite à Marie*, Paris: Gallimard.

Darwin, C. (1871/1981) *The Descent of Man and Selection in Relation to Sex*, Princeton, NJ: Princeton University Press.

Darwin, C. (1872/1965) *The Expression of the Emotions in Man and Animals*, Chicago, IL: University of Chicago Press.

Dawkins, R. (1989) *The Selfish Gene*, Oxford: Oxford University Press.

Dawkins, R. (1998) *Unweaving the Rainbow*, Boston, MA: Houghton Mifflin.

Dennett, D. (1991) *Consciousness Explained*, Boston, MA: Little, Brown and Co.

Foster, M.L. (1978) The symbolic structure of primordial language, in Washburn, S.L. & McCown, E.R. (eds.) *Human Evolution: Biosocial Perspectives*, pp. 77–121, Menlo Park, CA: Benjamins/Cummings.

Foster, M.L. (1992) Body process in the evolution of language, in Sheets-Johnstone, M. (ed.) *Giving the Body Its Due*, pp. 208–230, Albany, NY: State University of New York Press.

Foster, M.L. (1994) Language as analogic strategy: Suggestions for evolutionary research, in Rolfe, L.H., Jonker, A. & Wint, J. (eds.) *Studies in Language Origins*, vol. 3, pp. 179–204, Amsterdam: John Benjamins.

Foster, M.L. (1982) Meaning as metaphor I, *Quaderni di Semantica*, 3 (1), pp. 95–102.

Foster, M.L. (1996) Reconstruction of the evolution of human spoken language, in Lock, A. & Peters, C. (eds.) *Handbook of Symbolic Evolution*, pp. 747–772, Oxford: Oxford University Press.

Grudin, R. (1990) *The Grace of Great Things: Creativity and Innovation*, New York: Ticknor and Fields.

Haldane, J.S. (1931) *The Philosophical Basis of Biology*, New York: Doubleday, Doran.

Husserl, E. (1973) *Cartesian Meditations*, Cairns, D. (trans.), The Hague: Martinus Nijhoff.

Keeton, W.T. & Gould, J.L. (1986) *Biological Science*, 4th ed., New York: W.W. Norton & Co.

Lawrence, D.H. (1932) *Apocalypse*, New York: Viking.

Liberman, A.M. & Mattingly, I.G. (1985) The motor theory of speech perception revised, *Cognition*, 21 (1), pp. 1–36.

Love, G. (1999) Science, anti-science, and ecocriticism, *Interdisciplinary Studies in Literature and Environment*, 6 (1), pp. 65–81.

Portmann, A. (1967) *Animal Forms and Patterns*, Czech, H. (trans.), New York: Schocken Books.

Saroyan, W. (1940) *The Time of Your Life*, New York: Harcourt, Brace.

Sheets-Johnstone, M. (1990) *The Roots of Thinking*, Philadelphia, PA: Temple University Press.

Sheets-Johnstone, M. (1994) *The Roots of Power: Animate Form and Gendered Bodies*, Chicago, IL: Open Court Publishing.

Sheets-Johnstone, M. (1999/exp. 2nd ed. 2011) *The Primacy of Movement*, Amsterdam/Philadelphia, PA: John Benjamins.

Williams, G.C. (1993) Mother nature is a wicked old witch, in Nitecki, M.H. & Nitecki, D.V. (eds.) *Evolutionary Ethics*, pp. 217–239, Albany, NY: State University of New York Press.

Chapter XI

The Enemy
A Twenty-First-Century Archetypal Study[1]

Abstract: This chapter delineates the biologically based archetype of the enemy, showing how it derives ideationally and affectively from the archetype of the stranger, the latter an evolutionary given within the lives of animate creatures. In doing so, it both extends Jung's classic exposition of archetypes and sustains their relationship to instincts. It shows how globalization magnifies the archetype of the enemy; how, in a living sense, stranger and archetype are taxonomically distinct; and how, just as the enemy is the cultural elaboration of the biologically based archetype of the stranger, so war is the cultural elaboration of male–male competition. In elucidating these aspects of the enemy, it makes explicit reference to Darwin's lengthy descriptive writings about male–male competition across invertebrate and vertebrate species. Key implications and ramifications are discussed on the basis of both Jung's and Darwin's insights into what is commonly known as "the mind/body problem."*

I. Introduction

In this strife-ridden, seemingly incurable fratricidal and fractionated twenty-first-century human world, the recognition of basic and powerful psychic dispositional attitudes appears increasingly mandatory to the survival not only of humans, but of the diversity of animate life and of the planet Earth itself. Basic and powerful psychic dispositional attitudes drive people to oppress, torture, and exterminate one another, often enough in ways deleterious to the world beyond the immediate human one. The attitudes are fueled by basic and powerful psychic ideational figures that motivate feelings and behaviors on par with biologically basic and powerful in-the-flesh alpha males. *The enemy* is just such a psychic ideational figure, an archetype in Jung's classic sense. In whatever guise and at

1   First published in *Psychotherapy and Politics International* (2010), Vol. 8, No. 2: 146–161.

whatever time *the enemy* comes culturally to the fore, threat and danger loom, and fear and loathing germinate in equal measure.

The archetype indeed emerges across cultures and is of pan-cultural import. It represents a plurality of others who are not simply inimical to one's group's, tribe's, or nation's values and the meanings one's group, tribe, or nation holds dear. It is an ever-present potential source of the group's, tribe's, or nation's consummate undoing, its total and absolute annihilation. That *the enemy* bestirs fear and loathing is hardly surprising.

The aim of this chapter is to delineate the psychic nature of the enemy as a uniquely human archetypal figure that arises culturally on the basis of a phylogenetically based psychic archetype, the archetype of the stranger. In earlier writings, I identified and described in detail phylogenetically based *corporeal* archetypes. Some but not all of these archetypes are inter-corporeal spatial ones in the service of power; for example, being larger or smaller than another, being above or below another, being in front of or behind another, and the like. Pilo-erection and whole body inflation, both of which increase one's apparent size, nonhuman primate presenting (its submissive context to be distinguished from its mating context), nonhuman primate mounting (its dominance context to be distinguished from its mating context), and the assumption of a bipedal stance in relation to another are further examples of phylogenetically based corporeal arche-types, specifically interanimate spatial ones carried out in the service of power (Sheets-Johnstone 1994). The aim here is to enlarge this archetypal frame to include a phylogenetically based *psychic* archetype, and in a manner that, while extending Jung's classic conception of archetypes, at the same time sustains Jung's notion of archetypes as related to instincts. In the course of enlarging the frame, I will be crossing a hurdle, namely, demonstrating the reality of a biologically based and driven *psychic* arche-type, a hurdle similar to that of demonstrating the reality of biologically based and driven *corporeal* archetypes. Crossing the hurdle essentially requires fleshing out in a psychic sense the evolutionary source of the cultural archetype, that is, laying out the phylogenetic ground of the arche-type of *the enemy*. A sense of this biological rooting, in what Jung would term the human "collective unconscious," is given by psychology editor and religion scholar Sam Keen in a prose poem titled "To Create an Enemy" (1991). Keen's book *Faces of the Enemy: Reflections of the Hostile Imagination* is rich in Jungian thought and insights. Keen in fact notes in the very beginning pages of the book that his "initial quest is for what Jung would have called 'the archetype' of the enemy" (1986, p. 13). In its analytic of war, violence, and killing, it provides exceptionally timely reading for twenty-first-century humans. I quote the following lines from his prose poem:

Start with an empty canvas
Sketch in broad outline the forms of
men, women, and children.
Dip into the unconscious well of your own
disowned darkness
with a wide brush and
stain the strangers with the sinister hue
of the shadow.
Trace onto the face of the enemy the greed,
hatred, carelessness you dare not claim as
your own.
[…]
When your icon of the enemy is complete
you will be able to kill without guilt,
slaughter without shame.
[…]

II. Stranger and Enemy:
Archetypal Forms in Phylogenetic Perspective

The stranger is an evolutionary given within the animate world, a given from which virtually no animate form is sealed off. Strangers are in other words a fundamental biological fact of life and the typical affective reaction of animate creatures to strangers is equally a fundamental biological fact of life. Indeed, the typical wariness or outright fear reaction is an adaptive biological response in the classical sense. The stranger, after all, is an unpredictable quantity; his or her possible actions, motives, and intentions are unknown. Animate creatures are understandably wary of what is unfamiliar because what is unfamiliar may injure or inflict pain. In short, a stranger is the harbinger of possible harm and as such is the embodiment of a psychic archetype across the animal kingdom. The psychic archetype comes typically to the fore when any animate form unexpectedly comes upon a stranger, is accosted by a stranger, or otherwise encounters a stranger.

Human history consistently validates the psychic archetype of the stranger in its typical ideational and affective guise. What is evolutionarily given, however, may be and commonly is culturally reworked, that is, shaped in different ways: it may be elaborated, suppressed, exaggerated, or neglected (Sheets-Johnstone 1994). Hence, strangers may be welcomed and accepted rather than disdained and avoided. Herodotus, for example, points out that foreign customs are avoided by Egyptians and Scythians but that "There is no nation which so readily adopts foreign customs as the Persians" (Herodotus, *The Persian Wars*, I.135). In addition to observing that the Persians "have taken the dress of the Medes, considering it superior to their own," and that "in war they wear the Egyptian breastplate," Herodotus notes too that "[a]s soon as they hear of any luxury, they instantly make it their own: and hence, among other novelties, they have learned pederasty from the Greeks" (I.135). Insofar as strangers are differentially perceived according to cultural practices and beliefs—in a general sense, perceived as either contaminating or enriching—one is affectively moved to move differentially in relation to them. One may feel open toward them, enfolding them or their customs into one's own community, or closed toward them, shunning them or their customs. It is notable that in both the Old and New Testament, the Bible specifies in exacting ways how strangers are to be recognized and treated (see Kidd 1999 for a thoroughgoing account of strangers in the Old Testament; Luke 10:29-35, for example, in the New Testament). The specifications constitute an implicit recognition of the elemental biologically driven inclination to be wary of strangers, to fear them as a source of possible harm. But the Bible also at times explicitly admonishes people to change their primary inclination, to turn toward strangers rather than away from them.

Archaeological evidence further validates the biologically driven inclination. Archaeologist Lawrence Keeley's extensive and meticulous field studies of weaponry and human populations show conclusively that "a pacified human past" is a myth (Keeley 1996). In other words, human history is replete with instances in which one group of humans whose social organization as a whole—whose values, ways of living, and so on— is different from that of another group of humans enters into a destructive combat with the alien group for the purpose of eradicating its values, ways of living, and so on, or of taking its land and resources for its own use, or for both purposes such that the alien group can, and in fact does, no longer survive. In sum, others who are unlike oneself and one's community are a persistent possible danger and may in addition hold in their possession assets one would like because they would enhance one's own community.

Tennyson's observation that Nature is red in tooth and claw—a stark contrast to God's love—is notably relevant in this context. Human history —biblical texts included—shows indisputably that what is red in tooth and claw are human groups, tribes, and nations. While their redness is obviously rooted in inter-species prey/predator relations for the purpose of procuring food, it is their redness rooted in intra-species relations that is of sizeable moment. In a word, humans have *human* blood on their hands. That redness comes naturally too, but naturally in a way exponentially greater than other animate creatures who at times are brutally unwelcoming to intra-species strangers (see, for example, Wrangham and Peterson 1996). The intra-species xenophobic proclivities and practices of humans are indeed unmatched in the animate world. They are unmatched because whatever the intra-species xenophobic proclivities in the nonhuman animate world and whatever the exterminative practices associated with them, they have no archetypal *cultural offspring en par with the enemy.*

Human blood on human hands derives from what might thus be termed "archetypal descent with modification." In other words, while the phylo-genetic archetype of the stranger and the cultural archetype of the enemy both contribute to humans being red in tooth and claw, they are quite distinct archetypal figures. Their common ground and difference warrant detailed specification.

The archetypal enemy is like the archetypal stranger: a psychic social entity or figure one does not in actuality know in any personal sense. One can of course have what one considers a personal enemy, a person whom one knows, a person who is working against one and is even out to destroy one, but such an enemy is precisely not a cultural elaboration of the stranger. The cultural archetype of the enemy is on the whole a faceless horde of others who have an overpowering socio-political-economic and/or religious significance. This culturally elaborated rather than individually defined enemy cannot just take things from you and deprive you of your livelihood — your job or your standing in a group of people, for example. This enemy can enslave you, rape you, torture you, behead you, depriving you not just of your livelihood but your life — precisely as might, con-ceivably, the archetypal stranger whose actions, motives, and intentions are totally unknown. The archetypal enemy, however, derives not just in a purely ideational sense but affectively from the archetype of the stranger. As so derived, the enemy is to begin with not a source of *possible* harm but of *unquestioned* harm. It is not just that the values one holds dear are anti-thetical to those of the enemy, but that the aim of the enemy is to wipe out those values along with those holding them. The enemy is hence a psychic figure evoking not just fear but hatred, and in turn, a figure from whom one does not in actuality just turn away or even run from as one might from a stranger, but a figure whom one wants in turn to kill and exterminate.

It bears notice that an archetype, whatever its form, may not only rise powerfully to the fore, but, as Jung indicates, be quiescent. An archetype is indeed a latent psychic form that arises circumstantially, situationally, according to conditions of life. It is thus not an abiding presence, but what one might call an abiding absence that can be awakened into presence; it comes from within, but in conjunction with distinctive awarenesses of the world in which one lives. In effect, it can arise as a collective phenomenon. The enemy in present-day American-Western European life, for example, is a conscious manifestation consequent to the events of 11 September 2001. Prior to that date, and even with the threat of communism, the Korean and Vietnam wars, there was no immediate overarching *enemy*, and certainly no *global enemy*. The culture-spawned archetypal figure took root and grew palpably after 11 September. Its manifestation parallels in a striking if eerie way the rise of the archetypal figure of which Jung wrote in 1936. Prior to identifying the figure, Jung describes thoughts and feelings that were prevalent in Europe:

> When we look back to the time before 1914, we find ourselves living [now] in a world of events which would have been inconceivable before the war. We were beginning to regard war between civilized nations as a fable, thinking that such an absurdity would become less and less possible in our rational, internationally organized world. (Jung 1970, p. 179)

He then goes on to describe events in the 1930s in conjunction with the archetypal figure, "the long quiescent Wotan," who has awakened "like an extinct volcano, to new activity, in a civilized country that had long been supposed to have outgrown the Middle Ages" (Jung 1970, p. 180). He points out specifically, "We have seen him come to life in the German Youth Movement, and right at the beginning the blood of several sheep was shed in honour of his resurrection" (Jung 1970, p. 180). With respect to the seemingly irresistible power of an archetype, Jung suggests at a later point that outsiders can judge those irresistibly caught up in an archetype both inaccurately and too harshly, specifically when they accuse them of not being "responsible agents." He states, "perhaps it would be nearer the truth to regard them also as *victims*" (Jung 1970, p. 192). Whatever its nature — and outside judgements aside — when an archetype comes to the fore, its aura, tenor, and energy can clearly permeate an entire nation, mobilizing it in ways heretofore unimagined. In contrast, "When it is quiescent," Jung writes, "one is no more aware of the archetype [...] than of a latent epilepsy" (Jung 1970, p. 187).

Just so with the archetypal figure of the enemy at the beginning of the twenty-first century: prior to 11 September 2001, the archetype was a "latent epilepsy" in America and Western Europe. Awakened into presence, *the enemy* rose to the fore "like an extinct volcano," and continues to erupt, perseverating feelings of fear and hatred, and motivating ongoing killings. In contrast to its ancestral form — the stranger who lurks about or appears out of the blue and is the perennial symbol of danger and possible harm in the animate world — the enemy is a decidedly augmented offspring in terms of power, unpredictability, and scope of potential destruction.

III. The Psychic Import of Globalization: A Beginning Sketch

With the advent of globalization, the stakes increase, for with ease in monetary flow, air travel, and the like, the enemy can be anywhere and everywhere. Globalization in fact diminishes or at least attenuates the archetype of the stranger and correlatively augments the archetype of the enemy. It diminishes the former archetype for a fairly obvious reason:

globalization shrinks the world, bringing all others into close and consistent if not immediate contact with one's own kind. It augments the latter archetype for a variety of reasons: because covetousness and greed can readily accompany an otherwise humanistically oriented global economy, as can political territorial pursuits; because if, or as, human populations outgrow their resources, they can opportunistically seek the pastures of others through weaponry readily acquired from foreign industries, which thrive on such business; because the now proximate (rather than distant) existence of theological belief systems radically different from one's own can threaten the authenticity of one's own god or gods; and so on. It is hardly surprising then that, with globalization, the capacity to defend oneself from attack or encroachment by others is of considerable and consistent moment.

The enemy can rise to the fore at any time and at any place. Fear of the enemy in fact emerges within a larger affective field than fear of the stranger not only because his presence is totally unpredictable, but because he is the personification of death in the most radical and far-reaching sense: someone to be vanquished precisely because he is not simply out to kill you personally, but to extinguish the very cultural ground, meaning, and values that sustain your group, tribe, or nation.

In just this sense the archetypal enemy is known: he is the one who is out to destroy you and all that you stand for or symbolize. At the same time, however, he is essentially unknown in that, unlike the stranger, he is not commonly present in the flesh. When and if he is there in the flesh, he is a human being; he is not an alien figure, but just like you, not only with his two eyes, his nose, and his mouth, but with his blinkings, grimaces, gestures, feelings, and thoughts. One reads stories of earlier wars when enemies met face to face, then mutually turned their backs on each other without either of them harming the other. In archetypal guise, however, the actual humanness of the enemy is subverted: he is regarded and treated as a nonhuman or subhuman object to be mutilated, tortured, or done away with, here and now, *in the flesh*. The treatment of *enemy combatants* at Guantánamo readily documents the subversion as do the suicide bombings in Mumbai.

It is furthermore not surprising then that, with globalization, the twenty-first-century enemy emerges on a much broader affective field than mere wariness, i.e. the wariness of strangers. There is no attempt at understanding the motivations and actions of *the enemy*, for example, as there might be of a stranger. The enemy is simply branded, sometimes, as indicated above, in ways not totally unlike the way humans used to brand nonhuman animals—by putting hot irons onto their flesh. Because the archetypal enemy is depersonalized and dehumanized, he can be hated and killed in the flesh with impunity, indeed with sanction from confrères, applause from the home front, and honor from leaders—or gods—who rule with supreme authority. In effect, the archetypal enemy in a global world is an overriding blanketed human abstraction and affectively charged obsession; he is the psychic rendition of all those anonymous others who directly or indirectly threaten one and one's way of life, the psychic expression of all those anonymous others who are out to kill one and nullify the meaning and values that structure one's life.

IV. Livingly Present Taxonomic Contrasts

Stranger and enemy are clearly related but differentially configured psychic archetypes. Moreover, as intimated, they are taxonomically distinct in a living sense as well. Essential among these distinctions are the following markers:

(1) The one is a possible or potential threat to one's existence; the other, a certain and absolute threat.

(2) The one is encountered bodily, face to face even if not eye to eye, and even if commonly ignored as when one walks down the street, boards an airplane, or shops in a supermarket; the other is commonly unencountered bodily, though certainly at checkpoints in Israel, for example, and in hostage-takings and beheadings, face to face encounters take place.

(3) The humanness of the one is subliminally recognized—a common humanity obtains; the humanness of the other is denied or conjured as monstrous, and in either instance is bent on destroying what is truly human.

(4) The one is marginalized; the other is tortured, maimed, or straightforwardly exterminated.

(5) A latent question of power obtains with respect to the stranger; a definitive ever-present question of power obtains with respect to the enemy.

(6) Fear of strangers is adaptive in an evolutionary sense; there is nothing analogously adaptive in an evolutionary sense about either fear or hatred of the enemy, for neither the fear nor the hatred is rooted in the unfamiliarity of the other, that is, in the possibility of harm from someone unknown. Moreover while fear is indeed the pivotal emotion with respect to both stranger and enemy, fear of the enemy is not uncommonly veiled by unabated hatred.

The above livingly present taxonomic distinctions are notable and certainly worthy of further analysis. There is, however, a further taxonomic distinction, one definitive of the enemy in a classic evolutionary sense quite apart from the stranger and thus of such significance that it should not only *not* be overlooked but be of prime concern.

The culturally spawned psychic archetype of the enemy gives rise to certain kind of actions, actions that are combative in nature, that are rooted in the biological matrix of male–male competition and in the ascension to and maintenance of power in conjunction with that competition, and that are instantiated in the human practice of war. Indeed, the archetype of the enemy is a cultural elaboration of the biologically based archetype of the stranger in a manner parallel to the way in which war is the cultural elaboration of the biological matrix of male–male competition (Sheets-Johnstone 2008). The enemy is thus in the most fundamental sense male through and through: he is *archetypally* male. Women and children— civilians, i.e. those who do not fight—are classically outside the archetypal denomination "*enemy.*"

It warrants emphasis and in fact sizeable underscoring that Darwin devoted 12 chapters to male–male competition in *The Descent of Man and Selection in Relation to Sex*. In particular, he devoted upward of 460 pages to intra-species male morphological and behavioral differences, starting with mollusks and crustaceans and beetles and working his way through fish, amphibians, reptiles, birds (four chapters), mammals (two chapters), then finally and specifically human mammals (two chapters). In these pages, he consistently describes male–male competition as "the law of battle." The "law" is certainly *not* sanctioned or obeyed by every human male, but, given human history, it is an undeniable law all the same. Male–male competition should thus surely be examined, at minimum cease being ignored in the way it is presently ignored, and in biology itself. Buried under the sobriquet of *sperm competition*, it never surfaces. Though sperm competition, an area of study for many years now (e.g. Birkhead and Moller 1998; Parker 1998; Birkhead 2000; Simmons 2001) keeps the phenomenon of male–male competition indirectly tethered to its original evolutionary context, i.e. competition for females, it puts *real-life* male–male competition as it is culturally elaborated by humans in the practice of war under wraps and out of sight. Sperm competition may be a more com- pelling and engaging academic area of study precisely for that reason. But it is not the only way of putting *real* human male–male competition under wraps. *Real* human male–male competition is regularly buried as well under the aegis of aggression, a culturally safe, and, in a sense, refined way of investigating what is at base a biological reality. Aggression, specifically male aggression, is viewed, in other words, as a purely cultural product, not a biologically based or driven phenomenon.

A further incisive light may be cast on *real* human male–male com- petition by recalling an observation of cultural anthropologist Ernest Becker, whose book, *The Denial of Death*, won a Pulitzer Prize in 1973.

Becker's observation elaborates psychiatrist Otto Rank's seminal insights concerning immortality ideologies, their anchorage in forms of soul-belief, and their development into the enduring scientific pursuit of truth-seeking. In particular, Rank showed how soul-belief lives on in the guise of truth-seeking not only in psychology and psychoanalysis, but in all fields of scientific inquiry (Rank 1998). Becker takes up this broader theme in a striking way. He states that if anyone doubts Rank's conception of truth-seeking as an immortality ideology,

> let him try to explain in any other way the life-and-death viciousness of all ideological disputes. Each person nourishes his immortality in the ideology of self-perpetuation to which he gives his allegiance; this gives his life the only abiding significance it can have. No wonder men go into a rage over the fine points of belief: if your adversary wins the argument about truth, *you die*. Your immortality system has been shown to be fallible, your life becomes fallible. History, then, can be understood as the succession of ideologies that console for death. (Becker 1975, p. 64)

The law of battle is indeed culturally elaborated at an individual ideological level as well as at national, ethnic, and tribal socio-political levels in the form of war. As Becker comments, "If we had to offer the briefest explanation of all the evil that men have wreaked upon themselves and upon their world since the beginnings of time right up until tomorrow, [...] it would be simply in *the toll that his pretense of sanity takes*, as he tries to deny his true condition," i.e. that he is an abysmal worm, an insignificant nothing, and that his fear of death is *dreadful*, too dreadful to be faced (Becker 1973, pp. 29–30). Thus, where man turns against man in harmful and murderous ways, he turns in defiance of his own death: "If we don't have the omnipotence of gods," Becker writes, "we at least can destroy like gods" (Becker 1973, p. 85).

Killing their own kind in acts of war is never mentioned as a behavior that makes humans unique in the animal world. One might question whether the omission is due wholly to the fact that killing one's own kind is considered a purely cultural phenomenon or whether it is due also to the fact that killing one's own kind is a singularly *unlaudable* practice, far from the honorific practice of language, for instance, and of all those other fine practices offered in distinctive praise of humans and of human civilization. In other words, since war is a *beastly* practice, it can hardly differentiate "man" from "the beasts," and differentiating man from the beasts is not only easily and readily done by way of culture, but is vital to the self-esteem of *Homo sapiens sapiens*. That male–male competition can be disregarded in this context is both startling and inexplicable. With quite minor as well as altogether rare exceptions in the long course of human history, it is males who plan wars, who initiate wars, who fight wars, and who win and lose wars. Indeed, the omission of male–male competition is odd in the extreme, but then few humans seem prepared either to examine close-up the biological roots of war *or* to acknowledge something "beastly" as that which in fact readily distinguishes human animals from their nonhuman counterparts.

Real male–male competition clearly both supports and escalates the phylogenetically based cultural psychic archetype of the enemy. Indeed, it perpetuates, enshrines, and even vindicates the very archetype itself. Were the real-life biological phenomenon to be recognized and examined, the cultural archetype of the enemy might in time and in turn come to be quiescent and perhaps even remain quiescent, receding from its present-day prominence and perhaps even diminishing in power in the event of future awakenings. In this context, however, we should note that the enemy naturally needs a counterpart and that counterpart is obviously the cultural archetype of the warrior, he who fights the enemy. The cultural archetype of the warrior is concomitant with the cultural honing of heroes. Archetype and honing both warrant deep and serious study. They are relevant correlatives of the cultural archetype of the enemy and its biological relationship to male–male competition. Jung's remarks on the hero are notably relevant in this context. They implicitly highlight the archetypal reality of the enemy, a relationship that will be briefly but pointedly exemplified in the concluding section of this chapter.

V. The Fecundity and Import of Jung's Classic Notion of Archetypes

Archetypes arise from the transcendent ground of the psyche and remain an embedded "psychoid factor" (Jung 1969, p. 123). They are thus not immanent in experience but a psychic motif within it, a motif that "is a piece of life, an image connected with the living individual by the bridge of the emotions" (Jung 1968, p. 87). An archetype is similar to an instinct in this respect. It too is not controllable but arises *causa sui* in conjunction with a felt inclination or affinity, a felt reluctance or aversion to something in the world. As Jung astutely observes, "A man likes to believe that he is the master of his soul. But as long as he is unable to control his moods and emotions, or to be conscious of the myriad secret ways in which unconscious factors insinuate themselves into his arrangements and decisions, he is certainly not his own master" (Jung 1968, p. 72). Jung is in fact at pains to show that humans are "possessed by 'powers' that are beyond [their] control" (Jung 1968, p. 71). Emphasizing many times over that "we are moved by forces from within as well as by stimuli from without" and that we tend not to recognize our dependency on these forces, he specifically notes, "The one thing we refuse to admit is that we are dependent upon 'powers' that are beyond our control" (Jung 1968, p. 71). Thus, just as present-day humans separate themselves from "basic instincts," aligning the latter with "animals" (Jung 1968, pp. 72, 64, respectively), so they separate themselves from archetypal forms of thought. Instinct and archetype are indeed intimately related powers and their coincidence is highlighted by Jung: "instinctive trends" are represented by corresponding thought forms — that is, by the archetypes (Jung 1968, p. 67). Moreover, "[l]ike the instincts, the collective thought patterns of the human mind are innate and inherited. They function, when the occasion arises, in more or less the same way in all of us" (Jung 1968, p. 64).

The notion of instincts and of "collective thought patterns" — of a human collective unconscious — is patently distant from present-day cognitive science, neuroscience, and related fields of inquiry. So long as humans remain blind to psychic powers beyond their control, however, they are pawns of those powers, precisely as with their collective response to *the enemy*. They remain in the grip of a powerful, emotionally laden archetype that drives them and that can insinuate itself into virtually all aspects of their lives. They are, in a word, driven by fear, threatened by death, in constant battle with others to sustain their way of life, its values and meanings. The substantive emotional value of the archetype is the source of its power; it readily awakens humans. It moves them to move, both to protect themselves and to kill those who threaten them. Moreover the emotional charge of *the enemy* is rife with meanings that the realities of globalization augment, as noted earlier, meanings that a government can in fact ratchet up such that fear is indelibly branded onto the collective psyche. It is hardly surprising then that the emotional charge of *the enemy* is not simply fear but fury and vengeance, driving people to kill as well as to protect. It moves them to think and weigh their doings, to be concerned about risking their resources or themselves.

It is important to note in this context that the word *enemy* — and/or words associated with it — do not create the archetype or the emotions that fuel and engender it — any more than we ourselves create the archetype or emotions that fuel it. On the contrary, archetype and emotions create us in the sense that, as indicated, they move us to move in certain ways and correlatively to think and decide in certain ways. As Jung notes, the word *emotion* itself conveys the fact that emotions are "involuntary" (Jung 1968, p. 49): they "move out feelings," bodily felt feelings, and thereby "set in motion" (*OED*). With respect to the actual linkage of emotion and archetype, Jung explains, "That is why it is impossible to give an arbitrary (or universal) interpretation of any archetype. It must be explained in the manner indicated by the whole life-situation of the particular individual to whom it relates" (Jung 1968, p. 87). Jung's point is exemplified by his own descriptive account of the reawakening of Wotan in Germany in the 1930s. Wotan, he writes, "is the god of storm and frenzy, the unleasher of passions and the lust of battle" (Jung 1970, p. 182). He states, to avoid prejudice, we could of course dispense with the name "Wotan" and speak instead of the *furor teutonicus*. But we should only be saying the same thing and not as well, for the *furor* in this case is a mere psychologizing of Wotan and tells us no more than that the Germans are in a state of "fury". We thus lose sight of the most peculiar feature of this whole phenomenon, namely, the dramatic aspect of the *Ergreifer* and the *Ergriffener* [the one who is taken, moved, or touched, and the one who is taker, mover, or toucher]. (Jung 1970, p. 185)

A few pages later, he explains further: "Because the behaviour of a race takes on a specific character from its underlying images we can speak of an archetype 'Wotan'. As an autonomous psychic factor, Wotan produces effects in the collective life of a people and thereby reveals his own nature" (Jung 1970, p. 187). Noting that Wotan "simply disappeared when the times turned against him, and remained invisible for more than a thousand years, working anonymously and indirectly," Jung remarks more generally that "Archetypes are like river-beds which dry up when the water deserts them, but which [they] can find again at any time." Elaborating on the analogy, he states,

An archetype is like an old watercourse along which the water of life has flowed for centuries, digging deep channel for itself. The longer it has flowed in this channel the more likely it is that sooner or later the water will return to its old bed. The life of the individual as a member of society and particularly as part of the State may be regulated like a canal, but the life of nations is a great rushing river which is utterly beyond human control, in the hands of One, who has always been stronger than men. [...] Thus the life of nations rolls on unchecked, without guidance, unconscious of where it is going, like a rock crashing down the side of a hill, until it is stopped by an obstacle stronger than itself. Political events move from one impasse to the next, like a torrent caught in gullies, creeks, and marches. All human control comes to an end when the individual is caught in a mass movement. Then the archetypes begin to function. (Jung 1970, p. 189)

Archetypes are a central and perdurable theme not only throughout Jung's writings, but pivotal in what might be called his natural-history based socio-political psychoanalytic. His descriptive accounts specify not only the collective power of archetypes and their affective and temporal nature, they also delineate the grounding of archetypes in biological ways strongly suggestive of an evolutionary history:

[Archetypes are] the hidden foundations of the conscious mind, or, to use another comparison, the roots which the psyche has sunk not only in the earth in the narrower sense but in the world in general. Archetypes are systems of readiness for action, and at the same time images and emotions. They are inherited with the brain structure—indeed, they are its psychic aspects. They represent, on the one hand, a very strong instinctive conservatism, while on the other hand they are the most effective means conceivable of instinctive adaptation. They are thus, essentially […] that [aspect] of the psyche [that] is attached to nature, or in which its link with the earth and the world appears at its most tangible. (Jung 1970, p. 31)

Given their biological grounding if not natural history, archetypes are clearly not a theoretical construct on the order of "feature analyzers" (e.g. Bernstein et al. 1994, pp. 196–8), "cognitive maps" (e.g. O'Keefe & Nadel 1979; Golledge 1999), "eye-direction detectors" (Baron-Cohen 1995), or other such hypothetical entities present-day psychologists, neuroscientists, cognitive scientists, and others have conjured to exist in *the brain* to explain phenomena discovered in a laboratory or in experimental studies. Archetypes are an affectively-rich ideational or imagistic reality of life itself. They stem from Nature, an endowment on par with instincts. Indeed, Jung remarks that "To the extent that the archetypes intervene in the shaping of conscious contents by regulating, modifying, and motivating them, they act like the instincts" (Jung 1969, p. 115). In effect, archetypes influence us in ways no less primordial than instincts, precisely as detailed in the cultural archetype of *the enemy*. The cultural archetype of the enemy is indeed properly conceived as Jung conceives an archetype: "instinct raised to a higher frequency" (Jung 1969, p. 122). What exists at the frequency of instinct is xenophobia, the biologically based fear of strangers. The cultural archetype of the enemy elevates the intensity, scope, and import of this basic biological fear. Humans are thus clearly *by nature* attuned in both an instinctual and archetypal sense to *the enemy*, attuned in Jung's sense of both "spirit" and "matter": "In archetypal conceptions and instinctual perceptions, spirit and matter confront one another on the psychic plane," which is to say that "[m]atter and spirit both appear in the psychic realm as distinctive qualities of conscious contents" (Jung 1969, p. 126).

While Jung emphasizes that the archetype is a "psychoid factor," i.e. a transcendent form we experience only as a psychic motif and of which we are not and cannot be directly conscious, the cultural archetype of the enemy can nonetheless be specified as both a *psychic species*, one that may manifest in various forms, and an attendant *psychic reflex* in terms of the actions one is inclined to take. Jung intimates as much when he states, "Like the instincts, the collective thought patterns of the human mind are innate and inherited. They function, when the occasion arises, in more or less the same way in all of us" (Jung 1968, p. 64). Hence, though archetype and instinct are ontologically distinct and may be differentially manifest according to variations among individuals and to *circonstances*—to draw on a rich and useful concept from Lamarck—they are an abiding human inheritance. Indeed, archetypes are dynamic: they "manifest themselves in impulses, just as spontaneously as the instincts" (Jung 1968, pp. 64–5). In short, they coexist within an evolutionary framework.

VI. Key Implications and Ramifications

If "the hero figure is an archetype, which has existed since time immemorial," as Jung claims, so also is the enemy. Moreover the same may be said of their respective origins. Jung writes with respect to the hero:

> When and where such a motif originated nobody knows. We do not even know how to go about investigating the problem. The one apparent certainty is that every generation seems to have known it as a tradition handed down from some preceding time. Thus we can safely assume that it "originated" at a period when man did not yet know that he possessed a hero myth; in an age, that is to say, when he did not yet consciously reflect on what he was saying. (Jung 1968, p. 61)

The enemy, like the hero, originated ideationally on its own, unquestionably on the basis of a natural history of animate life, i.e. in the phenomenon of the stranger, and of a natural history of human experience, in the cultural elaboration of the stranger. The enemy was and is, in other words, not an *invented* idea. That the cultural archetype of the enemy has erupted and grown in this twenty-first-century world can hardly be denied. Its overarching and relentless presence derives from the biologically rooted archetype of the stranger and follows from the twenty-first-century globalization of virtually all individual human lives. As indicated earlier, strangers can indeed be a matter of life and death. They raise questions of survival not in so many words, of course, but in the immediate non-linguistic kinetic apparencies and interactions of animate life. The idea that twenty-first-century adult humans live in some form of radical psychic captivity deriving from globalization strongly suggests that Herbert Spencer's nineteenth-century ethics of amity and enmity was on the right track. In effect, ethical implications follow from globalization and warrant brief but pointed specification.

To begin with, the larger the global world, the more worries, the more threats, the more competition—in the end, the more *danger*. With an ever-more expanded world, with its ever-more extended conflicts, ever-more extended possibilities for territorial takeovers, ever-more extended resources to appropriate, and so on—much of it the result of more and more information about the world—people's focus of attention changes; their attitudes change; their feelings change. At the everyday level of everyday people, i.e. nonpoliticians and nonleaders, there is more and more—ostensibly—to be concerned about, while at the everyday level of many a politician and leader, there is more and more to be *actively pursued*.

Territory is an integral part of this picture because it is an integral part of the national history of a people. It is thus not surprising that, in a pan-cultural sense, danger, and specifically the danger of war, shapes and patterns human life. But territory has a much longer and more complex history, being an integral part not only of the national history of a people but of the natural history of humans. Its national history is in fact the cultural elaboration of its natural history, that is, an elaboration of what is evolutionarily given, as evidenced in the territorial behaviors of nonhuman animals, especially the behaviors of other primates, and equally, in light of the human archaeological record, the behavior of humans for untold centuries and more.

We glimpse these evolutionary relationships in a preliminary way in Robert Ardrey's 1966 book *The Territorial Imperative*, in which Ardrey fittingly identifies human nations as biological entities, showing how they are an extension of the territorial claims of nonhuman animals, a domain of research he documents extensively. In addition to dwelling pointedly on the concept of a biological nation, he dwells at length on Spencer's concept of amity and enmity that identifies the dual moral codes informing human action, emending the concept along the lines of evolutionary thought. Indeed, Ardrey remarks on the fact that, despite Spencer's knowledge of their obvious ties to evolutionary thought, the dual codes remain devoid of evolutionary reference: "Oddly enough," Ardrey writes, "it is Spencer, the evolutionist, who seems by some quirk to have clung to a belief in man's original good nature. He saw the code of enmity as something laid onto man, something that history must one day wash away" (Ardrey 1966, p. 286). He points out too that anthropologist Sir Arthur Keith was actually the first to take up Spencer's dual codes in a true biological sense, giving them a firm footing in territorial behavior, and quotes Keith's basic claim:

> Human nature has a dual constitution; to hate as well as to love are parts of it; and conscience may enforce hate as a duty just as it enforces the duty of love. Conscience has a two-fold role in the soldier: it is his duty to save and protect his own people and equally his duty to destroy their enemies. [...] Thus conscience serves both codes of group behavior; it gives sanction to practices of the code of enmity as well as the code of amity. (Ardrey 1966, pp. 287-8)

What Keith was at pains to show was how tribes occupying specific territories were the original human "evolutionary unit" (Keith 1946, p. 142), how nations are "the lineal successors of tribes" (Keith 1946, p. 146), and how amity binds the tribe or nation together in "group affection" and enmity separates the tribe or nation from other tribes or nations in "group aversion" (Keith 1968, p. 14). Of particular note is his emphasis on fear as the basis of the "enmity complex": "Fear is the tribal sentinel," he states. "Even at peace, fear is not asleep," but is present in "suspicions, dislikes, contempt, and so on" (Keith 1946, pp. 143-4). When roused by a perceived threat, fear sets off a "state of warlike exaltation [in which] there is pressed into action a passion to destroy, to kill, to exterminate the enemy, to terrify him by acts of cruelty and of inhumanity" (Keith 1946, p. 144). In short, Keith's insights into human nature and its capacity for enmity toward outsiders run deep, including not only understandings of the power of fear but the power of ambition to precipitate war. At the base of man's "competitive complex," he states, is "man's desire for place and power-ambition" (Keith 1968, p. 58), a desire he elsewhere speaks of as "the most compelling of human passions" and specifies as one of the two causes of war (Keith 1946, pp. 145, 141, respectively).

It should be noted that both Keith's and Ardrey's conceptions of the dual codes are firmly grounded in the world-wide field research of renown primate psychologist C.R. Carpenter, whose penetrating and insightful studies of the behavior of nonhuman social primates is seminal to their theses (see, for example, Carpenter 1963).

In sum, globalization brings nations, tribes, clans, and ethnic groups into closer and closer commercial and socio-political proximity to one another. The psychic archetype of the stranger runs along a continuum in these more closely lived circumstances. At one extreme, the archetype is prominenced, especially in one's actual and initial face-to-face encounter with a strange other; at the other extreme, the archetype recedes, especially as one's acquaintance with the stranger tempers and even nullifies his or her strangeness. The fear that Keith highlights is essentially an archetypal fear that runs along this same continuum. Fear waxes and wanes in accordance with the waxing and waning of strangeness because it foundationally defines the affective nature of the archetype. Accordingly, when one solidifies one's identity with one's own kind in amity, or "group affection," as Keith describes it, fear is defused precisely by group solidarity; when one turns against others in enmity, or "group aversion," fear may be similarly muted, but muted in this instance by hatred and contempt. On the one hand, globalization can turn the stranger into a known quantity; on the other hand, it can turn the stranger into *the enemy*. In the latter instance, more and more alien others who remain alien stream into one's life. More and more of these others disrupt one's familiar patterns of living. More and more of these others weigh in on the political moves of one's government. More and more of these others are out to destroy the meaning and values of one's life and one's life itself. These others are no longer strangers; they are precisely *enemies*. Clearly, what can follow and has in fact followed from globalization warrants painstaking study.

A key ramification of the cultural archetype of the enemy similarly warrants painstaking study. It has to do with what is generally referred to as the mind/body problem, but takes its bearings not from theoretical formulations but from biological facts of life.

To begin with, the idea that mind and morphology evolved together surely makes evolutionary sense. What Darwin observed in his travels and in his home studies, especially in his extended study of worms in his last years (Darwin 1881/1976), was movement—the habits and practices of living creatures. He observed that what they did and how they did it made sense in terms of survival. It is thus hardly surprising or odd that Darwin should write in one of his Notebooks, "Experience shows the problem of the mind cannot be solved by attacking the citadel itself—the mind is function of body—we must bring some *stable* foundation to argue from" (Darwin 1838/1987, p. 564). What Darwin meant by saying "experience shows" may be interpreted in two ways. He may have been referring to philosophers who attempt to show the nature of mind by attacking the citadel itself. But he may also very well have meant that his own experience —his own first-person experiences of animate life—showed him that the mind was not something distinct from the body but precisely, as he states, a function of body. In effect, animate bodies are mindful bodies. Jung's description of archetypes as systems of readiness for action that are infused with images and emotions and that are inherited with brain structure, constituting psychic aspects thereof, ties in readily with Darwin's observation that mind is a function of body.

The psyche is indeed rooted in nature—it is "part of nature," as Jung (1968, p. 6) avers. Moreover the neglect of the body was apparent and of moment to Jung. Writing in 1928 of "the spiritual problem of modern man," of modern man's "fascination" with the psyche in terms of the unconscious, i.e. what lies below the surface of consciousness and the possibility of this fascination bringing about "a new self-appraisal, a reassessment of our fundamental human nature," Jung presciently remarks,

> We can hardly be surprised if this leads to a rediscovery of the body after its long subjection to the spirit—we are even tempted to say that the flesh is getting its own back. [... T]he body lays claim to equal recognition; it exerts the same fascination as the psyche. If we are still caught in the old idea of an antithesis between mind and matter, this state of affairs must seem like an unbearable contradiction. But if we can reconcile ourselves to the mysterious truth that the spirit is the life of the body seen from within, and the body the outward manifestation of the life of the spirit—the two being really one—then we can understand why the striving to transcend the present level of consciousness through acceptance of the unconscious must give the body its due, and why recognition of the body cannot tolerate a philosophy that denies it in the name of the spirit. (Jung 1970, pp. 93-4)

Still another way of emphasizing the fact that mind and morphology evolve together and of understanding their relationship is to recall an observation by evolutionary anthropologist, William Howells, who rightly, if wryly, noted that "hands and a big brain would not have made a fish human; they would only have made a fish impossible" (Howells 1959, p. 341). Moreover the idea that the psyche is rooted in nature, that its roots are sunk deep into the earth in the narrower sense and in the world in general is methodologically significant. Darwin's ending line intimates as much: i.e. "we must bring some *stable* foundation to argue from" is quintessentially a question of methodology. Surely we can take a cue from evolutionary biology itself, that is, a cue from Darwin's formulation of the origin of species, selection in relation to sex, and the expression of the emotions in man and animals (Darwin 1859/1968, 1871/1981, 1872/1965, respectively). We can, in other words, take a cue from his basic writings about the animate world. They all have a *stable* foundation. They are based on observations of animate creatures making their way in the world. They are based on the observable forms and dynamics of life itself. But that is not all. Darwin meticulously transcribed the observable forms and dynamics into language that both captured and preserved their uniqueness. The stable foundation from which he argued was thus not immediately explanatory or theoretical in nature but *descriptive*. His consequent thesis concerning evolution and explanations of the interconnectedness of animate life rest on *descriptive foundations*. We might note that, in a related way, phenomenology rests on descriptive foundations as do literary, environmental, and ecological writings (see Sheets-Johnstone 2002).

What is the import of descriptive foundations? They are obviously the empirical foundation for verification by others who can corroborate or question the authenticity and aptness of a description. In addition, however, they are the basis of taxonomic analyses, which analyses, of fundamental import in themselves, in turn open the possibility of comparative studies that set forth relationships among the things described. With respect to archetypes, such studies would be of considerable value precisely for this reason. An archetypal taxonomy would delineate the nature of psychic forms and in turn open the possibility of showing relationships and lineages among them.

References

Ardrey, R. (1966) *The Territorial Imperative*, New York: Dell Publishing.

Baron-Cohen, S. (1995) *Mindblindness: An Essay on Autism and Theory of Mind*, Cambridge, MA: MIT Press.

Becker, E. (1973) *The Denial of Death*, New York: The Free Press.

Becker, E. (1975) *Escape from Evil*, New York: The Free Press.

Bernstein, D., Clarke-Stewart, A., Roy, E.J., Srull, T.K. & Wickens, C.D. (1994) *Psychology*, 3rd ed., Boston, MA: Houghton Mifflin.

Birkhead, T.R. (2000) *Promiscuity: An Evolutionary History of Sperm Competition*, Cambridge, MA: Harvard University Press.

Birkhead, T.R. & Moller, A.P. (eds.) (1998) *Sperm Competition and Sexual Selection*, San Diego, CA: Academic Press.

Carpenter, C.R. (1963) Societies of monkeys and apes, in Southwick, C.H. (ed.) *Primate Social Behavior*, pp. 24–51, New York: Van Nostrand Reinhold.

Darwin, C. (1838/1987) *Charles Darwin's Notebooks, 1836–1844*, Barrett, P.H., Gautrey, P.J., Herbert, S., Kohn, D. & Smith, S. (eds.), Ithaca, NY: Cornell University Press.

Darwin, C. (1859/1968) *The Origin of Species*, Burrow, J.W. (ed.) Harmondsworth: Penguin Books.

Darwin, C. (1871/1981) *The Descent of Man and Selection in Relation to Sex*, 2 vols., Princeton, NJ: Princeton University Press.

Darwin, C. (1872/1965) *The Expression of the Emotions in Man and Animals*, Chicago, IL: University of Chicago Press.

Darwin, C. (1881/1976) *Darwin on Earthworms: The Formation of Mould Through the Action of Worms with Observations on Their Habits*, Ontario: Bookworm.

Golledge, R.G. (ed.) (1999) *Wayfinding Behavior: Cognitive Mapping and Other Spatial Processes*, Baltimore, MD: Johns Hopkins University Press.

Herodotus, *The Persian Wars*, Rawlinson, G. (trans.), in Godolphin, F.R.B. (ed.) (1942) *The Greek Historians*, pp. 3–563, New York: Random House.

Howells, W. (1959) *Mankind in the Making*, New York: Doubleday & Co.

Jung, C.G. (1968) *Man and His Symbols*, New York: Dell Publishing.

Jung, C.G. (1969) *On the Nature of the Psyche*, Hull, R.F.C. (trans.), in Read, Sir H., Fordham, M., Adler, G. & McGuire, W. (eds.) *Collected Works*, vol. 8 (Bollingen Series XX), Princeton, NJ: Princeton University Press.

Jung, C.G. (1970) *Civilization in Transition*, 2nd ed., Hull, R.F.C. (trans.), *Collected Works*, vol. 10 (Bollingen Series XX), Princeton, NJ: Princeton University Press.

Keeley, L.H. (1996) *War Before Civilization*, New York: Oxford University Press.

Keen, S. (1986) *Faces of the Enemy: Reflections of the Hostile Imagination*, New York: Harper & Row.

Keith, A. (1946) *Essays on Human Evolution*, London: Watts.

Keith, A. (1968) *A New Theory of Human Evolution*, Gloucester, MA: Peter Smith.

Kidd, J.E.R. (1999) *Alterity and Identity in Israel*, Berlin: Walter de Gruyter.

O'Keefe, J.O. & Nadel, L. (1979) The hippocampus as a cognitive map, *Behavioral and Brain Sciences*, 2, pp. 487–533.

Parker, G. (1998) Sperm competition and the 'Evolution of ejaculates': Towards a theory base, in Birkhead, T.R. & Moller, A.P. (eds.) *Sperm Competition and Sexual Selection*, San Diego, CA: Academic Press.

Rank, O. (1998) *Psychology and the Soul: A Study of the Origin, Conceptual Evolution, and Nature of the Soul*, Richter, G.C. & Lieberman, E.J. (eds.), Baltimore, MD: Johns Hopkins University Press.

Sheets-Johnstone, M. (1994) *The Roots of Power: Animate Form and Gendered Bodies*, Chicago, IL: Open Court Publishing.

Sheets-Johnstone, M. (2002/this volume, Chapter X) Descriptive foundations, *Interdisciplinary Studies in Literature and Environment*, 9 (1), pp. 165–179.

Sheets-Johnstone, M. (2008) *The Roots of Morality*, University Park, PA: Pennsylvania State University Press.

Simmons, L.W. (2001) *Sperm Competition and Its Evolutionary Consequences in Insects*, Princeton, NJ: Princeton University Press.

Wrangham, R. & Peterson, D. (1996) *Demonic Males: Apes and the Origins of Human Violence*, Boston, MA: Houghton Mifflin.

Chapter XII

Strangers, Trust, and Religion

On the Vulnerability of Being Alive[1]

Abstract: *This chapter is far less a position paper or a descriptive analysis than an attempt to illuminate the lines that connect commonly recognized realities of human life: unfamiliar others in the form of strangers, interpersonal feelings in the form of trust, and organized belief systems in the form of religion. Its epistemological and even ontological conclusion may be sketched as follows: where belief overtakes wonder, religion fails in its mission to enhance life. When fear overtakes wonder, individuals fail in the promise of their aliveness. In particular, when belief overtakes wonder, religion fails in the sense of constraining or even shutting the individual off from investigation and exploration of the unknown or unfamiliar, or from what is not sanctioned as proper. When fear overtakes simple curiosity and the desire to know, the individual fails in the sense of simply reacting, prejudging a situation or a person as threatening or dangerous in advance of actual experience. When belief and fear together take over, human experience is shackled and crippled. It remains ideologically tethered and affectively maimed. The effect of this tethering and maiming has moral consequences having to do with a recognition or non-recognition of the foundational common humanness of humans.*

I cannot imagine a God who rewards and punishes the objects of his creation, whose purposes are modeled after our own—a God, in short, who is but a reflection of human frailty. Neither can I believe that the individual survives the death of his body, although feeble souls harbor such thoughts through fear or ridiculous egotism. It is enough for me to contemplate the mystery of conscious life perpetuating itself through all eternity, to reflect upon the marvelous structure of the universe which we can dimly perceive, and to try humbly to comprehend even an

---

[1] First published in *Human Studies* (2015), Vol. 38, No. 3: doi 10.1007/s10746-015-9367-z.

infinitesimal part of the intelligence manifested in nature. (Einstein 1990, pp. 204 ff.)

I experienced terror at what awaited me [...] I could not patiently await that end. The horror of darkness was too great, and I wished to free myself from it as quickly as possible by noose or bullet. That was the feeling which drew me most strongly toward suicide. [...] During that time ["seeing the truth of the situation and yet clinging to life, knowing in advance that nothing can come of it"] this is what happened to me. During that whole year, when I was asking myself almost every moment whether I should not end matters with a noose or a bullet—all that time, together with the course of thought and observation about which I have spoken, my heart was oppressed with a painful feeling, which I can only describe as a search for God. I say that that search for God was not reasoning, but a feeling, because that search proceeded not from the course of my thoughts—it was even directly contrary to them —but proceeded from the heart. It was a feeling of fear, orphanage, isolation in a strange land, and a hope of help from someone. (Tolstoy 1992, p. 354)

I. Introduction

Strangers, trust, and religion are critical dimensions within the sphere of human vulnerability. How are they experientially related? This chapter begins with an epistemological account of the stranger as an Other in the Sartrean sense of otherness: someone who is the embodiment of possible harm, a threat to both one's existence and the very meanings and values one's life embodies, hence an existential source of fear. The chapter then sets forth an account of trust as a palliative to fear, trust being a socio-affective "compensation" for all its risks. On the basis of observations by both Thomas Merton and Huston Smith concerning the stranger, the chapter in turn investigates the relationship of strangers, trust, and religion in the terms of life and death. In doing so, it draws on citations from the writings of Michel Foucault and Elaine Scarry who, in different ways, highlight provocative conceptions of the Other. The chapter ends with reflections upon what Rudolph Otto termed the "mysterium tremendum" —the experienced mystery of life itself—upon the fact that humans are vulnerable in the mere fact of being alive among other humans, and upon the fact that they have ways of transcending their vulnerability through a recognition and even celebration of their common humanity.

II. The Stranger: Fleshing Out the Epistemological Ground of Sartre's Ontological Other

A stranger is by definition someone unknown and as such the embodiment of possible harm. Being an unfamiliar Other, a stranger in a broader sense confronts one with a potentially inharmonious world. Feelings of vulnerability come readily to the fore and with them the immediate challenge to trust or distrust: should one turn toward the stranger and explore a relationship or turn away and avoid or even escape contact?

Feelings of vulnerability are basic human feelings put vividly on the line by a stranger. The anxiety intrinsic to these feelings and the gravity of these feelings run deep. We can begin to grasp both by examining them in the context of the Other, in particular, in the context of Sartre's meticulous and penetrating exposition of "The Existence of Others" (1956, pp. 221–302). As we will see, though not identified as such, the stranger underlies the whole of his exposition, beginning with his initial identification of the Other as the source of the feeling of shame and concluding with his questioning concern about "manifest bodies" (Sartre 1956, p. 302).

Although Sartre makes no distinction between familiar and unfamiliar Others, the existentially significant epistemological distinction is implicit from the start in his affirmation that "inseparable" structures define "my *being*" and "the being of the Other" (1956, pp. 222 ff.). In particular, while his concern and the structures he proceeds to elucidate are clearly ontological rather than epistemological, it is nonetheless evident throughout that the Other is not someone familiar—familiar in any way, shape, or form; on the contrary, the Other appears consistently as a total and utter stranger. Consider, for example, the following passages that attest to an unknown, unpredictable Other who in one way and another threatens one's aliveness. Each passage brings a central but differently nuanced dimension of vulnerability to light:

> "Through the Other's look I *live* myself as fixed in the midst of the world, as in danger, as Irremediable" (1956, p. 268); "[F]or me the Other is first the being for whom I am an object" (1956, p. 270);[2] "[T]he death of my possibilities causes me to experience the Other's freedom" (1956, p. 271); "Fear is therefore the discovery of my being-as-object on the occasion of the appearance of another object in my perceptive field. It refers to the origin of all fear, which is the fearful discovery of my pure and simple object-state in so far as it is surpassed and transcended by possibles which are not my possibles" (1956, p. 288).

Consider further, Sartre's descriptive account of an experience that culminates in the look and its corollary, "being seen." Though highlighting a distinctively ontological rather than epistemological relationship, the

---

[2] "The proof of my condition as man, as an object for *all* other living men, as thrown in the arena beneath millions of looks and escaping myself millions of times—this proof I realize concretely on the occasion of the upsurge of an object into my universe if this object indicates to me that I am probably an object at present functioning as a *differentiated this* for a consciousness" (Sartre 1956, p. 281).

descriptive account paradigmatically captures the core experience of
vulnerability with respect to a stranger:

> What I apprehend immediately when I hear the branches crackling
> behind me is not that there *is someone there*; it is that I am vulnerable,
> that I have a body which can be hurt, that I occupy a place and that I can
> not in any case escape from the space in which I am without defense — in
> short, that *I am seen*. (1956, p. 259)

Several pages later (1956, p. 264), this core experience is given fuller
description in the context of noting "possibilities that are present to my
unreflective consciousness in so far as the Other is *watching me*." *Unreflected
possibilities* are precisely not reasoned out options but a spontaneous mix of
possible actions and scenarios that arises spontaneously within immediate
experience. They include:

1. hiding — "the dark corner becomes a given possibility";
2. the use of weaponry or an electronic signal — the Other may be
   "ready for anything, his hand in his pocket where he has a weapon,
   his finger placed on the electric bell and ready 'at the slightest
   movement on my part' to call the police";
3. escaping — "[t]his inclination to run away, which dominates me and
   carries me along and which I *am* — this I read in the Other's watchful
   look";
4. a further look that augments the inclination to run away — the look
   of "the gun pointed at me";
5. the alienation or total annihilation of my possibilities — "[t]he Other
   is the hidden death of my possibilities in so far as I live that death as
   hidden in the midst of the world."

In short, while the look of the Other is foregrounded in Sartre's
descriptions, vulnerability in face of an unknown Other is the grounding
experience. "Being seen" is thus instrumental, not fundamental, in "the
death of my possibilities." What is fundamental is fear, fear of an unknown
Other and what an unknown Other might do. As Sartre himself pointedly
observes, "fear [is] the feeling of being in danger before the Other's freedom" (1956, p. 268). Moreover if the feeling of danger is epitomized in the
knowledge that "I have a body which can be hurt," then surely it matters
when "the 'situation' escapes me," that is, when "*I am no longer master of the
situation*" (1956, p. 265). Indeed, when Sartre states, "I am *in danger*," and
then immediately states, "[t]his danger is not an accident but the permanent structure of my being-for-others" (1956, p. 268), there is no doubt but
that an incisive bodily-felt vulnerability is a core human experience, that it
is a primordial dimension of human life, and that a strange Other cannot
but loom large and in fact figure as an ineffaceable central presence within

"the permanent structure of my being-for-others." In effect, the epistemological dimension of the core experience cannot be ignored: an affectively-
charged existential abyss separates familiar and unfamiliar Others.[3]

In sum, Sartre's Other is unequivocally a stranger, and a stranger is
unequivocally the personification of vulnerability. Vulnerability is indeed
at the core of basic human affects, not only shame but terror, apprehension,
depression, and abjection. Its foundational existential presence in these
affects is evident in the same distinctive temporal dimension Sartre
describes specifically with respect to the lived relation of oneself to oneself
in shame, namely, "the consciousness of being irremediably what I always
was: 'in suspense' — that is, in the mode of the 'not-yet' or of the 'already-

---

3   Further examination of Sartre's exemplary descriptions reveals additional
    perspectives on how affectively-charged epistemological facets are funda-
    mental. Sartre describes the feeling of shame as "an intimate relation of
    myself to myself" (1956, p. 221), emphasizing from the start that such a
    relation is not a reflective relation but an immediately lived one, i.e. "in so
    far as the Other *is watching me*," I immediately experience myself as an
    object. It is thus clear how "the Other is the indispensable mediator between
    myself and me" (1956, p. 222), and in particular, how "I am ashamed of
    myself as I *appear* to the Other" (1956, p. 222), namely, as an object caught in
    an unseemly act of some kind. As indicated above, however, the primordial
    vulnerability of humans is not a matter of being seen; it has nothing to do
    with "appearance" as such. When we distinguish between a purely ontol-
    ogical rendition of the Other and an epistemologically inflected ontological
    rendition of the Other — between a theoretical concern with the being of the
    Other *tout court* as distinct from a living concern with the being of the Other
    as familiar or unfamiliar — we find that the primordial vulnerability of
    humans has to do not with *the look* of the Other, but with the *full-bodied
    presence* of the Other and the potential harm that full-bodied presence
    embodies, above all with respect to its familiarity or unfamiliarity. The pri-
    mordial vulnerability of humans, like the primordial vulnerability of all
    animals, is indeed tied to the existential condition of being alive, and alive
    among full-bodied Others. Shame is in truth only one possible form of
    communal vulnerability and a highly sophisticated one at that. The starkest
    form is tied to the simple fact of being communally alive. It hinges on the
    unpredictability of unknown Others and on the incipient to full-fledged fear
    that unpredictability evokes or may evoke. Sartre himself points up the
    "unpredictability" of the Other in the fact of his being "*no longer master of the
    situation*" (1956, pp. 265 ff.). Clearly, an epistemological gap exists, a fore-
    boding scissure engendered in the very presence of an unfamiliar Other.
    The gap is implicit in Sartre's descriptions of his "situation" before the
    Other: "I am in a world which the Other has made alien to me" (1956, p.
    261); "I experience a subtle alienation of all my possibilities" (1956, p. 265);
    "every act performed against the Other can on principle be for the Other an
    instrument which will serve him against me" (1956, p. 264); "I grasp the
    Other [...] in a fear which lives all my possibilities as ambivalent" (1956, p.
    264).

no-longer'" (1956, p. 288). In a word, the experience of vulnerability is the tantalizingly frozen yet ongoing moment in which one's aliveness is and remains on the line, in which the meaning and values of one's life hang in the balance.

Whatever the particular affect which literally embodies it, the experience of vulnerability runs along a continuum of being "in suspense" because vulnerability is an Ur-existential condition of human life. It lies *in potentia* and is brought to fore full-force in the form of a stranger whose unknownness has the power to hold one's life in suspense, in an ongoing, all-enveloping anxiety of the unfamiliar.

Like virtually all animals, humans cultivate familiarity. It is not that they turn from exploring new terrains, discovering new edibles, or trying new techniques, however. On the contrary, they investigate novelty. As pointed out and cited in a discussion of infant learning: "Infant researchers have long remarked on the fact that infants are attracted to novelty; they habituate to what is regular or expected and pay particular attention to what is unusual. The latter phenomenon— 'preferential looking,' as infant and child psychologist Lois Bloom at one point describes it (1993: 43)—is regularly used as an empirical measure of an infant's perceptions, expectations, interests, and so on" (Sheets-Johnstone 1999, p. 499/exp. 2nd ed. 2011, p. 432). Once explored, discovered, or tried, however, any novelty is encompassed within the realm of the familiar. That a terrain proves hostile, an edible indigestible, or a technique ill-conceived is immaterial. What matters is that the initial novelty is no longer novel; it no longer has the status of the unknown but enters the realm of the known. A stranger undergoes just such an epistemological metamorphosis when he or she becomes familiar and is no longer avoided or feared but enfolded into the group.[4] Yet there is something familiar, even *already indubitably known*, about a human stranger, namely, his or her humanness.

A human stranger is indeed in essence both a known and unknown quantity. On the one hand, he or she is what we would colloquially describe as "one of us," a biological consociate we immediately recognize as human; on the other hand, he or she is feared, feared precisely because we know the possibilities of being human. Our fear emanates from our knowledge of the possibilities for harming that lie within humans—all humans. Even if—or even as—we deny the existence of these possibilities in ourselves, we take for granted that they lie within a strange Other. The double standard is quintessentially epitomized in Jung's concept of "the

---

4   An exceptionally lucid and detailed account of just such acceptance is given by evolutionary anthropologist Shirley Strum, who describes the patient and protracted lengths to which a strange male olive baboon (*Papio anubis*) went prior to being accepted within a new group (1987, pp. 23–37).

shadow," that commonly un-owned realm of our psyche that we keep in the dark even as we unwittingly project aspects of it onto others.[5] If we would actually examine our shadow side, we would find that we are vulnerable to our own felt proclivities, that is, to carrying out acts that harm others. Jung put the matter tersely and sharply when he wrote, "[s]ince it is universally believed that man is merely what his conscious-ness knows of itself, he regards himself as harmless and so adds stupidity to iniquity. He does not deny that terrible things have happened and still go on happening, but it is always 'the others' who do them" (1970, p. 296).[6]

Of specific moment here is less the fact that we humans are all psychically shadowed, so to speak, commonly projecting facets of our shadow Other onto real-life others and remaining opaque to our own capacity for doing harm—psychoanalytic facts that surely warrant examination in their own right—than the fact that we know the harmful possibilities of humans. We know in concrete, graphic ways not simply *that*, but *how*, humans can and do harm each other, and we know further, in concrete, *affective* ways the difference between being among familiar and unfamiliar humans. In short, we know that our fundamental vulnerability in being alive among other humans is augmented in the extreme when it is a question of unfamiliar others. A stranger can be a danger not just to our life but to our way of life, a threat to both our existence and the very meanings and values our life embodies.

III. On Trust and Its "Compensations"

We can begin to unravel the religious consequences and implications of our epistemologically inflected vulnerability by considering first the experi-ential difference between trust and distrust. As elsewhere noted and discussed at length (Sheets-Johnstone 2006), trust is a palliative to fearful feelings: it diminishes fear, but neither automatically nor necessarily banishes it conclusively for all time. Bodily feelings of fear and trust, how-ever, are oppositional. The dynamics of fear are in a corporeal-kinetic sense antithetical to trust. Fear *moves through* the body in ways different from trust, and it *moves* the body in ways different from trust (Sheets-Johnstone

---

[5] Jung's concept of the shadow and his analyses of the practice of projection are highly relevant to understandings of the stranger and warrant full examination in their own right.

[6] Jung also comments provocatively in his essay "The Undiscovered Self" on the fact that "resistances to psychological enlightenment are based in large measure on fear—on panic fear of the discoveries that might be made in the realm of the unconscious. [...] Often the fear is so great that one dares not admit it even to oneself. This is a question which every religious person should consider very seriously; he might get an illuminating answer" (1970, pp. 271 ff.).

2006, 2012). In effect, the emotional resonance of the feelings is such that the two cannot be present simultaneously. In the one, an overall feeling of ease and openness toward the future obtains along with a concomitant fluidity of motion; in the other, a tightness grips the body in preparation for the worst of futures and eventuates in a taut irregularity of motion. Both the tensional mode of the body and the flow of movement are palpably distinct. A striking resemblance is in fact evident with respect to the relationship Epicurus observed between life and death: when fear is present, trust is not; and when trust is present, fear is not. Moreover, at any moment fear may banish trust just as, at any moment, trust may banish fear.[7]

The oppositional dynamics of trust and fear testify affectively to the fact that, as sociologist Niklas Luhmann affirms, trust "rests on illusion" (1979, p. 32) and is "a risky investment" (1979, p. 27). Yet however illusory and risky the nature of trust, it is in our interest to trust and to cultivate trust both in ourselves and in others,[8] for in a way almost totally unlike other creatures, humans are at risk not only by way of natural accidents or ageing; they are at risk in being alive among their own kind: as indicated above, humans are at risk "*in being alive among other humans*" (see Sheets-

---

[7]   The deftly programmed relationship of the federal government to the electorate in the United States from 11 September 2001 until the bursting of the Republican bubble on 7 November 2006 is a sterling example. Fear of terrorism was willfully injected into public life — via duct tape and other such measures — to secure trust in the federal government, which trust, of course, kept fear of terrorism at bay. See footnote 8. In short, trust was politically cemented by the social manipulation and control of fear. Injections of fear not only kept trust in federal governments alive but strengthened its social hold.

[8]   If one were a sociobiologist rather than a systems theorist, one would attempt to show that trusting and cultivating trust are behaviors enhancing reproductive success, not behaviors reducing complexity; that is, one would attempt to explain trust adaptively in terms of ultimate causation rather than functionally in terms of proximate causation. The explanations, however, would run basically along similar lines, i.e. they would determine "the benefit" that comes from trust. In contrast to posing and answering the question, "what is it good for?" or "how does it work?," one could pose and answer the question, "where does it come from?" If phenomenologically inclined, one might thereby trace out the origin and development of trust, elucidating it as an existential condition of human aliveness. For a beginning attempt in this direction, see Sheets-Johnstone (2006). But see also Endress and Pabst for a phenomenological exposition of "basic (operating) trust" (2013, p. 95) as a "non-thematic" constituent (2013, p. 95) and "persisting background premise" (2013, p. 96) of actions and interactions in everyday life, a trust that can "only be analyzed *ex negativo*" (2013, p. 102), that is, in the context of interpersonal violence that shatters trust.

Johnstone 2002, p. 52). The existential value of trust is to mitigate this human condition, that is, to preserve human sanity by mitigating the potential threat of others and the concomitant anxiety that that threat poses. To put the value in terms of sanity is not to say that the relationship of uncertainty to trust is a reasoned out relationship; one does not think, "[o]ther people have an 'uncontrollable power to act' (Luhmann 1979: 41); I cannot be certain what they will do, therefore I will trust them to offset my anxieties about what they might do." Trust, after all, is not an adult affect but originates in ontogeny, in feelings of well-being, and in subsequent feelings of attachment.

From an ontogenetic viewpoint, the learning of trust begins in non-linguistic experience, i.e. in tactile-kinetic social interactions, notably those in the context of nurturing and play. In such infant/adult interactions, affective experiences are generated. In particular, feelings of ease (e.g. comfortableness, pleasure, contentment) and uneasiness (e.g. apprehension, startle, fear) are generated (see Sheets-Johnstone 2006). These primary experiences, documented in a variety of literature on human infant and child development (e.g. Stern 1977, 1985; Trevarthen 1977; Bugental et al. 1991) — and on nonhuman infant development as well (van Lawick-Goodall 1971; Strum 1987; Dolhinow 1972) — are the foundation of developing attitudes of trust; they are the ontogenetic basis of learning to trust. In effect, and precisely as Luhmann implicitly affirms, trust is in the very nature of human nature. It develops naturally in specific sociological ways on the basis of its natural affective origins. Its existential value is in turn a naturally arising value. Luhmann recognizes this naturally arising existential value implicitly when he states, "[o]ne of the most elementary mechanisms of complexity reduction is the *stabilization of feelings* towards particular objects or people" (1979, p. 80; italics added).

In sum, trust has sizeable socio-affective compensations for all its risks. Its power to stabilize feelings of ease in a world of others is a substantive part of its nature. In a limited way, something similar may be said of religion; that is, for all its risks, not only as classically articulated by Pascal, but by others as well, it too has the power to stabilize feelings of ease in the world. Indeed, "In God we trust" is emblazoned on all US money, seemingly to assure Americans of the absolute goodness of capitalism, thus perhaps assuring corpulent corporate Americans in particular of being able to squeeze through the eye of a needle after all.

Though unconcerned with trust in any focal way, philosopher Konstantin Kolenda's conception of religion as compensatory is topical to feelings of ease in the world. Kolenda conceives religion as compensation for human finitude. With respect to the notion of God and the human awareness of death, his aim is to show how the essence of religion is not to trust in a God — an object or image of some kind — but to enrich individual human lives to the fullest. In his book *Religion without God*, he writes, "[t]he notion of God is the limiting target of compensation. It encapsulates the desire to escape finitude, the search for realization of highest potentialities, the urge to translate ideals into actuality. God is the embodiment of perfection, but if compensation as the tendency toward perfection is logically prior to perfection, then the notion of compensation is a more primitive, more fundamental religious concept" (1976, p. 75). Kolenda goes on to show that religion as compensation links us to the *radiance* of the world, both the world of nature and the human-made world; the latter including music ("an ingenious invention"), knowledge ("a display of intellectual power"), and so on, all of which "compensations" enhance and intensify the meaning of our lives (1976, p. 86). Such "religiousness," as he terms it, is a "superontological" proof of the existence of God that bypasses the notion of God as a transcendent object but is the very essence of religion (1976, pp. 76 ff.). Through participation in the radiance of the world and arriving at such states as wonder, well-being, assurance, security, safety, and joy (Kolenda 1976, pp. 78 ff.) — all of them "manifestations of finding the world *good*, as God found it to be when he beheld it following the act of creation" (1976, p. 79) — we are, according to Kolenda, at the heart of religion. "[T]he world," as he affirms, "provides suitable material for religious feeling" (1976, p. 81).

One might say, in effect, that, for Kolenda, religions offer compensation for death by way of celebrating life itself.[9] If worldly compensations answer to the desire to escape finitude by providing "material for religious feeling," however, religion becomes no more than a way of avoiding the fearful reality of death. Well-being, joy, security, safety, and the like are attributes of compensation, but they do not answer in any depth to the fear and trembling of humans, to the fundamental vulnerability embodied in their very aliveness. Moreover however self-deceptively reconfigured or even offset by quite other worldly means than those mentioned by Kolenda, by the accumulation of *more*, for example — more power, more money, more real estate holdings, or more fame, all of which putatively

---

9   Although well-being, security, safety, and the like figure in the compensatory spin-offs of religion that Kolenda describes, trust does not figure substantively and centrally in the equation in any way. What does figure centrally is death. As philosopher David Stewart points out, Kolenda attempts to find an alternative to the personal and transcendent God of the Jewish and Christian traditions through the notion of compensation: "The religious impulse, Kolenda argues, arises from our awareness of human finitude; another way of saying this is that religion grows out of our awareness that we all die. Because religions — at least some religions — give us hope for continued existence after death, they attempt to provide what Kolenda calls *compensation* for human finitude" (1992, p. 340).

maximize the compensatory feelings Kolenda specifies, bringing greater and greater well-being, joy, security, safety, and the like — the fact of death remains. Thus, whatever the mode or modes of compensatory subversion that keep it veiled, death continues to loom large in human affairs. That it does so perhaps explains why it is uncannily presenced in the form of a stranger. The presence of a stranger is akin to a presentiment of death, evoking a foreboding, fear-laden awareness of what might be termed the ultimate unknown Other: oneself as dead. In light of our epistemologically-inflected vulnerability, the linkage of a stranger with death is far from odd. Yet another quite different sense of the stranger turns us toward the possibility of a distinctly different — indeed, positive — experience.

Huston Smith, renowned authority on comparative religions and their history, asks at the end of his book, *The World's Religions*, "[w]ho today stands ready to accept the solemn equality of peoples? Who does not have to fight an unconscious tendency to equate foreign with inferior?" (1991, p. 390). He asks these questions in the context of proposing an altogether different sense of the stranger, that is, in the context of an emphasis on listening, on striving for open and compassionate understandings of all ideologically-tethered religious ways of life, and in particular those ways that are foreign to one's own. In the process of doing so, he reminds his readers of Thomas Merton's observation that "God speaks to us in three places: in scripture, in our deepest selves, and in the voice of the stranger" (Smith 1991).

Clearly, if we take Smith's emphasis on listening to the stranger and Merton's observation regarding the voice of the stranger seriously, then we perforce take both our "unconscious tendency," "our deepest selves" — that is, the shadow dwelling in our own psyche — and the foreigner — that is, the stranger dwelling in our midst — seriously, and seriously in a double sense: both shadow and stranger are in different ways a threat to our comfortable, familiar existence and at the same time harken us to a fuller, richer life by opening us to *their* existence. Granted, listening with searing clarity to the affective swells and inclinations of our deepest selves commonly puts us less in touch with radiance than with pain, evoking less than joyful, less than secure, less than assured aspects of ourselves. Indeed, we are less in touch with feelings of well-being than of *un*well-being. Yet the dark side of our psyches warrants examination, for it provides us with insights into our true motivations, into the true consequences of our actions, and so on. The Bible does not speak to us about investigating our shadow side. It does, however, speak straightaway of strangers, of traditional attitudes toward strangers and the proper attitude toward strangers. A circuitous route to these biblical conceptions and admonitions provides substantive experiential and theoretical understandings that follow through on Huston's and Merton's promptings to listen openly to the stranger, that correlatively suggest openings toward our own shadow side, and that lead back full circle to the epistemologically-inflected Other discovered earlier in the examination of Sartre's descriptive ontology of the Other. The circuitous route consists in my hazarding two comments, each followed by pertinent citations, from Michel Foucault in the one instance, from Elaine Scarry in the other, comments and citations that situate oneself and the Other in relation to life and death.

IV. The Circuitous Route

First, the larger one's lifeworld and the larger the perceived globality of the world itself, the greater the weight of eternity and the more infinitesimal the meaning and value of one's life. What can God possibly do with all these dead humans, billions upon billions of them, far more than a trickle of whom believed or may have believed in an assortment of Gods altogether different from the one any particular religion venerates? Does the real God take into account moreover that uncountable numbers of humans believe and have believed in God but be on the wrong God-track, so to speak? Does the real God offer eternal life or salvation equally to all those well-meaning and well-believing but off-track humans? However unacknowledged, the weight of eternity weighs heavily indeed regardless of the track one is on. At the same time, the greater the weight of eternity and the more infinitesimal the meaning and value of one's life, the tighter one clings to one's beliefs and the more strongly one is threatened by and counters the beliefs of others that are different from one's own. In short, fear of strangers and their strange beliefs increases exponentially with an expanding world. In effect, trust in strangers easily falls by the wayside as xenophobic fears hold greater and greater sway. Foucault recognized something on the order of this socio-spatio-temporal relationship when, in suggesting that an Other is someone who disturbs the familiar order of things and is thus commonly perceived as a threat, he wrote, "[i]t is [...] [a]s if we were afraid to conceive of the *Other* in the time of our own thought" (1972, p. 12).

"[...] in the time of our own thought": a provocative thought in itself. We have so little time to think and think so little in the sense of being "at the pains of a little thought" as Berkeley genteelly put it (1709/1929, p. 85; see also, 1709/1929, pp. 72f., 79) — and especially as concerns the Other, not only in the sense of thinking so little but thinking belittlingly. Most notably too, we are affectively stirred, precisely "*afraid*," as Foucault observes, "to conceive of the Other in the time of our own thought." Foucault might have had in mind not only a stranger — an unfamiliar, threatening-because-disturbing live Other — but "Other" in the form of death itself, an Other equally unfamiliar and threatening. We are indeed afraid to conceive of death — most commonly, our own death — "in the time of our own thought." Most of us think of death along the lines of our projected shadow, indeed, along the literal lines of Jung already cited and readily paraphrased: "Man does not deny that death has happened and still happens, but it is always 'the others' who die." (There are obvious tie-ins here with Heidegger's "they" and their idle talk.) Whether stranger or death, the more distant we keep the Other in space, time, and thought, the less we are engulfed in fear. In effect, the less we recognize that we are vulnerable, that we are, as Sartre affirmed, *"in danger,"* that "[the felt] danger is not an accident but the permanent structure of my being-for-others," and that "fear [is] the feeling of being in danger before the Other's freedom." Whether as stranger or death, we protect ourselves precisely by not, in Foucault's word, "conceiving" the unfamiliar.

A different sense of the Other can nonetheless haunt us. The strange Other whose freedom evokes fear and before whom we are vulnerable may be God, who looms in a towering, ascendant, and far more sweeping sense than any mundane stranger. It may be He who controls the seemingly accidental time of our birth and ordains the seemingly accidental time of our death, "the time of our own thought" thus being a matter of His judgement of us. The second comment I hazard enlarges on this theme.

The price of not believing is spelled out explicitly in the Bible and leaves no doubt that not just death, but life itself will be the punishment. Deuteronomy 28:67 unequivocally describes the price of not believing: "[T]he Lord will give you an anxious mind, eyes weary with longing, and a despairing heart. You will live in constant suspense, filled with dread both night and day, never sure of your life." In short, you will be punished for disbelieving: you will live dying, in the constant throes of vulnerability. Elaine Scarry has written in penetrating and corporeally enlightened ways on the biblical theme of disbelief and disobedience. She cites passages showing that both disbelief and disobedience are "habitually described as a withholding of the body, which in its resistance to an external referent is perceived as covered, or hard, or stiff" (1985, pp. 202 ff.). We might note, of course, that a hard, stiff, and/or covered body is commonly a dead body, but this is not Scarry's theme. Her keynote idea is rather that "the withholding of the body — the stiffening of the neck, the turning of the shoulder, the closing of the ears, the hardening of the heart, the making of the face like stone — necessitates God's forceful shattering of the reluctant human surface and repossession of the interior" (1985, pp. 203 ff.).[10] She comments

---

[10] She notes that "[p]erhaps the most overt acting out of this [shattering and repossession] occurs in the final plague on the house of the Pharaoh, the final entry into his hard heart, the massacre of the innocents in which the interior of the body as it emerges in the firstborn infant is taken by God (Exodus 12)" (1985, p. 204).

that "[t]he fragility of the human interior and the absolute surrender of that interior that does not simply accompany belief, that is not simply required by belief, but that is *itself belief* [...] are in this history acted out with terrible force and unequivocal meaning" (1985, pp. 203 ff.). Not only this but "the willing consecration of the Israelite infants, the willing consecration by the Israelites of their own interiors" follows in the form of God's command-ment to "[c]onsecrate to me all the first-born; whatever is the first to open the womb among the people of Israel, both of man and of beast is mine ([Exodus] 13:1, 2)" (1985, pp. 203 ff.).

In her chapter on "Body and Voice in the Judeo-Christian Scriptures," Scarry speaks specifically of "the imperfection and vulnerability of the human" (1985, p. 183), and goes on to describe how "[t]he relation between man and God [...] becomes a power relation based on the fact that one has a body and the other does not, a relation that is itself radically revised in the Christian scripture where the moral distance between man and God is as great as in the Old Testament but no longer depends on a discrepancy in embodiedness" (1985, p. 184).[11] In support of her corporeal readings, she shows how "[i]t is through the human body that belief is substantiated and [...] it is in its capacity of substantiation that the body, the interior of the body, is often represented in these stories. The most overt instances of this occur in those passages describing the actual passage of children out of the mother's body" (1985, p. 188). Finally, we should note Scarry's claim that "however more powerful the Word of God is than the Body of man, it is within these [biblical] stories always the case that the Word is never self-substantiating: it seeks its confirmation in a visible change in the realm of matter" (1985, p. 193).[12]

What becomes evident on the basis of Scarry's reading of biblical texts is that the transition from verbal to physical is a transition that existentializes belief by materializing it in some form. Trust in God is, as it were, corporeally cemented. The Word is indeed made flesh. The price of not believing is, in contrast, to suffer one's flesh, to live not only precisely as the Bible indicates, excruciatingly and morbidly "in constant suspense," but, strikingly enough, precisely as Sartre indicates with respect to the temporal relation of oneself to oneself in shame, namely, being "conscious-ness of being what I always was: 'in suspense' — that is, in the mode of the 'not-yet' or of the 'already no longer'." Being locked in suspense is in both

---

11 Scarry's theme is furthermore to show how "God's most intimate contact with humanity, His sensory contact with the human body, is in the Hebraic scriptures mediated by a weapon [e.g. a flaming torch, a burning bush, a rod, a stick, a stone (1985, pp. 200 ff.)] and in the Christian scriptural additions is mediated by Jesus" (1985, p. 213).

12 The relation between the "Word of God" and the "Body of Man" is mediated.

instances a matter of living irremediably in a relentless vulnerability, in a tantalizingly frozen yet ongoing moment when one's life is on the line, when the meaning and value of one's life hang in the balance.[13]

V. Closing the Distance: Bringing Stranger, Trust, and Bible into Conjunctive Alignment

Scarry does not write of strangers as such, but in the context of specifying forms of disbelief and disobedience she points out that "to be a foreigner [...] is also an extreme form of disbelief, a state of existing wholly outside the circle of faith" (1985, p. 202; see also pp. 128–33). Categorical denigration of foreigners is surely widespread among religionists within doctrinaire circles of faith, but certainly the enlightened concept of a stranger as it appears in the Bible is well-known, even if not put into serious active practice by the religious faithful (but see Fasching 1992).[14] The biblical concept can in essence be condensed as follows:

---

[13]   The Bible and Sartre aside, one has a readily available contemporary point of reference that documents the experience of living in a sheer and ongoing corporeally-gripping vulnerability: American-held prisoners at Guantánomo.

[14]   An incident in the United States points up the lapse in a homely but plainly incisive way:

"Less than 10 years ago I found myself one Sunday in a white Baptist church in rural South Carolina listening to a sermon titled 'Surrounded' and sincerely wishing I was somewhere else. For more than an hour I sat there, gradually realizing that my own considerable discomfort was dwarfed by that of the worshipers around me. The stares I received betrayed not hostility but genuine confusion. In a segregated town that was 60% black, my presence in this white space was itself a statement. But about what, no one knew. The eyes fixed upon me desperately sought answers. 'What are you doing here? You know the rules. Everybody knows the rules. We don't go to your churches, and you don't come to ours. Why are you doing this to us? What do you want?'

When the sermon was over, I tried to leave as quickly as I could, but a hand caught my shoulder. 'Welcome. I'm so glad you came,' said one woman. 'Thank you. I'm glad to be here,' I said. On hearing my voice her face relaxed a little. 'You're not from here, are you?' she said. 'No, I'm from England,' I said. As the words were repeated all around me a small crowd formed. 'He's from England,' 'He's English,' I could hear people muttering as a mini-stampede came to shake my hand and greet me. I was English. I was not their problem I would not be coming back" (Younge 2006, p. 12).

Gary Younge, a columnist for *The Nation*, later notes that "American racism has me pegged somewhere between the noble savage and the idiot savant—it adds twenty points to my IQ for my accent but docks fifteen for the bell curve" (2006, p. 12).

A scapegoat, the negative focal point of a community, figures in a similarly excluded way, but a way that is definitively hostile and vindictive. An insightful analysis of a biblical scapegoat in the person of Job is given by

First, we humans are ourselves strangers here on Earth. Heaven is our real home; we abide properly with God. Second, God is strange in being totally Other, not only outside and apart from the mundane human world, but an Other of whom there is no Other and in relationship to whom there is no Other. Third, Jesus appeared as a stranger to those about him as the gospels of Matthew, Luke, and John attest: "I was a stranger and you invited me in" (Matthew 25:35);[15] "[f]oxes have holes and birds of the air have nests, but the Son of Man has no place to lay his head" (Luke 9:58); "[h]e was in the world, and though the world was made through him, the world did not recognize him" (John 1:10). Fourth, strangers can be "good," as Jesus taught in the lesson of the good Samaritan, who was himself a stranger, a reviled one, and who, in traveling from Jerusalem to Jericho, treated and helped a stranger who was robbed and beaten (Luke 10:29–35).

Clearly, the biblical concept of a stranger is far from one-dimensional.[16] Its encompassing richness is epistemologically reinforced by a subtext that permeates both Old and New Testaments and in fact permeates the general everyday concept of a stranger. The subtext and everyday concept are haunted by language; they are "nominally obsessed." Naming is typically a way of making the strange familiar, not just cursorily familiar, but known and in turn potentially if not fully trustworthy. In Genesis, for example,

---

religion scholar René Girard, who shows how Job becomes the innocent victim of opprobrium, persecuted by his own people, including even his wife. The "scapegoat mechanism," as Girard terms it, operates on the principle of "*all against one*" (1987, p. 24). On a smaller scale, the same principle is at work with respect to "the black sheep" of a family. Church intruder, scapegoat, black sheep—all are strangers in their own communal midst, foreigners outside the "circle of faith." All are treated counter both to the way in which the Bible conceives and has been interpreted as conceiving strangers and to the way in which it admonishes us to treat strangers. The biblical thematic can in essence be condensed in quadrant form.

15 Note too, "I tell you the truth [...] no prophet is accepted in his hometown" (Luke 4:24).

16 See also the analyses of José E. Ramírez Kidd in his finely researched book *Alterity and Identity in Israel: The Stranger in the Old Testament* (1999). Kidd documents in thorough fashion the prescribed treatment of strangers specified in the Old Testament. He shows that the Hebrew word for stranger in the text, for example, refers both to individuals and to Israel, that both orphans and widows are included in the former use of the word and that a distinct notion of resident aliens prevails that is not found in any of the ancient texts of the surrounding cultures. The laws the Old Testament sets forth as governing behavior toward strangers is particularly remarkable in light of present-day behaviors in the Middle East. See too theological scholar Bernhard A. Asen's essay "From Acceptance to Inclusion: The Stranger (*ger*) in Old Testament Tradition," which also contains a short but informative section on the stranger in the New Testament (1995).

Jacob appeals to the strange man who wrestles him at Jabbok "Please tell me your name" (Gen 32:29); in Exodus, Moses says "Suppose I go to the Israelites and say to them, 'The God of your fathers has sent me to you', and they ask me, 'What is his name?' Then what shall I tell them?" (Exodus 3:13); in Isaiah, God says in answer to the question who controls the world, "I, the Lord [...] I am he" (Isaiah 41:4), and later, "I am the Lord, that is my name!" (Isaiah 42:8). Jesus asks "Who do men say that I am?" His disciples variously name John the Baptist, Elijah, and other prophets, and when asked who they themselves say he is, they answer with the name "the Christ" (Mark 8:27–30).

Naming confers identification and identification confers a sense of familiarity. What is named can be trusted to be something rather than nothing and to be what it is and not another thing. Naming thus stabilizes our feelings of ease in the world: whatever the object or individual, it now inheres by linguistic authority in the world of the known and thereby lives under our wings, so to speak. In truth, *naming* dupes us into thinking we *know* something—as when we specify "feature analyzers" and "cognitive maps" in the brain, or phlogiston, quarks, and the Big Dipper in the external physical world. What is nonlinguistic remains by contrast strange until we secure it a reality, a knowability and potential trustworthiness by naming it. The idea that *what* or *who* we don't know can hurt us is thus not simply a colloquialism or banal truism, but an expression of our fundamentally-felt, epistemologically-inflected vulnerability, the bite of which can be muted by naming.[17] The Bible in fact showers us with names, not only as in the begat sequences (Genesis), the listings of clan memberships and their numbers (Numbers), and the like, but throughout in its pinpoint naming of individuals and places—e.g. "Then the men of Judah went with the Simeonites their brothers and attacked the Canaanites living in Zephath, and they totally destroyed the city. Therefore it was called Hormah" (Judges 14:17). Naming casts a net of familiarity over the world. It operates in everyday life in the service of what Luhmann (1979) termed "complexity reduction," but in a biblical sense, it does much more. It not only gives us the sense of knowing an individual or place, but instantiates the individual or place as real, providing proof as it were of its existence.

What would otherwise be the point of naming all these people and places and of emphasizing names from the beginning if not to secure the reality of the history being told, to assure the reader that the genealogy, the cities, the regional areas, and so on, are not a fiction or fairy tale but emanate from the word of God? Indeed, biblical naming is as much flesh

---

17 When we are at a loss to name something, the typically unnoticed challenge of languaging experience is directly experienced and even heightened. For more on the challenge, see Sheets-Johnstone (2009).

made Word as Word made flesh. The Bible historicizes God, humans, and God's relationship to humans by naming. The significance of this historicizing can hardly be ignored. Historicizing confers reality, all the more emphatically as that history is not just spoken but recorded. Writing makes real and true the tale of what happened when, where, and to whom. The rite of baptism with its christening motif is the ceremonial epitome of the transformation of flesh made Word, the sanctification of the body by word of mouth and therewith the enfoldment of an erstwhile stranger into a circle of faith.

That the biblical concept of a stranger is richly textured cannot be doubted. That stranger anxiety is a core human experience cannot be doubted either. Anxiety in face of a stranger in fact commonly begins in infancy,[18] and is in further fact, to begin with, an evolutionary fact of life. Vulnerability is in other words an ontogenetically and phylogenetically-derived existential reality and religion is one of its cardinal cultural elaborations; religions commonly provide an answer to the existential reality of human vulnerability. Religious belief systems are indeed

---

[18] As classically identified, stranger anxiety commonly appears at eight or nine months of age, but infant anxiety in face of a stranger might also be identified as vulnerability; the first stirrings of vulnerability, not in any ideological sense, religious or otherwise, but in the sense of an immediately felt openness to danger or harm from others, that is, a raw, culturally unembellished experience of the Other as unfamiliar, wholly unknown and thus threatening. Stranger anxiety from this perspective constitutes the ground floor of the experience of being at risk in the presence of a strange Other and of the possible harm that the full-bodied presence of the Other embodies. The response, in other words, is obviously in the service of survival. Looking back on our own infancy from this adult perspective, we find that it is not only conscience in the sense of reflection that "makes cowards of us all," as Shakespeare has it, but strangeness and strangers. The stranger must prove himself trustworthy, someone whose actions we can count on, someone whose words we can believe—thus, the later religious connection with knowing the name of the stranger and in turn trusting. Someone whose words can be believed—"I am the Lord"—is someone who will keep his word, someone who can do what he says he can do and will in fact do what he says he will do, someone who can thus be venerated and who will protect one from harm. It is of interest to note in this context that the first words of an infant are typically "Mama," the naming of someone already familiar, but now made even more familiar by naming, more familiar in the sense of having a distinctive *call*, so to speak. One can articulate the already familiar, and in articulating the already familiar, make the familiarity a *felt* presence, not just heard but presenced in and by the body. To be emphasized too is the fact that stranger anxiety is an evolutionarily-rooted phenomenon, as might be apparent from earlier references to nonhuman infant behaviors. See, for example, van Lawick-Goodall (1971), Goodall (1990), Strum (1987).

culturally and familially inculcated. We are taught what is religiously true of the world. Whether religious knowledge is esteemed a spiritual blessing, a sacred covenant linking us with God, an indubitable story of creation, and the like, or whether esteemed a compensation, a placater, a tranquilizer, an opiate (as per Marx), or whatever, we are not born with this knowledge.[19] The opening quotation from Tolstoy testifies to, and speaks eloquently of, both our fundamental existential ignorance and our terror of death: his words reverberate with the felt vulnerability of being a stranger in the world, of being alive without appeal—helpless, alone, bereft of meaning, fearful of the inevitable end. Tracing this ignorance and terror to its biblical core, we find the simple fact that if death were not, biblical religions would be not. If, in the Garden of Eden, humans had not tasted of the tree of knowledge, they would not know of death, or of good and evil, *nor* would God have immediately decreed thereafter that man "must not be allowed to reach out his hand and take also from the tree of life and eat, and live forever." Nor, furthermore, would God, after banishing man from the Garden and to assure his not living forever, have placed "cherubim and a flaming sword flashing back and forth to guard the way to the tree of life" (Gen 3:22–4). But the simple fact too is that if a stranger were not a quasi-symbol of death, the living embodiment of possible harm, a permanent danger that, as Sartre would affirm, brings on a near-death experience in the form of the death of my possibilities, the dissolution of myself into an object, my wholesale saturation in fear, then biblical religions would not analogously be pervaded by concerns with the stranger and conceive the stranger in all manner of guise. The coincidence of stranger and death resonates in the vulnerability of being alive.

Sartre's description of shame at being caught peeking through a keyhole is indeed oddly akin to being caught naked in the Garden, that is, oddly akin to being aware of oneself before an Other, an unfamiliar Other who stops you in your tracks and robs you of your freedom, who causes an

---

[19] In this respect it is of substantive import to note that naming talk—what we might call veritable Heideggerian "idle chatter" about the world and its occupants—is an adult occupation and preoccupation, not the occupation and preoccupation of infants and young children whose experiential knowledge of the world is nonlinguistically constituted and whose basically tactile-kinesthetic constitution of the world lays the foundation for its later linguistic constitution (Sheets-Johnstone 1999/exp. 2nd ed. 2011). Infants and young children, after all, have yet to be indoctrinated into the epistemological name-game by which what is unfamiliar is made putatively familiar by naming. Learning the world originally, regardless of one's ancestry or religious environment, means making one's way not by dint of language but in the flesh, *exploring* it, not naming it. In doing so, infants and young children take what is initially strange directly into their world, familiarizing themselves with it in the process.

internal hemorrhaging of the world, who makes you an object.[20] There is indeed an uncanny resemblance not just between oneself at the keyhole and oneself in the Garden of Eden, but between the Other watching at the keyhole and the Other watching in the Garden. The presence of the Other in each instance means "I am no longer master of the situation"; it means "I *live* myself as fixed in the midst of the world, as in danger, as irremediable"; it means "[t]he Other is the hidden death of my possibilities in so far as I live that death as hidden in the midst of the world."[21]

A totally different Other, however, warrants recognition. A strange Other distinctively unlike the Other that either Sartre or Scarry describes, and furthermore having no link either symbolically or otherwise to the Otherness of death, is described in painstaking detail by Rudolf Otto in *The Idea of the Holy*. Nothing mundane approximates to the "wholly Other" that Otto (1928) captures in his seminal notion of the *mysterium tremendum*, a phenomenon he categorically distances from everyday conceptual understandings of mystery or unfamiliarity, and the felt experience of which he categorically distances from everyday experiences of fear or dread.

The experience of the *mysterium tremendum* is an experience of the numinous that begins in a sensory experience of some kind, but is not itself sensory. It is an emotional experience in which "a creature [feels] abased and overwhelmed by its own nothingness in contrast to that which is supreme above all creatures" (Otto 1928, p. 10). The experience is a uniquely religious one that is resoundingly positive, a "harmony of contrasts" (1928, p. 42), as Otto describes it, a complex of fascination as well as fear, wonder as well as terror, felt in relation to a transcendent Being. Otto emphasizes many times over that the *mysterium tremendum* is a natural, spontaneous experience, i.e. it is not derived from any teachings, and that the words he uses to describe it are to be understood not conceptually but affectively. Moreover while his descriptive analysis of "the stupor before

---

20 Shame is close to guilt and guilt is close to sin in that feelings of shame can open onto feelings of guilt for doing or having done what one did, and feelings of guilt for doing or having done what one did can open in a religious context onto feelings of sinfulness.

21 Moreover Sartre's description of the look of the Other as "eyeless" is akin to Scarry's description of God's voice as bodiless: "[M]y apprehension of a look turned toward me appears on the ground of the destruction of the eyes which 'look at me'" (1956, p. 258); the voice of God "is exclusively verbal [...] [God] has no body" (1985, pp. 19–23). Both look and voice are a pure and awesome presence distilled absolutely from anything corporeal. But like the voice of God, the look of the Other is actually physically substantiated, namely, in the Other's corporeally-grounded ontological freedom, or, in Luhmann's words, in the "uncontrollable power [of Other people] to act" (1979, p. 41). In actuality, then, we live continuously on the edge of the death of our possibilities, on the edge of the unfamiliar.

something 'wholly Other'" (1928, p. 27) is clearly weighted in Christianity and Judaism, it encompasses references to Hinduism and Buddhism. It in fact harks back to Plato, a fact Smith points out in the course of answering his own question, "[w]hat does holiness involve?" He observes that, "[t]o many moderns the word is empty; but those who feel the stir of wonder and can sense the ineffable pressing in on their lives from every side will know what Plato was talking about when he wrote, '[f]irst a shudder runs through you, and then the old awe creeps over you'" (1991, p. 301). He comments that "[t]hose who have had such experiences will know the blend of mystery, ecstasy, and the numinous, which received classic description in Rudolph Otto's *The Idea of the Holy*" (1991, p. 301).

Smith himself writes of mystery in the context of his studies of religion, an abiding epistemological mystery similar to that of Einstein but not wholly removed from Otto. "Reality," he states, "is steeped in ineluctable mystery; we are born in mystery, we live in mystery, and we die in mystery. [...] A mystery is that special kind of problem which for the human mind *has* no solution; the more we understand it, the more we become aware of additional factors relating to it that we do not understand. In mysteries what we know, and our realization of what we do not know, proceed together; the larger the island of knowledge, the longer the shore-line of wonder. It is like the quantum world, where the more we under-stand its formalism, the stranger that world becomes" (1991, p. 389). The epistemological affinity with Einstein notwithstanding, the affinity with Otto is equally strong: in the same way that nothing mundane approxi-mates to the *mysterium tremendum* of which Otto writes, so nothing in the way of a definitive answer approximates to the mystery of which Smith writes. Indeed, in a permanently and ever-increasingly strange world, it is as if a "wholly Other" holds absolute and permanent sway, a "wholly Other" whose presence is not rooted in affective experience as with Otto, but is a matter of ever elusive knowledge.

Whether an awareness of that "wholly Other" eventuates in the numinous experience that Otto describes or in forms of mystery that Smith and Einstein describe, or in fact eventuates in a vacuum of no particular experience at all, the reach of the world clearly extends beyond us in a never-ending unfamiliar space and time filled with a never-ending presence and emergence of "strangers"—natural phenomena as well as animate beings—whose possibilities for action for or against us are beyond our ken. These are immutable facts of life. We are indeed vulnerable by the mere fact of being alive. A supernatural redemption of our vulnerability by way of the *mysterium tremendum* invites our trust but with no guarantee of fulfillment. Other mysteries say nothing of the vulnerability of our alive-ness but bequeath us an interminably strange natural world to comprehend and contend with as we will. Indeed, they invite our trust in nothing more than our own understanding, including the limits of our own understanding. With respect to these mysteries, the origin and terminus of the natural gift of life remain unfathomable; precisely as Smith (1991) indicates, "[r]eality is steeped in ineluctable mystery." At the end of his book titled *Apocalypse*, D.H. Lawrence echoes this thought. He eloquently concedes the unfathomability of our punctuated existence,[22] but with a wondrous twist. He writes, "[w]hatever the unborn and the dead may know, they cannot know the beauty, the marvel of being alive in the flesh. The dead may look after the afterwards. But the magnificent here and now of life in the flesh is ours, and ours alone, and ours only for a time" (1932, pp. 199–200).

In essence, Lawrence's words attest to the fact that the natural gift of life can invite trust with no strings attached, either fearful strings of death or their personification in strangers, and with no tetherings either to religion. His alternative vision of the human world is eschatologically and doxically unencumbered. Neither the prospect of death nor a terror of death, neither belief in a transcendent Being nor in an afterlife, enters into his vision. As Einstein affirms, "[t]he mystery of conscious life" and "the marvelous structure of the universe" suffice in themselves. Lawrence in fact extols their sufficiency in expansively rich first-person plural terms. In his affectively-charged closing words following immediately upon those quoted above, he fervently summons us to awaken to the wonders of life: "We ought to dance with rapture that we are alive and in the flesh and part of the living incarnate cosmos" (1932, p. 200). The words recall those of Nietzsche: "I could only believe in a God who could dance." A god who dances celebrates life, reveres life, is alive to the wonder of life. A god who dances is creative rather than destructive and vengeful, life-enhancing rather than life-destroying. A god who dances joins together rather than renders asunder; a god who dances is yea-saying of life in all its wondrous forms.[23]

---

[22] For more on "punctuated existence," see Sheets-Johnstone (1990), Chapter 8, "On the Conceptual Origin of Death."

[23] The teachings of the Buddha, we might note, focus in a related way on the preciousness of life. Moreover Lawrence's and Nietzsche's words might recall those of Aristotle with respect to the source of all nature, the unmoved eternal that imparts motion, the Prime Mover. Further still, the words might prompt us to ask why the stranger who wrestled with Jacob all night till dawn did not dance with him instead. The stranger was God. We might well wonder what would have happened if God had danced with Jacob. What would have been different if they had danced together rather than fought? Surely an intercorporeal attunement and spiritual rejoicing would have been present throughout the night. At the very least, Jacob would not have been injured by God in the hip and limped ever after.

Unsentimentalized reflection on Lawrence's closing words brings us to a closing thought on the challenge of our aliveness. Would we humans actually dance with rapture "that we are alive and in the flesh and part of the living incarnate cosmos," we would not escape the sheer vulnerability of our aliveness, but we would surely escape the vulnerability of being alive among unfamiliar Others, for no strangers would be among us, dancing with rapture. Rapture, like trust, *moves* the body and *moves through* the body in ways contrary to fear.[24] In effect, none of us would be clutched "in suspense," frozen in an ongoing vulnerability. On the contrary, we would each be open toward a world of others and toward moving with a world of others. In Smith's evocative image, we would all be moving along the shoreline of wonder, the shoreline that stretches continuously beyond us, extending our interpersonal understandings to their limit and profiting from the interpersonal understandings of others along the way.

Fanatical and fundamentalist ideologies would find no place along this never-ending shoreline of wonder: motivated by life itself, none would feel inclined toward any such ideology. Being in the company of fellow humans, we would each of us be experiencing a common aliveness in the here and now, a common being in the flesh, a common rapture and interconnected presence in the living incarnate cosmos. Our communal dance would transcend language and prominence our foundational communal humanness, strengthening religious moral teachings concerning strangers by living them in the flesh. Our movement together would clearly not be a panacea for all ills of the human world—deep and conscientious probings into the commonly disowned shadow side of our human psyche would be equally essential—but it would surely be a point of departure for ameliorating the violent ideological conflicts that adult humans proliferate within the world and moreover teach their children to proliferate within the world.[25] Experiencing the rapture of our aliveness would refocus our attention to life itself, awakening us to the fact that we are all mortal humans who are of a piece with the ongoing, interwoven wonders of nature.

Acknowledgement: This chapter was originally presented as a guest lecture sponsored by the Templeton Foundation for Science and Religion at the State University of New York at Stony Brook in 2007 and as a guest lecture in the Department of Philosophy at Durham University in the same year.

---

[24] For a further discussion of such kinetic distinctions, see Sheets-Johnstone (2006).

[25] Vengeance and terrorism are paradigms of just such human adult-generated ills that heighten to an extreme the fear of strange Others, of death, and of the "uncontrollable power [of Others] to act" (Luhmann 1979, p. 41).

References

Asen, B.A. (1995) From acceptance to inclusion: The stranger (*ger*) in old testament tradition, in Nichols, E.W. (ed.) *Christianity and the Stranger: Historical Essays*, pp. 16–35, Atlanta, GA: Scholars Press.

Berkeley, G. (1709/1929) An essay toward a new theory of vision, in Calkins, M.W. (ed.) *Berkeley Selections (Berkeley: Essay, principles, dialogues with selections from other writings)*, pp. 1–98, New York: Charles Scribner's Sons.

Bloom, L. (1993) *The Transition from Infancy to Language: Acquiring the Power of Expression*, New York: Cambridge University Press.

Bugental, D.B., Kopeikin, H. & Lazowski, L. (1991) Children's responses to authentic versus polite smiles, in Rotenberg, K.J. (ed.) *Children's Interpersonal Trust*, pp. 58–79, New York: Springer-Verlag.

Dolhinow, P.J. (ed.) (1972) The north Indian langur, in *Primate Patterns*, pp. 181–238, New York: Holt, Rinehart and Winston.

Einstein, A. (1990) Strange is our situation here upon earth, in Pelikan, J. (ed.) *The World Treasury of Modern Religious Thought*, pp. 202–205, Boston, MA: Little, Brown and Company. (See also Einstein, A. (1931) Untitled, in *Living Philosophies*, pp. 3–7, New York: Simon and Schuster.)

Endress, M. & Pabst, A. (2013) Violence and shattered trust: sociological considerations, *Human Studies*, 36 (1), pp. 89–106.

Fasching, D.J. (1992) *Narrative Theology after Auschwitz: From Alienation to Ethics*, Minneapolis, MN: Fortress Press.

Foucault, M. (1972) *The Archaeology of Knowledge*, Sheridan Smith, A.M. (trans.), New York: Harper & Row.

Girard, R. (1987) *Job: The Victim of his People*, Freccero, Y. (trans.), Stanford, CA: Stanford University Press.

Goodall, J. (1990) *Through a Window: My Thirty Years with the Chimpanzees of Gombe*, Boston, MA: Houghton Mifflin.

Jung, C.G. (1970) *Civilization in Transition*, 2nd ed., Hull, R.F.C. (trans.), Bollingen Series XX, Princeton, NJ: Princeton University Press.

Kidd, J.E.R. (1999) *Alterity and Identity in Israel: The [Stranger] in the Old Testament*, Berlin/New York: Walter de Gruyter.

Kolenda, K. (1976) *Religion without God*, Buffalo, NY: Prometheus Books.

Lawrence, D.H. (1932) *Apocalypse*, New York: Viking Press.

Luhmann, N. (1979) *Trust and Power*, Burns, T. & Poggi, G. (eds.), Davis, H., Raffan, J. & Rooney, K. (trans.), New York: Wiley.

Otto, R. (1928) *The Idea of the Holy: An Inquiry into the Non-Rational Factor in the Idea of the Divine and its Relation to the Rational*, Harvey, J.W. (trans.), Oxford: Oxford University Press.

Sartre, J.-P. (1956) *Being and Nothingness*, Barnes, H.E. (trans.), New York: Philosophical Library.

Scarry, E. (1985) *The Body in Pain: The Making and Unmaking of the World*, New York: Oxford University Press.

Sheets-Johnstone, M. (1990) *The Roots of Thinking*, Philadelphia, PA: Temple University Press.

Sheets-Johnstone, M. (1999/expanded 2nd ed. 2011) *The Primacy of Movement*, Amsterdam/Philadelphia, PA: John Benjamins.

Sheets-Johnstone, M. (2002) Size, power, death: Constituents in the making of human morality, *Journal of Consciousness Studies*, 9 (2), pp. 49–67.

Sheets-Johnstone, M. (2006) Sur la nature de la confiance, in Ogien A. & Quéré, L. (eds.) *Les moments de la confiance: connaissance, affects et engagements*, pp. 23–41, Paris: Economica.

Sheets-Johnstone, M. (2009) On the challenge of languaging experience, in Sheets-Johnstone, M. (ed.) *The Corporeal Turn: An Interdisciplinary Reader*, chapter XV, Exeter: Imprint Academic. (Originally presented as a guest lecture, German–American Institute, Heidelberg, Germany, 2006.)

Sheets-Johnstone, M. (2012) Steps entailed in foregrounding the background: Taking the challenge of languaging experience seriously, in Radman, Z. (ed.) *Knowing without Thinking: Mind, Action, Cognition, and the Phenomenon of the Background*, pp. 187–205, New York: Palgrave Macmillan.

Smith, H. (1991) *The World's Religions: Our Great Wisdom Traditions*, (revised and updated edition of *The Religions of Man*, 1958), San Francisco, CA: Harper Collins.

Stern, D.N. (1977) *The First Relationship: Infant and Mother*, Cambridge, MA: Harvard University Press.

Stern, D.N. (1985) *The Interpersonal World of the Infant: A View from Psycho-analysis and Developmental Psychology*, New York: Basic Books.

Stewart, D. (ed.) (1992) *A World without God: Exploring the Philosophy of Religion*, pp. 340–342, Englewood Cliffs, NJ: Prentice Hall.

Strum, S.C. (1987) *Almost Human: A Journey into the World of Baboons*, New York: W.W. Norton.

Tolstoy, L. (1992) A confession, in Stewart, D. (ed.) *Exploring the Philosophy of Religion*, 3rd ed., pp. 351–356, Englewood Cliffs, NJ: Prentice Hall. (See also Tolstoy, L. (1983) *Confession*, Patterson, D. (trans.), New York: W.W. Norton.)

Trevarthen, C. (1977) Descriptive analyses of infant communicative behavior, in Schaffer, H.R. (ed.) *Studies in Mother–Infant Interaction*, pp. 227–270, London: Academic Press.

van Lawick-Goodall, J. (1971) *In the Shadow of Man*, New York: Dell Publishing.

Younge, G. (2006) Obama: Black like me, *The Nation*, 283, p. 16.

Chapter XIII

Movement

Our Common Heritage and Mother Tongue[1]

The world of dance is testimonial to the kinetic possibilities of human bodies. The possibilities are not merely anatomical ones. Their significance is in fact inadequately understood when specified simply in terms of a facilitating anatomy. Their fundamental significance lies in having a foundation in human ontogeny, namely, in the spontaneous disposition to learn one's body and to move oneself, and in the correlatively spontaneous disposition to think in movement. These native dispositions of infancy are basic to dance. Being ontogenetically pan-cultural, they are basic to dance in any culture. Because they are human universals that define foundational aspects of our humanness, they warrant study in themselves. Such study can pinpoint ways in which standard conceptions of infancy are wayward. The characterization of infants as pre-linguistic is a prime example. When we examine closely the corporeal facts of the matter, or more specifically, the corporeal-*kinetic* facts of the matter, we find that, rather than infants being pre-linguistic, *language is post-kinetic*. An inquiry into the basis of our kinetic possibilities brings to light just such corporeal-kinetic matters of fact, not only correcting our illusions concerning infancy, but pointing us in the direction of basic truths about ourselves. It does so by elucidating both the essentially kinetic way in which humans—like all other animate forms—come to make sense of themselves and the world, and the kinetic structures at the foundation of dance across cultures. In what follows, my major focus will be on the former, that is, I will focus in particular on the conceptual import of our common kinetic ontogeny and pinpoint its cultural implications and aspects in the process.

---

1   First published in *Dance Knowledge*, ed. Anne Margrete Fisvik and Egil Bakka (2002), (Proceedings of the 5th NOFOD Conference, Trondheim, Norway, 10–13 January 2002): 37–50.

I. Learning Our Bodies and Learning to Move Ourselves

In the beginning, we are apprentices of our own bodies. No one teaches us how to move nor do we come equipped in the beginning with an owner's manual that instructs us about heads and how they turn, arms and how they extend, torsos and how they bend, and so on. Quite on our own, we learn our bodies and learn to move ourselves. We literally discover ourselves in movement. We grow kinetically into our bodies. More specifically, we grow into those distinctive ways of moving that come with our being the bodies we are. In the process, we develop concepts of space, of time, and of energy or effort. In other words, on the basis of self-movement, we develop fundamental concepts having to do with speed, distance, direction, amplitude, intensity, evenness, abruptness, attenuation, straightness, jaggedness, and so on. We develop these concepts through the experience of movement itself, through our tactile-kinesthetic bodies.

Because the concepts originate in kinetic/tactile-kinesthetic experience, they are qualitative, not quantitative, concepts. In other words, the concepts are not reducible to *mechanics*. In experiencing self-movement, an infant (or a human of any age, for that matter) does not experience itself as a machine but as a qualitatively moving dynamic form, an *animate* form. It is thus clear why and how movement *creates* the qualities it embodies and why and how it is erroneous to think that movement simply takes place *in* space and *in* time. By extension, it is clear why and how *dance* creates the qualities it embodies and how it is erroneous to think that a dance simply takes place *in* space and *in* time. In both instances, what is of moment is not mechanics but qualitative kinetic dynamics.

From the moment we are born—and even before we are born, as fetuses in the womb—we are kinesthetically aware of kinetic qualities. When an infant moves—as when any adult moves—it formally creates a certain space, time, and energy in the process of moving; it thereby creates a certain spatial and temporal dynamic by the very nature of its movement: a tight, resistant space as when its movement is constrictive and effortful, a relatively large, open space, as when its movement is expansive and unimpeded; a regularly sequenced temporality as when it kicks repeatedly and with the same intensity each time, an erratic temporality as when it flails its arms about; and so on. Concepts generated in and through movement in the course of learning our bodies and learning to move ourselves are fundamental to all of our later kinetic capacities as adults, whether a matter of reaching for a glass without knocking it over, stepping off a curb at just the right moment with respect to oncoming traffic—or doing a *plié* or *tour jeté*. We do not need recourse to a body schema or to a body image to explain either our conceptual familiarity with our bodies or our conceptual familiarity with movement. We need only a recognition of kinesthesia, or more specifically, a recognition of tactile-kinesthetic awarenesses of our bodies and of our bodies in movement that have developed from infancy onward, and a recognition of how these awarenesses have generated fundamental human concepts.

In addition to spatial, temporal, and energic concepts, we discover causal concepts, again, not in a mechanical sense, but in a dynamic sense. We progressively attain complex conceptual understandings of consequential relationships: if I close my eyes, it gets dark; if I turn my head, the mobile comes into view; if I make a fist, the inside of my hand disappears; and so on. These if/then relationships are empowering experiences, but they are not on that account mere physical accomplishments. On the contrary, they are conceptually rich experiences. Basic concepts having to do with opening and closing, with weight, with containment, with closeness, with distance, and with myriad other spatio-temporal-energic dimensions and effects of self-movement are inherent in the experience of if/then relationships. There is thus no bridge to be crossed between thinking and doing. Concepts develop not only in the same sense that abilities and skills develop; they are coincident with the development of those abilities and skills—whether you are an infant in China, Madagascar, the Fiji Islands, in Constantinople, Helsinki, or Yachats, Oregon.

On the basis of a common kinetic apprenticeship and repertoire, all humans in the beginning forge a sense of themselves as animate forms: they experience themselves changing shape as they move, and moving as they change shape from the very beginning. Moreover, from the very beginning, they see animate forms in the world about them doing the same: horses, sheep, cows, cats, flies, ants, wolves, bees, and so on. While each moves in its own distinct manner, all change shape as they move and move as they change shape. It is not an overgeneralization to claim that living creatures perceive themselves and other living beings as *animate* forms.

Now with respect to this generalization, we may well ask: What is it like to build up knowledge of the world by moving and touching one's way through it, apprenticing oneself by way of one's body, rather than by way of information, language, or any kind of formal instruction? Consider, our own human situation. Consider, for example, how keenly attuned we are to the slightest movements of others—a flickering of the eyes, a pulling in of lips, a waywardness of gaze, a tremoring of hands, a fleeting constriction in the torso, a sudden intake of breath, a softly beating foot. We are kinetically attuned to each other, and kinetically attuned cross-culturally, whether we immediately grasp the kinetic specifics of a person of a culture other than our own or not. We are kinetically attuned to the world. No one teaches us how to be attuned. We teach ourselves—nonverbally. In a word, movement is our mother tongue.

However implicitly, the literature on infant and child development over the past thirty years gives rich and eloquent testimonial to this original tongue, even literally, or quasi-so, in the fact that infants as young as 42 minutes old can imitate the tongue protrusion, lip protrusion, and lip rounding of an adult (Meltzoff & Moore 1977, 1983). These specific movements that infants see resonate dynamically with their own tactile-kinesthetic bodies. Close study of just such empirical findings on infants is of fundamental significance to showing "the primacy of movement." In my own case, phenomenologically informed readings of the literature on infancy allowed me not only to demonstrate generally how empirical onto-genetical findings complement phenomenological ones, but allowed me to show specifically how, from both a phenomenological viewpoint and a phenomenologically-informed empirical viewpoint, movement is our matchpoint; that is, movement is our original epistemological link with the world. The world may be initially unfamiliar, but there is a familiar point of origin, a familiar way by which we all go about making sense of it in the beginning. Moreover, that corporeal-kinetic beginning is not something that is lost or forgotten but remains the abiding foundation of our self-understandings, our interpersonal understandings, and our under-standings and explorations of the world in which we live.

A series of experiments by well-known infant psychologist T.G.R. Bower that dates back to the 1960s and 70s are of signal interest in this respect, particularly Bower's own comment on the results of his experi-ments. Bower's aim was to determine how an infant puts the world of objects together, specifically, "[how] an infant begin[s] to associate qualities such as solidity with objects that he sees" (Bower 1971, p. 30). The experi-ments focused on both the featural differences of objects—their size, shape, and color—and on their movement differences—that is, whether they were moving, whether they stopped, whether they disappeared, whether they reappeared. In discussing his experimental research, Bower states that "These results show that younger infants [6 weeks to 22 weeks] are not affected by featural differences. For them movement is predominant. They respond to a change in motion but not to a change in size, shape or color" (ibid., p. 37). His subsequent comment is as insightful as it is startling. He states that infants "ignore features to such an extent that I would suggest they respond *not to moving objects but to movements*" (ibid.; italics added).

Given a pre-eminently kinetic/tactile-kinesthetic body, the kinetically-tethered response of infants makes sense. An infant's primary path to knowledge is through movement. Moreover Bower's distinction between objects in motion and movement is of quintessential significance. To per-ceive movement is to perceive a dynamic form, specifically, a dynamic form-in-the-making, a form dynamically unfolding before our eyes. Most commonly, and in contrast, to perceive an object in motion is to perceive an *object doing something*: running, throwing a ball, pushing, stooping, washing a dish—or doing a *plié* or *tour jeté*. Perceiving an object in motion is thus commonly not the same as perceiving movement. This is *not* to say that objects in motion lack dynamics or that one is necessarily unaware of dynamics in perceiving objects in motion. It is only to say that to perceive objects in motion is commonly to perceive just that: a moving *object*, pre-eminently a *thing* that is moving and *doing something* in the process of moving, the emphasis being precisely on what the thing is doing or accomplishing. Noticing its dynamics, in contrast, is contingent on perceiving movement. In other words, to notice the dynamics of an object in motion is to foreground movement—a qualitative dynamic form-in-the-making—and to put in relief the object that is moving—just as the infants did in Bower's experimental studies.

We should note that Bower's findings on the central place of movement in infancy are neither idiosyncratic nor culturally relative. Studies of other researchers implicitly if not explicitly substantiate the claim that movement is initially our matchpoint with the world. The substantiation is evident not only in the studies of infant imitation mentioned earlier, but in studies of joint attention—studies of the spontaneous way in which an infant and its parent or caretaker focus on the same object—and in studies of turn-taking—studies of the spontaneous way in which an infant responds to, and itself initiates a response from, its parent and or caretaker. Though unacknowledged as such, even Piaget's findings substantiate an infant's attention to *movement*, in this instance, the sheer movement of its own body. Piaget writes of a two-day-old infant opening and closing its mouth, and notes that it is an increasingly frequent behavior in the absence of any object. Oddly enough, though he states that the behavior subsequently becomes more frequent, he says that "we shall not take it up again" (Piaget 1952, pp. 25–6).

When the significance of the phenomenon of self-movement and the phenomenon of the tactile-kinesthetic body go unrecognized, as in Piaget's observational report, then the foundational, cross-cultural significance of movement can hardly be appreciated, much less acknowledged. On the other hand, with respect to the kinetic/tactile-kinesthetic body and the capacity of infants to imitate adult mouth gestures, there is no need to invoke a common pan-cultural brain mechanism—a "psychological primitive" or "body scheme" as an explanatory device—as do infant psychologist Andrew Meltzoff and philosopher Shaun Gallagher (Meltzoff 1990, p. 160; Meltzoff & Gallagher 1996, p. 216). If we carry forward the kinetic thematic, we readily explain the extraordinary ability of infants to imitate adult mouth gestures as a kinetic/tactile-kinesthetic dynamic matching. In fact, recalling what was said of the integral and epistemologically rich linkage between learning our bodies and learning to move ourselves and our conceptual development, we readily come to fundamental under-standings of why binary oppositions such as right/left and light/dark are cross-cultural conceptual oppositions. The opposition right/left, for example, is not a cultural artifact, as anthropologist Rodney Needham (1987) tries to show, but a human universal. Whether in the Suez, in Antarctica, or in the Tierra del Fuego, all humans walk: first this leg, then this leg; first this side, then this side; first this foot impact, then this foot impact; first this arm swing, then this arm swing. What is more natural than walking? What is more natural than a binary dynamic gait with its attendant laterally-anchored binary rhythm and binary accents? Everyday generic human experience is the source of fundamental human concepts, which is to say that bodily movement is the source of our initial knowledge of ourselves and of the world, a knowledge that is not lost, but on the con-trary, grounds all further adult knowledge regardless of our cultural origins.

This foundational, developmental, bodily-based knowledge is closely tied to our sense of self. It is of interest in this context to point out, first, that infant psychiatrist and developmental psychologist Daniel Stern (1985) has shown that the core sense of self generated in infant experience is never lost but is the foundation of the developing sense of self that ultimately achieves stability in adulthood, and second, that the core sense of self Stern describes, deriving as it does from experiences of self-agency, self-coherence, self-history, and self-affectivity, may be shown to be funda-mentally proprioceptive in nature, that is, to derive from tactile-kinesthetic experience (Sheets-Johnstone 1999). In particular, what Stern identifies as self-agency constitutes "I cans" in phenomenological terms. As an infant might say if it put its developing "I cans" into words: "I can kick my legs, I can lift my head, I can reach the bottle." As an adult might say in describing some of his or her I cans: "I can leap, speak, turn my head this way, balance on a beam, read a book, judge accurately how far to stretch my hand to pick up the ball or how far to lift my foot with respect to the size of the stone on the path." Self-agency is, in other words, tied to tactile-kinesthetic experience, experiences that ground the very possibility of voluntary movement because they are experiences of one's body in motion. What Stern identifies as self-coherence refers basically to the spatio-temporal-energic unity of one's body and one's body in motion. Contrary to estimations of infants as incompetent know-nothings—contrary, for example, to Lacan's identification of an infant as a *corps-morcelé* and as an "uncoordinated turbulence" (Lacan 1977, pp. 19, 2, respectively)—self-coherence refers to an infant's sense of itself as a unified whole. However unable yet to reach effectively or to sit up, for example, an infant is aware of itself as a singular locus of feeling and movement. An interesting experiment documents this awareness. Siamese twins joined ventrally often sucked each other's fingers as well as their own. When Stern and colleagues attempted to pull the arm of a twin sucking its own finger away from its mouth, the twin would resist the pulling movement of its arm. When they attempted to pull away the arm of its sibling whose fingers it was sucking, the twin would strain its head forward in pursuit of the retreating fingers (Stern 1985, p. 78). The experiment documents both a sense of self-agency and a sense of self-coherence. What Stern identifies as self-history has to do with memory, including what infant psychologist Jerome Bruner (1969) calls "memory without words," but memory that is more commonly — and most unfortunately — called "motor memory." I say most unfortunately because whether infants or adults, moving creatures are not machines. Hence their memory of movement is ill-conceived and ill-defined in terms of a mechanics. Their memory of movement is proprioceptive in nature, and, with respect to neuromuscular systems in particular, is naturally dynamic. Hence it is both more precisely and appropriately termed *kinesthetic memory* (Sheets-Johnstone 2003). Kinesthetic memory is conjoined with affective memory and cognitive memory and is obviously linked to the formation of myriad kinetic habits — not only habitual ways of walking and talking, but habitual ways of being angry, sad, joyous, reflective, curious, and so on, that develop in infancy and in the course of growing up. An infant's sense of self-history is thus intimately related to what Stern identifies as self-affectivity. Self-affectivity is tied to the tactile-kinesthetic body through bodily activations and changes in tonicity, and in particular, by the way in which affective feelings play out dynamically with respect to bodily movement. Whether an infant is feeling agitated, delighted, frustrated, dejected, or whatever, its affective feelings are linked to movement, and thus, to tactile-kinesthetic feelings. The linkage between affectivity and movement is not of course peculiar to infants, let alone human infants, but is an essential dimension of animate life. A phenomenological analysis of the intimate relationship between affectivity and movement has in fact shown how there is a fundamental *dynamic congruency of form* between emotion and movement in everyday life (Sheets-Johnstone 1999a), the dynamics of movement mirroring the dynamics of the particular emotion. The fundamental dynamic congruency is in fact attested to not only by a phenomenological analysis of emotion and movement in everyday life, but by modern dance, especially dances such as Graham's *Lamentation* or Cunningham's *Rainforest*, dances which are non-narrative in form.

In sum, what Stern describes as dimensions of an infant's sense of self are grounded in the experience of self-movement and in a correlative bodily-based knowledge.

II. Our Disposition to Think in Movement

Given that movement is our mother tongue, it is not surprising that thinking in movement is our original mode of thinking. What we see, what we hear, what we smell, taste, or touch is always a function of where we are in relation to something in the world. In other words, we learn about objects originally by moving in relation to them and by noticing their changing appearances in concert with our movements. Moreover even when infants are merely looking at objects and are not themselves moving in relation to them, what they notice is movement. We saw this fact dramatized in Bower's studies of infants. Infant-psychologist Lois Bloom, whose research studies are focused on language development, recalls Bower's studies in her most recent book *The Transition from Infancy to Language* and in that context points out that "infants as young as 2 to 4 months of age [...] track a moving object and anticipate its reappearance" (Bloom 1993, p. 40). The attribution of anticipation to infants testifies to the fact that infants are thinking in movement. To *anticipate* first of all to think ahead, as in expecting something to happen; in other words, to expect the reappearance of an object that has been moving along a certain path and that disappears at a certain point on that path, i.e. *to think ahead dynamically*, i.e. to think in movement. This kinetically tethered "theory of objects" acknowledges the fundamentally dynamic character of life and the fundamentally dynamic character of the world. Moreover even if or when an object is static, our knowledge of it is forged dynamically. Thus Bloom calls attention to the fact that objects such as bottles and blankets have a "dynamic quality" for infants (ibid., p. 38) according to where the infant is in relation to them, how the infant moves or is moved by others relative to the them, or, in the case of mobile objects, how the objects themselves move or do not move. As Bloom points out, the movements of a blanket, for example, "are integrated with the baby's own twisting, turning, trying to rise up, and so forth" (ibid.); in other words, the blanket moves in relation to the infant's movements.

Bloom's account of dynamic quality recalls Stern's more elaborate account of what he terms "vitality affects" (Stern 1985). Stern coins the phrase "vitality affects" in order to call attention to the many qualities of feeling that, he says, "do not fit into our existing lexicon or taxonomy of affects" (ibid., p. 54). He states that "These elusive qualities are better captured by *dynamic, kinetic terms*, such as 'surging', 'fading away', 'fleeting', 'explosive', 'crescendo', 'decrescendo', 'bursting', 'drawn out', and so on" (ibid.; italics added). He goes on to say that "These qualities of experience are most certainly sensible to infants and of great daily, even momentary, importance" (ibid.). In short, the sensitivity of infants to "dynamic quality" or "vitality affects" is evidence of our initial kinetic bond with the world; it is evidence as well of our own primal animation, that is, of the fact that we are movement-born (Sheets-Johnstone 1999b). Not only do we experience vitality affects with respect to the world about us, but we create and experience our own vitality affects in the process of moving ourselves. There are thus dual experiential grounds for Bloom's statement regarding an infant's theory of objects. She states that "A theory of objects clearly begins very early in infancy, and experiments have shown its beginnings in perceptions of objects that *move* in relation to a physical field" (Bloom 1993, p. 45; italics added). Though we are ourselves not objects as such but animate forms, we too move in a surrounding world, or "physical field," as Bloom calls it. Thus it is not surprising that thinking in movement is our primary way of making sense of both ourselves and of the world.

There is a further conceptual linkage that attests to our original mode of thinking in movement. What Bloom terms "relational" concepts are concepts that develop outside of language on the basis of observation. Bloom defines them by saying that "Children learn about relationships between objects by observing the effects of movement and actions done by themselves and other persons" (ibid., p. 50). These relationships are akin to what Stern describes as "consequential relationships" (Stern 1985) and what phenomenological philosopher Edmund Husserl terms "if/then relationships" (Husserl e.g. 1970, pp. 161–2, 1989, p. 63), relationships I described earlier with reference to learning our bodies and learning to move ourselves. All three terms are descriptive of the same basic phenomenon. An infant notices, for example, that slapping bath water causes a splash; that closing one's mouth impedes the insertion of food into it; that pulling on a blanket brings it closer; that pushing against a bottle or a ball causes it to roll on the floor; and so on. Whether termed relational concepts, consequential relationships, or if/then relations, the attendant concepts are the backbone of our knowledge of objects, motion, space, causality, and time. The concepts derive from experiences in which and by which we, as infants, attained understandings of different objects and gained what is loosely termed "physical knowledge" about the world, knowledge that is oftentimes erroneously trivialized in comparison with "mental knowledge," the latter being most commonly tied to the ability to use language. Just such so-called physical concepts and knowledge, however, are basic to the acquisition of language, that is, basic to an infant's ultimately having something to talk about. Moreover at least some of these concepts and some of this knowledge may never wend their way into language. In other words, nonlinguistic concepts are not necessarily ultimately articulated or even articulable. What a blown-up balloon does, for example, when it is suddenly untied is hardly expressed by the word "deflates" or the words "splutters about." The actual dynamic kinetic event is not reducible to a word or even to a series of words. We all have knowledge of just such physical events just as we all have nonlinguistic concepts of their dynamics. We have this knowledge and these nonlinguistic concepts because we have all been nurtured by an original capacity to think in movement, a capacity that does not diminish with age but merely becomes submerged or hidden by the capacity and practice of thinking in words.

Psychologist Jerome Bruner's focal emphasis upon narrative as the primary form of discourse, and upon the central place of action in that discourse, affirms this very insight. He writes that when young children "come to grasp the basic idea of reference necessary for any language use [...] their principal linguistic interest centers on *human action and its outcomes*" (Bruner 1990, p. 78). His point is that narrative structure is, in the beginning, concerned with movement, in particular, with what he calls "agentivity" (ibid., p. 77). "Agent-and-action, action-and-object, agent-and-object, action-and-location, and possessor-and-possession," he says, "make up the major part of the semantic relations that appear in the first stage of speech" (ibid., p. 78). A particularly interesting experiment implicitly demonstrates the ready concern of infants with movement in Bruner's sense of "agentivity." In this experiment, luminous points are placed at eleven anatomical joints strategic to human walking—e.g. ankles, knees, elbow, and so on. When set in motion, the luminous points create the illusion of a person walking (or running or carrying or throwing or involved in other acts). Not only do adults readily see a person walking (or engaged in other acts: see for example, Runeson and Frykholm 1981, 1983), but three-month-old infants do also. When the eleven luminous points are randomly organized and set in motion in computer simulations, or when the moving point-figure is turned upside down and set in motion, infants no longer perceive a coherently moving shape (Bertenthal and Pinto 1993; Bertenthal, Proffitt & Cutting 1984). Though some infant researchers have tied the experimental findings to the notion that infants have a "body schema"—a body schema "that permits not only the control of their own bodies but also the recognition of their fellow humans" (Mehler & Dupoux 1994, p. 108)—no such hypothetical explanatory entity is actually necessary. Even as a fetus in utero, an infant has a sense of gravity, i.e. of the vertical; even as a fetus in utero, an infant has a sense of its joints, i.e. through kinesthesia. Moreover though as an infant, it has itself never walked, it has seen others walking; and again, even as a fetus in utero, it has a tactile-kinesthetic sense of its own body as an articulable, essentially dynamic form.

"Agentivity" specifies a dynamic concept of action coincident with this articulable, essentially dynamic form. "Agentivity" is thus intimately related to *primal animation*: we come into the world moving. We are originally indeed infants—meaning etymologically (from Latin) that we do not speak — and we are originally indeed *animated*. Our primal animation is the epistemological ground on which *thinking in movement* develops, hence the ground on which the concept of "agentivity" develops, agentivity in conjunction with both our own actions and the actions of others.

From this perspective, thinking in movement makes language conceptually possible both through the development of corporeal concepts deriving from the qualitatively dynamic, tactile-kinesthetic experiences of our own bodies, and through the development of correlative kinetic, nonlinguistic concepts deriving from our sensitivity to dynamic qualities or vitality affects in our surrounding world. In effect, our standard conceptualization of infancy should be corrected: *infants are not pre-linguistic, language is post-kinetic*. Lacking a dynamic backbone of kinetic experiences, and lacking tactile-kinesthetic bodies, we would be at a loss for language. We might highlight the significance of this fact by putting it in evolutionary perspective: we might ask ourselves how a verbal language could even have been invented short of kinetic/tactile-kinesthetic bodies. Surely verbal language did not arise *deus ex machina* such that one fine day, out of the blue, earlier hominids opened their mouths and words poured forth. Surely, in other words, language did not sprout "full-blown from the mouths of hominids like the Goddess Athena [...] from the head of Zeus" (Sheets-Johnstone 1990, p. 118). Verbal language was indeed *invented*. The very concept of a verbal language had first to arise. In order for such a concept to arise, other concepts generated corporeally and nonlinguistically would have had to have been present, concepts that anchored living in a nonverbal world (Sheets-Johnstone 1990). Moreover verbal language initially required, and still requires, lingual fluency and regularities undergirded by kinetic/tactile-kinesthetic invariants. Clearly, kinetically attuned bodies were at the origin of the invention of verbal language, bodies already conceptually attuned to movement, to concepts generated in and through movement, and to thinking in movement.

In sum, what allows us to dance in the first place, and in turn, to appreciate, analyze, and understand dance both culturally and pan-culturally, is our common apprenticeship in learning our bodies and learning to move ourselves, and our common capacity to think in movement. However diversely articulate we are in a kinetic sense, that is, however diverse our individual kinetic possibilities, and however dynamically variable our cultural heritage in dance, we share a common kinetic ancestry. An exclusive focus on cultural differences blinds us to the kinetic ties that bind us in a common humanity and in a common creaturehood. Dance is a cross-cultural phenomenon because movement is our mother tongue.

References

Bertenthal, B.I. & Pinto, J. (1993) Complementary processes in the perception and production of human movements, in Smith, L.B. & Thelen, E. (eds.) *A Dynamic Systems Approach to Development: Applications*, pp. 209–239, Cambridge, MA: Bradford Books/MIT Press.

Berenthal, B.I., Proffitt, D.R. & Cutting, J.E. (1984) Infant sensitivity to figural coherence in biomechanical motions, *Journal of Experimental Child Psychology*, 37, pp. 214–230.

Bloom, L. (1993) *The Transition from Infancy to Language: Acquiring the Power of Expression*, New York: Cambridge University Press.

Bower, T.G.R. (1971) The object in the world of the infant, *Scientific American*, 225/4, pp. 30–38.

Bruner, J. (1969) Modalities of memory, in Talland, G. & Waugh, N. (eds.) *The Pathology of Memory*, New York: Academic Press.

Bruner, J. (1990) *Acts of Meaning*, Cambridge, MA: Harvard University Press.

Husserl, E (1970) *The Crisis of European Sciences and Transcendental Phenomenology*, Carr, D. (trans.), Evanston, IL: Northwestern University Press.

Husserl, E. (1989) *Ideas Pertaining to a Pure Phenomenology and to a Phenomenological Philosophy: Book 2 (Ideas II)*, Rojcewicz, R. & Schuwer, A. (trans.), Boston, MA: Kluwer Academic Publishers.

Lacan, J. (1977) *Ecrits: A Selection*, Sheridan, A. (trans.), New York: W.W. Norton.

Mehler, J. & Dupoux, E. (1994) *What Infants Know*, Southgate, P. (trans.), Cambridge: Blackwell.

Meltzoff, A.N. (1990) Foundations for developing a concept of self: The role of imitation in relating self to other and the value of social mirroring, social modeling, and self practice in infancy, in Cicchetti, D. & Beeghly, M. (eds.) *The Self in Transition: Infancy to Childhood*, pp. 139–164, Chicago, IL: University of Chicago Press.

Meltzoff, A.N. & Gallagher, S. (1996) The earliest sense of self and others: Merleau-Ponty and recent developmental studies, *Philosophical Psychology*, 92, pp. 211–233.

Meltzoff, A.N. & Moore, M.K. (1977) Imitation of facial and manual gestures by human neonates, *Science*, 198, pp. 75–78.

Meltzoff, A.N. & Moore, M.K. (1983) Newborn infants imitate adult facial gestures, *Child Development*, 54, pp. 702–709.

Needham, R. (1987) *Counterpoints*, Berkeley, CA: University of California Press.

Piaget, J. (1952) *The Origin of Intelligence in Children*, Cook, M. (trans.), New York: International Universities Press.

Runeson, S. & Frykholm, G. (1981) Visual perception of lifted weight, *Human Perception and Performance*, 114, pp. 733–740.

Runeson, S. & Frykholm, G. (1983) Kinematic specification of dynamics as an informational basis for person-and-action perception: Expectation, gender recognition, and deceptive intention, *Journal of Experimental Psychology*, 112 (14), pp. 585–615.

Sheets-Johnstone, M. (1990) *The Roots of Thinking*, Philadelphia, PA: Temple University Press.

Sheets-Johnstone, M. (1999a) Emotion and movement: A beginning empirical-phenomenological analysis of their relationship, *Journal of Consciousness Studies*, 6 (11–12), pp. 259–277.

Sheets-Johnstone, M. (1999b/exp. 2nd ed. 2011) *The Primacy of Movement*, Amsterdam/Philadelphia, PA: John Benjamins Publishing.

Sheets-Johnstone, M. (2003) Kinesthetic memory, *Theoria et Historia Scientiarum*, VII (1), special issue on Embodiment and Awareness: Perspectives from Phenomenology and Cognitive Science, Gallagher, S. & Depraz, N. (eds.), pp. 69–92.

Stern, D.N. (1985) *The Interpersonal World of the Infant: A View from Psycho-analysis and Developmental Psychology*, New York: Basic Books.

Chapter XIV

Globalization
and the Other
Lifeworld(s) on the Brink[1]

Abstract: *This chapter specifies how globalization is not only an economic reality, but is also a socio-political-psychological and ecological one. It demonstrates how globalization, as an institution created by humans, not only fosters fear and greed among humans, but also decimates nonhuman animal lifeworlds, and, in doing so, threatens planet Earth itself. The chapter explores the relationship of globalization to Otherness in the form of the "enemy," whether religious, national, ethnic, political, or ecological, the latter specifically in the form of coral reefs. The exploration highlights the fact that if there are endangered species, it is because a dangerous species exists. Globalization foments an "us against them" mentality; heightens human competition between groups; and, not surprisingly, draws on what Darwin described as "the law of battle." namely, male–male competition. What in a phylogenetic sense originated in the service of mating now functions in the service of power and war. Recognition of this socio-political-psychological-ecological reality leads to an inquiry into the enemy that is not only outside but also within. Notable descriptions of the "Other within" are found in Socrates's and Plato's commentaries on the nature of humans, in Jung's concept of the Shadow, and, strikingly, in the observations of David Shulman and Mahmoud Darwish on the Israeli–Palestinian conflict and impasse. This investigation of the relationship between globalization and the Other leads ultimately to the realization that, if socio-political-psychological – and ecological – ills are to be treated and cured, then we need to examine the Other within.*

I. Introduction

Shortly after George Bush disavowed the United Nations' search for weapons of mass destruction in Iraq, declared a war on terror, and invaded the country, a global proclamation appeared in a cartoon. It pictured the

---

[1]   First published in *Psychotherapy and Politics International* (2012), Vol. 10, No. 3: 246–260.

global earthworld, duly labeling Bush's own country "US" and all other countries "THEM" (see The Student Room, 2011).

Though having its origin as an economic strategy, globalization is not simply an economic phenomenon; it is a socio-political-psychological phenomenon that brings with it a decided augmentation of "the Other." Prior to the formal institution of a global economy, "others" were what one might call distant relatives: real-life, individual humans whom one would not see, visit, hear about, or even be interested in hearing about in one's lifetime. Now, with the advent of instant communication and news, they are worldwide virtual kinfolk. If one does not see them or visit them, one hears or reads about them every day, not just in terms of failing national economies as in Greece and Portugal; of the billions of dollars being spent on military operations or wars; and of natural and man-made disasters; but simply and starkly in terms of individuals killing and being killed by others for religious, political, territorial, or national reasons. Religious beliefs, political ideologies, territorial claims, and ever-ready "national interests" run rife in our newly acclaimed globalized world, driving us to obliterate our virtual kinfolk as Other and them to obliterate us as Other. A polarized "Us against Them" mentality holds sway: in a speech in 2011 on the fight against terror, George Bush said famously: "You're either with us or against us." Thus a combative course of action is ever-present, a motivation to exterminate those who pose a threat or stand in the way, whether obstacles, competitors, or infidels. Of course, by virtue of their political and/or corporate positions and ties, our virtual kinfolk also make lucrative killings: they gouge others for money, destroy jobs, ruin individual means of livelihood in the process, and bring on real-life, real-time national and global as well as individual economic catastrophes. Indeed, their financial killings pointedly belie the positive economic values promoted by global free market enthusiasts.

In short, globalization brings to the fore and from virtually every corner of the Earth others whose proclivities and outright acts may be rapacious and violent as well as thoroughly self-serving. In effect, there are fewer and fewer strangers and more and more enemies or potential enemies. The move to globalization has thus meant living in a world too close for comfort. Though putatively secured by economic agreements, in the full scope of its socio-political-psychological dimension, the global world is in fact riddled with fear.

Surveillance is indeed mandatory: security forces, security codes, security checks, security fences, and so on, become a way of life. In a socio-political-psychological sense, globalization ironically shrinks the world of each human individual. Certainly one can still travel and explore distant lands. The global horizons of one's surrounding world are still open and beckoning, but *the singular and common lifeworld of humans* has changed.

There is a pervasive undercurrent of fear generated by those no longer distant relatives whose paths may cross your own at any moment and place and whose motives and intentions may spell your doom. The word "lifeworld", we might note, is a direct translation of the German *lebenswelt*, a word Edmund Husserl (1931/1973), the founder of phenomenology, used to describe the immediate surrounding world in which we live our everyday lives, a directly experienced world distinct from the world of science that investigates humans, other forms of life, and the world "objectively." As Husserl (1935/1970) wrote, we are "here and there," "in the plain certainty of experience, before anything that is established scientifically, whether in physiology, psychology, or sociology." Moreover "we are subjects for this world [...] experiencing it, contemplating it, valuing it, relating to it purposefully" (pp. 104–5).

In our economic practice of globalization, we humans have changed not only our own singular common lifeworld, but the lifeworlds of other living creatures. Nonhuman and human animals alike have been and are being affected, decimated, and, in many instances, made extinct. Humans have long killed other species not simply for food, but for land, for resources, for money, for putative medicinal benefit, and so on. The present rapacity of human beings in this age of economic globalization, however, knows few if any bounds.

In this context, it is of interest to recall the two standard and preeminent values given for human bipedality: a consistent upright stance allows humans to see to greater distances and to plan ahead. "Ah!" one might exclaim, "What unparalleled stature in the world—a definitive space-time amplification over and above nonhuman animal talents." In particular, given their unique bipedality, humans can see a wider world beyond their immediate spatial frame of reference and look temporally to the future, taking it into consideration in terms of the present. These unique talents and awarenesses, these possibilities for thoughtful enterprise, are encapsulated in the doubly vaunted rationality of *Homo sapiens sapiens*: we modern humans, a subspecies of the genus *Homo*, the genus of bipedal primates, are doubly named for our peerless and unsurpassable wisdom.

But is human bipedality really doing its job, so to speak? Are the purportedly positive values of our upright stance in the world duly vindicated? Are they vindicated, for example, by what "shock and awe" brought about in Iraq? Does the global outsourcing of jobs by companies, the worldwide overfishing in our oceans, or the lack of global action on climate change attest to our human space-time talents and wisdom? In the sense of greed, the answer is "Yes." In each instance, seeing to greater distances means to exploit more resources, to make more money, and to plan ahead to exploit and to make even more. With apologies to Shakespeare, one might say that "gluttony by any other name would smell as sour." In a tangential but equally pre-eminent sense, the answer is again "yes" — that sense being ideological self-righteousness. Making the world conform to one's religious or political beliefs may readily be seen as a form of greed: raking in the believers at the existential expense of the "non" believers, thus satisfying the craving for the supremacy of one's own religion or one's own political program. Again, one might exclaim "Ah!" in this instance, in light of the self-righteous power and glory that come with religious or political dominance, not to mention the afterlife — a concept which speaks of the insatiable greed for more.

What has so far been said of globalization and the other, and of fear and greed, may sound to some like soapbox oratory, which is why I want now to document what has been said more closely. I begin with nonhuman animal life, perhaps a surprising place to begin but, in fact, the essential place to begin, for nonhuman animal lifeworlds are fundamental to full understandings of the relationship between globalization and the Other.

II. The Otherness of Nonhuman Animal Lifeworlds

I focus on coral reefs as an example of the Otherness of nonhuman animal lifeworlds for several significant reasons:

(1) because coral reefs are global;
(2) because they are presently endangered, indeed under radical threat of extinction;
(3) because they house such small forms of life — corals are the calcareous skeletons of marine polyps, minute sedentary creatures;
(4) because most of us have never seen coral reefs and are not likely to experience them directly; and
(5) because, as we shall see, they were the first natural phenomenon about which Darwin wrote lucidly and in enlightening detail with respect to evolution.

Coral reefs are, of course, not the sole nonhuman animal lifeworld at risk of being decimated or going extinct at the hands of humans; so are gorillas, polar bears, and multiple species of frogs, to list only a few examples. All are endangered species, but, as I have written elsewhere (Sheets-Johnstone 2008a), if endangered species exist, *it is because a dangerous species exists*. Just as this existential relationship is commonly overlooked, so also is a seminal conceptual relationship having to do with biodiversity:

> Present-day concerns with endangered species focus attention on a vast range of imperiled creatures in the animal kingdom and on the concomitant ecological hazards of a diminished biological diversity. The diminished biological diversity may be described in twentieth–twenty-

first-century terms as a lack of biological pluralism. Just as a belief in and valuing of pluralistic societies demands respect for others, so also does a belief in and valuing of biological diversity. From a moral stand-point, biodiversity and sociological pluralism are indeed sister concepts. In each instance, the "Other" is commonly recognized as morphologically different in some way from oneself, but not so different as to be ranked inferior, deemed expendable, and so on. Indeed, in a Darwinian sense, i.e., in the sense of a conjoint human/non-human evolutionary history within the Kingdom Animalia, morphological difference is a matter of degree, not of kind. Conceptions and valuations of others thus logically reflect natural gradient differences rather than egoistically inflected "Us against Them" categorical differences. The former kinds of differences propel us toward thoughtful, equitably negotiated decisions concerning Nature and other living beings, the latter toward per-emptory and myopic acts that sever relational bonds. (Sheets-Johnstone 2008a, pp. 343–444)

We might well add to Darwin's fundamental truth of differences in degree and not in kind, and emphasize that, were we indeed to recognize a singular and common lifeworld with, as Husserl (1931/1973) put it: one "common time-form" (p. 128), and one "[o]penly endless Nature […] that includes an open plurality of men (conceived more generally: [an open plurality of] animalia)" (p. 130), we might have far more ecologically enlightened citizens, along with a far more informed and respectful sense of evolution and of our own human evolutionary history within the evolution of the Kingdom Animalia.

The state of coral reefs today is the result of precisely those kinds of human acts that sever relational bonds. The report issued by the World Resources Institute (Burke, Reytar, Spalding & Perry 2011) says as much. Seventy-five percent of coral reefs around the world are at a three-fold risk: from overfishing, from industrial pollution which causes ocean acidification, and from climate change. Overfishing constitutes the most immediate threat, and has affected approximately half the world's reefs. Overfishing in the Indian and Pacific oceans poses the biggest threat because dynamite and other explosives are used to blast fish out of the water. Moreover, in Southeast Asia and the Caribbean, 275 million people live within less than 15 miles of the reefs, and rely on them for food as well as for tourism. As for climate change, global warming warms water which, in turn, bleaches the normal color of coral reefs by killing the marine polyps that live on the reef and give the reef its color. By their inaction on global warming, humans are wantonly destroying the lives and lifeworld of these tiny creatures, and with their destruction the lives and lifeworlds of other forms of marine life and the source of food and economic stability for millions of humans, not to mention the natural beauties of the Earth.

Darwin's first published writing in 1842, the *Sketch* (see Darwin 1909), was devoted to coral reefs, and pre-dated publication of *The Origin of Species* by 17 years. Gordon Chancellor's (2008) excellent summary of Darwin's *Sketch* in *The Works of Darwin Online* aptly highlights the integral conceptual relationship of this earlier work to *The Origin of Species*, namely, in the fact that coral reefs evolve, their evolutionary sequencing running from fringing reef to barrier reef to atoll, a sequencing that hinges on the relationship between coastline level and water level. Chancellor describes this evolutionary sequencing as follows:

> [I]n clean, agitated, tropical seas corals will form fringing reefs just below low tide level. If the coastline is being elevated (as for example may happen if the island is an active volcano) this type of reef should persist but as soon as the living coral is raised above the surf it will die and become a strip of white limestone. If the coastline is stable, the coral will gradually grow out from the shore to become a barrier reef. If the coast is sinking, as Darwin thought was happening to hundreds of islands in the south Pacific, the coral might keep pace by growing upwards but as the land sinks beneath the waves all that would remain would be a more or less circular atoll. Eventually the rate of subsidence might prove too fast, or (perhaps as in our own times of global warming) sea level will rise too fast and the atoll will die.

As is evident from Chancellor's summary, Darwin thought globally in an ecologically interconnected and temporal sense. He could, indeed, see to greater distances because he had actually traveled great distances, and explored and described them in fine detail. He could also see to greater distances in a temporal sense, deriving present conditions from past conditions as well as possible future conditions from present ones, precisely as in his recognition of the evolutionary sequencing of coral reefs. Clearly, in today's world of global warming, he would be eminently capable of planning ahead precisely because he had a historical sense of nature and of the natural world.

Corals are *others* that barely if ever enter directly into our 21st-century human concerns with, or sense of, the natural living world. Moreover, though we humans are in fact consummately *others-dependent*, those others—both animate and inanimate—who sustain our immediate world barely, if ever, enter into our immediate concerns: we do not grow our own vegetables, cultivate our own fruit trees, raise our own chickens or livestock, make our own clothes, build our own houses, manufacture our own cars or computers, and so on. In great measure, the problem is that we fail to recognize the fact that we are *others-dependent in the positive communal interconnected sense it warrants*. On the contrary, that positive interconnected and communal sense has long been and remains for the most part reversed. Though not naming it as such, economists Paul Krugman and Robin Wells

(2011) have justly pinpointed and analyzed that reversed sense in their recent article: "Why Greed Gets Worse." With the institution of Reagonomics in the USA and with economist Milton Friedman's free-market solutions for every problem, a reigning doctrine prevails that Krugman and Wells (2011) term "a creed of *greedism*," namely, the idea that "unchecked self-interest furthers the common good" (p. 28). In this form of globalization, greed is the driving force, propelling humans to be exploitative, bilking (cheating), rapacious "others": others who overfish, pollute, and care nothing of global warming; others who, in making killings, in grabbing resources and land, and so on, are concerned with amassing more and more, satisfying their own self-interests at the expense of those they disdain to recognize as kinfolk, whether real or virtual. In effect, the plurality of lifeworlds that is part of what Husserl (1931/1973) described as "openly endless Nature" (p. 130) is endlessly exploitable—that is, until the moment that overkill exhausts or exterminates these worlds completely.

Is it surprising, then, that greed-driven others easily slip into being regarded not a distant relative but a close-up threat to one's existence, and indeed, an enemy of the common good? To examine this question concretely and to answer it effectively, understandings of our other-dependency in a positive, communally interconnected sense are mandatory. The conceptual relationship pointed out earlier between biological diversity and social pluralism suggests as much. By considering the relationship of nonhuman animals to human ones in finer terms, we will in fact bring to the fore Darwin's positive communally interconnected sense of the global world, a sense that duly and in detail recognizes competition as part of the natural order, and just as duly and in detail recognizes the natural foundational interdependence of living beings. As we shall see, lifeworlds are the existential terrain of the foundational interdependence of living beings and of competition between and among them.

III. Nonhuman and Human Animal Lifeworlds

As should be apparent from what was said about coral reefs, nonhuman animals have distinctive lifeworlds of their own. Differential lifeworlds exist because each species of animal has its own niche, its own particular surrounding world with its own particular "functional tones," as biologist Jakob von Uexküll (1957) so aptly described species-specific subject–world relationships. The lifeworld of humans is indeed but one form of lifeworld. When humans invade the lifeworlds of other animate organisms, they necessarily disturb those worlds, often enough bringing them to the point of extinction. A seminally important irony is thus evident—an irony that is notable precisely because the Earth is a singular planet, which is to say that, however differential the lifeworlds of animals, both human and non-human, they are inescapably interconnected, not just geographically but existentially. Darwin (1968/1859) observed this fact in *The Origin of Species*. He described at length the checks and relations between and among organic beings, giving detailed examples of the interconnectedness of life, even to the point of showing how the introduction of a single species of tree—a Scotch fir—can affect not only other trees but also insect and bird populations, and even cattle. As he succinctly stated: "*plants and animals, most remote in the scale of nature, are bound together by a web of complex relations*" (Darwin 1859/1968, pp. 124–5, my emphasis). On the basis of his extensive observations, he furthermore noted that competition is "most severe between allied forms, which fill nearly the same place in the economy of nature," but that "in no one case could we precisely say why one species has been victorious over another in the great battle of life" (p. 127). He added that "[a] corollary of the highest importance may be deduced" from competition, namely, that the structure of every organic being is related, in the most essential yet often hidden manner, to that of all other organic beings, with which it comes into competition for food or residence, or from which it has to escape, or on which it preys (p. 127).

In light of Darwin's empirically detailed studies of plant and animal life, the very idea of globalization might have given us an appreciation not just of economic competition in "the great battle of life," but of the positive communal interconnectedness of life on this singular planet; that is, it might have given us an appreciation of how, as Darwin wrote: "*plants and animals, most remote in the scale of nature, are bound together by a web of complex relations*" (pp. 124–5, my emphasis). Notwithstanding the dedicated work of organizations such as the Environmental Defense Fund (www.wdf.org), Earthjustice (www.earthjustice.org), Natural Resource Defense Council (www.nrdc.org), National Wildlife Federation (www.nwf.org), and many others, what globalization has done is quite the opposite. With its internationally sanctioned economic platform, globalization has heightened competition. It has done so because, as pre-eminently an economic strategy, globalization is a financially driven and financially focused program whose reigning motto is "More!"—a motto that as shown elsewhere (Sheets-Johnstone 2008a) is utterly devoid of any moral weightings.

Clearly, self-interest, devoid of moral weighting, justifies literal and metaphorical killings. The enemy of the common good is, in effect, hard to miss. The example of coral reefs demonstrates unequivocally how non-human species are at risk because humans put them at risk, and have the unquestioned capacity to put them at risk. Hence, if endangered species exist, it is indeed because humans exist. Human beings have become the most dangerous species ever spawned by Nature, and not only with respect to the Other, but also with respect to their own kind: "Their intra-species danger is in fact unique: no non-human animal species decimates its own kind as humans do and have done for millennia. And no non-human animal species decimates its environmental resources, fouls its own air and water, or puts the global planet itself at risk as humans do and have done over the last century in particular" (Sheets-Johnstone 2008a, p. 345). In short, as the American cartoon character Pogo long ago observed and declared: "We have met the enemy and he is us." To gain insights into this enemy that is us involves searching within for the destructive penchant of humans, to inquire into their self-deceptive side as Socrates described it, their "conceit" side as Plato described it, their shadow side as Jung described it, a side that is set forth in close-up, present-day terms and eloquently described in different but complementary ways by David Shulman, an Israeli professor of Humanistic Studies and activist in the Arab–Jewish Partnership (Ta'ayush), and by Mahmoud Darwish, a Palestinian poet. In short, insights into the enemy within demands recognition of another Other, that is, an Other who, through ignorance or fabrication, impacts on the socio-political-psychological realities of globalization.

IV. The Other Within

In an earlier article (Sheets-Johnstone 2008b), I pointed out that Socrates's dictum "Know thyself" was one whose import was apparent in many of Plato's dialogues. In the *Phaedrus*, for example, Socrates states, "I must first know myself, as the Delphian inscription says; to be curious about that which is not my concern, while I am still in ignorance of my own self, would be ridiculous" (Plato pp. 235–6). In the *Philebus*, he observes that self-ignorance is evident in three domains: wealth, beauty, and wisdom, and specifies each domain as follows:

> [T]he ignorant [person] may fancy himself richer than he is [... a]nd still more often he will fancy that he is taller or fairer than he is, or that he has some other advantage of person which he really has not [... a]nd yet surely by far the greatest number [of people] err about the goods of the mind; they imagine themselves to be much better men than they are. (Plato p. 384)

Consulting Plato directly, I noted further striking resemblances between ancient Greek thought and Jung's pivotal psychic figure: the Shadow. In the *Laws*, Plato writes that to imagine oneself a better human being than one actually is is to take on what the Athenian Stranger (Plato himself) describes as the "conceit of wisdom" (Plato p. 608). The Athenian Stranger, who ironically is Plato himself in the face of foreign Others (Clinias, the Cretan, and Megillus, the Spartan), declares that to take on the conceit of wisdom is to fall short of the highest virtue: one does not accurately assess one's own knowledge but professes to know what one does not know.

Stating specifically that this form of ignorance can have dire socio-political consequences, the Athenian Stranger affirms that when conceit of wisdom is "possessed of power and strength, [it] will be held by the legislator to be the source of great and monstrous crimes" (pp. 608–9). In finer terms, when ignorance is not merely simple, resulting in only "lighter offences," but is accompanied by a conceit of wisdom, ignorance doubles, and when "doubled ignorance" combines with power and strength, criminal action results (p. 609). Present-day testimony to the trenchancy of this observation is readily available. We have only to open our eyes to "the great and monstrous crimes" that are committed by certain leaders, among whom was President George W. Bush, in whom the embodiment of the conceit of wisdom combined with unparalleled "power and [military] strength."

Jung's (1937/1970a) emphasis on "know[ing] ourselves as we really are" (p. 170; see also Jung, 1955/1970b) is present in multiple perspectives across his writings. He points out, for example, that a patient's illness "is not a gratuitous and therefore meaningless burden; it is *his own self*, the 'other' whom, from childish laziness or fear, or for some other reason, he was always seeking to exclude from his life" (Jung 1937/1970a, pp. 169–70). As to that "Other" and to the challenge of confronting one's own psychic shadow, Jung (1967/1983) succinctly observes: "One does not become enlightened by imagining figures of light but by making the darkness conscious," adding, wryly, "The procedure, however, is disagreeable and therefore not popular" (Jung 1967/1983, pp. 265–6).

Succinct though it be, his observation is telling and leads us to consider how, by keeping ourselves in the dark with respect to our own self-deceptions and conceits, we fail to illuminate the darker corners of our humanity and fail to see their ever more disastrous socio-political consequences in today's globalized world. Indeed, Jung's observation leads us to a central and critical question posed in an earlier article:

> What is the nature of a being who cannot live in peace with others of its own kind, who is obsessed with power and who has the power in equal measure to create and to destroy, and to destroy not simply his own kind but other kinds as well and indeed the whole earth? More finely, what is the nature of a being who cannot live without killing, not in order that he may eat but in order that others, whether termed the enemy or the devil, the intruder or the insurgent [...] are obliterated? (Sheets-Johnstone 2008b, pp. 22–3)

Before proposing a beginning answer to that question, let us consider Jung's insights into the Shadow in broader contexts.

Jung spelled out the socio-political consequences of self-ignorance in *Civilization in Transition* (Jung 1937/1970a), the tenth volume of his collected works. The temporal span of the book runs from the close of World War I to World War II and more than a decade beyond. A fitting epigraph of the book with respect to his essays on both wars might well read — in his own words — that "for man to regard himself 'harmless' is to add 'stupidity to iniquity'" (Jung 1937/1970a, p. 296). The opacity of humans to their shadow side might be tied to the vapidness of Heidegger's "*they*," the "everybodies" who fail to live authentically, who are cowards to confront their own fears, in particular, the fear of their own death, and are instead consumed in "idle talk" (Heidegger 1962, pp. 211–4, my emphasis). It might also be tied, however, to the self-opacity of those who literally thrive on manly competition, who take pleasure in the pursuit of power and war, and in the excitement and bravado of killing others. Darwin (1871/1981) rightly identified male–male competition as "the law of battle" (p. 182), an evolutionary fact of male life in the service of reproduction. He described the living realities of the law in 12 chapters (over 460 pages in *The Descent of Man and Selection in Relation to Sex*), detailing the competitive behavior of males in species across the animal kingdom, aquatic and terrestrial, beginning with the secondary sexual characters of mollusks, annelids, and crustaceans; moving from there to spiders, beetles, and other insects; from there to butterflies and moths; from there to fish, amphibians, and reptiles; and finally, to birds (four chapters); mammals (two chapters); and man (two chapters). In the first of the last two chapters, Darwin pointedly comments, "Man is the rival of other men; he delights in competition, and this leads to ambition which passes too easily into selfishness. These latter qualities seem to be his natural and unfortunate birthright" (p. 326). His second sentence notwithstanding, however natural the birthright, there is variation among characters or traits common to a species, including sexual characters or traits. In other words, all males are not equally competitive. On the contrary, it is essential to recognize *variation*, Darwin's first central observation of differences among individuals of the same species. Thus, *all* human males are not given to violence, all do not revel in the excitement and bravado of battle, all are not so-called "killers at heart," and so on. What hardly needs saying, however, is that "the law of battle" has been culturally elaborated in infinitely barbarous and violent ways by male humans. What in a phylogenetic sense began as male–male competition in the service of mating has mushroomed into an ever larger cloud that threatens to erase not only humanity, but also the 99 million other species that inhabit this planet, and the planet itself.

Male–male competition is in fact an overlooked if not deliberatively ignored topic of study. Its neglect in terms of human history and our barbarously violent 21st-century world is astounding: *real* male–male competition is nowhere on the academic map, let alone on laymen's or politician's lips, even though its real-life presence is all about us, as in the 2010 Football World Cup competition, for example, where winning at all costs meant injuring, cheating, and lying (Parks 2010). It will not do to distract ourselves with discourses on aggression. Aggression is a cultural euphemism for the essentially biological phenomenon of male–male competition (Sheets-Johnstone 2008a), something akin to *les préciosités* in earlier French literature where authors, rather than speaking of teeth, for example, spoke of "the furniture of the mouth." Neither will it do to distract our attention with studies of sperm competition (see, for example, Parker 1998; Birkhead 2000; Simmons 2001). Sperm, after all, are rightly doing their job in a quite laudable biological sense – a sense totally unlike the savagery to which real male–male competition is devoted nationally and honed culturally. Those whose motivation lies in the pleasure of killing others, in the sheer excitement and bravado of war are, to reverse Jung's words, adding iniquity to stupidity. In this context, it is pertinent to point out that were the present scientific surge toward reductionism a truly credible pursuit, then surely the most significant study a geneticist could pursue would be a search for the gene that drives male–male competition and expresses itself in the pursuit of power and war. The idea is patently ludicrous, yet the following report concerning the cardinal role of a singular hormone in the service of cooperation and trust supports it. Science writer, Sharon Begley (2007) states that "Being hunted brought evolutionary pressure on our ancestors to cooperate and live in cohesive groups," and that such cooperation and cohesion, more than aggression and warfare, "is our evolutionary legacy" (p. 56). Subsequent to this bald statement, she states:

> Both genetics and paleoneurology back [up] that [evolutionary] legacy. A hormone called oxytocin, best-known for inducing labour and lactation in women, also operates in the brain (of both sexes). There, it promotes trust during interactions with other people, and thus the cooperative behaviour that lets groups of people live together for the common good. (pp. 56-7)

If such a series of claims were true – including the claim that "cooperation and cohesion, more than aggression and warfare, is our evolutionary legacy," a claim that ignores Darwin's detailed studies of "the law of battle" – why would oxytocin not be made clinically available and administered worldwide? To affirm that a hormone "promotes trust during interactions with other people" is an outlandish and irresponsible claim: it not only overlooks the evolutionary reality of male–male competition, but overlooks the experiential source of our social proclivities and feelings and indeed their developmental progression in the course of ontogeny. We are not born with trust; trust is learned (Sheets-Johnstone 2008a). Indeed, were such a reductionist claim plausible, it would follow that if oxytocin promotes cooperation and trust in the brains of both sexes, and thus "lets" people live together for the common good, then surely a certain other hormone operates in the brain and promotes male–male competition in the service of "aggression and warfare"—the other half of our "evolutionary legacy"—and thus "lets" people live together for the common bad. Were this conditional statement true, then hormonal treatment of males competing for power and "delighting" in the rivalry of war should receive immediate medical and worldwide public attention.

In sum, nothing can compete with self-knowledge. This socio-political-psychological truth is eloquently stated by David Shulman (2011) when, writing of the retraction of UN Commissioner Richard Goldstone of part of his Commission's report on the behavior of Israelis in the 2009 Gaza war, he discussed what remained true in Goldstone's report, for example, that

> Israel unleashed firepower of an unprecedented intensity in Gaza, despite its dense civilian population [... and that] though efforts were made to warn civilians to leave the combat zone—the combat zone was by no means emptied of ordinary people. (Shulman 2011, p. 28)

As Shulman states, "[a] great many were killed—primarily because as a high-ranking Israeli officer told *The Independent* [newspaper], 'We rewrote the rules of war for Gaza'" (p. 28). Shulman, who served in the Israeli army in the 1982 (Lebanon) war and whose three sons also served in the Israeli army, goes on to note that: "Soldiers interviewed by the Israeli veterans group Breaking the Silence [...] report being told literally to shoot first and put troubling doubts aside for later" (p. 28). He notes too, for example, that the Gaza war

> began with an attack on newly trained Gaza policemen at their induction ceremony; some eighty-nine police officers were killed, along with members of their families who had come to attend the celebration. The majority were *not* known Hamas fighters but simply police cadets, some of them apparently trained as traffic cops or for other minor, clearly noncombatant jobs (including five who were musicians in the police orchestra). (p. 29)

Shulman's critical analysis of the factual truths in Goldstone's report bears precisely on a full understanding of "the Other." Although Shulman himself does not recognize the two distinct forms of the Other, that is, *the Other without* and *the Other within*, his two closing observations give voice to each of them. After observing first that the colonial enterprise that defines the ongoing Israeli occupation is of a piece with the Gaza war in terms of "the willingness to sacrifice innocents on an ever wider scale" (p. 29), thus recognizing violence to the Other without, he goes on to make an observation that strikes resonant chords with self-ignorance, self-deception, and the conceit of wisdom as described by Socrates, Plato, and Jung. Following his surmise that "Israel may well repeat its earlier mistake in Gaza and eventually make some sort of niggardly, unilateral withdrawal from, say, Area B in the West Bank—anything except cutting a meaningful deal with the Palestinians, anything except making peace," Shulman then, with great acuteness, points out: "There is nothing more precious than an enemy, especially one whom you have largely created by your own acts and who plays some necessary role in the inner drama of your soul" (p. 29).

Mahmoud Darwish's (2008) poem "A Ready Scenario" reads like a validation of that created enemy in its descriptive enactment of the "necessary role" the "precious enemy" plays in "the inner drama of your soul." The poem centers on two men and begins as follows:

> Let us now suppose that we fell, I and the enemy,
> Fell from the sky
> In a hole …
> So, what will happen?

What will happen, as Darwish's poem shows, will be conditioned precisely by what "I and the enemy" think of each other, that is, what each of us has largely created by our own acts on behalf of the inner drama of our respective souls. The accordance of this notion of a self-conditioned future with the Buddhist concept of *karma* is notable; in both instances, it is a recognition of the fact that "what we do and how we act create our future experiences" (Goldstein & Kornfield 1987, p. 4). Furthermore, the "precious enemy" that we largely create by our own acts, i.e by our self-created "Other," is nowhere to be found in contemporary phenomenological discourses on "The Other." Indeed, while "The Other" has risen to great prominence in phenomenology, that Other remains a wholly *outside* Other, a non-self-contaminated Other. In a recent article by Françoise Dastur (2011), for example, we find Sartre's (1956) confrontational or "hemorrhaging of the world" conception of the Other, Merleau-Ponty's (1968) "anonymous intercorporeity" conception of the Other, and Levinas's (1969) "hostage-holding facial" conception of the Other. The *Other* that emerges from the shadow side of our own individual psyche is not recognized. Yet, clearly, that concealed Other is a powerful Other in the global realities of life, one substantively permeating the affective character of our relations with other world-living beings. In short, the affective character of our relations with other humans across the globe is incontrovertibly conditioned by our own acts and the "inner drama" of our own soul that motivates those acts. Darwish's poem gives substantive evidence of the reality of this psychic Other.

V. Expositions and Ruminations on Darwish's Poem

In her meticulous analysis of Darwish's poem, Honaida Ghanim, General Director of the Palestinian Forum for Israeli Studies and former postdoctoral fellow at the Center for Middle Eastern Studies and the Department of Sociology at Harvard University, states that what Darwish is doing is exploring possibilities that the I/enemy relationship—or, as she herself calls it, "this partnership"—generates, both "in the metaphorical hole itself, and more broadly in the predicament of hostility in which it figures" (Ghanim 2011, p. 1). Quoting the continuing lines of the poem, she points out that "[q]uickly, a conflict arises over whose right it is to exit first" (p. 1):

> At the beginning, we wait for luck …
> Rescuers may find us here
> And extend the rope of survival to us
> He says: I first
> And I say: I first
> He curses me then I him
> In vain,
> The rope has not arrived yet …

Most importantly, Ghanim goes on to point out that "*salvation* from outside the hole never arrives, and no one extends the rope of survival. Time passes and enmity remains within their *common* hole, and so they share the same fate against their will. Extending enmity, each one is occupied with his own willingness to get out alone from their common entrapment, without regard for what the enemy–partner says or does" (Ghanim 2011, pp. 1–2).

The backdrop of the poem is obviously the ongoing Israeli–Palestinian conflict over land, resources, livelihood, and life itself. In a general sense, that backdrop is a common human one: the oppression of one group of humans by another. What the poem so eloquently captures is the futility of life in the hole and what Ghanim so accurately describes is the hole's "temporary permanence" (pp. 10–11), that is, the putative temporariness of the occupation until a peaceful solution is reached, and the actual permanence of the putative temporariness in the ongoing construction of "settlements." Validation of this temporary permanence is apparent in Israel's final approval of a plan to build 1600 settlement homes in east Jerusalem (Heller 2011). As Ghanim observes, until the conditions that define the hole and the kind of "enemy" relationship that exists within it change, "attempts to triumph over the enemy inside the hole" not only will continue to fail but will broaden "the divisions between the two sides and [deepen] the hole" (Ghanim 2011, p. 14). With what might be called "the audacity of hope," Ghanim concludes that the solution lies in the possibility that "the 'hole residents' […] turn their gaze to the opening of the trap" (p. 15), seeing a future in which there is no longer an "enemy–partner" but a future modeled on a past that echoes actual cultural history—a history in which, in part quoting Darwish's words, Ghanim writes:

> "Jews would not be ashamed to find the Arabic element in [themselves], and the Arab would not be ashamed to say that he [is] composed of Jewish elements," and this because people realize that they are "a

product of all the cultures that [have passed] in this place—Greek,
Roman, Persian, Jewish, Ottoman," and that "[e]very developed culture
left something." (p. 15)

This notion—that multicultural threads run through our human lifeworld,
that humans of any particular time and place are the lineal descendants of
mixed racial, ethnic, religious, and/or social pasts—can hardly be denied.
Civilizations have come and gone; empires have been built and destroyed;
people have migrated from one place to another; racial, ethnic, tribal, and
religious intermarriages have taken place; and so on. In this historical
sense, we can only be our own enemy; we are in truth temporally and
globally interconnected in the here and now. Moreover, from an evolutionary perspective, we undeniably share a common humanity and a
singular common lifeworld to begin with. The multicultural threads that
run through that lifeworld are historically akin to the foundational taxonomic threads of our evolutionary heritage: all present-day humans are a
species of the genus *Homo*, of the Family Hominids, of the Order Primates,
of the Class Mammals, of the Subphylum Vertebrates, of the Phylum
Chordata, of the Kingdom Animalia. What warrants our attention is thus
paradoxical: namely, the communally concealed negative Other of our
positive phylogenetically and culturally interconnected otherness. However paradoxical, what in finer terms clearly warrants our attention is "the
precious enemy" that constitutes our iniquity and stupidity, and that
sanctions us to commit foul deeds. Indeed, our communal human psychic
divide warrants our undivided attention. Until we give it such attention,
our own Other will continue to loom destructively within our being. Our
neglect of it can only spell a self-inflicted doom, the doom of the lifeworlds
of other forms of animate life, and the doom of the planet on which all
these lifeworlds were spawned in the first place. If the socio-political-
psychological—and ecological—ills of globalization are to be treated and
even cured, then our us-against-them mentality, our greed, our iniquities
and stupidities, male–male competition and its co-option from its origins in
sexual selection to its transfiguration into warriorhood and the honing of
heroes to fight our precious enemy—whoever it may be—all need to be
recognized in terms of the full scope of Otherness: the Other within and the
Other without.

    From the perspective of these socio-political-psychological-ecological
ills, the moral equivalent of war is not sports and other kinds of sanctioned
public displays of competition, vigor, power, manliness, and so on. The
moral equivalent of war is making the darkness conscious: assuming
responsibility for one's own self-lucidity, for one's own Other, for living up
to one's own doubly vaunted sapiential wisdom; in effect, recognizing that
our positive communal interconnectedness and singular common lifeworld

can come to light only in the light of the inner drama of our own soul and of the enemy that is us.

References

Begley, S. (2007, 19 March) Beyond stones and bones, *Newsweek*, 149 (12), pp. 53–58.

Birkhead, T.R. (2000) *Promiscuity: An Evolutionary History of Sperm Competition*, Cambridge, MA: Harvard University Press.

Burke, L., Reytar, K., Spalding, M. & Perry, A. (2011) *Reefs at Risk Revisited*, Washington, DC: World Resources Institute.

Chancellor, G. (2008) Introduction to coral reefs, *Darwin Online*, [Online], http://darwin-online.org.uk/introductions.html [26 June 2011].

Darwin, C. (1842/1909) *The Foundations of The Origin of Species: Two Essays Written in 1842 and 1844*, Darwin, F. (ed.), Cambridge: Cambridge University Press.

Darwin, C. (1859/1968) *The Origin of Species*, Harmondsworth: Penguin.

Darwin, C. (1871/1981) *The Descent of Man, and Selection in Relation to Sex*, Princeton, NJ: Princeton University Press.

Darwish, M. (2008) *Scenario Jahez*, [Online], http://www.mahmouddarweesh. org/index.php?option=com_content&view=articl&id=55:q-q-&catid=35: his-books

Dastur, F. (2011) The question of the Other in French phenomenology, *Continental Philosophy Review*, 44, pp. 165–178.

Ghanim, H. (2011) The urgency of a new beginning in Palestine: An imagined scenario by Mahmoud Darwish and Hannah Arendt, *College Literature*, 38 (1), pp. 1–20.

Goldstein, J. & Kornfield, J. (1987) *Seeking the Heart of Wisdom: The Path of Insight Meditation*, Boston, MA, & London: Shambhala.

Heidegger, M. (1962) *Being and Time*, Macquarrie, J. & Robinson, E. (trans.), New York: Harper & Row.

Heller, J. (2011, 11 August) Israel okays 1,600 settler homes for East Jerusalem, *Reuters News Service*, [Online], http://www.reuters.com [11 August 2011].

Husserl, E. (1935/1970) *The Crisis of European Sciences and Transcendental Phenomenology*, Carr, D. (ed.), Evanston, IL: Northwestern University Press.

Husserl, E. (1931/1973) *Cartesian Meditations*, Cairns, D. (trans.), The Hague: Martinus Nijhoff.

Jung, C. (1937/1970a) *Civilization in Transition*, 2nd ed., Hull, R.F.C. (trans.), Princeton, NJ: Princeton University Press.

Jung, C. (1955/1970b) *Mysterium Coniunctionis*, Hull, R.F.C. (trans.), Princeton, NJ: Princeton University Press.

Jung, C. (1967/1983) *Alchemical Studies*, Hull, R.F.C. (trans.), Princeton, NJ: Princeton University Press.

Krugman, P. & Wells, R. (2011, 14 July) Why greed gets worse, *New York Review of Books*, pp. 28–29.

Levinas, E. (1969) *Totality and Infinity: An Essay on Exteriority*, Lingis, A. (trans.), Pittsburgh, PA: Duquesne University Press.

Merleau-Ponty, M. (1968). *The Visible and the Invisible*, Lefort, C. (ed.), Lingis, A. (trans.), Evanston, IL: Northwestern University Press.

Parker, G. (1998) Sperm competition and the "evolution of ejaculates": Towards a theory base, in Birkhead, T.R. & Moller, A.P. (eds.) *Sperm Competition and Sexual Selection*, pp. 4–23, San Diego, CA: Academic Press.

Parks, T. (2010, 19 August) The shame of the World Cup, *New York Review of Books*, pp. 48–49.

Plato (1937) *Laws*, in *The Dialogues of Plato*, Vol. 2, Jowett, B. (trans.), pp. 407–703, New York: Random House.

Plato (1937) *Phaedrus*, in *The Dialogues of Plato*, Vol. 1, Jowett, B. (trans.), pp. 233–282, New York: Random House.

Plato (1937) *Philebus*, in *The Dialogues of Plato*, Vol. 2, Jowett, B. (trans.), pp. 343–403, New York: Random House.

Sartre, J.-P. (1956) *Being and Nothingness: An Essay on Phenomenological Ontology*, Barnes, H. (trans.), New York: Philosophical Library.

Sheets-Johnstone, M. (2008a) *The Roots of Morality*, State Park, PA: Pennsylvania State University Press.

Sheets-Johnstone, M. (2008b/this volume, Chapter VII) On the hazards of being a stranger to oneself, *Psychotherapy and Politics International*, 6 (1), pp. 17–29.

Shulman, D. (2011, 26 May) Goldstone and Gaza: What's still true?, *New York Review of Books*, pp. 28–29.

Simmons, L.W. (2001) *Sperm Competition and its Evolutionary Consequences in the Insects*, Princeton, NJ: Princeton University Press.

The Student Room (2011) *Map*, [Online], http://www.thestudentroom.co.uk/showthread.php?t=1710073&page=346 [23 July 2012].

von Uexküll, J. (1934/1957) A stroll through the worlds of animals and men, in Schiller, C.H. (ed. and trans.), *Instinctive Behavior*, pp. 5–80, New York: International Universities Press.

Index of Names

Printed in the USA
CPSIA information can be obtained
at www.ICGtesting.com
LVHW021202190724
785901LV00001B/64

9 781845 409043